SUSTAINABLE DEVELOPMENT AND THE INDIAN ECONOMY:

Issues and Challenges

Edited by

Sailabala Debi
V.B. Annigeri

Serials Publications
New Delhi

for

सा विद्या या विमुक्तये

CENTRE FOR MULTI-DISCIPLINARY DEVELOPMENT RESEARCH
(CMDR)

D.B. Rodda Road, Alur Venkatrao Circle, Dharwad – 580 001, KARNATAKA

Edited by
Sailabala Debi & V.B. Annigeri

First Published - 2006

ISBN: 81-8387-054-6

The view expressed in the book are those of the authors and are not necessarily shared by CMDR, editors, publisher or printer.

Published by
SERIALS PUBLICATIONS
4830/24, Prahlad Street, Ansari Road
Darya Ganj, New Delhi-110002 (India)
Phone : 23245225. Fax : 91-11-23272135
E-mail: serials@satyam.net.in

Contents

Foreword

The Centre for Multidisciplinary Development Research (CMDR), Dharwad, is recognized by Indian Council of Social Science Research (ICSSR) as one of the 27 such Institutes. The Centre serves as a unique Think -Tank on different socio-economic issues of North Karnataka. Despite the location disadvantage, the Institute has made sincere and concerted efforts to come to the limelight by involving actively in social science research with a special focus on 'capacity building programme' and 'action research' especially for the deprived sections of population and at the grass-root level.

The ICSSR Institutions located in South India have been conducting the Development Conventions every year since 2001-02 to promote social science research awareness among young researchers/scholars. The Convention provides a Forum for the ICSSR institutions located in South India to establish processes of mutual learning from each other's experiences in carrying out Social Science Research, Doctoral Programme, Publications and Policy Contributions. The most important goal of the Convention, however, is to extend an opportunity to young scholars to share their work in progress or recently completed research, thereby to let the wider academic world know of their potentials.

Recently, The Fifth Development Convention of 2006 was organized on 27th and 28th April, 2006. This is the first of this type in the city of Dharwad which is known as the 'Knowledge Capital' of North Karnataka. The theme of the convention for this year was "Sustainable Development and the Indian Economy- Approaches and Challenges in the New Millennium". About 60 participants from different parts of the country attended the Convention and the deliberations during the two days were of very high standard.

The Convention was academic in rigour with which it sought to address almost all the relevant issues of development. Also it had a strong policy focus and I hope this will help to address most of the important problems of the Indian Economy facing in the New Millennium. Publication of the papers presented in the Convention I believe will reinforce the message. The main idea behind this publication is to promote the knowledge of young social scientists.

I take this opportunity to convey my appreciation to the Director, CMDR, her Colleagues and well wishers of CMDR for the successful completion of this Convention. I am sure, the Centre will act as a 'light house' for the social science research community in days to come.

M.S. Gore
Chairman, CMDR

Acknowledgements

Economic Science has been undergoing significant changes in respect of its approach and contents from time to time. While initially this discipline was aiming at inquiring into the causes and consequences of value and prosperity and depression of nations, the later developments seem to have given rise to several sub disciplines. There is a paradigm shift on the focus of development when UNDP launched its Human Development Report in 1990. There is also enough evidence that the socio-economic development in India suffered a major set back with the introduction of economic reforms as a part of the process of globalization. Then the question of not only scaling up the development of India but also its sustainability faced the major challenges. In this backdrop, the topic selected for discussion in the recent convention was in order.

The ICSSR Institutions located in South India have been conducting the Development Conventions every year since 2001-02 to promote social science research awareness among young researchers/scholars. The Convention provides a Forum for the ICSSR institutions located in South India to establish processes of mutual learning from each other's experiences in carrying out Social Science Research. The 5th Development Convention was organized by the CMDR in Dharwad.

I express my gratitude to Prof. M. S. Gore, Chairman, CMDR, who is constant source of inspiration in research and developmental activities of the Centre.

CMDR expresses its sincere thanks to the all Directors of partner Institutes of Development Convention. Dr. Padmini Swaminathan, Director, Madras Institute of Development Studies (MIDS), Channai (Tamil Nadu), Dr. G.K. Kadekodi, Director, Institute for Social & Economic Change (ISEC), Nagarabhavi, Bangalore, (Karnataka), Dr. P.R. Nair, Director, Centre for Development Studies (CDS), Ulloor, Thiruvananthapuram , (Kerala), Dr.Mahendra Dev, Director, Centre for Economic & Social Studies (CESS), Begumpet, Hyderabad, (Andhra Pradesh), deserve special thanks for their continued guidance and support in successfully holding the Convention.

I express my sincere thanks to members of the Advisory Committee; Prof.P.R.Panchamukhi, Professor Emeritus and Founder Director, CMDR,

Prof.K.R.Madi, Member, CMDR, Dr.A.N.Kabbur, Member, CMDR, who constantly advising to successful completion of Convention.

Thanks are due to members of the Screening Committee; Prof. S. Subrahmanyam, CESS, Hyderabad, Dr. S. Janakarajan Professor, MIDS, Chennai, Prof. Usha Devi, Education Unit, ISEC, Bangalore, Prof. P. Sivanandan, Professor, CDS, Thiruvanthapuram, Dr.V.B. Annigeri, Reader, CMDR, for their patiently screening the papers to be presented at the Convention.

Thanks are also due to Member of the Organizing Committee of the Convention; Dr.V.B. Annigeri, Ms.Nayanatara Nayak, Dr. A.R. Kulkarni, Mr. V.T. Hungund, Mr. A.S. Raichur, Ms. Jayashree Kulkarni, Mr. B.P. Bagalkot, Mr. Gururaj V.H., Mr. D.R. Revankar, Dr. S.G. Purohit, Prof. & Head, Dept. of Eco, Nehru Arts, Sci & Comm College, Hubli. Dr. S.G. Das, Prof. & Head, Dept. of English, Nehru Arts, Sci & Comm College, Hubli. Shri Suresh Kini, Advocate, Hubli, who have supported in all the way in organizing this convention.

I also render my sincere thanks to the Commissioner, Hubli-Dharwad Municipal Corporation, Hubli, Dr.Masood Ali Khan, Director, Southern Region Centre, ICSSR, Hyderabad; Planning Commission, New Delhi; Canara Bank, Main Branch, Dharwad; Indian Overseas Bank, KHRS Extension Counter, Dharwad; Sanmati Computers, Dharwad; Omkar Electricals, Dharwad; Shreenidhi Builders, Dharwad, B.D.K.Process Controls Pvt. Ltd.,Hubli, Intel Book Distributors Pvt. Ltd. Bangalore; Shrihari Publications, Bangalore; and Svenpa Systems, Hubli for their kindly extending financial support to successfully hold the convention.

I take this opportunity to express my thanks and appreciation to all the colleagues and well wishers of the Centre, who have sincerely extended their cooperation and support in completing this convention.

Last but not the least I would like to place on record our gratitude to the scholars who have contributed their valuable papers for the book. My thanks are due to the Serials Publications to bring out the book in time. I also owe a debt of gratitude to NABARD for its financial assistance of the publication of this book.

Dr. Sailabala Debi

Contributors

1. **Prof. P.R. Panchamukhi,** Professor Emeritus & Founder Director, C.M.D.R., Dharwad. *panchamukhipr@yahoo.com*

2. **Dr. Sukhpal Singh,** Associate Professor, Centre for Management in Agriculture (CMA), Indian Institute of Management, Ahmedabad (IIMA), Vastrapur *sukhpal@iimahd.ernet.in*

3. **Dr. K. Sivasubramaniyan,** Assistant Professor, Madras Institute of Development Studies, 79, II Main Road, Gandhi Nagar, Adyar, Chennai-600 020, *siva@mids.ac.in* & Dr. Sakthivadivel, Senior Fellow, International Water Management Institute, Srilanka.

4. **Himanshu Sekhar Rout,** Lecturer in Economics, Department of Economics, Dr. SRK Government Arts College, Yanam- 533 464, Pondicherry, *hsreco@hotmail.com*

5. **Dr. Bahnisikha Ghosh,** Professor of Economics, Department of Economics, University of Kalyani, Kalyani- 741 235, West Bengal, *insparc@cal2.vsnl.net.in* & Mr. Avijit Brahmacharya, Research Scholar, Department of Economics, University of Kalyani, Kalyani - 741 235, West Bengal, *avijiteco@rediffmail.com*

6. **Mr. S.K. Hegde,** Lecturer in Economics, MM Arts & Science College, Sirsi, Teacher Fellow under FTP, CMDR, A.V. Circle, Dharwad-01.

7. **Mr. Sanjeev Kenchaigol,** Research Scholar, CMDR, Dharwad.

8. **Ratna Reddy, M. Gopinath Reddy, V.M. Ravi Kumar & M. Srinivasa Reddy,** Centre for Economic and Social Studies (CESS), Hyderabad-500016, *mr_vejandla@yahoo.com*

9. **Dr. A.R. Kulkarni,** Associate Fellow, Centre for Multi-disciplinary Development Research (CMDR) A.V. Circle, D.B. Rodda Road, Dharwad-580 001, *cmdr@sancharnet.in*

10. **Dr. G.S. Sastry,** Assistant Professor, Centre for Ecological Economics and Natural Resources Institute for Social and Economic Change, Nagarabhavi, Bangalore-560 072, *gssastry@isec.ac.in*

11. **Mr. Rajesh Raj S.N.,** Research Associate, Centre for Multi-disciplinary Development Research (CMDR), Dharwad-01, *cmdr@sancharnet.in* & Dr. Malathy Duraisamy Professor of Economics, Department of Humanities and Social Sciences, Indian Institute of Technology Madras, Chennai-600036 (Tamil Nadu, India), *mdurai@iitm.ac.in*

12. **Md. Zakaria Siddiqui** Centre for Development Studies, Trivendrum- 695011, Kerala, *zakkulus@yahoo.com*

13. **Nandana Baruah** Ph.D Student, Centre for Development Studies, Trivendrum-695011, Kerala, *nandanabaruah@gmail.com*

14. **Syam Prasad,** Ph.D Scholar, Centre for Development Studies (CDS), Prashantnagar Road, Ullor-, Trivendrum, Kerala- 695011, *shyammail04@yahoo.com*

15. **Sandeep Sharma,** 344-E, Brahmaputra Hostel, Jawaharlal Nehru University, New Delhi-110 067, *sandeep07@gmail.com*

16. **Harilal M.S.,** Ph.D. Scholar, Centre for Development Studies, Prasant Nagar, Ullor, Thiruvananthapuram- 695011, *harivenganoor@rediffmail.com*

17. **Dr. V.B. Annigeri,** Reader, Centre for Multi-disciplinary Development Research (CMDR). A.V. Circle, D.B. Rodda Road, Dharwad- 580 001, *vinodann@yahoo.com* & Dr. Sailabala Debi, Director, CMDR, *s_debi_99@yahoo.com*

An Integrated Method for Research in Social Sciences: Some Reflections Key Note Address

P.R. Panchamukhi

This keynote address, which is of somewhat unconventional contents, is directed towards the young social scientist researchers, particularly economists with an open mind who wish to make research as their career. It is not directed so much to those researchers who have become less innovative in their research approaches and for whom research has become almost a routine, monotonous and a mechanical activity. Research, it must be remembered, is always an ever fresh and an innovative activity. I am aware that the Conventions, like the present one, have been visualized as the forums for helping young social scientists in particular, with innovative ideas, when senior social scientists are also available on the spot to extend their help. I may mention here that over the past more than a decade or so, CMDR has adopted in its own way this type of approach in its Ph.D. programmes in particular, through what it has termed as the *Research Scholars' Colloquium,* when a scholar/researcher, particularly a beginner from the Centre or from outside, is expected to present her/his research study, a proposal or a draft of the study, in front of all the senior faculty including the research supervisor from within and outside CMDR. We have found this activity to be a very useful programme for the young researchers. I am happy that such an idea is implemented on an extended scale under these Southern Institutes' Conventions and that CMDR has got an opportunity to organize the present Convention. The senior researchers may like to consider whether some of the ideas that I wish to present in this Key Note Address can be adopted on a wider scale through their own research students.

Research means examining something 'carefully', 'intensively', 'closely' or 'critically', in order to discover something. In the case of social science research this intensive examination relates to certain socio-economic issues, about which much more needs to be known.

Social Scientists, particularly economists have adopted a standard approach of research in most of their research inquiries, which has come to stay. According to this approach a research report or a dissertation should have the following components:

(a) Statement of the Problem

(b) Literature Review

(c) An Approach for An Empirical investigation consisting of Sampling Frame and description of the Location of the empirical investigation

(d) Instruments for Empirical Research such as a checklist or questionnaire with an explanation of the rationale for each question in the questionnaire, coding diagram, tabulation chart, etc

(e) Discussion of the Empirical Results

(f) Summary and Conclusions, Policy implications of the Study, Limitations of the Study and Leads for Future Research.

The above is a standard approach in any research study particularly in economics. There may be minor innovations and adjustments under each of the above components. For example, the literature review may be sometimes done in an unconventional way, being thematic and critical, throwing light on the importance of the problem chosen for the study instead of a chronological review of studies by different authors, quoting their names, references etc. Similarly, instead of full-fledged sample study the empirical investigation of the study might consist of a case study or case studies. Further, sometimes, research reports at the stage of Ph.D. are expected to focus more on the analysis of the problem chosen rather than on drawing policy inferences, etc. All the same, the format- the sequence in the research process and its presentation remains the same as above.

Friends, now I wish to share some of my ideas about social science research, particularly relating to the empirical investigation aspect (covered under c, d and e above, which obviously are the crucial aspects of research on socio economic problems). The ideas that I am trying to present might be quite familiar to many of my senior colleagues, particularly those from sociology and social work. But, I take the courage to outline them here, for the information of my younger friends and senior colleagues from economics, who probably have not yet adopted them in the main line economic research. These ideas have evolved over the past more than a decade of our research work here in CMDR and we have found them quite rewarding. I wish to name these ideas about research as *Integrated Method of Research in Social Sciences.*

Research, the Nobel Laureate T.W. Shultz, said, essentially consists of asking questions: asking relevant questions. When one is asking questions, one tends to develop pertinent insights about the issue under question. In other words, research is not so much directed towards seeking answers to the questions but is directed towards asking the insightful and relevant questions. This process may consist of posing questions before oneself or asking questions to the people about whom research is initiated or asking questions to others in order to elicit their responses about the issue under consideration. The checklist approach or questionnaire/interview schedule approach is essentially a method of collecting the quantitative and qualitative information relating to the issue being researched. The objective of this information gathering may be to strengthen the existing insights about the issue in question or to validate or verify the understanding, which already exists, or to *falsify* the accepted insights. All such initiatives are essentially the initiatives of a person who is trying to understand the problems of others. In this sense, there is a wedge between the researcher and the researched in the process of this type of research, which may be termed as the *'conventional research approach'*. A close scrutiny of this approach gives an impression that there is an implicit assumption/presumption that the researcher has better competence as compared to the researched even in understanding the problems of the latter. This 'hegemonic' approach is obviously a method of ascribing superiority to the researcher and the victim of the problem being researched is on the receiving end. Whether this approach is proper in social science research or not is not just an ethical question. It is indeed a question about the usefulness of the approach for a better understanding of the problem itself. It is a common knowledge now that the responses that the questioner gets from the respondents squarely depend upon the way the questions are put to him and in what mood both the questioner and the respondent are at that particular point of time. An innocent child when asked for example, what she/he would like to have- a brother or a sister, is reported to say in reply as sister and when the sequence is changed in the question- as sister or brother is found to say brother! In the same way the respondents in an empirical investigation also respond depending upon the way the questions are put, their sequence and the language of the question, etc. The questionnaire-based or checklist-based investigation therefore cannot ensure the objectivity in the entire research process. In order that the level of the objectivity of investigation improves it is better to involve the investigated also in the research process. It is in this background that some of the social sciences seem to have adopted what is termed as *'participatory research methods'* in their inquiries. It should however be admitted that the subjectivity may not be completely eliminated under this also as there is likely to be the subjectivity of the investigator and the investigated who are the partners now in the research process. This joint product of subjective investigation might however, result in a better acceptability of the outcome of the investigation by both the cooperators in the research process, as they are party to that process.

Participatory research method obviously provides scope for participation for both the researcher and the researched in the task of understanding the problems being examined. There is a joint reflection. The researched also is a researcher in a sense, in this approach of research. It is said that Darwin spent years in Beagle expedition and conducted surveys in the Cocos (Keeling) Islands living with the people over there. Cultural anthropologists following Bronislaw Malinowski have been adopting this method of intensive observation fully immersing into the other cultures, which they want to study. It has been said that this immersion is to the extent of even getting married to a member of other cultural groups in order to develop an insider view of other cultures. This form of *cooperative research or participant research* has paid immense dividends to the researchers in so far as developing insights about the problems is concerned. If the objective of an inquiry is only to understand the problem in question and not so much on evolving a solution to it then this type of approach might be considered useful. However, if the objective is to evolve approaches for resolving the issues in question then something more is needed.

The approach of research that attempts to consider this aspect is action research, which is gaining acceptability in recent years amongst unconventional researchers/organizations. Action research is not incompatible with social sciences as in most of them there is a problem solving approach.

Most of the social sciences have been considered not only as positive sciences but also as normative sciences, in the sense, they not only aid our understanding about the problem in question with facts and figures but they are also expected to help the process of reaching a desired end result. They call for positive intervention into the problems of the people. The debate about economic science whether it is a positive science or a normative science was quite intense during yester years. This debate seems to have got settled in favour of considering economics both as a positive science and a normative science. Adding a branch of welfare economics to economics as one of its important sub-disciplines is an important landmark, wherein value judgments about what is good for the society are allowed for. Even though much ink has been spilt in defining social welfare, welfare economists do indulge in developing theories for welfare improvement through several interesting propositions. The Pareto optimality criterion is one such proposition, which unfortunately is distribution neutral. Various compensation principles evolved by Hicks, Kaldor, Scitovsky, etc are attempts to lay down approaches for improvement in social welfare, keeping in mind sometimes the equity compulsions. In the case of reaching higher welfare positions through political process also such equity and efficiency integration is attempted in various systems of voting such as simple majority voting, qualified majority voting due to Wickell, rank voting, point voting, etc. Out of these the Wicksellian suggestion for qualified majority provides for a due weightage to the views of minority in arriving at a collective decision through a political process suggesting that the distributive equity considerations are duly incorporated so that the social welfare improvement is not distribution neutral. Thus, there is a normative dimension here, viz. that the minority views also ought to be considered in collective decision making. Thus, economic science is viewed under this dispensation as a normative science and not simply a positive science.

Having accepted this premise it follows that any economic research inquiry should help not only in improving our understanding about the problem under investigation but should also help validating the approach for resolving that particular problem. It is true that the conventional research studies do draw policy implications from the empirical investigations conducted in the study. However, there is no attempt at verifying the validity or otherwise of the policy suggestions made. The researcher continues to remain passive in this inquiry. Even the respondent- the researched people-remain indifferent to the policy inferences hoping for somebody to appear to solve their problems. In the action research this does not happen. The researcher intervenes into the problem having understood its nature with a purpose of resolving it. Both the researcher and the researched participate both in the process of understanding the problem under investigation and in the implementation of the policies to solve the problem.

Thus, it is clear that participatory research need not be necessarily oriented towards action. What is implied therein is that there are definite roles for both the professionals and the people in the process of research. On the other hand, in action research, research is necessarily oriented towards action. One should also note that not all action research need be participatory, though most often in actual practice, it is. Simply speaking, action research consists of research for action and action for research. Since most economic research is library research and some of it is based upon data collected from the field, it is essentially reflective and not action based. This practice of research had gives an impression that action research is not compatible with economic research. However, it should be clarified that *action research is not incompatible with even economic research.* Economics being one of the social sciences also happens to be a normative discipline, as elucidated above. Economic research also entertains a desire or it is even under a mandate to bring about a desired change through its own contributions.

Action research is defined as a *'study of a social situation carried out by those involved in that situation in order to improve their practice and the quality of their understanding'*.[1] In participatory action research there is a cycle of reflection–action-reflection and action and so on. 'Action without reflection and understanding is blind just as theory without action is meaningless'[2] I am reminded of in this connection the debate of thirties of last century about theory without measurement and measurement without theory, which got concluded with the need for theory with measurement in our inquiries. In the same way in social sciences, in economics in particular, we need to integrate action with reflection.

Action research is considered to be due to the contributions of Kurt Lewin.[3] However, I wish to highlight that action research was prevalent in India over centuries. In the Indian philosophical traditions, for example, action was considered as an integral part of learning. This *learning by doing* is picturesquely illustrated through an anecdote of *Chandogyopanishat,* where Shvetaketu an arrogant son of Uddalaka is told that human beings are so small in the world, which is controlled by an *invisible hand.* With nine action studded illustrations this is explained to the conceited boy. In the same way, in the discipline of ancient linguistics a theory has been enunciated to show that meanings of the words are understood by a child only through verbal statements followed by action and not just by verbal statements by the *prayojaka vruddha (an elderly person who initiates action) and the prayojya vruddha (an adult who undertakes action at the instance of the elderly person)*. Thus, when the elder brother tells the younger brother-take the pot and bring water, the child who is supposed to be keenly observing and reflecting, notices that the younger brother takes a pot, goes to the river, fills it with water and places the pot before the elder brother, saying here is water. By these actions the child comes to know about the meaning of the word 'water'. In fact, most of ancient Indian education consisted of learning by doing, which seems to have been replaced by the modern system of liberal education. There is even a school of thought, which says that the entire *Vedas* are guidebooks for action and not so much the treatises on Brahman, the supreme power. In this background, action research need not be considered as something, which is not compatible with the thinking of the Indian social scientists and scholars in humanities.

Thus, *participatory action research can be a useful approach for research in social sciences in general and in economics in particular.* Of course, this participatory action research needs to be integrated with the conventional research approaches consisting of base line data gathering even to identify the nature of the social problem and the nature of the approach to solve the problem, before plunging into action. All these aspects need to be participatory. There is a cyclical nature of the typical action research process consisting of four steps; plan, act, observe and reflect. As has been rightly observed, 'there are five phases to be conducted within each research cycle. Initially, a problem is identified and data is collected for a more detailed diagnosis. This is followed by a collective postulation of several possible solutions, from which a single plan of action is implemented. Data on the results of the intervention are collected and analysed and the findings are interpreted in the light of how successful the action has been. At this point, the problem is reassessed and the process begins another cycle. This process continues until the problem is resolved.'[4][4][4] I call this as an *Integrated Method of Research for Social Sciences.* Under this method social science research is continuous. It is a method of *rolling research. Such a research approach is necessary in social sciences, for the social problems never terminate but they only roll over to next set of problems.*

This opens up a question; *are all issues in the society/economy amenable to this type of integrated method of research (IMR)?* I do not have a ready answer to this question. The researcher herself or himself has to reflect and take a view in the matter. So far as CMDR researches of late are concerned we have tried out this approach in two areas, viz agriculture and health. And we had very fascinating experiences in both of them.

The IMR in agriculture related to economics of shifting from tobacco cultivation. We adopted a village in the bidi tobacco belt in Belgaum district of Karnataka for trying out our ideas for shifting from tobacco cultivation I am sure our colleagues enjoyed what we tried collectively and jointly with farmers in this research exercise, consisting of understanding the nature of determinants of tobacco cultivation, developing insights about the socio economic conditions of tobacco farmers based upon a thorough survey of nearly 2000 tobacco farmers, intervening with 100 selected farmers from among them, facilitating shifting from tobacco to other livelihoods based upon their decision and showing to the policy makers that tobacco farmers have high level of willingness to shift to other livelihoods if proper alternatives are shown to them, etc. We discovered that farmers are not so much guided by only the commercial considerations of tobacco cultivation, as is normally thought of. They would be interested in voluntarily shifting from tobacco cultivation to other livelihoods once they are made aware of the ill health effects of not only tobacco consumption but also of tobacco cultivation. We discovered that what is needed is an integrated approach of social awakening with a multidisciplinary thrust that can really trigger of their decision and action. I am happy to mention here that this successful action experiment, was floated by the International Development Research Centre Canada, which sponsored this project, on their web site. The results of this action research did have further ripples in the sense that a large number of tobacco farmers in the region willingly took a decision in due course of time to shift to other livelihoods like sugarcane cultivation, soya-bean farming, dairy farming etc. The Centre is planning to bring out the results of this action research in the form of papers, though it has already brought out a few papers and monographs on these experiments under its Monograph Series.

The other action research experiment undertaken by CMDR was in the field of health. On the basis of a thorough field investigation and country reviews we noticed that during economic reforms the social services in general and health services in particular become costlier making the poor suffer on account of non availability of quality health care services and that self help by the people is necessary under the circumstances. After a number of studies about the health service development in a macro setting we tried out an action experiment developing a Peoples' Health Clinic in a village (Morab) that we adopted for the purpose, in Dharwad district. With the cooperation of the people from the village and our partial but carefully worked out intervention (which also was the outcome of joint reflection) we could notice that all people in the village, including those who are relatively poor, are willing to pay for health care services, if care is taken to ensure their quality and timely availability. It was also true that with the newly started Peoples' Health Clinic people did get good medical care service. This experiment also had its positive externalities in the sense that the Primary Health Centre (PHC) under the government's programme of rural health care services, which merely existed in that village without much activity, became more alert and started functioning properly ! We discovered that this triggering off of people's action by a small action research intervention could act as a countervailing power to reform the prevailing service delivery system of the government! A number of studies under this action research project are now published[5] by the UNDP who had sponsored this project on Economic Reforms and the Health Sector. I have also presented our interesting action research experiences with the responses of the District Health Officer and PHC in the form of a novel entitled *Oh! Our People,* just to bring home the message of our action research for the benefit of lay readers and government officers.

Thus, it is possible to pick and choose the issues for action research under the *Integrated Method of Research,* with an action research component. I feel that this IMR, which has micro perspectives is a better suited research method in the background of economic reforms; for, the micro level issues may hardly receive the attention that they deserve in the course of the economic reforms of globalization, liberalization and privatization, which sweep the entire economy and society. It is true that generalizations from a single action research experiment may not be possible. But, action experiments in different locations relating to the same issue might provide useful insights for policy making.

The message from this address for the young researchers is that they may adopt unconventional research approaches in their research initiatives and may not get bogged down to the monotonous stereotype approaches. This strategy would make research thrilling, enjoyable and useful. I am happy to mention that the Indian Council of Social Science Research has taken kindly to the action research studies and studies adopting this IMR. I do hope that the social science fraternity, particularly economists also would take kindly to this.

NOTES

Prof. P.R. Panchamukhi, Professor Emeritus & Founder Director, Centre for Multi-disciplinary Development Research (CMDR), Dharwad on the occasion of 5th Development Convention of Southern ICSSR Institutes held at CMDR on 27-28th April 2006.

1. Richard Winter and Carol Munn-Giddings: *Action Research in Health and Social Care.* Rotledge, London and New York; 2001. p. 8.
2. Peter Reason & Hilary Bradbury: *Action Research: Participatory Inquiry & Practice* Sage Publications. 2001.
3. Lewin Kurt. "Action Research and Minority Problems", *Journal of Social Issues* 2 (1946) pp. 34-46.
4. Gerald Susman "Action Research : A Socio-technical Systems Perspective." In Ed. G.Morgan: Sage Publications; 1983.
5. 1. Annigeri. V.B: *Private Doctors Amidst Economic Reforms: Reflections from Survey.*
   2. Annigeri. V.B., Myageri D.R.: *Analysis of Budgetary Health Expenditure in the Public Sector using a Health Accounting Framework: Reflections from Maharashtra, Karnataka and Orissa.*
   3. Nayanatara S.N: *Economic Reforms and Health Sector in India with special reference to Orissa, Karnataka and Maharashtra : Reflections from NSS 28th, 42nd and 52nd Rounds.*
   4. Panchamukhi P.R. and Nayanatara S.N. *People's Participation in Health: Prepayment Mechanism Through Health Care Cooperative.*
   5. Badiger Aravind, Kadekodi G.K. Nayanatara N.S.: *Economic Reforms and Drug Policy : A Micro Level Analysis.*

Chapter - 1

Leveraging ICTs for Inclusive and Sustainable Agricultural and Rural Development in India

Sukhpal Singh

INTRODUCTION

Sustainable development involves not only economic aspects, but also equity, ecology, and indigeneity. In the context of global economy and competitive markets, developments in Information and Communication Technologies (ICTs) such as satellite television broadcasting, radio, long-distance telephony, computers, Internet and telecommunications have sparked optimism about their potential to accelerate the pace of social and economic development in developing countries. It is argued that the ICTs can be harnessed to meet basic human needs of the poor and marginalised communities in rural and remote areas, and to create new structures for governance and commerce. They can also be used to create markets with the poorest of the poor ('bottom of the pyramid') as argued by CK Prahalad for some time now (Prahalad, 2005). But, the development outcomes depend on economic factors on the supply side as well as demand side mediated by institutional factors which include private firms, NGOs, government agencies, and social norms and institutions (Kaushik and Singh, 2004). Despite the hype, ICT spending accounted for only less than 10% of GDP during the 1990s across nations with as much as 9.3% in New Zealand and only 2.1% in India, which is one of the lowest. Further, there is digital divide between the rich and the poor users. For example, over 90% of the internet users came from the richest 20% of the world's population and the poorest 20% make only 0.2% of the world's internet users. This divide or inequality exceeds income inequality and can lead to further inequalities of income and livelihoods (Joseph, 2002; Clarke, 2003).

The important research questions about the role of ICTs in sustainable agricultural and rural development are:

1. How Internet as a technology is made accessible to rural people? What is the context in which it operates? Which factors help or hinder its use? (*system/technology*).
2. What kind of knowledge and information is made available to the farmers on agriculture? Who defines this knowledge? What kind of agricultural knowledge and information they find useful and how? How? Why? (*content*).
3. Who are the users of Internet for agricultural/rural knowledge and information? What are their perceptions about Internet and its relevance for agricultural development? (*users*).
4. Who really benefits from introduction of Internet in rural/local communities? (*equity*).
5. How are ICTs being used by the government, NGOs, and international development agencies to bridge the digital divide and promote sustainable development? (*strategies*).
6. What is the extent and nature of social exclusion, reasons for it, and ways to make ICTs more accessible and participatory? (*exclusion and participation strategies*).
7. What is the financial and technological sustainability of the ICT projects over the longer term? (sustainability).

In India, however, diffusion of ICTs in rural areas is hampered by the lack of infrastructural development. In 1998, India had only four computers per 1,000 population, 0.01 internet hosts per 1000, 20 telephone lines per 1000, and 13.17 US$ per capita ICT, all of them being the lowest in Asia (Clarke, 2003). Nonetheless, some efforts have been made in the recent years to take Internet to the rural communities. These include mainly the e-governance projects like the Gyandoot of the Government of Madhya Pradesh in Dhar (a tribal district), the Warna wired villages project in Kohlapur district of Maharashtra (Rajora, 2001), Village Information Centres (VICs) of the M.S. Swaminathan Research Foundation (MSSRF) in Pondicherry, The Friends and the IT@School projects in Kerala, Drishtee.com in many states of India starting from Sirsa district in Haryana, and the TARAkendras of the Development Alternatives (DA-an NGO) in Bathinda (Punjab) (Sreekumar, 2003), besides the well known e-choupal project of the ITC in agricultural input supply and procurement sector. This paper reviews some of these projects for drawing lessons about their developmental impact in terms of above stated questions and possible strategies to enhance the impact on agricultural and rural producers, more so, marginal and small of them.

THE PROJECTS AND THEIR PERFORMANCE

The Gyandoot Project

The Gyandoot (meaning 'purveyor of knowledge') Project involved, to begin with, setting up of 26 *soochanalayas* (information centres) at the village level in Dhar District of M.P., which has 60% households below poverty line, by the state government in 2000, in collaboration with local bodies, which provide farmers information on agricultural produce prices, land records, and other agricultural issues besides other types of e-governance. The purpose was to reduce time and cost involved for the villagers in accessing the government officials. These ICT kiosks, placed in villages which hold weekly markets or are located on major roads to facilitate access by people in neighbouring villages, are operated by unemployed rural (at least) matriculate youth (Soochaks) who are selected and trained to run these centres (Cecchini and Raina, 2004).

At the local level, there are two models of governance-one where village committee manages the kiosk and the other where it is given to a private entrepreneur. In the former case, village committee pays for set up costs and the operator has to bear the operational costs and does not receive any salary. Bu, he keeps 90% of the earning after remitting 10% to the panchayat. The private model, on the other hand, gives full ownership of the kiosk to the soochak, he keeps all earnings and pays fixed amount of Rs. 5000 to the Gyandoot Samiti annually (Cecchini and Raina, 2004). In the Panchayat model, the kiosk operator is one of the three persons selected by the Panchayat who are sent for training and who is finally chosen after an interview and practical examination. On the other hand, in private model, an entrepreneur who has capital to invest or manages a loan gets the job of a soochak. Thus, by virtue of the need for capital, private soochkas mostly came from economically stronger backgrounds, higher castes, and with higher education.

The entire project is managed by a committee called Gyandoot Samiti registered under the M.P. Societies Registration Act with the District Collector as the President. The CEO of the District Panchayat functions as the Secretary of the Committee and various departmental heads are members of the Committee. It has a project manager, an assistant project officer, a technical head and a few computer operators. But, the Samiti does not have any authority or the financial means to improve the information processing methods of the government departments or the quality of service which rests with the state government. Therefore, Samiti has limited scope to improve back end processes though it has improved the front end processes with kiosks (Cecchini and Raina, 2004).

Each Soochanalaya caters to 15 gram panchayats and 25-30 villages. On the whole, the project benefits about half a million people living in 311 gram panchayats and 600 villages. A Soochak is expected to earn an income of Rs. 2500 per month. The cost of setting up a Soochanalaya is Rs. 75,000 and all the money has come from the panchayat funds with no cost to the government exchequer. Some of the Soochaks have also been given the power of petition writing and stamp vending (Rajora, 2001). In fact, a programme called Gramhaat is being used to facilitate buying and selling of produce and animals within the intranet villages. The project was awarded the Stockholm Challenge Award in 2001 which considered aspects like innovation, user need, transferability of the project, and accessibility of the project benefits to people who need it the most, besides sustainability of the project (Krishan, 2003).

The information of various types about different departments can be accessed from the *Soochanalaya* on payment of a nominal fee. These *Soochanalayas* which numbered 38 in 2004 (Cecchini and Raina, 2004) offer services such as agricultural prices, internet surfing, job work, data entry, computer training, offset printing, video games, cassette recording, screening of CD films, preparation of horoscopes, online applications, complaints, e-mails, matrimonial, government programmes, and technical advice for villagers and students, the cost of which ranges from Rs. 5- 500 each (Krishan, 2003). It caters to the ICT requirements of a wide section of rural community as part of social engineering and development and has marked a major shift in the way government functionaries relate to the needs of the rural poor. But the project remains an administered programme with little relationship with the society (Sreekumar, 2003). The new services include gram daak, mandi rates, gram haat, and weather report (Krishan, 2003). The major factors in the success of the Gyandoot project has been clear identification of information needs of the villagers, use of the soochak as the intermediary, and ensuring tangible benefits to local people. But, the dangers are that of the new dependence of the farmers on soochaks and the divide between those who have all the access to information and those who have little access. This necessitates monitoring (Choenni, 2003).

A more recent study of the project shows that though the service satisfaction among users was high, the usage was low (10 users per day against a target population of 25,000 i.e. 0.3% of total (Dossani, et al, 2005)) due to low awareness among potential users and long distances to travel, and the project was not reaching the poorest people. Only 74% of the kiosks were operational and only 31% of the poor people were aware of the project or facility compared with 77% in the case of rich people. There were also gender and caste barriers in making use of the kiosks due to their location in upper caste or class households especially when they were run by private entrepreneurs. There were only two women kiosk operators in 2002 who were managing panchayat owned soochnalayas. Further, though 20 services were offered, there were a few services which people found useful like agricultural prices which was useful for large farmers with large surplus produce to sell and grievance redressal and advisory modules. Further, the revenue from a kiosk was not sufficient to generate a good livelihood. But, soochaks were found be co-operative, helpful and polite (Cecchini and Raina, 2004).

The Warna Project

The project is operational across 70 villages covering 350,000 people with 54 booths at the village level. It is run by Warna Vibhag Shikshan Mandal in districts of Warna Nagar, Kohlapur and Sangli and serves largely the sugarcane growers with the objective of making the sugar co-operatives more efficient and to support cooperatives with agricultural and medical information besides facilitating continued enskilling and education (Sreekumar, 2003). The booth is run by an employee trained by the sugar co-operative and has a PC, a printer and a UPS besides a modem with dial up connectivity. It is in Marathi and about 40 users use the facility every day on an average (Dossani et al, 2005).

Gyandoot and Warna compared

The Gyandoot project has been set up at a cost of Rs. 25 lakh which is perceived to be very cost effective compared to the investment of Rs. 2.5 crore in the case of Warna Wired Village Project. Also, in the later case, the benefits go to members of sugar and dairy cooperatives only (Rajora, 2001). But, it is only the men who make use of most of the facilities at the Soochanalayas in M.P. In fact, most of the users were children and young people. Therefore, there is exclusion of the aged and the women (Sreekumar, 2003). Further, the usage level was much higher in the Warna project (4.4%) compared with Gyandoot (0.3%) (Dossani et al, 2005).

The VICs of MSSRF

MSSRF Village Information Centres (VICs) launched in 1998 aim to provide sustainable food security in rural areas of Pondicherry–a Union Territory of India. The centres were originally designed to provide information and technical assistance to farmers through packages prepared locally making use of both indigenous knowledge and modern science. The project not only provides access to ICTs and trains rural youth in ICT but also provides information on various government programmes and mobilizes data for action research. The VICs receive information by voice mail and dispense it through a public address system. The farmers receive advice on rotation of crops, fertilizers and pesticides. There are wireless sets connecting the villages and most of the project work is fueled by solar power. This project is a part of a larger project called Bio-village being implemented by the MSSRF to cover seven lakh villages in India by 2010 (Ram, 2000). But, here, most of the operators are women and users both women and men. In fact, the entire project is being managed by 10 women volunteers who faced opposition from their family members initially. The centre provides two websites: *www.pondicherryagri.com* for price of agricultural commodities and farm policies, schemes of the government, and subsidies, and *www.cnn.com* for weather information for the farmers and the fisherfolk. It also brings out a local publication (Our Village News) containing all farming related news and information, of which 5000 copies are distributed in villages as farmers can not afford to buy a Tamil newspaper (Menon, 2005). Interestingly, as it was more participatory in its design, the usage levels were much higher (5.2%) compared with other projects and comparable to Warna (4.4%) and e-choupal (8.9%). In 2005, there were 12 such centres in 12 villages covering 35,000 people (Dossani et al, 2005).

The ICT Projects in Kerala

The FRIENDS and IT@School are two projects in Kerala. The FRIENDS stands for Fast, Reliable, Instant, Efficient Network for Disbursement of Services. Local bodies and seven government agencies collaborated to create these integrated service centres which accept utility bills, taxes and fees meant for participating departments in 14 districts of the state. It is perceived as a single window scheme for the consumer. But, in practice, the centres have not made a major headway and suffer from official negligence besides poor financial performance in the first year of their establishment. The IT@School Project has also suffered from similar obstacles. It was an E-Learning initiative and was to cover 65 lakh students from class 1 to class 10. The project has been a non-starter and criticized for its collaboration with Microsoft (Sreekumar, 2003).

The TARAkendras of Tarahaat

TARAkendras are a project of TARAHAAT which is sponsored by Development Alternatives (DA), an NGO based in Delhi. TARA stands for Technology and Action for Rural Advancement and is a marketing wing of DA. TARAHAAT which has a mix of business and development objectives, is an internet portal supporting a network of franchised computer kiosks (TARAkendras) launched in 2000 in Bundelkhand region of M.P. and U.P. and then in 2001 in Bathinda, Sangrur and Ludhiana districts in Punjab. Today, it has 19 centres. It is a body registered under the Companies Act and has 51% ownership with a non-profit foundation. It is run as a franchising business (for each kiosk) where each operator franchisee invests Rs. 2.4-3 lakh per kiosk with bank finance available on 25% margin money contribution by the franchisee operator. A franchisee earns about Rs. 3.5-4 thousand per month but has to pay 25% to the franchisor (TARAhaat), which was earlier 40%, besides a fixed annual fee. He is given initial training and periodic visits by local TARAhaat officials (Kaushik and Singh, 2004). It delivers a wide range of services i.e.

information on government schemes, health, law, weather and commodity prices; communication like e-mail and Taradaak in Indian languages; and education like job oriented courses in IT, English and personality development, through ICTs and expects to earn revenues by pricing the services as well as levying membership fee and commissions (source: TARAhaat.com).

An interesting feature of this project is that it was not conceived as a voluntary venture from the very beginning. The villages and towns are identified with the help of local agencies like DRDA and other influential people and opinion leaders in the villages. In order to meet the training needs of TARAkendras, a TARA Academy has been set up. In order to promote participation of women which is low at present, it has set up TARA Baatcheet. But, it has not been very successful in most of the places (Sreekumar, 2003). Tarahaat was also awarded the Stockholm Challenge Award in 2001. TARAhaat has moved more to commercial operations for viability reasons and has suffered from poor connectivity. Thus, it could start only eight kiosks instead of the planned 32 in Punjab due to various institutional constraints like transfer of facilitating govt. officials and the very business model it chose. It also had high start up costs for its franchisees and getting bank loans was not that easy. Besides, the franchisees were not always local people which hindered rapport building for faster business growth as they were perceived to be outsiders. Thus, it has not been able to deliver the promised deals to franchisees as well as customers of these kiosks. It could also not penetrate the real rural people and its users were more of students and other relatively well off people who sought connectivity for various other reasons, not production or business activity. This was partly due to the fact that TARAhaat left promotion activity to the franchisees (Kaushik and Singh, 2004).

The Drishtee.com

On the other hand, another e-governance initiative in Sirsa District of Haryana by Drishtee.com, a private commercial organization operating its kiosks in many states, which also adopted the franchisee model and had its origins in Gyandoot project, was successful as it had lower investments per kiosk (Rs. 60-80 thousand), covered lesser population, charged lower franchiser royalty (20%), had more of state and local public services like registration of vehicles, driving license applications, Below Poverty Line (BPL) applications, and complaints, provided field support and was also supported by local administration. Its clear focus on poor people, mobilizing franchisees as a pressure group for making state respond quickly, and aggressive expansion of operations which led to economies of scale, also helped. But, its over-dependence on government services alone can prove to be risky in future (Kaushik and Singh, 2004).

In addition, several portals have been created by the government, donor agencies and the private sector in the broad areas of development, such as agricultural marketing, health, education, and environment. One such portal is *www.krishiworld.com*, an agricultural portal, currently in English and Marathi, which is developed to encourage the widespread use of critical information in agriculture and related fields among farmers. This portal is used by farmers of Maharashtra for information on fruit and vegetable preservation and canning, use of inputs, current market prices of various agricultural produce and inputs, imports and exports, and government policies for farmers. Recently, the Government of India has launched 1551 toll free Kisan Call Centres at eight places in the country which provide the farmers with technical and market information round the clock and already receive 2500 calls each every day.

ICTs for Agri-supply Chain Efficiency: The E-choupals of ITC Ltd.

The experience of agricultural development in India has shown that the existing systems of delivery of agricultural inputs and purchase and use of agricultural output have not been efficient in reaching the benefits of better linkages between agriculture and agro-processing industry to the farmers or the agro-industry. The timely, quality and cost effective delivery of adequate inputs still remains a dream despite the marketing attempts of the corporate sector and the developmental programmes of the state. The farmers are not able to sell their produce remuneratively. There are frequent gluts in the markets, resulting in low prices and losses to the farmers. On the other hand, processors and/or marketers face problems in obtaining timely, cost effective, and adequate supply of quality raw materials. Though various models are being attempted in India to build better linkages with farmers, but there is no doubt that biotechnology and ICTs will play a decisive role in bringing about competitiveness in Indian agribusiness sector both for quality and cost reasons (Streeter et al, 1991). The role of ICTs in agricultural development can be viewed in terms of role of information provision and its use for decision making at the farmer level. The information asymmetries created by lack of information lead to market inefficiencies and market failures and consequently sub-optimal outcomes for farmers both in input as well as output markets. From the production side, information can be used to increase the efficiency of extension input and thereby improving the input use efficiency and returns. The provision of information can be catalyst in making farmers switch to new crops and technologies and they can become progressive farmers. But, the context in which information is provided and used is critical as that determines the ultimate use of such information and its effects for wider agricultural and rural development.

The information needs of India's marginal and small farms which make up more than 80% of the total operational holdings include information about input markets, technologies, output markets, financial (credit) markets, weather, and policies of the state. And, the present system of information flow is slow, time taking, inadequate in content, less interactive, and expensive besides being multi-step. It is here that ICT can play a role in bettering the agricultural scenario for these farmers.

ITC is one of India's leading private companies with annual turnover of US$ 2 billion in 2003. Its international business division (IBD), which operates the e-choupal (choupal means a gathering place in a village in Hindi) project, was created in 1990 as an agricultural trading company and generated revenue of the order of US$150 million in 2003 (Annamalai and Rao, 2003). The ITC Ltd.'s e-choupal project is an ICT based project which aims at building effective farmer-agribusiness linkages. The existing system of agricultural markets in soyabean was found to be inefficient leading to higher costs for the farmer and the company. In Madhya Pradesh, the agribusiness division of the company (IBD) has set up e-choupals for soyabean which provide the farmers access to market information and quality inputs. The model had reengineering, not reconstruction, and holistic approach as its principles. In these e-choupals, the farmer takes his produce to the ITC procurement center located at the block or district level after knowing price of the crop from the sanchalak in the village. He has the option to sell the produce to the company warehouse, factory, collection center or the sanchalak (Company agent who interacts with farmers for output and input transactions). The produce is bought under standardized weighing and grading systems. In the e-choupal system, the farmer takes only a sample of his produce to the local *sanchalak* and receives a spot price quote from the sanchalak. The previous day's mandi price is used to determine a benchmark fair average quality price at the e-choupal for a given day and it is static for that day (Annamalai and Rao, 2003). If the farmer accepts the price, he can deliver directly to the company's collection center and get paid within a few hours. The ITC offers Rs.15-20 per quintal higher price than the mandi price to the farmers for their produce. The sanchalak gets a commission of 0.5% on the sales through him. The farmer produce is accepted by the company procurement centers only with a slip from the sanchalak. The farmers are reimbursed cost of transport if they deliver to the procurement or processing center, in order to remove another constraint in accessing the market i.e. transport cost (Kumar, 2004). The company has maintained a role for the traditional commission agents by making them *sanyojaks* (coordinators) in this project who manage physical flows in the supply chain and collect price information from local mandis and maintain records. Thus, the company has chosen to reintermediate, and not disintermediate (Sawhney, 2002).

The sanchalak is an interface between the computer terminal and the farmers. He provides information to the farmers about the company and the mandi price of the produce, samples produce and even procures it sometimes, sells products (agricultural inputs) of the company and other partner companies to farmers, and builds relationship with farmers. The sanchalaks are overseen by sanyojaks appointed by the company who coordinate groups of farmers, document information at the procurement center level, collect information about market prices, ensure transport of produce to the processing center, supply inputs to the sanchalak and build relations with sanchalaks and farmers, and sometimes also make payments to the farmers for their produce sold to the company (Figure 1). The sanyojaks are more often traditional commission agents in local mandis and the company leverages their strengths in trading and dealing with farmers. A sanyojak gets a commission of 1% on the sales through him.

Figure 1
The ITC e-choupal network

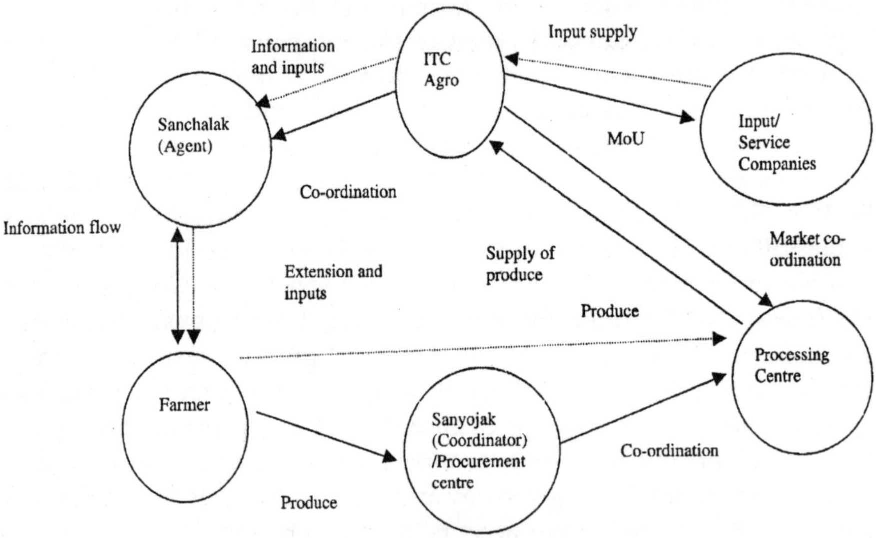

In this backwards vertical e-co-ordination, the company provides and maintains the infrastructure and equipment for the sanchalak and trains him. Each e-choupal costs Rs. 1.3-2.5 lakh in terms of set up costs and Rs. 4000 per year for maintenance (Annamalai and Rao, 2003). The sanchalak bears all the operational costs. In some villages, where there is no computer made available, the information exchange is carried out through telephone. In some other places, there are computers without Internet connectivity (Gupta, 2003). The sanyojak identifies sanchalaks in the villages and recommends them to the company which finally appoints the sanchalaks. A sanchalak is interested in e-choupal as it gives him/her a profitable business, functional computer which is a matter of prestige, and a role to help the local community. A sanchalak is given three day training to run the e-choupal- for a day each after recruitment, after a week of operations, and after a month of operations. It is ensured that the sanchalak should be a medium farmer so that he is acceptable to other farmers and has interest in e-choupal. On the other hand, local arthiyas (commission agents) are interested in becoming sanyojaks as the company promises to work with them over the long term and through the mandi, it offers attractive commission, and the fear among the agents that if one does not take it up, others may grab the opportunity (Annamalai and Rao, 2003). There are many advantages to the farmers which an e-choupal offers compared to those offered/not offered by mandi (Kumar, 2004). The farmers find that e-choupal gives them better prices, reduces wastage of produce, ensures transparency and is faster and less costly compared with the market based transactions. The figure 1 shows the linkages among various participants in the e-choupal project.

A farmer saves Rs. 25-27 per quintal on soyabean marketing as he no longer pays bagging, transporting, loading and unloading charges, and avoids wastage and wrong weighment at the mandi. On the other hand, the company saves about Rs. 20-27 per quintal even after paying for transport cost to the farmer (Shenoy, 2002; Kumar, 2004). Thus, the farmer gets 2.5% higher price and the company is able to procure at 2.5% lower cost (Annamalai and Rao, 2003). In fact, during 2001-2002 (16 months), the company saved about 1.7% on transaction costs and about 2.8% on account of improved quality produce (Kumar, 2004). In wheat, the company has managed to save Rs. 5-6 per quintal which is almost 10% of the procurement cost. The traditional market players in soyabean have responded to this supply chain innovation of the company by adopting its practices like higher prices, credit facility, and fairer trade (Gupta, 2003). The e-choupal model has been designed to tackle the problems of fragmented farms, weak infrastructure, and large number of intermediaries in the Indian farm sector. This modal leverages information technology to cluster all the value chain participants to reap benefits of vertical coordination. It makes use of the physical transmission capabilities of current intermediaries like aggregation logistics, counter party risk and bridge financing while disintermediating them from the chain of information flow and market signals. The information provided is in local language. The leveraging of Information Technology in this model takes place through (a) delivery of real time information and customized knowledge to the farmers to improve their decision making ability for better alignment of produce to the market and better quality and productivity; (b) aggregation of demand at the village level for accessing higher quality farm inputs and knowledge at lower costs; and (c) setting up of direct marketing channel linked to the mandi system for price comparison and simultaneously eliminating wasteful intermediation. This reduces transaction cost and makes logistics efficient (Paul, 2003). Some infrastructural inadequacies like power supply and telecom connectivity have been addressed with innovative solutions like solar battery power backups, installation of V-SAT equipment and mobile choupals (itcportal website).

Within two years of its launch (since June 2000), the project reached 6 lakh farmers in 6000 villages through 1000 e-choupals (Sanganeria, 2003). The project became the largest initiative among all internet based interventions in rural India in 2002 reaching more than 10 lakh farmers in 11000 villages through 1900 kiosks in four states i.e. Madhya Pradesh, Karnataka, Andhra Pradesh and Uttar Pradesh in crops of soyabean, coffee, fish, and wheat respectively (Annamalai and Rao, 2003). M.P. alone had 1750 e-choupals in 2005 with a total of 5500 throughout the country covering 31,000 villages and 3.1 million farmers in 2005 (Dossani et al, 2005). It is also planning to get into other crops such as bajra, basmati rice, sesame seeds and handpicked groundnut besides spices and fruits and vegetables. These projects will be spread across 14 states over the next few years (Sanganeria, 2003). But, so far, the company has been purchasing only soyabean and not providing much of other services like inputs or information on farm practices. However, the company has tied up with Monsanto and MP Seed Corporation for seeds, NFCL for fertilizers, ICICI Bank for credit, and ICICI Prudential for insurance, for the supply of these inputs to farmers through its network system. It charges a commission of 10% on the sales of these services of which 50% goes to the sanchalak and the sanyojak. In the Madhya Pradesh project, the tie up with input companies makes it possible for the sanchalaks to earn a commission of 2-3% on sales, and for the sanyojaks who is distributor for the sanchalak, a commission of 1-3%. The company collects between 2-3% commission for itself for lending its network to input sellers (Assisi and Gupta, 2003). Thus, it is taking care of other hurdles like credit for the farmers to access e-choupal markets (Kumar, 2004).

Though during 2001-02, only about 60% choupals sold soyabeans to the company (Kumar, 2004), the value of e-choupals to the company is not for their ICT role per se but what they do to the supply chain in which the company deals. Therefore, viability of the e-choupal is not dependent upon its ICT transactions, but on the volumes of produce traded due to it (Kumar, 2004). This is a case of use of ICT by an enterprise in an agri-supply chain to improve its supply chain efficiency which was crucial to maintain and improve global competitiveness due to opening up of its markets (Kumar, 2004). It had led to both, cost reduction for the two players in the chain i.e. company and farmers, and better product quality for the company which is must for competitiveness (Salin, 1998). It is the case of a firm which has knowledge and resources and strategy for sustained growth through partnership with local people. It (ITC) will make money while helping others, including farmers, make money. Their strategies involve bundling of inputs and linking up of credit with input supply which is the agribusiness of the 21st century (Boehlje et al, 1995). It is interlocking of factor markets coming back in another form. But, what is wrong with it if it can provide what state and co-operatives have not been able to provide for so long i.e. timely and cost effective supply of quality inputs and finance and even tractors, and combine harvesters etc. on hire basis and assured market for produce? Theses agribusiness services focus on more efficient use of modern inputs with a two-pronged strategy i.e. yield increase or cost reduction through inputs and value addition (market improvement). This is a must for competitiveness whether domestic or international where quality and cost effectiveness are the driving forces. The factors in success include extensive knowledge of agriculture in the company, retaining the existing channels to reach farmers, and the company's commitment to the project and fair dealing with growers (Annamalai and Rao, 2003).

Of course, there are issues of access to poorer users of e-choupal due to its location in a larger, higher caste, and richer farmer's house most of the time. Further, most of the e-choupals are in prosperous villages and the e-choupals leading to a monopsonistic situation for the ITC-IBD is not ruled out (Kumar, 2004).

CONCLUSIONS

From a developmental angle, there is a need to look at the relationship between ICTs and development in terms of role of information in development which can be in terms of processes which are processing of data and communication of the same, and outcomes which include learning and decision making (Heeks, 2002). The lessons from some of the projects implemented are worth a mention here. Firstly, the benefits of ICT should be broad based from the beginning itself which helps viability and gets credibility and local support. Secondly, the partnership between private and public institutions should be handled carefully and be sustainable. Thirdly, it is important to ensure right incentives to people involved like the field staff and the franchisees. Fourthly, the services menu should be chosen carefully and expanded overtime as per local demand. Finally, the franchisee model suits better than any other model provided adequate incentives are built into the agreement for the franchisee, as it ensures commercial viability and local involvement and enterprise. Further, there are issues of appropriate technology, community participation and ownership, pro-poor services, and financial sustainability of the ICT initiatives which need to be considered at the project design stage itself (Cecchini and Raina, 2004).

So far as agricultural business is concerned, there is a need to understand local systems of buying and selling at the farmer level and bring in bundling of benefits like input supply and output purchase, besides credit facility as seen in the case of ITC's e-choupal and many other contract farming arrangements throughout the country more recently. The existing players in agricultural markets like traders, input sellers, and commission agents who often operate in more than one market (input/output/credit) need to be managed as partners as well as competitors through disintermediation or reintermediation. This requires continuous institutional innovations at the user and the provider levels.

The major factors in the success of an ICT project include useful content, awareness among users, involvement of the local community into the project, local language content, proper operator selection and training, transfer of adequate capabilities to the local population, realistic financial model, and government perception of the project (Dossani et al, 2005). Finally, it is important to remember that ICTs are not an end in themselves but a means to improve the efficiencies in existing or new business or development settings.

REFERENCES

Annamalai, K. and S. Rao (2003), *What Works: ITC's E-choupal and Profitable Rural Transformation-Web-based information and procurement tools for Indian farmers,* What Works Case Study, University of Michigan.

Assisi, C. and I. Gupta (2003). "ITC's Rural Symphony", *Business World*, 22 (34), January 14-20, 30-37.

Boehlje, M., J. Akridge and D. Downey (1995), "Restructuring Agribusiness for the 21st Century", *Agribusiness*, 11 (6), 493-500.

Cecchini S. and M. Raina (2004), "Electronic Government and the Rural Poor: The case of Gyandoot", *Information Technologies and International Development*, 2 (2), Winter, 65-75.

Choenni, S.R. (2003), "Summarising the Gyandoot Story", *Case Folio*, 3(11), November.

Clarke, M. (2003), *e-development? Development and the New Economy*, UNU-WIDER Policy Brief No. 7, UNU-WIDER, Helsinki, Finland.

Dossani, R., D.C. Mishra and R. Jhaveri (2005), Enabling ICT for Rural India, Asia-Pacific Research Center (APARC) of Stanford University and the National Informatics Centre (NIC), November.

Gupta, R.K. (2003), *'e-choupal so far and ahead': A Case Study in a Village in M.P.*, Theme paper, Fieldwork Segment, PRM 2002-2004, IRMA, February.

Heeks, R (2002): "i-Development Not e-Development: Special Issue on ICTs and Development", *Journal of International Development*, 14, 1-11.

Joseph, K.J. (2002), *"Growth of ICT and ICT for Development–Realties of the Myths of the Indian Experience"*, UNU-WIDER Discussion Paper No. 2002/78, UNU-WIDER, Helsinki, Finland.

Kaushik, P.D. and N. Singh (2004), "Information Technology and Broad Based Development: Preliminary Lessons from North India", *World Development*, 32(4), 591-607.

Krishan, A. (2003), "Gyandoot: An E-Government Initiative in India", *Case Folio*, 3(11), November.

Kumar, R (2004): "e-Choupals: A Study on the Financial Sustainability of Village Internet Centres in Rural Madhya Pradesh", *Information Technologies and International Development,* 2(1), Fall, 45-73.

Menon, J. (2005), "In Pondicherry, Women Script Quiet Revolution", *The Indian Express,* September 29, Ahmedabad.

Paul, P. (2003), "The Mandi is now on the Net", *Deccan Herald,* January 6 (from: wwwitcportal.com).

Prahalad, C.K. (2005), *The Fortune at the Bottom of the Pyramid-Eradicating Poverty through Profits,* Wharton School Publishing, N.J. (USA).

Rajora, R.K. (2001), "Gyandoot: Cybercafe-cum-Cyber Officers for the Masses", *Management in Government,* 32 (4).

Ram, A. (2000), "Wired to the Future", *India Today,* December 11, p. 12.

Salin, V. (1998), "Information Technology in Agri-Food Supply Chains", *International Food and Agribusiness Management Review,* 1 (3), 329-334.

Sanganeria, S. (2003), "ITC e-chaupal in UP wheat buying spree", *Business Standard,* February 13, 12.

Sawhney, M. (2002), "Fields of Online Dreams", *The CIO Magazine,* October 15 (www.itcportal.com).

Shenoy, M. (2002), "Transforming Agribusiness the e-way", *Business India,* 634, June 24 -July 7, 102-104.

Sreekumar, T.T. (2003), "e-Governance and Social Exclusion: Evidence from the Field", a paper presented at the ICAS-3 held at Singapore during August 19-22.

Streeter, D.H., S.T. Sonka and M.A. Hudson (1991), "Information Technology, Co-ordination and Competitiveness in the Food and Agribusiness Sector", *American Journal of Agricultural Economics,* December.

Chapter - 2

Land and Water Productivity in Tank Irrigation: A Comparative Analysis

K. Sivasubramaniyan &
R. Sakthivadivel

INTRODUCTION

In India, utilisation of water in agriculture varies considerably across states and between seasons depending upon the availability of supply. The availability of water from various sources also makes differences in its utilisation. Even though water is used from different sources with specified quantity there have been wide variations in the productivity of same crop. Although several factors are responsible for productivity variations, if other things remain constant, water and its proper application is considered to be the prime factor for major productivity variations. For instance, when water is provided through drip or sprinkler irrigation, productivity of certain crops increases considerably apart from a considerable quantum of water saving (this practice of timely, adequate and assured supply of water is otherwise called quality of irrigation). If this practice is adoptable for all regions then it would be possible to reduce a large quantum of water, which is currently applied for many crops. But we do not know actually what happens at field level when water is applied from different sources. Hence, a better understanding of the agri-business helps one to provide an optimum quantity of water required for crop production, which in turn reduces the over use of water and its savings help to bring more area under irrigation.

The earlier study carried out by Vaidyanathan and Sivasubramaniyan (2004)[1] pointed out the gaps in our understanding of the consumptive use of water and also its efficient utilisation by crops in India. The study has also suggested exploring possibilities of filling the gap with available data.

In a micro-level study, it is possible to find out the water use efficiency not only in the aggregate but also by crop, crop groups and seasons in a normal rainfall year and a dry year. For this purpose, a field survey in seven tanks in the Cheyyar sub-basin was undertaken to observe and compute farm level land and water productivity. The overall objective of this paper is to find out the land and water productivity of paddy between normal and dry years.

METHODOLOGY: SELECTION OF TANKS FOR THE STUDY

For the purpose of this study, five system tanks and two rainfed (non-system) tanks in the Cheyyar River basin are selected (table 1) representing the head, middle and tail reaches of the basin. The system tanks are selected at random and the non-system tanks are selected purposively to observe the differences between the two types of tanks. All selected tanks are located in Tiruvannamalai district. The locations of selected tanks are shown in figure 1.

Table 1
Salient Features of Selected Tanks under Cheyyar Basin

Sl. No.	*Name of Village*	*Tank*	*(S/NS)*	*Taluk*	*Capacity (MCM)*	*Registered Ayacut Hectares*	*Water Spread Area*	*Catchment Area*	*Zone*
							← Sq.Km.→		
1.	Vakkadai	Tank	(S)	Cheyyar	3.96	471.40.0	0.813	2.80	LC
2.	Kovilur	Tank	(S)	Cheyyar	0.82	133.15.5	1.953	3.24	LC
3.	Erumbur	Peria Eri	(S)	Vandavasi	0.48	352.42.0	0.470	2.40	KR
4.	Purisai	Peria Eri	(S)	Cheyyar	2.66	184.49.0	3.375	4.53	KR
5.	Irumbedu	Tank	(S)	Arni	1.69	180.57.5	1.175	3.97	KN
6.	Pelasur	Peria Eri	(NS)	Polur	2.59	166.09.0	1.265	7.45	UC
7.	Semmia-mangalam	Tank	(NS)	Polur	1.15	72.09.0	0.581	2.91	UC

Note: S = System Tank. NS = Non-System Tank. Zonewise Classification of Tanks: LC = Lower Cheyyar. KR = Kiliyar. KN = Kamandalanadhi. UC = Upper Cheyyar.
Source: PWD Memoirs of Respective Tanks.

Figure 1
Location of Tanks in Tiruvannamalai District

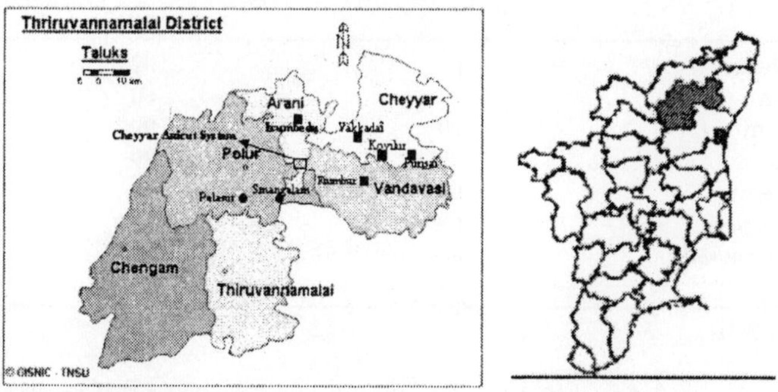

▪ System Tanks • Non-system Tanks

Tamil Nadu Districts

SELECTION OF SAMPLE FARMERS

This study has used primary and secondary data sources. As a first step, in each selected tank, the command area of each sluice is demarcated in the village map and the sluices are divided into three segments as head, middle and tail reaches according to their distance from the tank sluice along the main field channel. From the village map, in each segment two sample survey numbers are randomly selected. While selecting survey numbers if at least one of the selected survey numbers did not have wells, then one survey number was replaced with an adjacent one with wells. All the owners *(Pattadars)* of the plots within the selected sample survey numbers are the sample farmers for the survey. If the land has been leased in, the tenant is interviewed.

Altogether, there are 99 sample farmers selected for the survey. Among the sample farmers 50 of them owned wells and 49 non-well farmers. A questionnaire is used to collect information from the sample farmers. The area held, operated, season wise cultivation, source of irrigation supply from tank/well and both are collected. This is done for three agricultural seasons in a normal tank supply year (1998-99) and a dry year (2003-04) in the seven study tanks.

LIMITATION OF THE STUDY

This study takes into account only gross productivity (output (kg) per ha) and based on that value land and water productivity per ha is derived. Hence it may be considered as partial productivity.

FARM LEVEL LAND AND WATER PRODUCTIVITY: TANK LEVEL ANALYSIS

Based on tank wise productivity analysis the following results are presented.

Table 2
Gross Irrigated Area During Normal and Dry year: System level

Name & Type of tank	*% of well farmers*	*% of GIA*	
		Normal	*Dry*
Vakkadai-System	67	102	61
Kovilur-System	35	60	14
Erumbur-System	29	99	35
Purisai-System	35	89	37
Irumbedu-System	91	89	43
Pelasur-Non-system	69	95	32
Semmiamangalam-NS	42	62	5
Average %	51	86	32

Source: Survey, 2004.

Gross Irrigated Area (GIA): The average percentage of farmers having wells is 51 (table 2). It may be seen that the percentage of gross irrigated area in the system tanks in the normal tank supply year is relatively more compared to the non-system tank farmers. However, in the dry year one could not find any clear pattern but the area irrigated is grossly reduced due to paucity of well supply and also no tank supply was possible. Figure 2 gives a graphical form of tank-wise percentage of gross area under irrigation. In the Semmiamangalam tank, in the dry year, cultivation is possible only to a limited extent; hence the percentage of GIA is negligible.

Figure 2
Gross area irrigated Across Tanks

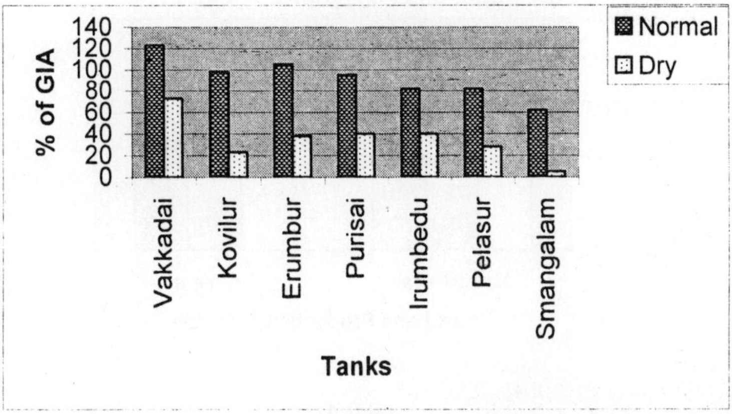

Table 3
Gross Land Productivity of Paddy in the Sample Tanks

Tank	*Gross Land Productivity per Hectare*	
	Normal Year Kg / Ha	*Dry Year Kg / Ha*
1	2	3
Vakkadai-(S)	3482	4418
Kovilur-(S)	3708	6152
Erumbur-(S)	3450	1588
Purisai-(S)	2455	2245
Irumbedu-(S)	3881	3799
Pelasur-(NS)	2374	3246
Smangalam-(NS)	2048	0
Average	3067	3575

Source: Survey, December 2004.
Note: S=System. NS=Non-system.

Gross Land Productivity: Table 3 gives the gross land productivity of paddy in the selected tanks. In the normal year, the gross productivity (output (kg) per hectare) is the highest in the Irumbedu system tank (3881 kg/ha) which is nearly two times that of the lowest gross output reported in Semmiamangalam non-system tank. However, in the dry year this output differs. The productivity in three tanks is lower than all tanks average (3575 kg/ha). The overall tank average productivity is three-fifths of the highest output attained in Kovilur tank (6152 kg). Again one may note in Semmiamangalam due to non-availability of water, farmers incurred loss due to withering of crops. The figure 3 shows the productivity levels of paddy crop.

Figure 3
Maximum, Minimum and Average Land Productivity

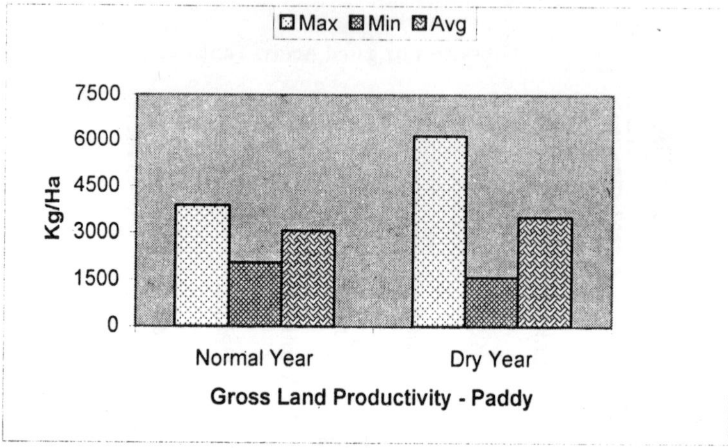

Table 4
Gross Water Productivity of Paddy per Cubic Metre of Diverted Water: System Level

Tank	*Gross Diverted Water PDY/Cubic Metre*	
	Normal Year Kg	*Dry Year Kg*
1	2	3
Vakkadai	0.33	0.59
Kovilur	0.35	0.72
Erumbur	0.26	0.25
Purisai	0.18	0.22
Irumbedu	0.48	0.54
Pelasur	0.21	0.45
Smangalam	0.20	0.00
Average	0.29	0.46

Source: Survey, December 2004.

Gross Water Productivity: Water productivity is measured in terms of kg per cubic metre of water diverted/supplied for paddy. The diverted water productivity in three system tanks is higher than that of the overall tank average of 0.29 kg per cubic metre (table 4). The highest output (0.48 kg/cum) is reported in Irumbedu and the lowest is in Purisai tank where it is 0.18 kg/cum. It should be noted that the contribution of wells is the prime reason to the hike in values in the Irumbedu tank. Actually, this tank has 10 farmers who have wells out of 11 sample farmers. In the dry year one may observe wide variations in gross water productivity, which ranges from 0 to 0.72 kg/cum and the overall tank average being 0.46 kg./cum. Figure 4 provides these details in a graphical form.

Figure 4
Gross Water Productivity of Paddy

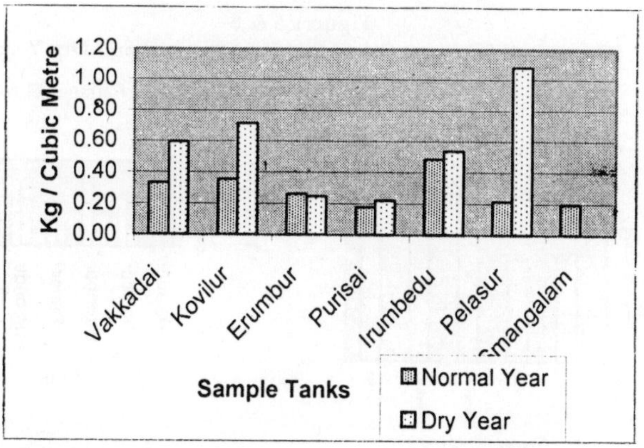

Water Use Efficiency: The importance of any irrigation management lies with achieving higher water use efficiency. Since the command area of tank irrigation system spreads over a limited extent compared to canal irrigation, the efficiency under tanks is relatively higher (around 50%) than the canal system. Our survey shows that at field level, the water use efficiency in the normal year is considerably higher with a percentage ranging from 57 to 98 for paddy in system tanks and in the non-system tanks it is around 70. In the dry year, only well irrigation is possible and due to water shortage the efficiency goes up to 122% in Erumbur (Table 5).

Table 5
Water Use Efficiency of Paddy in the Sample Tanks

NAME of Tank	*GWU (HaM)*		*% of well*	*CUR*	*WUE (%)*	
	NY	*DY*	*Farmers*	*M/Ha*	*NY*	*NY*
1	2	3	4	5	6	7
Vakkadai	1.049	0.743	67	0.785	75	106
Kovilur	1.046	0.860	35	0.785	75	91
Erumbur	1.310	0.644	29	0.785	60	122
Purisai	1.376	1.013	35	0.785	57	78
Irumbedu	0.804	0.709	83	0.785	98	111
Pelasur	1.106	0.726	69	0.785	71	108
Smangalam	1.044	0.000	42	0.785	75	0
Average	1.106	0.773	51	0.785	71	102

Note: CUR: Paddy (157+378+523+LP350mm=1.358 Meter/Ha).
Source: Survey, December 2004.

The volume of water used per hectare of paddy shows that in the normal year all the tanks had used more than 1 ham (except one) with little variation across tanks. However, in the dry year, due to paucity of supply from the wells the volume of water used is below 1 ham and only in one tank it is more than this level. Further in Semmiamangalam, a non-system tank, in the dry year water was not used by any of the sample farmers (Figures 5, 6 and 7).

Figures 5 & 6
Water use Efficiency (%) of Paddy in Normal and Dry Years

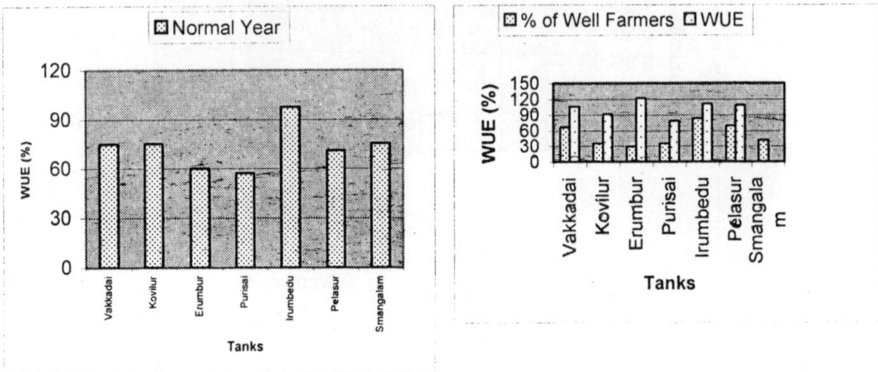

Figure 7
Volume of Water used per Hectare (ham) of Paddy in Normal and Dry Years

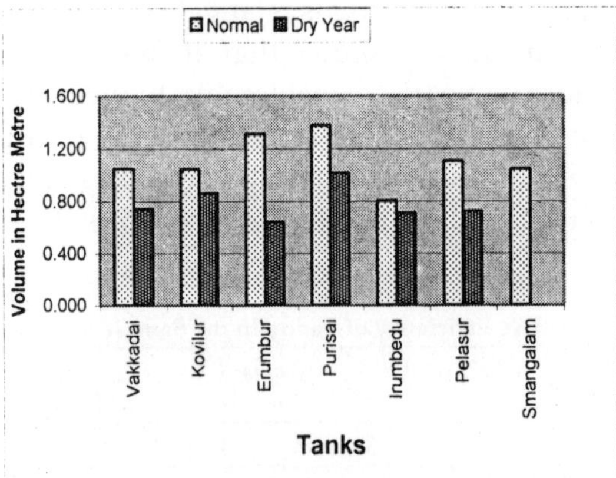

SYSTEM WISE LAND AND WATER PRODUCTIVITY

Differentiation of land and water productivity basically requires classification of tanks and farmers into specific categories such as (a) system and non-system tanks and (b) well and non-well farmers. Apart from these, other variables like area under crops, gross water use, and percentage of well water use also make differences in land and water productivity. Hence, by taking all these variables into account an analysis was carried out and the results are presented below. In our study, a majority of farmers (90 %) grow paddy during the cultivation period both in the normal and in dry years. Moreover, most of the other seasonal crops are grown purely by rainfed conditions in a few villages. If we leave these out, then the remaining other seasonal irrigated crops are only negligible in proportion. Hence, the season wise analysis concentrates only on the paddy crop.

AREA (ALL CROPS AND PADDY) UNDER CULTIVATION IN NORMAL AND DRY YEARS

Well Farmers: Taking all sample farmers together, a glance at Table 6 indicates that the percentage of land cultivated by the farmers in the normal year is invariably the highest in almost all seasons compared to the dry year. Further, the percentage of paddy cultivation is still the highest in the normal year. Across seasons, the mean total area cultivated per farmer dominates in season 1 (0.28 hectare). But there has not been much difference in the mean total area cultivated across seasons. Even for paddy, the variations in mean area devoted ranges between 0.30 hectare in season 1 and 0.26 hectare in season 3. Gross area devoted for paddy is comparatively higher in all seasons in non-system well farmers compared to system tank well farmers. It is important to note that in the dry year even among well farmers in the non-system tanks, the area cultivated among all types of crops in all seasons is negligible.

This indicates that crop diversification did not take place much for the non-system tank farmers. This shows that in the absence of tank supply and poor rainfall, well irrigation is not feasible for cropping for non-system tank farmers and adequate recharge of wells is possible only through the tanks, when they get filled.

Non-well Farmers: For non-well farmers paddy is the sole crop, which is grown in the first two seasons. Between system and non-system tanks, a sharp deviation in the percentage of farmers cultivating paddy is reported among non-well farmers. However, difference in the mean paddy area is negligible. The gross area under paddy indicates that non-well farmers under system tanks are more vulnerable than non-well farmers under non-system tanks.

The dry year paddy crop wholly depends upon the availability of well water supply. Between system and non-system well farmers the latter perform poorly. On the whole, the area analysis indicates that non-system tank well farmers perform better in the normal tank supply year and they are unable to crop the land in the dry year.

GROSS WATER USE FOR PADDY IN NORMAL YEAR: 1998-99

Well Farmers: The data indicate (table 7) that in the case of well farmers both in the system and non-system tanks, the mean water use per hectare in seasons 1 and 2 is more than the annual average of 1.01 hectare metre and it is the lowest in the third season (0.82 ham). This higher use in the first two seasons may be due to relative abundance of supply available from the tanks. But in the third season tank supply is a constraint and

Table 6
Percentage of Paddy Area under Cultivation and Mean and Coefficient of Variation for Cultivated Sample Farmers (Mean Area in Hectares)

Type of Sample Farmers	Season	% Cultivated M & CV	Total (System + Non-System)				System				Non-system			
			Normal		Dry		Normal		Dry		Normal		Dry	
			Total	Paddy	Total	Paddy	Total	Paddy	Total	Paddy	Total	Paddy	Total	Paddy
Well Farmers	S1	% Cultd	82	70	52	44	78	64	67	56	100	86	14	14
		Mean	0.28	0.30	0.25	0.27	0.23	0.26	0.23	0.25	0.36	0.38	0.47	0.17
		CV	0.73	0.73	0.60	0.58	0.69	0.63	0.45	0.42	0.74	0.77	0.97	0
	S2	% Cultd	92	82	30	18	94	86	39	25	100	71	7	0
		Mean	0.27	0.28	0.31	0.35	0.24	0.24	0.29	0.35	0.33	0.40	0.59	0
		CV	0.81	0.82	0.78	0.75	0.79	0.79	0.82	0.75	0.91	0.78	0	0
	S3	% Cultd	62	46	26	18	61	53	33	25	100	29	7	0
		Mean	0.26	0.26	0.22	0.21	0.24	0.26	0.19	0.21	0.19	0.26	0.59	0
		CV	0.59	0.64	0.67	0.53	0.69	0.68	0.56	0.53	0.87	0.50	0	0
Non-Well Farmers	S1	% Cultd	41	39	2	2	32	29	3	3	73	73	0	0
		Mean	0.26	0.27	0.26	0.26	0.26	0.26	0.26	0.26	0.27	0.27	0	0
		CV	0.56	0.57	0	0	0.67	0.69	0	0	0.42	0.42	0	0
	S2	% Cultd	69	69	0	0	74	74	0	0	73	55	0	0
		Mean	0.21	0.21	0	0	0.20	0.20	0	0	0.19	0.26	0	0
		CV	0.69	0.69	0	0	0.77	0.77	0	0	0.70	0.29	0	0
	S3	% Cultd	0	0	0	0	0	0	0	0	0	0	0	0

Note: S1, S2, S3 = Seasons 1, 2 and 3. Mean and CV represent the farmers who cultivated among the samples.

Table 7

Season wise Mean Area, Gross Water Use and Ratio of Consumptive Use Requirement to Gross Water Use for Paddy for Cultivated Sample Farmers (Paddy Area in Hectares; Gross Water Use in Hectare metre)

Type of Sample Farmers	Season	% Cultivated M & CV	Total (System + Non-System)						System						Non-system					
			Normal Year			Dry Year			Normal Year			Dry Year			Normal Year			Dry Year		
			Area	GWU	Ratio*	Area	GWU	Ratio*	Area	GWU	Ratio*	Area	GWU	Ratio*	Area	GWU	Ratio*	Area	GWU	Ratio*
Well Farmers	S1	% Cultd	70	70	70	44	44	44	64	64	64	56	56	56	86	86	86	14	14	14
		Mean	0.30	1.08	0.26	0.24	0.80	0.32	0.26	1.09	0.25	0.25	0.81	0.32	0.38	1.04	0.27	0.17	0.73	0.35
		CV	0.73	0.33	0.27	0.42	0.13	0.13	0.63	0.32	0.26	0.42	0.14	0.13	0.77	0.34	0.29	0.22	0.01	0.01
	S2	% Cultd	82	82	82	18	18	18	86	86	86	25	25	25	71	71	71	0	0	0
		Mean	0.28	1.06	0.57	0.35	0.72	0.85	0.24	1.00	0.60	0.35	0.72	0.85	0.40	1.22	0.46	0	0	0
		CV	0.82	0.42	0.59	0.75	0.34	0.81	0.79	0.43	0.61	0.75	0.34	0.81	0.78	0.40	0.40	0	0	0
	S3	% Cultd	46	46	46	18	18	18	53	53	53	25	25	25	29	29	29	0	0	0
		Mean	0.26	0.82	0.88	0.21	0.73	1.20	0.26	0.84	0.82	0.21	0.73	1.20	0.26	0.73	1.14	0	0	0
		CV	0.64	0.39	0.45	0.53	0.35	0.74	0.68	0.37	0.31	0.53	0.35	0.74	0.50	0.52	0.70	0	0	0
	Annual	% Cultd	90	90	90	48	48	48	92	92	92	61	61	61	86	86	86	14	14	14
		Mean	0.62	1.01	0.93	0.43	0.78	0.82	0.56	0.98	1.00	0.46	0.78	0.87	0.80	1.08	0.72	0.17	0.73	0.35
		CV	0.74	0.30	0.53	0.66	0.18	0.77	0.72	0.32	0.47	0.63	0.18	0.74	0.72	0.26	0.69	0.22	0.01	0.01
Non-well Farmers	S1	% Cultd	39	39	39	2	2	2	29	29	29	3	3	3	16	16	16	0	0	0
		Mean	0.27	1.22	0.23	0.26	0.99	0.26	0.26	1.34	0.21	0.26	0.99	0.26	0.27	1.05	0.26	0	0	0
		CV	0.57	0.29	0.29	0	0	0	0.69	0.28	0.33	0	0	0	0.42	0.25	0.21	0	0	0
	S2	% Cultd	69	.69	69	0	0	0	74	74	74	0	0	0	12	12	12	0	0	0
		Mean	0.21	1.30	0.40	0	0	0	0.20	1.32	0.39	0	0	0	0.26	1.17	0.46	0	0	0
		CV	0.69	0.27	0.31	0	0	0	0.77	0.24	0.29	0	0	0	0.29	0.39	0.36	0	0	0
	S3	% Cultd	0	0	0	0	0	0	0	0	0	0	0	0	0	0	0	0	0	0
	Annual	% Cultd	82	82	82	2	2	2	84	84	84	3	3	3	16	16	16	0	0	0
		Mean	0.30	1.27	0.37	0.26	0.99	0.26	0.26	1.32	0.36	0.26	0.99	0.26	0.47	1.08	0.40	0	0	0
		CV	0.91	0.25	0.32	0	0	0	1.07	0.24	0.33	0	0	0	0.39	0.21	0.28	0	0	0

Note: S1, S2, S3 = Seasons 1, 2 and 3. GWU = Gross Water Use. Mean represents the farmers who cultivated among the samples.
Ratio* = Ratio of Consumptive Use Requirement to Gross Water Use.

only well supply is possible. As a result, use of water is decreased considerably. The gross water use, in all seasons, indicates that well farmers in system tanks relatively used a less supply per hectare (0.98 ham) compared to well farmers in non-system tanks (1.08 ham). The effect of well water supply may be captured only in the third season when tank supply is almost nil. In season 3, well water used by system tank farmers is relatively more (0.84 ham) than that of the non-system tank farmers (0.73 ham). As this confirms clearly that gross water use (tank plus well supply) is more in the first two seasons compared to the third season. Further, it may be observed that the highest (1.22 ham) and lowest (0.73 ham) quantum of water use per hectare is seen only with the well farmers in the non-system tanks.

GROSS WATER USE BY WELL FARMERS IN THE DRY YEAR 2003-04

Contrary to the above situation, in the dry year (in terms of deficit seasonal rainfall which leads to no storage in the tanks) tanks do not get any supply even during the monsoon period. As a result, farmers had two options for cropping: (i) rainfed crop cultivation by using the scanty rainfall during the monsoon period; and (ii) cultivation by solely using the well water. There is difference between the two. Farmers using wells may also grow rainfed crops, but irrigated crops (by using wells) are not possible to non-well farmers. This situation was exactly prevailing in the dry year almost in all our survey tanks.

Even for the tank command wells, water availability depends upon both the seasonal rainfall and the tank storage. Most wells (especially in shallow depth) do not get adequate recharge. As a result, most well farmers do not crop the land. Even if they ventured for cultivating dry irrigated crops, expecting good showers, during monsoon but when it fails, immediately they incur total loss due to withering of crops. This situation is reported in many of the study tanks, especially in the non-system tanks. This type of unavoidable situation only makes agriculture to be referred as a "gamble in monsoon". In the light of the background, let us examine the gross water use by sample farmers in the dry year.

Regarding the quantum of gross water use for paddy a comparison (of well farmers) with the normal year shows that the dry year gross water use is relatively less both in the system and non-system tanks. Taking all seasons together, between system and non-system tanks, well water use per hectare is marginally higher in the system tanks (0.78 ham) compared to non-system tanks (0.73 ham). Further, in the non-system tanks, cropping was possible for 14 % of sample cultivators in the first season only. This indicates that in the absence of tank storage wells do not contribute much for better cropping even when they are located within the tank command.

Gross Water Use by Non-well Farmers in the Normal and Dry Years: Compared to well farmers, the non-well farmers tend to use relatively more quantum of supply per hectare both in the first and second seasons. The system tank non-well farmers relatively use more quantum of supply in all seasons compared to the non-system tank farmers. *Overall results indicate that system tank non-well farmers tend to use more water (1.32 ham) than non-system tank non-well farmers (1.08 ham).* However, between the system and non-system tanks the variations in water use among non-well farmers (the variability is only 24% and 21%) are much less. *This shows that non-well farmers are equally benefited from tanks of both types. No preference is possible for the non-well farmers in the system tanks.* In the dry year, cultivation is not possible for non-well farmers of both the system and non-system tanks.

RATIO OF CONSUMPTIVE USE REQUIREMENTS TO GROSS WATER USE

In our study tanks, paddy cultivation dominates over all other crops. Hence it is important to find out the ratio of how much water is required for paddy cultivation as per the crop water requirement and how much water is actually supplied by farmers for that crop. In this study, crop water requirement of paddy takes into account of both consumptive use (CU) requirement as well as land preparation (LP). Accordingly, the first season paddy requires 2570 cubic metre (CUM) of water per hectare (1070 CUM for CU and 1500 CUM for LP); second season requires 4780 CUM/ha (3780 CUM for CU and 1000 CUM for LP) and for the third season the requirement is 6230 CUM/ha (5230 CUM for CU and 1000 CUM for LP). By using these calculations one can easily compute season wise ratio of consumptive use requirements (CUR) to gross water use (GWU) for paddy crop.

Well Farmers: Normal Year: Taking all tanks together the mean ratio of CUR to GWU increases steadily from season 1 (26%) to season 3 (88%). This indicates that the quantum of water supplied is utilised more effectively in the third season compared to season 1. In other words, in season 3, 88 % of GWU is utilised for paddy and the same is only 26 % in season 1. Between system and non-system tanks the mean ratio of water use (or the efficiency of water use) is relatively higher in system tanks, which ranges between 25 % in season 1 and 82% in season 3.

Well Farmers: Dry Year: During the dry year, the non-system tank well farmers did not raise crop in seasons 2 and 3. But the system tank well farmers raised crop in all three seasons and the efficiency of water use in terms of mean ratio is gradually increasing from seasons 1 to 3. Especially in season 3 the mean ratio is 120%, which indicates that gross supply falls short by 20% of CUR.

Non-well Farmers: In the case of non-well farmers, cultivation in the normal year is possible only in the first two seasons. The efficiency of water use is relatively high in season 2 in both types of tanks compared to season 1. However, this efficiency is only less than 50%. This means that farmers are using 50% more water than what is required for CUR. In the dry year cultivation is not possible for non-well farmers.

LAND PRODUCTIVITY FOR PADDY IN THE NORMAL YEAR: 1998-99

Productivity of crop depends upon many factors. However, land and water are the prime factors to achieve crop's potential productivity. When other factors such as use of fertilizers, climatic conditions and crop management practices remain constant, the land and water are the twin factors deciding the crops maximum productivity. In the tanks under study let us examine the land productivity of paddy during normal and dry years (See table 8).

Some clear pattern on the levels of productivity exists between system and non-system tanks. Also, one can find that well farmers have achieved higher productivity than non-well farmers. Further, across seasons productivity in season 1 is less than that of Seasons 2 and 3 in system tanks. This is mainly because of the fact that during the tank supply period, especially in season 1, when the tanks reach its full capacity, the seepage effect of tank storage creates problems of drainage for the head reach farmers. If proper drainage is not available it retards productivity considerably. The table shows that all well farmers who served by system tanks have achieved only lower productivity (min. 3240 kg/ha in season 1) compared to seasons 2 and 3. Between seasons 2 and 3 under system tanks more yields are reported in season 3 (maximum yield is 3940 kg/ha). This is also due to better sunlight during seasons 2 and 3 and less pest attack.

Exactly the opposite picture is noticed in well farmers under non-system tanks. Here, in all seasons, well farmers achieved a lower productivity (max. 2350 kg/ha in season 3) than the system tank well farmers. This may validate our argument that well irrigation under system tanks helped to achieve more yields. Further, non-system tanks are not filled up frequently compared to system tanks. Hence, recharging capacity of wells is much less compared to system tanks.

Taking well farmers under system and non-system tanks together, a clear picture may be observed. Interestingly, all well farmers in all seasons have attained higher productivity (maximum is 3660 kg/ha in season 3) compared to non-system well farmers (highest yield is 2346 kg/ha). Mostly the same trend is noticed (but with lower productivity levels in all seasons) in the non-well farmers groups between system and non-system tanks.

On the whole, it may be observed between system and non-system tanks, the productivity levels are invariably higher in system tanks in all seasons compared to non-system tanks. Across seasons productivity is the highest in season 3 in both types of tanks. More importantly the productivity levels between these two types of tanks are more consistent with each other group and the variability seems to be very less in all seasons.

Table 8
Season wise Mean Land and Water Productivity of Paddy for Cultivated Sample Farmers
(Land Pdy in '000 Kg/Ha. Water pdy in Kg/Cubic metre)

Type of Sample Farmers	Season	% Cultivated M & CV	Total (System + Non-System)						System						Non-system					
			Normal Year			Dry Year			Normal Year			Dry Year			Normal Year			Dry Year		
			Land PDY	Water PDY CU	Water PDY Diverted	Land PDY	Water PDY CU	Water PDY Pumped	Land PDY	Water PDY CU	Water PDY Diverted	Land PDY	Water PDY CU	Water PDY Pumped	Land PDY	Water PDY CU	Water PDY Diverted	Land PDY	Water PDY CU	Water PDY Pumped
Well Farmers	S1	% Cultd	70	70	70	44	44	44	64	64	64	56	56	56	86	86	86	14	14	14
		Mean	2.86	1.11	0.29	4.33	1.69	0.54	3.24	1.26	0.33	4.43	1.72	0.55	2.13	0.83	0.22	3.35	1.30	0.46
		CV	0.37	0.37	0.48	0.30	0.30	0.29	0.33	0.33	0.46	0.29	0.29	0.29	0.31	0.31	0.40	0.28	0.28	0.29
	S2	% Cultd	82	82	82	18	18	18	86	86	86	25	25	25	71	71	71	0	0	0
		Mean	3.18	0.67	0.39	3.19	0.67	0.42	3.54	0.74	0.45	3.19	0.67	0.42	2.06	0.43	0.19	0	0	0
		CV	0.39	0.39	0.87	0.63	0.63	0.64	0.32	0.32	0.81	0.63	0.63	0.64	0.36	0.36	0.43	0	0	0
	S3	% Cultd	46	46	46	18	18	18	53	53	53	25	25	25	29	29	29	0	0	0
		Mean	3.66	0.59	0.51	3.63	0.58	0.47	3.94	0.63	0.54	3.63	0.58	0.47	2.35	0.38	0.39	0	0	0
		CV	0.31	0.31	0.44	0.54	0.54	0.53	0.26	0.26	0.42	0.54	0.54	0.53	0.26	0.26	0.47	0	0	0
	Gross	% Cultd	90	90	90	48	48	48	92	92	92	61	61	61	86	86	86	14	14	14
		Mean	3.19	0.37	0.36	3.88	1.01	0.51	3.57	0.41	0.42	3.93	0.98	0.51	2.14	0.26	0.21	3.35	1.30	0.46
		CV	0.36	0.56	0.69	0.35	0.73	0.32	0.29	0.54	0.64	0.35	0.77	0.33	0.27	0.36	0.31	0.28	0.28	0.29
Non-well Farmers	S1	% Cultd	39	39	39	2	2	2	29	29	29	3	3	3	16	16	16	0	0	0
		Mean	2.67	1.04	0.23	4.66	1.81	0.47	3.01	1.17	0.24	4.66	1.81	0.47	2.20	0.85	0.22	0	0	0
		CV	0.23	0.23	0.35	0	0	0	0.15	0.15	0.35	0	0	0	0.24	0.24	0.36	0	0	0
	S2	% Cultd	69	69	69	0	0	0	74	74	74	0	0	0	12	12	12	0	0	0
		Mean	3.20	0.67	0.27	0	0	0	3.45	0.72	0.29	0	0	0	2.04	0.43	0.20	0	0	0
		CV	0.48	0.48	0.57	0	0	0	0.46	0.46	0.56	0	0	0	0.34	0.34	0.63	0	0	0
	S3	% Cultd	0	0	0	0	0	0	0	0	0	0	0	0	0	0	0	0	0	0
	Gross	% Cultd	82	82	82	2	2	2	84	84	84	3	3	3	16	16	16	0	0	0
		Mean	3.13	0.66	0.26	4.66	1.81	0.47	3.40	0.73	0.28	4.66	1.81	0.47	2.05	0.37	0.20	0	0	0
		CV	0.45	0.54	0.52	0	0	0	0.42	0.49	0.52	0	0	0	0.22	0.35	0.30	0	0	0

Note: S1, S2, S3 = Season 1, 2, and 3. CU = Consumptive Use. Mean and CV for cultivated sample farmers. PDY = Productivity.

LAND PRODUCTIVITY FOR PADDY IN THE DRY YEAR: 2003-04

Contrary to our expectation (that use of more water will help to get more yield), the normal and dry year land productivity show that almost both in system and in non-system tanks the dry year land productivity is invariably higher than that of the normal year. The observations clearly indicate that in the normal year farmers tend to over use water than what it is required for crop needs. In other words, over use of water retarded the land productivity. Further, it may also be argued that in the dry year farmers are solely dependent on well water and in the normal year mostly tank water is used. It is known, that current system of tank water is not controlled to provide only the required quantum of supply for crop growth. Majority of farmers reported that daily supply was adopted for paddy crop in the normal year. Even that supply was not controlled and over supply was given as depicted below. In Purisai tank, one of the respondents revealed that due to over supply of tank water by the adjacent plot holder the respondent's plot manured with fertilizers was affected because of flooding of water from one field to the other.

In the case of well water use in the dry year, even though limited supply was provided compared to normal tank supply period, it was considered 'adequate', 'timely' and 'regular'. Consequently, well water supply helped farmers to achieve more yield. Hence, it is inferred that between the system and non-system well farmers, the land productivity among system farmers is relatively more (3930 kg/ha) compared to non-system well farmers (3352 kg/ha).

Our analysis clearly brings out the differences between the system and non-system tanks and indicates that higher productivity levels were achieved by system tanks. So, preference should be given to improve the system tanks in all possible ways, especially providing adequate drainage networks and other required infrastructure facilities to improve further and to achieve the potential yield levels. It should also be noted that non-system tanks are also equally important. As observed in some good years the productivity levels in the non-system tanks also reaches to appreciable level. Since, a major portion (about 60%) of area is still under unirrigated condition, attention should also be given to integrate the non-system tanks with run off from the local watersheds–to link/create facilities to withhold all precipitation during the monsoon rains.

DIVERTED WATER PRODUCTIVITY FOR PADDY IN THE NORMAL YEAR: 1998-99

In our analysis diverted water refers to the quantity of water used (both from tank and well supply) for the entire crop growth period. This water productivity (in terms of kilogram per cubic metre) analysis tells us farmers' effectiveness in utilisation of available water supply to maximize their crop yield. Since the land and water productivity are interdependent, one could expect the same type of results for water productivity also. This is evident from the table 8.

In the normal year, the mean diverted water productivity (kg/cum) of well farmers in the system tanks in all seasons is higher than that of non-system tank well farmers. The overall well farmers analysis indicates that in all seasons, system tank well farmers produce more output per unit of water applied compared to non-system tank well farmers. The annual water productivity under system tanks is 0.42 kg/cum compared to a half that level achieved by non-system well farmers. Between system and non-system non-well farmers, the system tanks non-well farmers relatively produce more output per cubic meter of water applied (overall 0.28 kg/cum). It should be noted that in the third season due to water scarcity, even in the normal year, not even a single farmer in the non-well respondents cultivated paddy. On the whole, it may be concluded that although system tanks perform much better in achieving higher productivity levels but the variability is much higher compared to non-system tank farmers. This means, that there is still a possibility to enhance system tank output levels if one introduces better water management practices.

PUMPED WATER PRODUCTIVITY FOR PADDY IN THE DRY YEAR: 2003-04

As it is noted, in the dry year due to efficient well water use, productivity is reported to be higher than the normal year. As a result, water productivity is found higher especially in season 1 in the dry year in both types of tanks and the variability is also found less. In the system tanks, mean pumped water productivity in season 1 is more (0.55 kg/cum) than the annual average of 0.51 kg/cum. However, in seasons 2 and 3, the productivity levels are lower than the annual average. In the non-system tanks, cropping was done only in season I, where the mean productivity is 0.46 kg/cum. The overall picture indicates that system tank water productivity is higher (0.51 kg/cum) than the non-system tank (0.46 kg/ ha). Since paddy is a water intensive crop the non-well farmers could not crop the land in the dry year in all seasons.

On the whole, taking both system and non-system tanks together, it may be observed that dry year pumped water productivity is higher in all seasons (except in season 3) and the annual mean productivity is 0.36 kg/cum in the normal year and the same being 0.51 kg/cum in the dry year. This clearly indicates that in the normal year over use of supply leads to a reduction in productivity levels, which is evident in comparison with the dry year water productivity values.

FARMERS' PREFERENCE OF PADDY OVER OTHER CROPS

It is interesting to note that why farmers mostly prefer paddy cultivation rather than any other crops even in the water deficit dry years. As one can observe from the table 9 that in the normal year average seasonal water productivity of paddy is Rs. 2.78 per cubic metre, whereas for sugarcane it is only Rs. 1.44 per cubic metre. Although 'other crops' water productivity in season 1 is comparatively very high which is Rs. 4.34 per cubic metre but its value is not consistent in other seasons. In the dry year also one can observe that water productivity of paddy is more than four times that of sugarcane values and more than three times that of 'other crops' values. This higher return of water productivity amply induces farmers to cultivate paddy even during the dry years when water scarcity is high. This specific trend is observed in almost all parts of Tamil Nadu with different sources of irrigation such as canals, tanks and wells.

Table 9
Comparison of Profitability of Paddy over Other Crops

Year	*Unit*	*Paddy Cultivation*				*Average/*	*Sugarcane*		*Other Crops*		
		S1	*S2*	*S3*	*Gross*	*Season*	*Annual*	*Average/ Season*	*S1*	*S2*	*S3*
NY	LPDY (kg/ha)	2860	3180	3660	9700	3233	136000	45333	-	-	-
	LPDY (Rs/ha)	20020	22260	25620	67900	22631	88400	24933	8081	-	5161
	WPDY (Rs/M³)	2.03	2.73	3.57	8.33	2.78	4.33	1.44	4.34	-	1.88
DY	LPDY (kg/ha)	4330	3190	3630	11150	3717	71000	23667	-	-	-
	LPDY (Rs/ha)	30310	22330	25410	78050	26019	46150	15383	18261	8306	-
	WPDY (Rs/M³)	3.78	2.94	3.29	10.01	3.34	2.18	0.73	1.01	0.99	-

Note: NY=Normal Year. DY=Dry Year. LPDY=Land Productivity. WPDY=Water Productivity. S1, S2, S3 = Season 1, 2, 3. Kg/ha = Kilogram per hectare. Rs/ha = Rupees per hectare. Paddy value is Rs. 7 per kg. Sugarcane value Rs. 0.65 per kg.

Source: Derived from Tables 42 and 43.

SUMMARY AND CONCLUSIONS

The study shows that the cropping pattern predominates with paddy that was grown in all the sample tanks in both the reference years. However, area devoted was very less during the dry year. Reduced supply to the tank leads to gross reduction in the area under cultivation in all the seasons. Supplementation of well supply was possible only during the normal supply year. In the dry year well water use was limited due to poor recharge from the aquifers. Taking all seasons and all tanks together, the average number of watering provided by a farmer for paddy crop was 75 and the average number of hours of water supplied per hectare was 12 per watering. Neither water sale nor water purchase was reported among the sample farmers.

It is found that crop diversification did not take place almost in all tanks even in the dry year because the area cultivated under less water intensive crops is negligible. Regarding the quantum of gross water use for paddy a comparison (of well farmers) with the normal year shows that the dry year gross water use is relatively less both in the system and non-system tanks. Taking all seasons together, between system and non-system tanks, well water use per hectare is marginally higher in the system tanks (0.78 ham) compared to non-system tanks (0.73 ham). Regarding gross water use in the normal year, the overall results indicate that system tank non-well farmers tend to use more water (1.32 ham) than non-system tank non-well farmers (1.08 ham).

The normal year well water use indicates that system tanks well water use is more consistent and hence the productivity levels may also be consistent among the well farmers. This is proved. Exactly the opposite picture is noticed in well farmers under non-system tanks. Here, in all seasons, well farmers achieved a lower productivity (max. is 2350 kg/ha in season 3) than the system tank well farmers. This may validate our argument that well irrigation under system tanks helped to achieve more yields. Further, non-system tanks are not filled up frequently compared to system tanks. Hence, recharging of wells under non-system tanks are much less compared to system tanks. Contrary to our expectation (use of more water will help to get more yield), the normal and dry year land productivity show that almost both in system and in non-system tanks the dry year land productivity is invariably higher than that of the normal year land productivity. This shows that over use of water retarded the land productivity in the normal year.

The analysis of the field survey amply indicates that the land and water productivity differ considerably with its location from the source of supply, access to well water and duration of tank supply available for cultivation. One of the important findings is that either the tank supply alone or the well water alone does not help the farmer to get more returns. The required condition is that both these sources should be used conjunctively to maximize returns from their cropping. The other interesting finding is that water productivity of paddy is invariably higher in both the reference years compared to all other crops cultivated, which induces farmers to cultivate paddy over other crops. Especially in the dry year, the values of water productivity of paddy are more than four times that of sugarcane and three times that of other crops cultivation. Further, it is suggested, that construction of a community well in each tank command and its proper management would help to enhance equitable sharing of available tank supply especially to non-well farmers even during the normal tank supply period.

NOTE

1. The pioneering basin level study involving all major river basins in all the states of India is brought out at the Madras Institute of Development Studies (Working Paper No. 183) in January 2004. The text version of this Working Paper is also published in the Economic and Political Weekly (3-9. Vol. XXXIX.

No. 27) in July 2004. Based on that macro level work this micro level field study was undertaken.

REFERENCES

Vaidyanathan, A. with K. Sivasubramaniyan. January 2004. Efficiency of Water Use in Indian Agriculture. *MIDS Working Paper, No. 183.*

Vaidyanathan A. with K. Sivasubramaniyan. July 2004. Efficiency of Water Use in Agriculture. *Economic and Political Weekly. Vol. XXXIX. No. 27.*

Sivasubramaniyan K. and R. Sakthivadivel. September 2005. Farm Level Land and Water Productivity in Tank Irrigation: Some Methodological Issues. *MIDS Working Paper, No. 194.*

Chapter - 3

Sustaining Secondary Education Through Public Private Partnerships: Reflections from Mahiti Sindhu Program (MSP) in Karnataka*

Vinod B. Annigeri & Sailabala Debi

EDUCATION AND DEVELOPMENT

Education has become an important area of interest to economists since empirical investigations revealed that output of goods and services had grown rapidly than the quantity of inputs (labor and capital) used to produce it. This difference in the values of input and output known as 'residual' was attributed to advances in knowledge, education of the labor force etc., The attempts for estimating the effect of each potential source of residual including education were initiated in some of the studies. All such studies resulted in the dawn of a new branch of economics in the form of 'Economics of Education'. T.W. Schultz being the pioneer in the field of economics of education was considered to be responsible for the current thinking on issues related to economics of education. In the latter years this thinking process came to be known as 'human capital revolution in economic thought'. Studies in the developed and developing countries have established a positive relationship between person's earnings and the amount of formal schooling received. (Becker, 1964, Schultz, 1963). Reviews of studies on cost benefit analysis in education have shown that returns to education exceed the rate of return to physical capital. Rate of return to primary education is generally higher than the rate of return to secondary education. (Psacharopolous 1975).

These developments in the domain of economic science have highlighted the importance of educated manpower for any economy in general and the type of industry where such manpower is located in particular. The human capital analysis was stimulated by concern for poverty, economic development, income distribution and the like. The analysis is also connected to human resource development and use of quantifiable base for decision-making process.

Such studies relating to the returns to the graduates in the discipline of electronics have also substantiated such findings especially in the state of Karnataka (Panchamukhi & Annigeri).[1] The sum and substance of these and other similar attempts bring out the important role played by the input of education to individuals as well as to the economy as a whole. In the recent past both academicians as well as policy makers are paying greater attention to secondary education. The challenges faced in retaining the child in the school till the completion of secondary education are many and many efforts are needed to enhance retention at this level of education.

Thus, the role played by education in promoting economic development is quite evident especially in the context of developing countries. This certainly brings forth the fact that there is a greater need to promote and sustain elementary education which would in turn act as the driver of development. The new millennium which is considered as the birth of knowledge society has thrown open new changelings especially in the background of liberalized global economies. If Indian community wishes to participate in such global opportunities, the need is felt to promote not only traditional education, but also education relating to information technology. The need of the hour seems to be ITBT wherein the core of the labor force would be engaged.

IT REVOLUTION AND EDUCATION AT SCHOOLS

In the present day context the rapid expansion of IT sector needs no explanation. Indian electronics industry has tremendous potential to become an engine of growth and productivity improvement for all sectors of the economy. With the continued thrust on liberalization, in order to make IT products cost effective and price competitive, the use and penetration of computers in the society is fast expanding with special emphasis on multi-lingual technologies. Investment in knowledge-based industries will determine a country's dominance in the present century. The software industry has emerged as one of the fastest growing sectors in the economy with a Compound Annual Growth Rate (CAGR) exceeding 50% over the last five years and with a likely turnover of US$ 6 billion and exports of US$ 4 billion during 1999-2002. The Government has targeted an export of US $ 50 billion by the year 2008 for the Indian software industry. In the state of Karnataka, the electronics industry is growing at a faster rate, and the growth potential seems to be quite promising. In this background the need for computer education assumes significance to provide the required manpower to meet the futuristic needs.

In this background, the early exposure of computer education to the school going children assumes significance. It would create the ground for the participating students to get prepared for the challenging opportunities that are waiting for them in their career ahead. The Government of Karnataka has made earnest attempt to impart computer education to students in Government schools through the 'Mahiti Sindhu Programme' (MSP). Now it is the opportune time to examine the impact of such programme on the student community to assess the contribution that the programme has made on the students to learn the basic of skills in computer related education. The ambition of the massive programme of MSP is to give computer education and computer aided education to the students of the Government High Schools in each of the revenue hobli, Morarji and Navodaya residential schools run by the social welfare and backward class department and thereby to enhance the quality of education. The programme has set forth various objectives and these objectives are realized through a well-designed strategy.

PUBLIC PRIVATE PARTNERSHIPS (PPPS) IN SECONDARY EDUCATION OF KARNATAKA STATE

As education is considered as a crucial input in achieving economic development, the need is felt to have government's intervention in the provision of education in any economy. Assessing the appropriate role of government requires recognition of the need for and the limitations of government action. Economic theory provides valuable guidance on the appropriate role of the state: market failure and distributional equity are the two frequent reasons for government intervention. In practice, a state's capabilities are often as important determinants of its actions as the theoretical rationale.

At the most fundamental level, the private sector can be defined as everything that is not government. Hence, the private sector is very large, quite varied and diverse. Thus, it may be interesting to know how a variety of selected public-private relationships can be effective in delivering educational services to the community.

The private sector and the nature of its relationships to the public sector can be thought of as a continuum of actors with varying degrees of relationship to the public sector.

The continuum moves from pure public provision of educational services to the extreme of pure private provision. In between, one can find a variety of mix of public private and private and private partnerships. Though the extremes may be ruled out in the present day context, one can visualize a mix of public and private actors in the provision of educational services.

A Continuum of Public-Private Partnerships

	1... Private institutions Providing services Using public funds	2... For profit institutions providing services (Privately financed)	3... Net work of for profit and non-institutions providing services	
Intense and Direct Involvement in Service delivery	←	———	→	No Public sector Involvement In service delivery; Public sector plays Regulatory role

Examples of activities located along continuum

1. Private schools/ colleges getting government financial assistances (Grant in aids)	2. Purely privately owned and managed schools /colleges	3. A partnership of educational institutions jointly managed by for profit and nonprofit organizations

PUBLIC PRIVATE PARTNERSHIPS AND MAHITI SINDHU PROGRAM IN KARNATAKA

In the present paper an attempt is made to understand the implications of PPPs, which intended to provide computer and computer, aided education to the students of secondary government schools. The program happens to the classic example of PPP wherein the private actors were involved in the provision of computer and computer aided education in government schools.

Elements of PPP in Mahiti Sindhu Program

The MSP was introduced in the right earnest to provide computer and computer-aided education to the selected schools in the state. The major features of the program are as noted below:

1. The MSP planned to provide computer education to 2.78 lakh students studying in 8th, 9th and 10th standards in one thousand schools out of 2667 Government. Secondary schools in Karnataka state.
2. Apart from Computer Education other subjects like Mathematics, Science, Social Science and English were also considered for teaching using computers. It also aimed at providing Internet facility to all students.
3. Teaching materials were to be provided according to the Medium of teaching (Kannada or English).
4. Computer Education would be provided to the extent of 4 periods per week per student. In addition to this, one hour would be devoted to each class for computer education.

Private computer agencies were involved in the prevision of computer education to the schools. Thus MSP also reflects the classic example of Public Private Partnerships (PPPs) in education sector.

In order to implement the program, following responsibilities were earmarked for different actors involved in the program.

Responsibilities for the Computer Agencies

1. The agencies were required to supply computers and other accessories like printers, operating system software, modem, telephone connection along with internet facility, furniture, electricity connection and the like.
2. Depending the number of students, the number of computers to be supplied to the school varies and following is the norm for the supply of computers to the schools.

Table 1

Category of School	*No. of Students*	*No. of Schools*	*No. of Computers*
A	Up to 150	261	1 Server and 5 PCs
B	151 to 250	273	1 Server and 9 PCs
C	251 to 550	466	1 Server and 14 PCs

Supply of UPS systems.
Supply of Two Qualified Computer Instructors.

Educating the children through Internet Active Multimedia

- Teaching different applications on computer and provide at least two hour Internet connection. Children would also be taught to open and operate an e-mail account.
- Providing computer training to regular teachers of the schools for a period of one month especially during the vacation.

Responsibility of the Department of Education

The government had the intention to provide computer education to schools run by the Department of Education, Morarji Schools run by the Department of Social Welfare, Minorities and Backward communities, Girls' Schools in rural areas. Keeping these norms as the basis the concerned officers in the concerned district prepared the list of schools to be included under the programme.

The proposed study has attempted an evaluation of MSP in the selected pockets of the state with the following objectives.

OBJECTIVES OF THE STUDY

Following are the specific objectives of the evaluation of MSP in Karnataka state.

1. To examine the performance levels of the students gained through computer and computer aided education in different subjects
2. To examine the flow of different components under the programme like computer hardware, software and human resources (computer instructors) and their training under the scheme. Hardware includes the number of PCs supplied, Generator, and other related inputs like furniture etc., Software would include the supply of computer education related software and the software for learning other subjects through computer aided education.
3. To review the training component of the computer instructors and other teachers of the school under the MSP.
4. To explore the impediments coming in the way of implementation of the scheme and suggest ways and means of overcoming them.
5. To assess the impact of the MSP on the enrollments in the schools. Here an attempt has been made to highlight the enrollments in the selected schools in the pre and during the MSP period. Though conceptually it is difficult to separate out the impact of MSP per se on enrollments, an attempt is made to have qualitative assessment of such impact through the case study approach with students, parents and teachers as the key informants in this regard.
6. To assess the impact of MSP with regard to the attendance levels of the students. The attendance levels have also bean reviewed for both pre and during the MSP periods.
7. To compare the attendance level of students in non-MSP schools with that of MSP schools. This provides an idea of increments in attendance if any attributed to introduction of MSP.
8. To examine the impact of MSP on dropout scenario at the schools. Here again one cannot ascertain the impact of MSP on the fall or otherwise with regard to the dropouts. However an attempt is made to ascertain the impact of the programme using the case study approach as stated above.
9. To compare the status of students with regard to the learning capacities, enrollments, dropouts of MSP schools with that in the non-MSP schools.
10. To assess and compare the performance of students in terms of computer aided education in MSP schools with that of non-MSP schools.

Sample Frame for the Study:

MSP Schools

Due to limited time for completion of the study, it was not possible to cover all the MSP schools for evaluation. Hence the study team firmed up the sample frame for the study, keeping in view to provide due representation to different provider categories who are engaged in the MSP. The following districts are chosen for the study.

Districts Selected for the Study

Districts Covered by NIIT	*Districts Covered by APTECH*	*Districts Covered by EDUCOMP*
1. Bangalore North	1. Bangalore North	1. Kolar
2. Bangalore Rural	2. Bidar	2. Chickmagalur
3. Chitradurga	3. Raichur	
4. Davangera	4. Bagalkote	
5. Shimoga	5. Gadag	
6. Tumkur	6. Haveri	
7. Madhugiri	7. Dharwad	
8. Mysore	8. Charmrajnagar	
9. Udupi	9. Kodagu	
10. Mandya	10. Chickmagalur	
11. Hassan		
12. D. Kannada		
13. Belgaum		
14. Chikkodi		
15. Bijapur		
16. U. Kannada		
17. Koppal		
18. Gulbarga		
19. Yadagir		
20. Bellary		
21. Kolar		
22. Chikkaballapur		

In the next step of selection of sample units, the taluks covered by these providers were selected. The table presented in the appendix gives the schools and taluks in different districts according to the provider category.

Non-MSP Schools

About 30 non-MSP government schools were surveyed as part of the study to capture the performance of such schools and to ascertain the impact of MSP with regard to the various indicators as stated above. These schools were concurrently surveyed along with the MSP schools. These schools were selected randomly from the same area where the MSP School is located, keeping in view its identical characteristics as that of MSP school.

IMPACT ASSESSMENT OF MSP-MAJOR FINDINGS

In the following discussion an attempt is made to present the major impact the MSP has made at the school level. The indicators relating to enrollment and attendance are examined to bring out the role of MSP. Since the factors influencing enrollment and attendance are many, it would be difficult to separate out the impact of MSP per se in this regard. However, our discussions with the Head Masters, Teachers and Computer Instructors have confirmed the fact the MSP is successful in attracting the children to the school as well in enhancing their attendance at the schools.

Enrollments in MSP and Non-MSP Schools

The class wise average enrollments in MSP and Non-MSP schools do indicate the fact that the enrollments in MSP schools are distinctly greater than the average number of students per Non-MSP schools. It is also interesting to observe that such enrollments have been showing an increasing trend for the MSP schools. Thus, there is every possibility that the enrollments in MSP schools could have been influenced by the information technology based education in these schools. The following graphs depict such a picture for different standards.

Chart 1

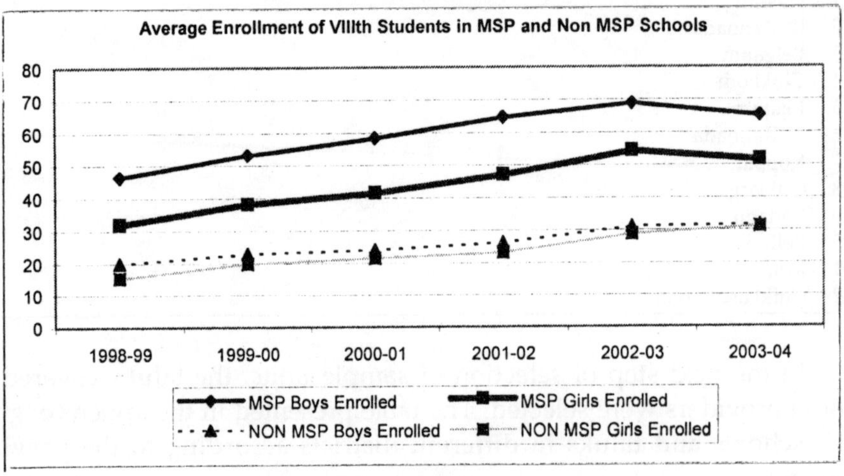

Chart 2

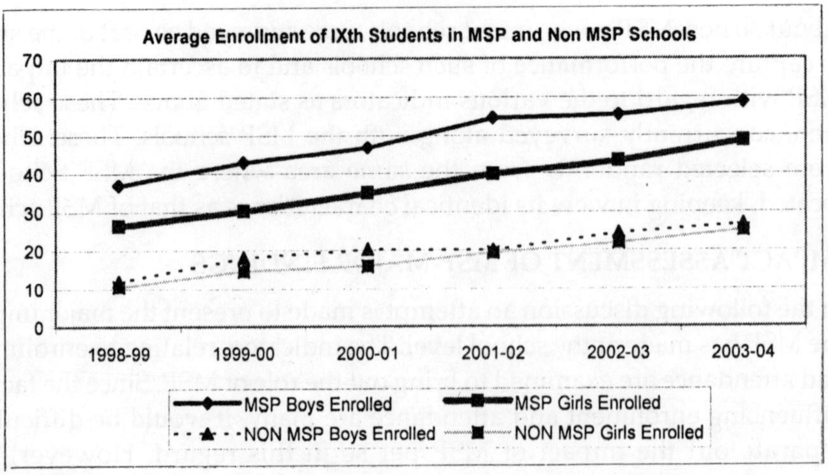

Chart 3

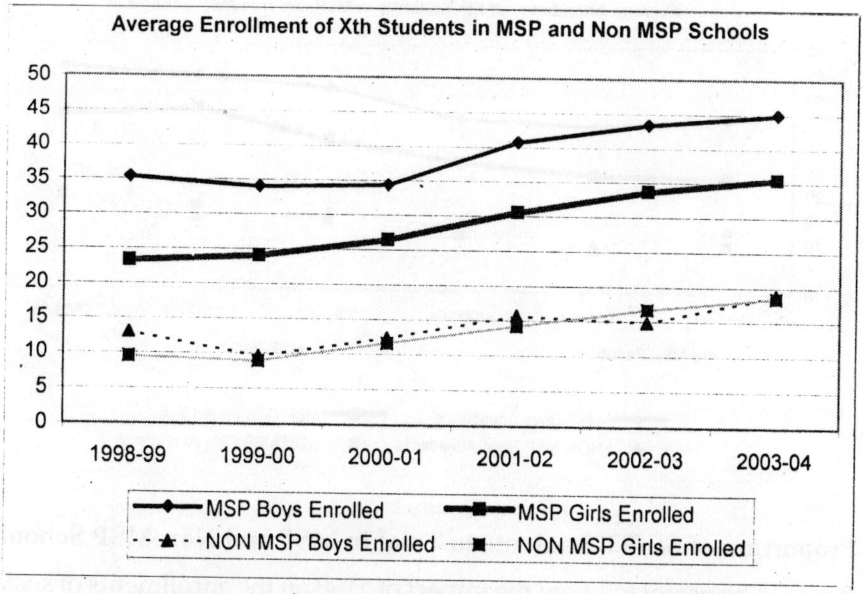

Attendance in MSP and Non-MSP Schools

The picture that emerges out of the analysis of the attendance data also supports the positive impact of the MSP. For example, in the Non-MSP category schools we can note that the average number of students attending the respective classes is significantly lower than the MSP schools. Following graphs do indicate this for different classes for MSP and Non-MSP schools. In view of non availability of data for VIII standard the respective graphs is not presented in the report.

Chart 4

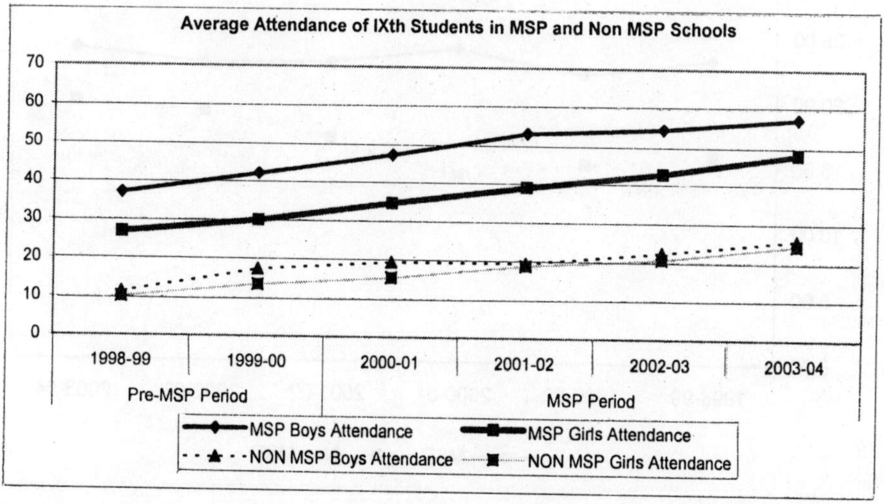

Chart 5

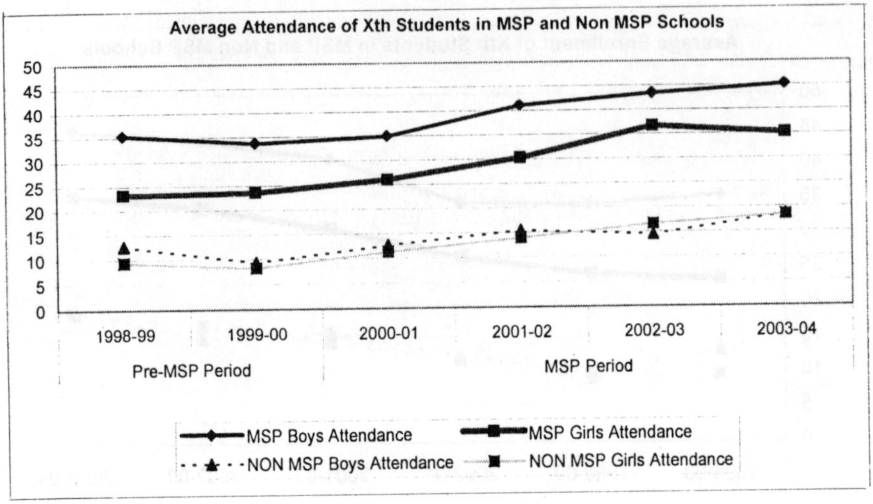

Proportion of SC/ST Students to Total in MSP and Non-MSP Schools

It would be useful to know the impact of MSP on the enrollments of socially disadvantaged groups like SCs and STs. This would have a bearing on the equity considerations of the program as far as the distributional effects are concerned. In this background an attempt was made to know the proportion of SC/ST enrollments to the total enrollments. This would tell us about the extent of participation of these socially backward groups in

Chart 6

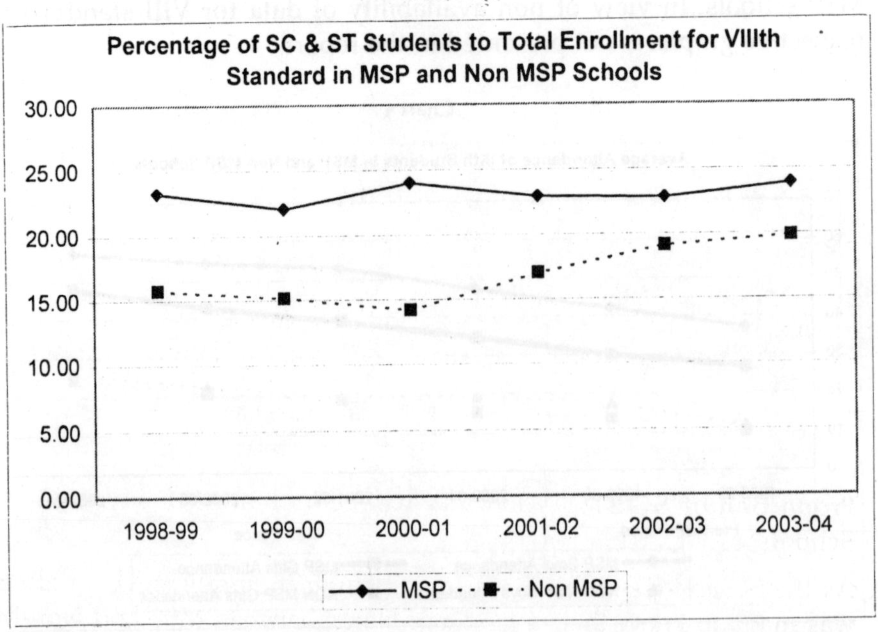

mainstream schooling. The analysis of the data clearly shows that the MSP has been successful in attracting greater number of students belonging to these groups in the schools under the program. Following graphs depict the picture for different classes for MSP and Non-MSP schools.

Chart 7

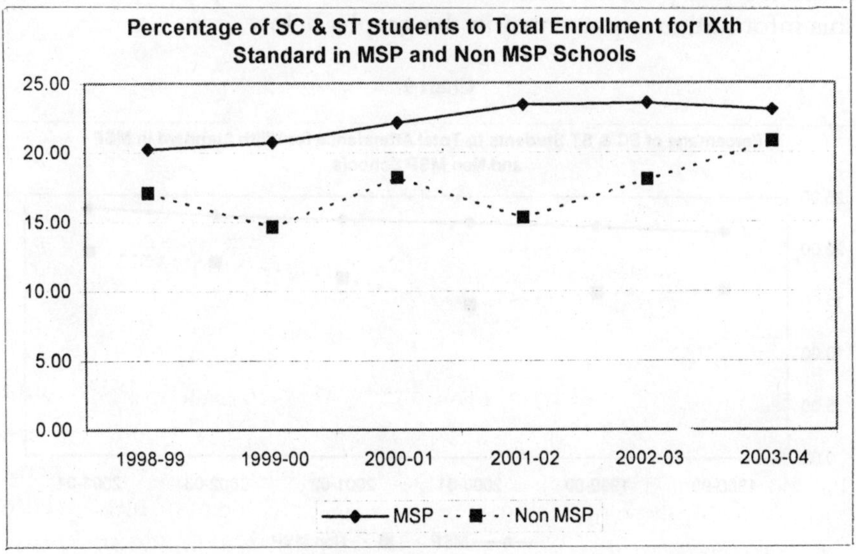

Chart 8

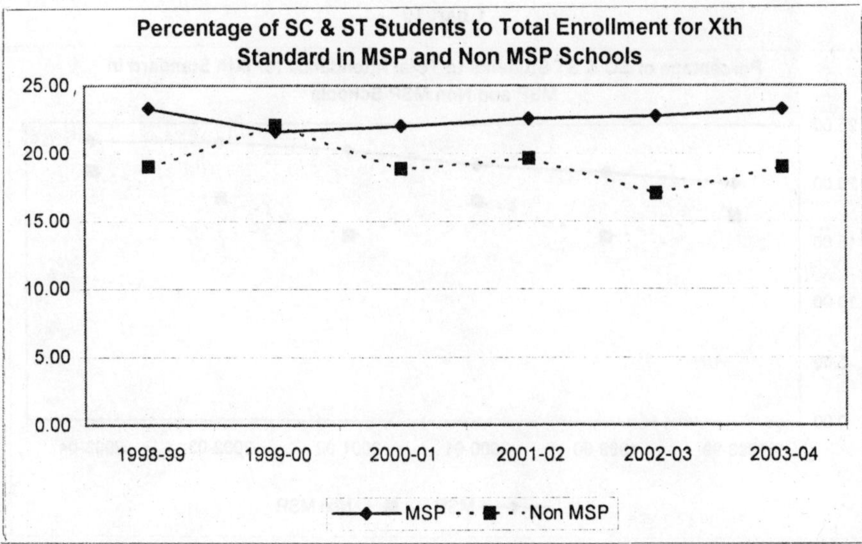

Proportion of SC/ST Students in Attendance in MSP and Non-MSP Schools

As the SC and ST students are doing better in enrollments, an attempt was made to know their attendance status between MSP and Non-MSP schools. The percentage of SC/ST students attending to the total attendance at the schools revealed that they attending on a higher scale in the MSP schools. Thus, the MSP seems to be instrumental in not only enrolling greater number of students but it is also encouraging the socially backward students to go the school regularly. But unfortunately the same set of students is not so punctual in the Non-MSP schools. Graphical presentation of this information is presented in the graphs below.

Chart 9

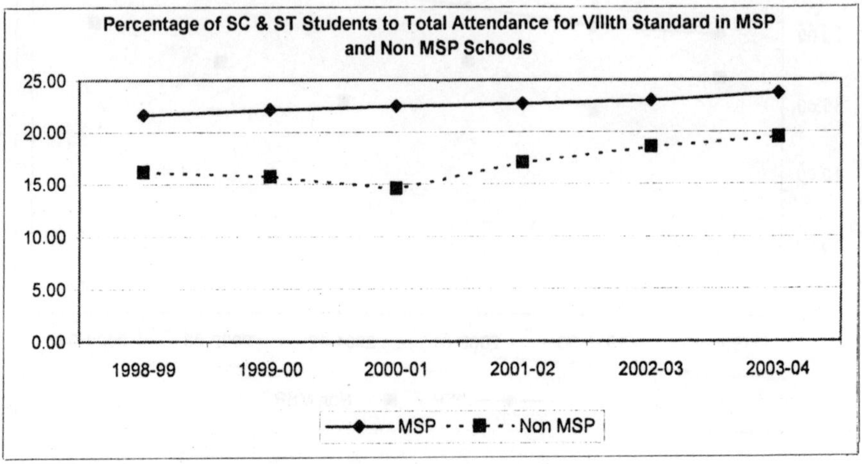

Chart 10

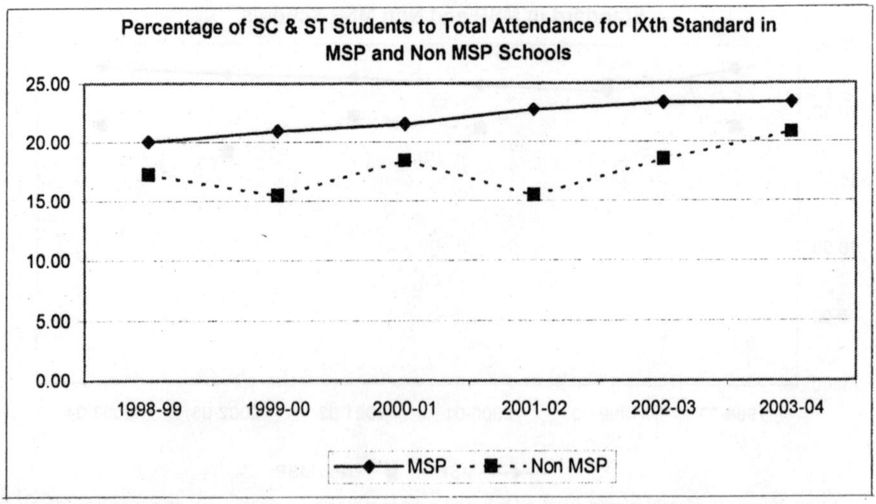

On the whole it appears that the enrollments and attendance have been influenced by the MSP quite favorably. One needs to be careful in attributing the effects on these crucial indicators. However, the qualitative impressions of different stakeholders' opinion on the issue of MSP favorably influencing

Chart 11

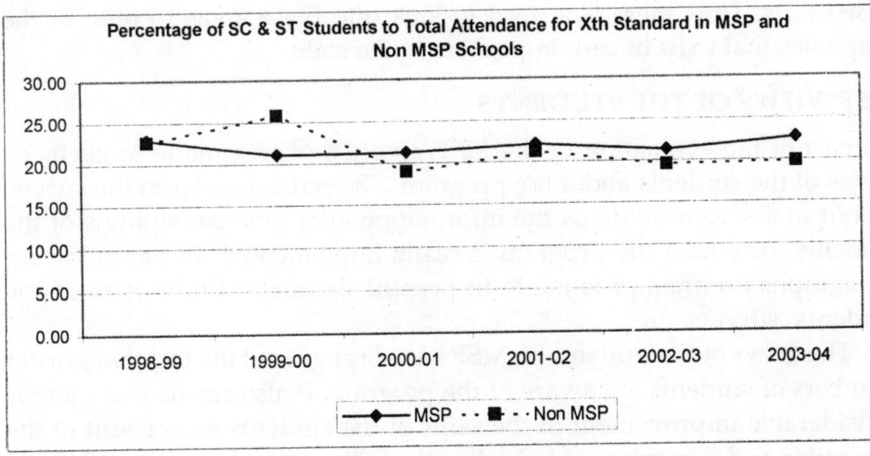

enrollments and attendance does support the fact that MSP indeed has done a lot on the performance of these indicators.

VIEWS OF COMPUTER AIDED TEACHERS

As part of the evaluation process of MSP an attempt was made to get the views of the different stakeholders of the program. The survey of teachers of the MSP schools has provided crucial information regarding various empirical aspects of the program.

The language of computer education was considered to be the major handicap when computer education was introduced. Every one believed that computers would require English language for imparting the knowledge. But the efforts by the DSERT to produce and distribute textbooks in the regional language deserve appreciation. The performance of the students also seems to have improved due to the teaching of subjects through the help of computers.

VIEWS OF COMPUTER INSTRUCTORS

The survey also covered the computer instructors in the selected MSP schools. Various issues relating to the program were included in the questionnaire. The opinion of the instructors should provide broad pointers about the strengths and weaknesses of MSP due to the fact that they are the major actors in the framework of MSP.

Teaching of different soft wares seems to be in good shape and the instructors also feel that crucial indicators like enrollments, attendance and performance of students have been doing well. Their opinion with regard to the repair and maintenance of equipments is encouraging and the supply of textbooks in local language is also quite student friendly. However, they have also expressed some concerns about the regularity of power supply, internet facility in far flung areas and supply of internet based CDs. Thus there is a need to look into these areas to plug in the loopholes that exist in certain pockets of the state.

MSP: VIEWS OF THE STUDENTS

As part of the evaluation of the MSP an attempt was made to elicit the views of the students about the program. The reflections from the survey would in a way provide us the information about the perceptions of the students for whom the program is really implemented. In the following paragraphs an attempt is made to present the major findings from the students' survey.

The views of the students on MSP have brought out the fact that greater numbers of students are aware of the program. It also seems that there is considerable improvement of the skills of the students on account of the computer and computer aided education. The attitudes of the students towards learning and participation in the activities of the school have also shown considerable improvement. The areas, which need improvement, could be the supply of Internet based CDs and provision of other inputs to the students. On the whole the student's community seems to be quite satisfied and they also enjoy this new and innovative method of teaching and learning.

VIEWS OF MSP STAKEHOLDERS AT DIFFERENT LEVELS

In the following paragraphs an attempt is made to summarize the qualitative information obtained through the discussion with various officials involved in MSP like Block Education Officers, DDPIs, Principals and Lecturers of DIETS, the officials of the computer agencies and lastly the key personnel at the state level who are in charge of the MSP.

Role of the Computer Agencies in Managing the MSP

All the three agencies have been effective in providing services and have been active in attending the problems. They have also provided the faculty with good experience. But in some remote areas the problems persist with regard to the up keep of the equipments and provision of electricity and Internet. However, the agencies are trying hard to do away with the problems. Such a prompt actions from the agencies is primarily due to the fear of penalty measures, which would be initiated by the DSERT. Thus the role of the DSERT in putting the things back on the track attracts appreciation.

Feedback Mechanism through Quarterly Evaluation of MSP

Quarterly evaluation seems to be effective and it brings out the shortcomings experienced by the schools. Nodal officers take prompt actions to initiate the corrective measures for those issues highlighted through such evaluation. Analyses of the information gathered through questionnaires as part of such evaluation needs to be utilized fully.

Taking stock of the reports, the nodal officers would act immediately and extend all kinds of co-operation to the schools. The chain of activities right from the school to the DIET and up to the state level seems to be quite effective in providing necessary assistance to schools in correcting the deficiencies.

Interaction between the Providers, Head masters, Teachers, SDMCs and DIET

There is a regular exchange of views and experiences among Head Masters of MSP schools, Principals of DIETs and representatives of computer agencies. The outcome of such interaction seems to be effective in addressing the problems faced by the MSP schools. Some of the Lecturers who are looking after MSP felt that the interaction between the agencies, Head Masters and the DIET is not very satisfactory and the agencies play hide and seek with regard to the provision of internet on the server and other PCs. This issue needs to be resolved to help the students to have access to Internet for a longer period of time. They also felt that sometimes the irregularity of payment to the agencies is affecting the services by the agencies. There were instances where the agencies did not provide original CDs to the schools, which have created problems in using the concerned soft wares.

Impact of the MSP

(a) Enrollment

The enrollment seems to have increased significantly in MSP schools. Almost all the respondents have unanimously endorsed which could be considered as a positive impact of the MSP.

(b) Attendance

Attendance of students on account of MSP has relatively improved in the schools. Most of the respondents have opined that the computer and computer based education at the schools has attracted students to the schools on regular basis. It was also observed by the school teachers as well as other block and district level officials that students prefer to stay at the schools even after the school hours. This indicates another significant achievement of the MSP.

(c) Dropouts

The drop outs scenario has also considerably improved. The obvious effect of the above two factors has naturally brought down the drop out rate at the schools. Of course one cannot easily attribute the reduction of drop out or improvements in enrollment and attendance, but nevertheless the wise judgment of the responsible people in charge of the programme does form the basis for such inferences.

(d) Examination

Many of the officials felt that the performances of the students have shown improvement in the examinations relating to the subjects as well as in computer related tests.

Opinion of the Officials and Teachers on the following

Regularity of Computer Instructors at Schools

Instructors are regular and they also do their duty effectively was the majority opinion. However there were instances of greater turn over of instructors, which have caused some concern at the school levels.

Training of Computer Instructors

Majority of the instructors are duly qualified and they have reasonable amount of training in this regard. The skills of such instructors seem to be quite effective in imparting the knowledge to the students.

Training of Computer Aided Teachers

Most of the regular teachers have received training and the training by INTEL seems to be the center of attraction for them. The training is conducted during the vacations and such training satisfies majority of the teachers. One important aspect in this regard is that the Head Master should also receive training so that he/she can play more effective role in promoting the cause of the programme.

Major Concerns Relating to Supply of the following

Hardware to MSP Schools

Hardware supplied at the beginning of the programme was good enough. But there are problems with regard to the supplies of floppies to the students. Every year floppies are not supplied and in place old ones are being re-distributed to the students. In some schools the net working problems exist.

Software to MSP Schools

The supply of CDs to schools containing soft wares seems to be all right. But problems persist with regard to the adequacy of such CDs on account problems with regard to the networking. In many cases anti virus kits are not supplied to the schools.

Telephone Connection

The problem of supply of telephone connection to schools is acute in rural areas. In taluka and district places there is satisfactory situation as far as telephone connection is concerned.

Internet Connection

The similar situation exists with regard to the Internet facility as well. The issues of extending the Internet to other PCs from the server exist due to problems faced by the proxy extensions.

Effective Electricity Supply (Un-interrupted)

Uninterrupted power supply is the major problem and needs immediate attention. Though in some schools generator is supplied, there are many issues relating to the maintenance of it as well as procurement of diesel/ petrol to the genset. Some people have opined that the possibility of supplying a solar based power system would be much more effective. The cost effectiveness of such option needs to be considered.

Repair and Maintenance

Prompt and effective attention to repair and maintenance is found in majority of places. However due to dearth of anti virus packages the computer down time has increased. In some remote places and in majority of places of the districts of north Karnataka, the attention paid to repair and maintenance is not very effective which needs immediate attention.

Performance of Students in Computer Education

Students do have acquired necessary skills as far as operation of computers are concerned. They have also learnt application of computers to their course work. The officials believe that there is a sea of change in the way students learn and report the subjects after the introduction of the scheme.

Performance of Students in Computer Aided Education

In majority of the schools students have learnt to use subject related CDs and they have also been acquainted with the use of computers in their project work. More time and space at the schools is needed to enlarge the student's participation in this regard.

Reasons for the best Performances under MSP

It is a general experience that wherever the Head Masters have taken a lead role in implementing the computer-based education; the success rate of the MSP has been good. The proactive role of the head of the institution and the teachers seems to be crucial in the effectiveness of the program. But, unfortunately in few cases though the staff is enthusiastic there are certain technical problems like effective telephone connection and uninterrupted power supply which have hindered the progress of the scheme. But there was also a feeling among the teaching community that the scheme is something exogenous to their system and in this regard efforts should be made to internalize the scheme so that it would be able to yield greater positive results.

THE FOLLOWING ARE THE MAJOR BOTTLENECKS/SUGGESTIONS WITH REGARD TO THE MSP

- Though there is a training a component under MSP it needs to be more comprehensive and the Head Master of the schools also needs training with regard to the use of computers in teaching.
- The evaluation by the Engineering colleges should also test the skills gained by the students with regard to computer education.
- Telephone connection and internet facility could be the major impediments and steps should be taken to improve the situation especially in rural areas.
- The power supply is another area where much needs to be improved. Some schools have suggested for the supply of solar-based power supply instead of a generator.
- There is a need to provide more furniture and additional room to the schools for the purpose of MSP activities.
- Since many agencies have started the process of terminating the instructors under the pretext of the end of MSP and hence the instructors are loosing interest in the teaching activities. Some sort of continuity needs to be assured to them to sustain their interest.
- Shortage of PCs is also one of the important handicaps faced by the schools.
- Medium of textbooks also seem to be significant bottleneck and effective number of text books each year need to be supplied to the schools.
- Since there are problems with regard to the supply of Floppies, CDs, Printing paper etc., the Head Master of the school needs to be given the authority and financial powers to procure these things.

Opinion of the officials at different levels has really brought an array of strengths and weaknesses of the MSP. We believe that such viewpoints are quite crucial and they would be instrumental in taking forward the efforts in strengthening the extended phase of MSP with greater coverage.

CONCLUDING OBSERVATIONS

On the whole it appears that the MSP has been successful in making a significant impact on the student community. The indicators of enrolment and attendance have shown considerable amount of improvement as compared for the periods prior to MSP and during MSP. It also appears that these indicators are in a better position as compared to the schools in Non-MSP category.

The program has made considerable in roads in providing Kannada medium learning materials for the benefit of the students. The skills gained by the students with regarding to computer per say as well as computer aided education need appreciation. However, there are certain weak spots, which deserve immediate attention. Regular and uninterrupted power supply and effective internet connection are the two major ones in this regard.

Computer instructors feel that they are satisfied by the MSP. Their views are important because of the fact that they are the people who are implementing the program at the school level and their interactions at the school would have given them good amount of insights about the impact of the program. Teaching of different soft wares seems to be in good shape and the instructors also feel that crucial indicators like enrollments, attendance and performance of students have been doing well. Their opinion with regard to the repair and maintenance of equipments is encouraging and the supply of textbooks in local language is also quite student friendly. However, they have also expressed some concerns about the regularity of power supply, internet facility in far flung areas and supply of internet based CDs. Thus there is a need to look into these areas to plug in the loopholes that exist in certain pockets of the state.

Views of the computer aided teachers have clearly brought out the fact that the language issue of computer education had been effectively dealt with by the officials who are in charge of implementing the program. The performance of the students also seems to have improved due to the teaching of subjects through the help of computers.

The views of the students on MSP have brought out the fact that greater numbers of students are aware of the program. It also seems that there is considerable improvement of the skills of the students on account of the computer and computer aided education. The attitudes of the students towards learning and participation in the activities of the school have also shown considerable improvement. The areas, which need improvement, could be the supply of Internet based CDs and provision of other inputs to the students. On the whole the student community seem to be quite satisfied and they also enjoy this new and innovative method of teaching and learning.

The program happens to be quite innovative and stands as a model for emulation by other state as well. Though it had some teething problems at the beginning, the sincere and tireless efforts by the officials have put the whole program on the right track. In view of the growing challenges and opportunities on account of the expanding IT sector in the Indian economy in general and Karnataka economy in particular, the novel idea of exposing students to the computer and computer aided education deserves full appreciation. The attraction of students to the schools on account of computer education needs to be utilized fully to sustain the secondary education which is usually crippled by high drop outs. Efforts should also be made to deal with the bottlenecks of the program effectively. Thus, the MSP has the potential to equip our student community to face the challenges of the knowledge society in the years to come.

NOTE

* This paper is part of the Study 'Impact Assessment of Mahiti Sindhu Program' sponsored by Department of State Educational Research and Training (DSERT), Government of Karnataka, Bangalore.

1. Human Resources in the Electronics Industry: A Case Study of Bangalore, CMDR, Unpublished.

REFERENCES

Schultz, Theodore W. (1963), The Economic value of Education. New York: Columbia University Press.

Psacharopoulos, G. (1975), Earning and Education in OECD Countries, Paris: OECD.

Becker, G. (1964), Human Capital. Ist edn (NBER).

Chapter - 4

Participation of Poor Households in Group-based Financial Institutions: Experience from Two Districts of West Bengal

Bahnisikha Ghosh & Avijit Brahmachary

INTRODUCTION

Microfinance is considered now as a powerful instrument for poverty alleviation and rural development. It is an effective intervention that is capable of reaching the otherwise unreached, by targeting and internalizing in the development process specific regions and social and economic groups. It is the supply of thrift, credit and other financial services and products of very small amounts to poor in rural, urban and semi-urban areas for raising their income levels and standard of living [Nair, 2001].

Financial institutions play an important role in channeling funds from surplus (savers) to deficit sectors (investors) [Dasgupta, 2001]. But unless mandated, formal financial institutions (FFIs) avoid dealing with poor people. Actually, the implementation of any formal lending programme directed towards the poor at small scale often suffers from four important difficulties. The first is the probleme of exact targeting, which would ensure that there are no Type-I or Type-II errors[Cornia and Stewart,1991]. Secondly, it faces the screening probleme of distinguishing the good from the bad borrowers. Thirdly, these agencies may not be able to monitor and ensure productive usage of the loan. And fourthly, due to high level of transaction costs incurred in lending to the poor and absence of collateral, formal lending agencies often leave the poor unbanked [Hulme and Mosely,1996].

The failure of FFIs to serve the rural poor effectively led to a review and look at the informal financial systems and lending groups. At present, informal groups world-wide play an important role in channeling fund for unbanked poor. The basic characteristics of such groups are that there is negligible information gap between the lender and the borrower and little transaction cost is involved for both parties. Besides, "peer monitoring" among the beneficiaries of the groups rectifies low repayment problems associated with lending activities [Khandaker, 1999; Goetz and Sengupta, 1996; Stiglitz, 1990].

In India, the failure of co-operatives, FFIs and government subsidized programmes(such as IRDP) to reach the targeted poor, acted as an inducement for the promotion of microfinance(henceforth 'mF') programme through Self-help groups(SHGs) as a viable alternative means of alleviating poverty. The first official involvement in promoting mF programme through SHGs in India has been taken by National Bank for Agriculture and Rural Development (NABARD) as early as in 1992, launching a pilot project for linking 500 SHGs with banks. Thereafter, FFIs, government agencies and NGOs involved themselves to encourage SHG formation and linking these groups with banks. In recent times mF programme through SHGs is operating across the country, albeit with multiple characteristics and performance magnitudes, to reduce poverty and empower the participants [Karmakar, 2001; NABARD, 2000, 1995; ACRC, 1993].

At present the group-based lending have spread over in many countries such as Bangladesh, Indonesia, Bolivia, India, Pakistan, Sri Lanka, Malawi and others and have occupied a central position in the government policy framework as an alternative poverty alleviation tool. By the end 2003 about 80 million clients across the world were being serviced by approximately 2900 microfinance institutions (henceforth, "mFIs), whereas India's share in the global mF market in 2003 was 13 per cent of all clients and 16 per cent of the poorest clients (Table 1) [Nair, 2005].

Table 1
Global Outreach of mF Programme, 1997-2003

Year	*No. of Reporting Institutions*	*No. of clients reached (million)*	*Poorest clients reached (%)*
1997	618	13.5	56.3
1998	925	20.9	58.4
1999	1065	23.6	58.5
2000	1567	30.7	62.9
2002	2572	67.6	61.5
2003	2931	80.9	67.7

Source: Morduch, 2004, Daley-Harris, 2004.

MF IN INDIA: DELIVERY MECHANISM AND OUTREACH

There is wide variety of institutions in India catering with various degrees of success to the mF needs of the poor families. In the Indian context mFIs can broadly be subdivided into three of organizational forms: (a) Not for profit mFIs (societies registered under Society Registration Act,1860, or public trusts registered under the Indian Trust Act,1882, or non-profit companies registered under section 25 of the Companies Act,1956 are fall in this category), (b) Mutual Benefit mFIs(State Credit Co-operatives, National Credit Co-operatives and Mutually Aided Co-operative Societies are fall in this category), and (c) For Profit mFIs(all Non-Banking Financial Companies registered under the Companies Act,1956 are fall in this perview).

Though banks themselves may form SHGs and after nurturing offer financial services, NGOs have a significant role in spreading mF programme among the unbanked poor. Besides their traditional activities NGOs are effective agents in organizing, nurturing and stabilizing SHGs and ultimately facilitating their linkage with formal banking system so as to improve the outreach of the financial services to the unreached and under-served poor. The working group on NGOs and SHGs (1995), set up by RBI, had observed that NGOs are one of the important agencies particularly suitable for empowering the rural poor and have generally been instrumental in the promotion of SHGs in different parts of the country.

In 1990s NABARD have started an experiment with MYRADA by promoting groups, mobilizing their savings and linking them with banks for credit support. Later NABARD replicated this project all over India under the SHG-Bank Linkage programme in 1992 and many NGOs came forward to implement this project with the co-operation of Banks. In 1994, following the success of NABARD, SIDBI also came forward to provide bulk lending to NGOs for on-lending to groups/individuals. Ministry of Human Resource Development, Government of India established Rashtriya Mahila Kosh (RMK) for providing loan to NGOs to on-lend to poor women.

In India Three Different Models of SHG-Bank Linkage have Evolved over time (NABARD, 2002)

Model I: SHGs formed and financed by banks

In this model, banks themselves take up the work of forming and nurturing the groups, opening their savings accounts and providing them bank loans. Up to March 2002, 16% of the total no. of SHGs was financed under this category.

Model II: SHGs formed by NGOs and formal agencies, but directly financed by banks

Here, NGOs and formal agencies act as an facilitators in the field of mF and up to March, 2002, 75% of the total no. of SHGs were financed under this model and occupies the major share among the three models.

Model III: SHGs financed by Banks using NGOs and Other agencies as financial intermediaries

This is the model wherein the NGOs take on the additional role of financial intermediation. In areas where the formal banking system faces constraints, the NGOs are encouraged to approach a suitable bank for loan assistance. Till March, 2002, only 9% of the total SHGs were financed under this category.

Although as yet not enough systematic formal official publication on different statistics about mF and SHGs in Indian context is available, NABARD, however, has brought out a publication on some basic data on SHGs in 2002. From this publication we get the cumulative progress of SHG-Bank Linkage programme in India since 1992 under NABARD model (Table 2).

Table 2
Cumulative Progress of SHG-Bank Linkage in India
(1992-2002)

Year	*No. of SHGs financed by banks*	*Bank Loan (Rs. Million)*	*Refinance from NABARD (Rs. Million)*
1992-93	255	02.9	02.7
1993-94	620	06.5	04.6
94-95	2122	24.4	23.0
95-96	4757	60.6	51.6
96-97	8598	118.4	106.5
97-98	14317	237.6	213.9
98-99	32995	571.0	521.0
99-2000	114775	1930.0	1501.0
2000-2001	263825	4809.0	4007.0
2001-2002	461478	10263.0	7965.0

Source: NABARD and mF, 2001-2002.

Although the programme of linking SHGs with bank finance was launched by NABARD in February, 1992 at all India level, it took some time to gain momentum in the state of West Bengal and the first breakthrough came only in the year 1993-94 when 3 SHGs were linked with Sagar Gramin Bank in 24 Pgs(S) district. However, thereafter the pace of growth of formation and linkage of SHGs continued to be tardy till 1997-98. From the year 1998-1999, the process of formation and linkage of SHGs started gathering momentum. During 1998-99 themselves, 1198

SHGs were credit linked through different commercial, co-operative and Regional Rural Banks, and this number went up to 3249 groups during 1999-2000 and 32868 groups' up to March, 2003. The district-wise performance in West Bengal up to March, 2003 in providing credit is shown in Table 3.

Table 3
District-wise Performance of SHG-Bank Linkage in West Bengal (Cumulative up to March, 2003)

Districts	*SHGs provided bank loan (No.)*	*Bank loan released (Rs. Million)*
Nadia	6156	439.580
24 pgs(N)	3647	209.392
Hooghly	5286	627.845
24 pgs(S)	3036	199.52
Darjeeling	130	36.065
Purulia	307	63.635
Coochbehar	562	84.095
Burdwan	599	77.246
Malda	1004	88.51
Jalpaiguri	1073	136.540
U. Dinajpur	1190	22.19
D. Dinajpur	468	8.61
Murshidabad	1816	233.288
Howrah	436	120.610
Bankura	2143	198.17
Midnapure	4529	228.346
Birbhum	486	296.6
Total	32868	3070.242

Source: NABARD (Kolkata Office), unpublished data.

The distribution of SHG-Bank linkage under different model in West Bengal is shown in Table 4.

Table 4
Model-wise Distribution of SHG-Bank Linkage in West Bengal (Cumulative up to March, 2002)

Model	*No. of SHGs*	*% of total SHGs in the State*	*Total Bank Loan (Rs. Million)*
Model-I	13686	79.83	105.21
Model-II	290	1.69	2.70
Model-III	3167	18.48	16.28
Total	17143	100.00	127.19

Source: State Focus Paper, NABARD, 2002-2003.

It has been observed that up to March, 2002 the outreach of SHG-Bank Linkage programme in West Bengal (17143 groups, cumulative) is much lower than other states such as Andhrapradesh (243714), Tamil Nadu

(63184), Karnataka (37032) and Uttarpradesh (33114). Though the programme picked up momentum since 1998-99 in West Bengal the comparative performance (in terms of linking SHGs with banks) with other states as stated above is not satisfactory. It clearly suggests that the outreach of the mF programme in West Bengal is not satisfactory and enough room is left for mFIs to improve and extend their services among the unbanked poor.

Against this background we have attempted in this paper to analyse the pattern of household participation in group-based financial institutions in the context of West Bengal. The analysis is based on field level data from two districts of the state. The econometric analysis focuses on the determinants of membership in group based financial institutions followed by the nature of loan transactions and loan repayment performance based on our sample survey. Whereas loan transaction pattern helps to explore the actual uses of group loan, the loan repayment performance, to some extent measures the economic sustainability of the programme in respective villages.

SAMPLE SELECTION AND SOCIO-ECONOMIC CHARACTERISTICS OF THE SAMPLE HOUSEHOLDS

The two districts chosen for this study are Nadia and 24 pgs (N). Here we have selected these two districts purposively due to the following reasons: (i) Nadia and 24 pgs (N) are among the first five districts in the state in terms of cumulative progress of SHG-Bank Linkage Programme (credit linked), (ii) All models of SHG-Bank linkage (i.e, the three models as stated earlier) are present here and (iii) though both the districts are neighbors according to geographical location, the outreach of the programme up to March, 2003 in 24 pgs (N) is far behind that in Nadia.

We randomly selected a total of five villages from these two districts - 3 from Nadia and 2 from 24 pgs (N). From these five villages we randomly selected 160 SHG member households who belong to those SHGs which are in operation for 2 years or more and collected required data through questionnaire based survey method. Besides, 30 non-member households were also selected randomly from these sample villages as a control group and requisite information was gathered from them. Thus we carried out our study considering 190 sample households-160 member households and 30 non-member households. It may be noted that all the member and non-member households belong to the same socio-economic class and geographic location. The sample design for this study is shown in Table 5. In case of non-member households we randomly selected 6 households from each village and hence, in total, 30 households are selected as control group for this study.

The socio-economic characteristics of the sample households are shown in Table 6.

Table 5
Sample Design

Village	*Districts*	*Group promoting agency*	*Group financed by*	*No. of Groups >2 year*	*Total Members (No.)*	*Group Surveyed (No.)*	*Members Surveyed (No.)*
Ruppur	Nadia	Nadia Gramin Bank (NGB)	NGB	12	159	8	30
Rabonbor	Nadia	Nadia District Central Co-operative Bank Ltd.	Nadia District Central Co-operative Bank Ltd.	10	115	7	30
Kulgachi	Nadia	Sreema Mahila Samity (SMS)	NGB	23	305	12	40
Datpur	24pgs (N)	SMS	NGB	12	121	10	30
Taraberia	24pgs (N)	Allahabad Bank	Allahabad Bank	13	143	10	30
Total				70	843	47	160

Table 6
Socio-economic Characteristics of the Sample Households

Characteristics	*Members*	*Non-Members*
Sample Size	160	30
Household Size (Avg.)	4.94	4.5
Sex of the respondents		
Male (%)	25.63	36.67
Female (%)	74.37	63.33
Sex of the household head		
Male (%)	68.75	73.33
Female (%)	31.25	26.67
Years of Schooling of the respondents (Average)	5.93	8.07
Years of Schooling of the household head (Average)	3.66	3.97
Agricultural land holding of the households (avg.)	2.66*	6.60*
Avg. Income of the Respondent	992.19	1113.33
Avg. Income of the household	2273.13	2636.66
Category of the households		
(%)	6.9	6.7
APL	78.8	63.3
BPL	14.4	30.0
AAY		
Principal economic activity of the households (%)		
Farm Production	19.37	33.33
Non-Farm Prod.	6.25	10.00
Farm Labour	20.62	3.33
Non-Farm Labour	16.25	10.00
Petty Trading, Vendors, Hawker, etc.	23.13	26.67
Livestock rearing	3.13	3.33
Fishery	3.75	6.67
Others	7.50	6.67

* Here agricultural land holding is measured by the unit "Katha", where 20 Katha= 0.33 acre. APL = above poverty level, BPL = below poverty level, and AAY = Antodaya Anna Yojana.

The average household size of the entire sample of 190 households is 4.87 persons. Among the member respondents 74.37% are female and 25.63% are male. In case of household head 31.25% are female and 68.75% are male. Therefore, it is clear that though the mF programme in our sample villages have included female members more significantly than the males, most of these respondents belong to the male-headed households. It is believed that mF programmes yield better results if it can be spread among the female poor who belongs to the female headed households. However, in our sample, though respondents report that they faced some obstacles from the male household head at the time of joining the groups, thereafter their participation has been accepted by the male member and everything has been adjusted gradually. Astonishingly, at present, senior males of the household have become strong advocates for their participation as a group member in such programmes.

DETERMINANTS OF MEMBERSHIP IN GROUP-BASED FINANCIAL INSTITUTIONS

In this section we have tried to address the determinants of membership in different SHGs promoted by Banks, NGOs or other institutions using survey data. Membership in a group-based programme is not solely a supply-side outcome since many individuals are not willing to apply for membership due to some reasons or other, even though they belong to the same socio-economic class and location as the members. Actually, participation in a group-based programme needs to be analysed as an outcome of the interaction between both the demand for and the supply of institutional services. From the viewpoint of the household, its decision to apply for membership depends on its calculations of the costs and benefits of joining the programme (Zeller, 2001).

The principal benefit for joining as a member in a group-based programme is the high probability of obtaining a loan at substantially lower interest rates. Besides, there may be some other secondary benefits as well. Risk-pulling in lending activities, collective bargaining for own and group's interests, opportunity to access in various training and skill development programmes, are such secondary benefits which an individual can enjoy as a group member.

Similarly, the cost of participation in such programmes has several components. First of all, there is a time cost. Actually, all group members are compelled to attend at all group meetings, which are held, in most cases, at bi-weekly/monthly intervals, and last up to 1.5-2 hours. The time cost is also associated with other compulsory activities such as attendance at training and social awareness programmes, routine transaction with banks, mandatory paper work to maintain balance sheet for every month, monitoring member borrowers for loan recovery, and so on. For the poor households whose main income-earning asset is labour, the opportunity cost of these activities can be significantly large. Secondly, the joint liability approach in group lending imposes an additional risk burden on members. It is because under these systems one member, or broadly speaking all group members, are partly responsible for the repayment actions of other group members. Many individuals, however, are not willing to bear such risks. Thirdly, it is mandatory for all group members to make small savings at a regular intervals(in our sample villages it is monthly intervals).Though the members have enough right to set their regular subscription amount but the opportunity costs of such saving with banks/NGOs generates an additional cost component for participation in a group-based programmes. However, if the expected benefits outweigh the expected costs, the ultimate decision of an individual is to apply for the membership.

The similar story is also present in the supply side as well. That is, the supplier of the group based programme accounts for the benefit and cost components in their accounting methods and decides about the supply of the programme provided that there is no pressure on the supplier (such as directed programme offered by the government through different agencies). However, in the context of granting membership, the condition is that the expected cost of lending to a particular borrower is lower than the expected marginal revenue.

But the objective of the group-based credit programmes under considerations often goes beyond simple profit maximization. Hence, the marginal benefits encompass considerations beyond purely financial returns. These programmes explicitly target the landless and near landless poor households and therefore, are offered selectively. All these considerations are crucial at the time of lender's decision to grant membership or forming a new group (Zeller and others, 2001).

However, the decision of an individual to apply for membership in group-based credit programmes and the decision of mF providers or mFIs to accept the application has been analysed by Zeller and others using the demand supply analysis as stated above in respect of Bangladesh (Research Report,IFPRI,2001). Using 0.5 acre of land holding as an eligibility cut-off point for membership, Zeller separated the demand and supply equations from each other and fitted a bivariate probit model. Though the findings of this study are in line with our expectations, but the above model cannot be used in our study due to following reasons.

Actually, Zeller and his colleagues used an eligibility criterion in the supply equation which they have defined by a cut-off level. In their study they used 0.5 acre of land holding as the cut-off point generally followed by mFIs in time of granting membership and thus households who have less than 0.5 acre of land holding are eligible for group membership. Unfortunately, no such eligibility criteria are practiced in our sample villages for granting membership. Actually, throughout West Bengal though the mF programme targets only the poor households, there is no unique criterion for granting a membership and very few institutions follow the strict eligibility criteria in time of forming or granting membership.

However, to make our study simple and transparent we have modeled the basic determinants of membership in a group-based programme as follows. We modeled the difference between benefit and cost for becoming a member (or granting a membership) in a group-based programme as an unobserved variable y_i^*, such that an individual decides to apply for (granting of) membership, when $y_i^* > 0$. y_i^* is functionally specified as,

$$y_i^* = f(X_i),$$

where vector X_i represents household-level characteristics. We do not observe the net benefit of any decision, only whether it is made or not. Therefore, the indicator variable y_i (in our model, it is the dependent variable which represents the current membership in a group based programme) can be defined as,

$$y_i = 1 \text{ if } y_i^* > 0,$$

$$y_i = 0, \text{ otherwise.}$$

That is, an individual is a present member if y_i^*, i.e, unobserved net benefit, is positive, and zero, otherwise. Similar explanation may be forwarded simultaneously for the supply side as well.

Within this formulation the probleme, therefore, can be cast in terms of a binomial probit model (Greene, 2003). The descriptive statistics of the independent variables used in the model are described in Table 7.

Table 7
Description of the Independent Variables used in the Regression Model

Variables	*Variable Description*	*Mean*	*Std. Deviation*
ALHOH	Agricultural land holding of the household	3.28	4.20
TFM	Total family member of the household	4.87	0.838
HEF	Highest education in the family/household	8.24	2.91
NWMH	Number of working members in the household	1.36	0.505
PLH	Poverty level of the household. It is a binary choice variable. If the household is below poverty level in terms of income PLH=1, Otherwise=0.	0.579	0.131

ALHOH or the agricultural land holding of the household at the time of joining in the group is measured by "*Katha*"-a local measuring unit, where 20 *Katha* = 0.33 acre. PLH is measured in terms of household income. According to the statistics of Planning Commission of India the per capita poverty line for rural area at 2003-04 prices is nearabout Rs. 375 for west Bengal (Reserve Bank of India Bulletin, 2005). We put PLH = 1 if the family income as reported is below the poverty line, and otherwise it is equal to zero. The estimated equations are presented in Table 8 and discussed below.

Table 8
Determinants of Membership in Group-based Programmes
(Binomial Probit Model)

Variable	*Coefficient*	*t-values*
Constant	4.1428	2.761*
ALHOH	-0.0979	-2.917**
TFM	0.4009	1.878
HEF	-0.4941	-3.964**
NWMH	-0.3544	-1.235
PLH	0.8975	2.870*

N = 190
Log likelihood= -49.7375
Chi-squared = 66.27
*= Significant at 5 per cent level and, **= Significant at 1 per cent level.

From table 8 it is clear that the probability of decision to apply for a group membership by the respondent declines as more land are owned by the household. The coefficient is significant at 10 per cent level of significance. The result is in line with our expectations. It is because as land increases, households are less likely to apply for membership because they know that the probability to deny their application is higher in these circumstances. Besides, an increase in landholding increases access to other sources of financial services. Households with more land are likely to be wealthier and have ability to adopt self-financed projects. Moreover, though group-based loan carry relatively low interest rates, they, nonetheless, carry some other indirect costs such as compulsory participation in different group level activities (such as training programmes, social activities, etc.), time devotion for group meetings and group monitoring and some amount of paper work for loan/saving transactions. Since all these activities are relatively labour intensive, the real cost of loans increases as the opportunity cost of household labour rises. Thus, as the increase in land size results in increase in the marginal productivity of labour (and hence its opportunity cost), loans from SHGs become less attractive when full labour costs are accounted for.

In case of TFM the coefficient is positive but not significant. As the family member of the household increases, the probability to join in the SHG from that family also increases. It is because; other things remaining the same, larger households imply poorer households and hence less access to alternative sources of credit. But these families have greater demand for financial services to combat various threats to their livelihood and so the tendency of larger household to participate in the group-based programme is positive.

The coefficient of HEF is negative and significant. Actually, as the education of a member in a household increases they can find different income earning activities more easily than a non-educated or lower educated persons. Besides, the mobility of higher educated persons outside the village is more than the others which in turn helps to find a new job or frequent change from the existing jobs and hence a higher income potentialities in the household. In such cases, willingness to join as a group from that household declines significantly. Besides, the main target of the SHG programmes from policy viewpoint is not only to enable the member to access in the financial services, rather also to generate awareness in respect of livelihood and others. So the targeted people of such programme are less educated poor and therefore higher educated families are not willing to apply for membership because of the expectations that their application faces the risk of being denied.

The coefficient for the number of working members in the household (NWMH) is negative but not significant. The result can be explained as follows. As the working member in the household increases the probability of earning by the household is expected to be higher than other families where NWMH is lower even though they have same or higher family size. These household has more ability to finance different household projects and less demand for livelihood maintenance loans. Since in our sample data the coefficient of NWMH is negative but not significant the above proposition, however, is not very much strong in our sample villages.

The coefficient of PLH is also negative and significant at 5 per cent level. However, the negative coefficient of PLH clearly indicates that wealthier household in terms of monthly income has lower probability to join as a member in SHGs and mF providers also has less interests about these households.

NATURE OF LOAN TRANSACTIONS

After sanctioning membership of individuals for joining in SHGs or forming a group, individuals are allowed to accumulate their thrifts/ savings and the concerned groups are linked with any FFIs, specifically with banks to mobilize their savings. Such process continues up to 6 months (the nurturing phase of SHGs) and then groups are eligible to apply for loan from banks. Noted that here 'individuals' are not eligible for applying a new loan. Rather, only 'groups' can apply for a new loan from banks for their members. According to NABARD's rule, at present, each group can borrow from FFIs up to 4 times of their accumulated savings as maintained with the banks.

After receiving a loan from banks group members are decide through a general meeting that how much loan should be disbursed among the members according to priority basis. All loans are not disbursed at a time. For emergency needs of the members, such as health hazard ness, education, natural disaster, etc. group maintains a minimum loan amount as reserves.

However, in this section we have described the sources, uses and repayment nature of loans obtained from our sample villages.

THE USE AND SOURCES OF LOAN

In table 9 we have described the information about the different use of loan (formal and informal) obtained from our 160 member respondents. Here they have reported only that amount of loan which they borrow in the last year in time of the survey date. By 'formal sector' here we want to mean-(i) all SHG-based mF programmes led by banks/ NGOs/ etc, (ii) all nationalized formal commercial banks, and (iii) specialized agricultural development banks. On the other, the informal sector includes family, friends, land lords, professional moneylenders, shop owners and different informal groups.

Table 9
The Use of Formal and Informal Credits

	For Members		*For Non-Members*	
	Formal Source	*Informal Source*	*Formal Source*	*Informal Source*
No. of observations that report they have taken loan	156	134	–	30
Avg. amount borrowed	3893.75 (Rs.)	3465.63 (Rs.)	–	7000.00 (Rs.)
Use of loan in (%)				
House repairing	7.70	12.69		10.00
Social events	5.13	8.21		13.33
Food	3.85	4.48		6.67
Health	8.97	20.15		3.33
Education	3.20	1.49		0.00
Farm production	17.30	13.43		23.33
Non-farm production	14.74	7.46		6.67
Livestock	12.18	5.97		13.33
Petty Trading	20.51	18.66		20.00
Others	6.41	7.46		3.33

However, in our sample villages, by formal sector we refer only the SHG-based mF programmes since in these areas poor people have zero/ or very low access to any other formal institutions as described above. Actually, people who have an access in other formal institutions for credit/ saving activities are not very much willing to become a member in a SHG due to their opportunity costs.

For comparison the use of loan pattern by non-member households are also described in the table. It may be noted that, since these households are not presently a member in any group-based programme and have no access to any other FFIs, they have not received any formal loan yet and therefore the column is left blank. Only the information about the uses of informal loan of these individuals has been gathered to assess the loan use pattern.

However, before the patterns of loan use are described it is important to address the issue of fungibility of financial funds. Loans are fungible since they affect the households by relaxing the intertemporal capital constraint. It is not analytically easy to classify loans as being either 'consumption loans' or 'production loans', unless it is possible somehow to observe how the household would allocate its resources had the loan been denied (Zeller, 2001). In sample survey method, collection of such data is not only complex but also generates some bias probleme overstating or understating the loan use category. To overcome such probleme we, therefore, classified the loan use into different types as shown in Table 7 and respondents are asked to report on what category they have spent the major portion of the loan.

From Table 9 it is clear that near about 47% of the member respondents have used the loan from informal sources to finance different expenditures such as house repairing, social events, food , health and education. Whereas the corresponding figure in case of group loan is 28.85%. Though in pure sense, expenditure on health and education can't be treated as consumption loan, in rural areas, however, the intertemporal outcome of such loan is very low and therefore we considered such loan as the consumption loans. This is an expected results due to two reasons–(i) loans from such formal sources are usually tied to income earning projects, and (ii) lower interest rates on group loan generates smaller pressure on the borrower and hence an inducement to undertake different income earning projects suitable for rural poor households. But in case of informal loans, they have less incentive to repay the loan within stipulated time due to high loan interests and have zero bindings to use the loan for productive purposes.

However, a significant portion of the member households (44.20%) have used the formal loans in productive activities, such as farm production, non-farm production, and livestock rearing. The corresponding figure in case of informal loan is 26.85%. In case of debt, credit needs of husband/spouses, etc. (all this category are named as 'others' in Table 7), 6.4% of the member households have used the formal group loans and 7.46% of the member households have used the informal loans. A significant portion of our member households uses both the formal and informal loan in petty trading activities, such as vending, hawking, petty businesses and others.

The loan use categories for non-members have also been shown in Table 7. Here 33.33% of the total non-member respondents used their informal loan in different direct consumption activities. Near about 43.33% of the total non-member households have spent their amount in productive activities and 20% of them have used their loan in petty businesses. Just 3.33% of these households have used their loan for other needs.

LOAN REPAYMENT PERFORMANCE

The loan repayment performance of the sample of member respondent has been shown in Table 10.

Table 10
Repayment Performance of the Sample of member Respondent

Repayment	*Group Loan (156 respondents)*	*Informal Loan (134 respondents)*
(a) Paid fully in time	34.62	17.16
(b) Paid fully, but late	27.56	60.45
(c) Paid partially, time left for repayment	37.18	16.42
(d) Loan defaulter(Partially/fully)	0.64	5.97
Total	100.00	100.00

In case of group loan near about 34% of the total borrowers have repaid their full loan in time, whereas the corresponding figure in case of informal loan is near about 17%, i,e almost half. On the other, 28% of the total borrowers have paid their loan fully, but late. The corresponding figure is near about 60% for informal loans. Whereas the per centage of loan defaulter in case of group loan is just 0.65%, in case of informal loans such figure is near about 6%, i,e almost 10 times as much as members. The basic reasons behind the differential nature of the same borrowers in case of repayment of their loans obtained both from formal and informal sectors can be explained as follows.

In case of formal group loans individuals are compelled to abide by the loan repayment schedule as designed by the groups and 'peer pressure' among the group members leads to successful loan repayment each month. Besides, lower interests on loan increases the loan repayment performance of the members. But the same member behaves in different ways in case of informal loans. Actually, due to high rate of interests on loans many individuals fail t6o repay their loan in time. Besides, such loans have no binding in respect of the loan use, individuals, generally consume a significant portion of such loans and therefore fail to repay it in time. But, due to close monitoring and strict pressure from the moneylenders make it difficult for the borrowers to shirk responsibility and ultimately are compelled to repay the full loan amount with a significant penalty over the time.

The nature of loan transaction in terms of loan use and the nature of loan repayment performance as derived from our sample villages clearly indicate that the mF programme is sustainable (the measurement of economic sustainability of group's operation is beyond the scope in this study, but at a glance we can say that the programme is sustainable since they are operating without any subsidy and no loss has been reported by the groups upto the survey date. It may be noted that the opportunity costs, however, have not been included here) and viable for the development of our sample villages. Though a significant portion (55.8%) of the group loan is still used for unproductive activities, but the proportion of households (44.20%) who have spent their loans in production activities is not negligible compared to other sources of loan.

CONCLUSIONS

There is no doubt that the mF programme through SHGs is an effective poverty alleviation tool in India. The growth of such programme in the state of West Bengal, however, is not satisfactory compared with other states such as Andhra Pradesh, Tamil Nadu, Karnataka, etc. Based on the results obtained from our analysis here, we propose the following policy issues in respect of West Bengal to achieve a greater success of the programme.

Firstly, in West Bengal up to March 2003 most SHGs have been formed and nurtured by the banks and only in few cases NGOs have played a role. However, banks are no longer willing to continue to spread the programme. This is because it imposes huge cost pressure on the banks. Besides, monitoring, provision of training, capacity building are also important issues for a successful mF programme. Banks do not offer such services and, only NGOs, in this respect, can achieve a better result. Unfortunately, in West Bengal, participation of good NGOs in these activities is very low. Therefore, policy should be directed to induce NGOs (obviously, good NGOs) to implement mF programme at a higher rate.

Secondly, in West Bengal mF providers generally target only low-income households for the implementation of the programme. But analysis of the primary data suggests that 'income' itself cannot be an important determinant for membership. With 'income' other important determinants are 'education', 'family size', etc. which generally are not considered by the mF providers in time of programme implementation. Therefore, the programme should not only be introduced to the low-income households, rather it should also be introduced among the low educated households as well. Low educated households have less capital (both physical and human) and suffer from same or more problems as the low-income households. Besides, due to the absence of any screening mechanism or cut-off levels, some high-income households also enter in the programme and erode its strength violating the homogeneity criterion of the group. Therefore, policy formulation should take these aspects into consideration.

Thirdly, the ultimate target of the mF programme is to up-lift the poor households through capacity building. But in West Bengal scenario, training programmes for capacity building for SHG members is very low and most of the SHG loan, therefore, goes to either in petty businesses or consumption purposes. Government and specialized rural development banks should take greater initiative for offering training, technology adoption and capacity building programmes suited for rural poor households so that they can use their loan in productive purposes. Besides, marketing of the output should also come under considerations as well. Such initiatives would not only help to use the loan of the existing members more productively, but also attract new households for joining in such programmes. Lastly, mF programme should increase its value by offering diversified financial services. In addition with usual savings and credit facilities, mF programme should offer other services such as insurance, housing finance, etc. for their clients. Besides, financial counseling is crucial for uneducated poor to increase the yield of micro loans. Policy should be diverted in this respect as well.

REFERENCES

Agricultural Credit Review Committee (ACRC) (1993), *A Review of Agricultural Credit System in India*, Reserve Bank of India, Mumbai.

Cornia, G.A. and F. Stewart (1993), *'Two Errors of Targeting'*, Economic Policy Series, UNICEF International Child Development Centre, Italy.

Dasgupta, Rajaram (2001), *'An Informal Journey through Self-Help Groups'*, Indian Journal of Agricultural Economics, Vol. 56, No. 3, July-Sept. 2001.

Daley-Harris, Sam (2004), *'State of the Microcredit Summit Campaign Report 2004'*, World Bank, New York.

Goetz, Anne Marie and Rina Sengupta (1996), *'Who Takes Credit? Gender, Power, and Control over Loan Use in Rural Credit Programmes in Bangladesh'*, World Development, Vol. 24, No. 1, pp. 45-63.

Greene, William H. (2003), *'Econometric Analysis'*, Fifth Edition, Pearson Education.

Hulme, David and Paul Mosley (1996), *'Finance Against Poverty'*, Vol. 1 and 2, London; Routledge.

Karmakar, K.G. (2001), *'Rural Credit and Self-help Groups: Microfinance Needs and Concepts in India'*, Sage Publication, New Delhi.

Khandker, Shahidur R. (1999), *'Fighting Poverty with Microcredit–Experience in Bangladesh'*, The University Press Limited, Bangladesh edition, 1999.

Morduch, Jonathan (2004), *'Microfinance: Transactions at the Bottom of the Pyramid'*, World Bank, November.

NABARD (1995), *'Linking Self-Help Groups with Banks–An Indian Experience'*, NABARD, Mumbai.

NABARD (2000), Annual Report, 1999-2000, NABARD, Mumbai.

NABARD and Microfinance, 2001-2002; Ten Years of SHG-Bank Linkage (1992-2002).

Reserve Bank of India Bulletin, August, 2005.

State Focus Paper (West Bengal), NABARD, 2002-2003.

Nair, Tara S. (2001), *'Institutionalising Microfinance in India: An Overview of Strategic Issues'*, Economic and Political Weekly (EPW), January 27, 2001.

Nair, Tara S. (2005), *'The Transforming World of Indian Microfinance'*, EPW, April 23, 2005.

Stiglitz, J.E. (1990), *'Peer Monotoring and Credit Markets'*, The World Bank Economic Review, Vol. 4, No. 3, pp. 351-366.

Zeller, Manfred and Others (2001), *'Group-Based Financial Institutions for the Rural Poor in Bangladesh: An Institutional-and Household-Level Analysis'*, Research Report, IFPRI.

Chapter - 5

Fission or Fusion: An Assessment of Decentralization of Forest Management in Andhra Pradesh*

V. Ratna Reddy, M. Gopinath Reddy, V.M. Ravi Kumar & M. Srinivasa Reddy

INTRODUCTION

The forest policies formulated and implemented by the Government of India, in recent times, have been influenced by three concepts, i.e. equity, sustainability and participatory. The main purpose of these concepts has been to craft a system of governance that fosters accountability and transparency for sustainable management of forest resources. The attempt to involve people in forest management was translated into formulation and implementation of community based forest management systems in the form of the Joint Forest Management (JFM) in India. The Government of Andhra Pradesh (AP) has converted JFM into the Community Forest Management (CFM), by incorporating several innovative rules to facilitate active involvement of local communities in forests management. The main object envisaged in the CFM is to diffuse the decision making process to local communities. The present study attempts to assess how the decentralized forest management initiated by the CFM has been implemented at ground level and what are the outcomes of this strategy in AP.

For analyzing the institutional dynamics of the CFM policy and practice, the present study is organized into four parts: part one deal with objectives, methodology and review of literature; part two analyzes the CFM scheme at policy level; part three demonstrates nature of policy implementation and constraints that have effected the process in our filed sites and finally, part four analyses the impact of CFM on livelihood pattern of forest dependent communities in our sample village and outcomes of the CFM policy.

Review of Literature

Decentralization has become popular mantra for developmental planners and policy makers. Though the concept of decentralization in state administrative structures has a long pedigree, its degree and applicability has phenomenally increased in the recent times (Sharma 2006). After 1980s, there has been an emphasis on decentralized forest management with the involvement of local communities for management of forests as a remedy to bring trade-off between livelihood concerns and environmental protection (Tang 1991, Becker and Ostrom 1995 and Jeffery and Sunder 1999). Involvement of communities in management of forests by creating local institutions prescribed as an appropriate option for arresting the degradation of forests (Hechter, et al, 1982 and Grafton, 2000). Having recognized necessity of involvement of people in forest management, participatory policy framework for management of forests was introduced in 1990s (Kulakarni et, al. 1994, Profomberger and McGreen 2000). After nearly one and half decades, some studies evaluated the outcome of Participatory Forest Management (PFM). Some of the recent studies show that the expected results are not being achieved in various states in India (Agrwal and Gupta 2005, Kumar 2002, Reddy et al. 2004, Samata 2005). Some studies documented the constraints for success of the programme, those are: lack of clearly defined property regimes (Vyrastekova and Soest, 2003, Jonshon and Forsyth, 2002); unequal socio-economic structure of communities and lack of commitment by Forest departments (Sundar 2001 and Sunder et, al, 2001a). However, some studies have shown that the PFM brought both positive and negative results (Twyman, 2000, Ravindranath et al, 2000).

Some of the recent studies have shown that in most of the states, community involvement in forest management has been undermined by several factors. In countries like India, where socio-economic fabric consists of sharp inequalities, decentralized governance has inherent problems like caste and class and gender inequalities (Johan Manor 2004) and estate management attitude of Forest Department (FD) undermined the effective functioning of decentralization process in forest management (Nicholas 2004). With this background, the present study attempts to demonstrate the factors that have influenced the institutional governance process of forest resource management in A.P.

Methodology of Study

For the purpose of evaluating the CFM programme in AP, nine sample villages scattered in the three geophysical regions of AP were selected: Kadapa district represents Rayalaseema; Visakhapatnam district represents the Coastal Andhra and Adilabad district represents the Telangana region. For analysis of CFM, the present study mainly depended on qualitative methods like focused group discussions (FGD) with different stakeholders i.e., Managing Committee members, women, youth, leaders, NGOs, FD officials and others; semi-structured discussions; personal interviews; case studies, transect walks and village public meetings.

Table 1
Details of the Sample Villages

District	*VSS Villages*
Adilabad	Pandhirlodhhi
	Sainagar Thanda
	Heerapur
Kadapa	Ramachandrapuram
	S.R. Palem
	Mudireddypalle
Visakhapatnam	Sobhakota
	Gudlamveedi
	Nandivalasa

Source: Filed Survey.

COMMUNITY FOREST MANAGEMENT POLICY PRONOUNCEMENTS

PFM in AP was introduced in the form of JFM in 1992 and it was converted as CFM in 2002 by incorporating several flexible rules to facilitate active participation of people in forest management.[1] Under CFM, 5000 villages, spread over 14 districts and covering 13, 79,862 hectares of forests were covered. It is funded by the World Bank with total outlay of Rs. 652 crores for the period of five years. The CFM targeted to benefit 55,000 families living in below poverty line (Andhra Pradesh Government 2002).

The basic difference between JFM and CFM is, while JFM was more a partnership between the people and state, CFM proposes more democratic nature of decision-making process to the local communities. The main object of the CFM scheme is to quote: "to reduce rural poverty through improved forest management with community participation" (Andhra Pradesh Government 2002).

The above-mentioned rules in the CFM policy are aimed at devolving more autonomy to the communities in management of forests. And it also intended to reduce the role of FD in the management of VSS.

COMMUNITY FOREST MANAGEMENT POLICY AND IMPLEMENTATION PROCESS

The Government of AP had taken some new measures for effective implementation of CFM. For instance, VSS HH sizes were reduced then in JFM. For instance, in Visakapatnam, Gudulem Vedi and Nandi Valas

Table 2
Number of VSS Covered under Andhra Pradesh CFM programme (World Bank sponsored)

S. No.	*District*	*APCFM (Number of VSS)*	*Area in (Ha)*
1.	Adilabad	1015	327608
2.	Warangal	205	83663
3.	Karimnagar	371	111905
4.	Khammam	355	210339
5.	Nizamabad	202	58133
6.	Medak	202	43740
7.	Mahabubnagar	233	67503
8.	Srikakulam	241	35115
9.	Vizianagaram	189	38941
10.	Visakhapatnam	876	100810
11.	East Godavari	466	152343
12.	Nellore	148	28633
13.	Chittoor	245	82605
14.	Kadapa	252	38524
	Total	5000	13,79,8612

Source: Facts and Figures, 2005. Andhra Pradesh Forest Department

Table 3
Major Policy changes from JFM to CFM

JFM	*CFM*
Management Committee	**Management Committee**
1. Total members 10	1. Total members 15
2. Women membership 30%	2. Women membership more than 50%
3. Attendance of women, no specific number	3. 50% women should attend.
4. Tenure two years	4. Tenure three years
5. Surpanch and forest officials were members of MC committee.	5. Only elected members consist of MC committee.
Financial transactions	**Financial tractions**
1. One account called joint account was provided.	1. Dual account system i.e. joint account and VSS account were created.
Micro Plan Preparation	**Micro Plain Preparation**
JFM plan was prepared by MC and Range Officer.	CFM micro plain prepared by MC and in consultation with VSS members. No official interference was sought.
Role of FD	**Role of FD**
FD played crucial role as a partner in guiding VSS in forest management	FD is a facilitator and technical adviser
Forest advisory committee existed in village level	Forest advisory committee from village to state level, elaborative advisory committee, were mentioned
Usufructary Rights	**Usufructary Rights**
NTFPs were divided into reserved and unreserved, and communities have rights only on selected items. Initially share was 50% to FD and 50% to VSS, on forest products excluding the NRFP items for GCC (Girijan Cooperative Corporation) monopoly.	All NTFPs, (100%) and 100% incremental volume of timber.

Sources: Government of Andhra Pradesh Orders issued from 1992 to 2004.

villages were being bifurcated into two VSS areas. In CFM, 40-50 HH considered as ideal number. Decentralized governance for forest management designed to install new management approach where, local people's interests are incorporated into forest management. CFM scheme formulated to strengthen the decentralized forest management approach, however, at operational level this process has to go through several inherent constraints.

Constraints analysis

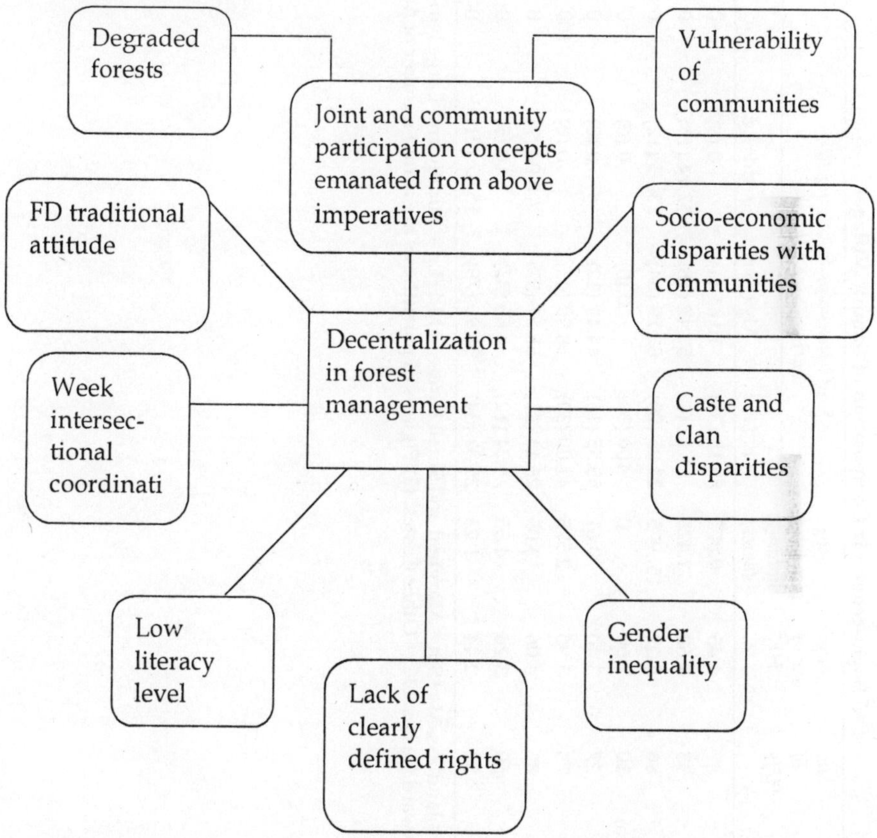

The above table shows that the social composition of the households in our sample villages indicates that STs are exclusive social group in Visakhapatnam, though there are number of subgroups within the STs. In Adilabad, STs are dominant in two VSS and while BCs are the dominant in the other village. In Kadapa one village has exclusive SC population, one village has complete tribal population and another village consists of STs and BCs. Land composition in VSS shows the economic inequalities in villages. Even in tribal villagers, large inequalities in land owing pattern are visible. Majority of them are land less, and small section of population had own land. Land owning community constitute village elite group in

Table 4

% Socio-economic Composition of Sample Villages

Districts	Village VSS	No. of HHs	Avg. size of HH	Avg. size land holding (acres)	% of households belonging to various Size Classes			% of HH belonging to various Social Categories			
					Ln. Less	Mg+Sm	Md+Lg	SC	ST	BC	OC
Adilabad	Pandhirlodhhi	37	4.45	0.875	89.18 (33)	10.81 (4)	0 (0)	0	100	0	0
	Sainagar	35	4.62	1.425	11.42 (4)	51.42 (18)	37.14 (13)	0	100	0	0
	Heerapur	86	5.27	15..975	23.25 (20)	62.79 (54)	13.95 (12)	0	38.76	61.24	0
Kadapa	Ramachandrapuram	30	2.60	0	100 (30)	0 (0)	0 (0)	0	100	0	0
	S.R.Palem	27	3.40	0.61	55.55 (15)	44.44 (12)	0 (0)	0	54	46	0
	Muddireddypalle	73	3.90	2.575	41.09 (30)	58.90 (43)	0 (0)	100	0	0	0
Vishakhapatnam	Sobhakota	87	4.06	3.05	26.43 (23)	65.51 (57)	8.04 (7)	0	100	0	0
	Gudlamveedi	50	3.26	4.55	24 (12)	66 (33)	10 (5)	0	100	0	0
	Nandivalasa	53	2.44	1.23	25.37 (34)	58.95 (79)	15.67 (21)	0	100	0	0

Note: (1) HH = Households, Ln.Less = landless, Mg+Sm = Marginal and Small Farmers, Md+Lg = Middle and Large Farmers, SC = Scheduled Castes, ST = Scheduled Castes, BC = Backward Castes, OC = Other Castes. (2) Figures in parenthesis are actual number of households in the village.

village. This information shows that communities in the plain as well as in hill areas have explicit socio-economic inequalities. Tribal society divided into different clans and explicit inequalities in terms of socio-economic status.

VSS Formation Process

In India, decentralization in forest management has not come from grassroots, four reasons mainly responsible for it: one, five decades of centralized management regime in forest management could not reduce the hostile relations between state and forest dependent people, second, participatory modals are being pushed by the donors agencies attention and third, as Odi study states decentralization was a response to demands from ascendant agrarian groups for acquiring benefits from state schemes (Baumann and Farrijgon 2003), and finally, state inability in baring high protection costs and constant conflicts with people. However, in our filed study it is observed that demand to form VSS has not come from VSS members. The main reason as for most of the respondents that, the income from wage has come down towards the end of JFM, so people did not show much interest in PFM.

It is found in our study sites during the period 2000-2002 (gap between JFM and CFM) neither FD nor NGOs went to village to monitor VSS functioning. It shows that while modifying the JFM into CFM, local people's opinions and suggestions were not taken into consideration into policy process. This process described by Ajit Menon that: 'JFM policy based on 'strait-jacketed' notion of what the local is and should be. As a result of, instead of allowing for local solution, JFM is in danger of imposing those solution from the outside' (Menon, 1995. 1933). Thus, instead of bottom up approach that was envisaged in CFM policy documents, remained top down policy that was imposed on communities.

Management Committee Formation and Decision Making Process

More people's representatives in (MC) have been incorporated in CFM (15). Women membership has been increased from three in JFM to eight in CFM. Vice-chairperson post is created in CFM. Interims of election, there are several changes from JFM to CFM. Though PFM was designed to take into cognizance the local factors, at practical level it remained a tightly 'Structured Package" which mainly translated by FD into local situation. In JFM, MCs in all our study sites were unanimously elected, however, chosen by FD. In CFM, it is general trend that competition for VSS chairperson and Vice-chairperson and MC membership has increased. In Kadapa, serious conflicts for MC membership and chairperson post were reported. In our study sites, out of nine, five chairpersons were replaced in CFM. It shows the competition with the dominant sections of village elite to capture MC posts.

Our FGD with different sections of people revels that MC posts are perceived as lucrative and prestigious. In Kadapa, out of three, two VSS have undergone election process. There were struggles in election for MC posts. In Adilabad, two MC were changed and in Visakhapatnam, two MC are changed in CFM. Surprisingly, in Sobhakota VSS in Visakhapatnam had undergone election for three times in CFM. This trend shows competition for membership in MC committee in CFM. This trend shows that instead of fission of decision-making process, fusion of decision-making process in the hands of village elite happened in CFM.

Table 5
Socio-Economic and Political Profile of the VSS Presidents of the Sample VSS Villages in the Districts

Name of the VSS	*Name of the District*	*Sex*	*Age*	*Education*	*Caste/ Category*	*Size Class*	*Political Affiliation*	*Membership in other Groups*
Pandhir-lodhhi	Adlibbed	Male	25	9th	Gond (ST)	SF	-	-
Heerapur	"	Male	47	3rd	Palle Kapu (BC)	SF	-	VSS, JFM President
Sainagar Thanda	"	Male	50	5th	Lambadi (ST)	LF	TDP	VSS President (JFM)
Ramachan-drapuram	Kadapa	Female	60	Just Literate	Lambadi (ST)	LL	-	SHG Leader, President in JFM
Sri Ranga-raju Palem	"	Female	35	7th	Lambadi (ST)	MF	-	VSS, MC Member (JFM)
Mudireddy Palle	"	Male	34	SSC	Harijan (SC)	MF	Cong.	-
Sobhakota	Visakha-patnam	Male	39	7th	Bagata (ST)	SF	TDP	-
Gudlam-veedi	"	Male	48	5th	Konda Kummari (ST)	SF	-	Rytu Mitra
Nandivalasa	"	Male	33	10th	Nuka Dora(ST)	SF	Cong.	VSS President (JFM)

Note: Cong: Congress; TDP: Telugu Desam Party; SHG: Self Help Group; Rythu Mitra (Farmer Association)

The table five shows that socio-economic profile of VSS chairpersons of our study sites. Except in Ramachandra (RC) Puram, all Chairpersons are landholders ranging from small to large farmers. Being the land owning community in village, they had easy access with state administrative apparatus. In CFM, FD picked up such groups with whom they have easy access and nexus.

In elections for MC, FD has manipulated with unfair election process. In Mudireddy (MR) Palli of Kadapa district, there was a struggle between Madiga and Malas communities (sub-castes in SC community) for MC posts. In this village, 51 families belong to Madiga and 25 belonging to Mala. The Malas are numerically less but socially, politically and economically strong group. Out 15 MC posts, 9 were owned by Malas and 6 were by Madigas. Though the Malas constitutes 32% in total population of village they secured 60% of MC membership and the Madigas are 67% in total village population have only 40% representation in MC membership. However, with the intervention of FD, MC chairperson post was given to numerically dominant Magidas. This kind of power game was common in many VSSs to bring about balance of power. As result of it, as Malas more in MC, they frequently opposed the VSS decisions and there was unanimity on VSS works. Consequently, no VSS works undertaken by this village for one year. It attests the fact that the intra community conflicts undermined the community participation in VSS management.

In Heerapur VSS in Adilabad, BCs being in majority (10 members out of 15) excluded the STs from decision-making process and in VSS works. As a result of this, STs breached the VSS rules and allowed cattle in VSS area for grazing. In other two sites of Adilabad district, though entire population belongs to STs, there are explicit inequalities and were observed. In Visakhapatnam, same trend is observed. VSS chairperson posts were occupied by socially and economically dominant sections within the tribal society. For instance, in Sobhakota, it is observed that chairperson favored people his group in VSS works, in Gudlamveedi, the *Konda Kapus* being dominant tribe, excluded other tribes from VSS works.

Micro Plan (MP) Preparation and Dominance of Forest Department

Micro Plain is a blue print for management of VSS. It registers the agenda to be followed in VSS works by incorporating local needs in forest management. The objective of MP is to allow 'need based' approach in forest management. In CFM policy, emphasis is given on involvement of various actors like Panchyayats, NGOs and FD, after conducting the Participatory Rural Appraisal.

Though priority is given on incorporation of local resource and their importance in livelihoods, FD, perceived MC as an integral part of working plan, which is a technical manual for management of forest zones. Though the CFM policy emphasized on enhancement of livelihoods, generally working plan prescriptions prepared by FD reflected in MP content. For instance, in Adilabad district, the forest area allocated to VSS has been converted into teak timber zone for generation of revenue. In our field study, villagers informed that conversion of VSS areas as teak plantation zones prevents sun light into forests. As a result of it, grass and procurement of Tendu leaves (Beedi leaves) became hard task. Consequently, the beedi leave collection, which is important NTFP item for peoples' livelihoods and grass crucial for cattle have been jeopardized. In Visakhapatnam, Silver Oak trees were promoted by the FD to increase green cover. This exotic plant undermined the growth of native plants consequently; availability of NTFPs like broom grass, adda leaves and others became scarce. Thus, the forest management models included in MC, on many occasions negatively affected people.

Though majority of the respondents in our (FGD) informed that they were not consulted at the time of PRA, but in case of species selection and other works, FD officials played an important role in MP preparation. The drafting of MP has received criticism from civil society, though it is supposed to be prepared with participation of the general body, in practice, the FD staff played an authoritative role than a facilitator. It is observed in our field sites that FD dictated the preparation of MC models. In Adilabad, all MC are prepared by FD. And in Visakhapatnam, MPs were prepared under the instruction of FD. In spite of strong NGO network, it is observed in Kadapa district that FD officials dictated the MP models. Regarding the devolution of forest management, A. Menon pointed out that: ' At one level JFM seems to be giving more powers to the local, but at the same time, the state through the FDs assumes significant powers in terms of constituting, organizing and monitoring VSS' (Menon, 1995).

Table 6
Nature of the Decision Making Process in VSS Management

	Functional aspects	*VSS*	*FD*	*Other, NGO*
1.	Organisation of meetings, GB/MC	√	√	√
2.	Selection of Forest areas for VSS		√	
3.	Micro Plan preparation	√	√	√
4.	Identification of works		√	
5.	Species selection			
6.	Carrying out of works		√	
7.	Supervision of works		√	
8.	Estimating the costs		√	
9.	Funds allocation		√	
10.	Distribution of harvesting income		√	
11.	Distribution of forest products	√		
12.	Entry point activities	√	√	√
13.	Minute writings	√	√	√
14.	NTFP value editions		√	
15.	Distribution of livelihood enhancement activities		√	
16.	Marketing of forest products		√	
17.	Selection of training programme		√	

Source: Field Survey.

The above-mentioned table shows the different actors and their role in VSS management. Important decisions like the identification of forest area, works, species selection, supervision of works, management and conservation models and other important decisions are mainly taken by FD. The above table also shows that though the CFM policy devolved decision-making powers, the important decisions related to VSS management are practically taken by FD. Thus, decentralized governance for management of forest resources given to communities was jeopardized by the dominant role played by the FD in decision-making process.

Management Committee Meetings and Decision-Making Process

MC is being constituted on behalf of community to execute VSS works. Literature on political ecology argues that the communities, which have better mediating and negotiating access to state apparatus, appropriated benefits of state sponsored programmes (Sabrwal, 2004). It is observed that on many occasions, MC members are hand picked by the FD with whom they have access. In Kadapa district, it is found that RC Puram and Srirangaraju Palem (SR Palem) chairpersons act as spokespersons of FD. In fact, all chairpersons in Kadapa hail from elite background. For instance, in SR Palem, women chairperson is a wife of school headmaster, RC Puram Chairperson is also from rich background, as her son with his family went to Gulf and in MR Palli, and chairperson works in Bangalore as drivers. Similar trend is observed in Visakhapatnam and Adilabad districts. It shows the fact that chairpersons elected for VSS are from dominant sections with whom FD has easy access and nexus. Thus, elite domination in nexus with FD officials had narrowed down the scope of benefits that were envisaged by the CFM policy.

MC is a vehicle to carry out CFM and peoples' participation. The execution of CFM is dependent upon the decisions that are taken in the MC. As for CFM policy, MC meeting should be conducted in every month. But it is observed that MC meetings were not conducted regularly in our VSS sample studies. The community halls constructed for MC meetings in all our study sites are used as storerooms of chairpersons and MC members. MC meetings are conducted in VSS chairperson's house and as a result of it, decisions related to VSS works are taken by chairpersons, vice-chairpersons and their group members in MC. For instance, in Sainagar Thanda of Adilabad district, MC meetings are conducted in VSS chairperson's house, similar trend is found in Visakapatnam and Kadapa districts.

In important decisions like species selection, identification of works, fund allocation to works are taken by the FD officials in MC meetings. The above table also shows that the decisions related to VSS works are mostly taken by the FD officials and VSS chairperson. It observed from the above table that women and other members of MC do not participate in decision-making process related to VSS works.

Women Participation

Some studies have shown that though there were efforts to involve women in forest management at policy level, there are no mechanisms to ensure their participation at practical level (Correa, 1996). Information percolation with regard to VSS management to women found to be poor in many states in India (Kameswari, 2002) In spite of increase number of women members in MC in CFM, women participation in decision-making process in VSS works found to be significantly low.

Table 7
Women Representation in Management Committee

District/VSS	*No. of MC members*	*CP*	*VCP*
Kadapa			
MR Palli	8	Male	Woman
SR Palem	8	Woman	Male
RC Puram	8	Woman	Male
Adilabad			
Sai Nagar Thanda	8	Male	Woman
Pandhirloddhi	8	Male	Woman
Heerapur	8	Male	Woman
Visakhapatnam			
Sobhakota	8	Male	Woman
Gudlamveedi	8	Male	Woman
Nandivalasa	8	Male	Woman

MC= Management Committee CP= Chairperson, VCP= Vice-chairperson

As laid down in the CFM policy, women membership in the MC has been implemented in all our study sites. In CFM policy, Vice-chairpersonship has been created. In our study sites, in seven out of nine VSS were headed by men (CP), while two are headed women and *vice-versa* in the case of VCP. It is common knowledge that Vice-chairperson post remained nominal in the decision-making process.

The realistic women participation in VSS activities was undermined by three factors: one, socio-economic conditions of women chairpersons. In Kadapa district, Chairperson of SR Palem is a wife of a government teacher. In our FGD, it is observed that village women did not have easy access to the chairperson. In RC Puram, it is reported that chairperson behaves arrogantly and don't even inform the decisions taken in MC meetings. Second factor is, FD officials dominate the women chairpersons and prevent them from taking any independent decision. Third factor is that husbands or sons of women chairpersons take lead in actual management of VSS. In RC Puram of Kadapa district, Chairperson's son takes most of the decision on the behalf of his mother.

In tribal areas of Adilabad and Visakhapatnam districts, women participation remained at a superficial level. Practically, men decided the nature of works and all decisions relating to VSS works. A woman from Adilabad district informed that to quote: "All decisions related to VSS works are being taken by men and after decisions being they inform us, practically we do not have any role in VSS functioning" (Field Study). Thus, at one level, numerically women participation has increased, at another, practical participation has not improved.

LIVELIHOOD IMPACT OF COMMUNITY FOREST MANAGEMENT

In AP, as per latest estimates, about 14% of population, predominantly belong to tribes; have been critically deepened on forest products as an important source of livelihood. The CFM programme, aimed meeting the livelihood needs with multidimensional strategies. The following table shows the livelihood dependency of people on forests in our study sites.

Table 8
Percentage share of Different Livelihood Activities in Study Cities

District/VSS	*Own cultivation*	*Podu*	*Farm activities, labour*	*Non farm activities*	*Forests/ NTF P/podu*	*VSS Works*	*Migration*	*Total*
Kadapa								
MR Pelly	10		45	30	5	5	5	100
SR Palem			60	10	15	10	5	100
RC Puram			20	25	45	5	5	100
Adilabad								
H. Pur	10		20	30	10	5	25	100
S N Tanda	50		20	10	10	5	5	100
P. Luddi	60		20	-	15	5	-	100
Visakapatnam								
S. Kota	10	35	25	-	25	10	-	100
G. Veedi	15	40	15	-	20	10	-	100
N. Valasa	20	25	20	5	20	5	5	100

Source: Field study.

The above-mentioned table shows that forests provide an important source of livelihoods, particularly in agricultural slak season. In tribal villages, forest dependency is significantly high, together with VSS works. In Visakhapatnam, it constitutes above 50%. Having completed most of the treatment practices in JFM, CFM focused on income generating activities with diversified practices. Due to this, wage based works have significantly declined. The following table shows the wage works undertaken in CFM.

Table 9
Wage Employment in CFM During 2003-05 in Study Sites

District/VSS	*No days of employment, accrued during 2003-05*	*Time taken for payment of wages (days)*
Kadapa		
MR Pelly	–	
SR Palem	30	40
RC Puram	35	45
Adilabad		
H. Pur	20	40
S N Tanda	–	–
P. Luddi	35	35
Visakapatnam		
S. Kota	25	45
G. Veedi	20	40
N. Valasa	30	35

Source: Field Study.

Villagers informed that amount of funding allotted to VSS works is insignificant in CFM. Due to this, not many villagers had an opportunity to partake in VSS works. The above-mentioned table shows, number of employment days were less and moreover, time taken for payment of wage is on an average about 40 days. In CFM, sanction of funding for works involves in a lengthy process. The FGD with MC members in MR Pelly of Kadapa informs that FD officials' sanctioned insufficient funds to the estimated works in CFM. In Heerapur of Adilabad, it is reported that wage works in CFM are insufficient, and provide employment only to a few. This resulted in widespread discontentment on VSS works among people.

Since treatment practices have come to an end, FD attempted to undertake income generating activities with diversified strategies like NTFP value addition like initiatives, honey bees keeping, preparation of vermi compost, supply of leaf plates preparation machinery, harvesting of valuable wood and other initiatives. These are meant for generating income from forest products under the supervision of VSS MC Committee. However, our interviews with FD officials in Adilabad and Visakhapatnam inform that these experiments were not been successful due to lack of conducive atmosphere.

The above-mentioned table shows the nature of income generation initiatives undertaken by FD to benefit communities in CFM. However, this policy is still in formative stage, and just introduced and results are not yet known. But in our FGD with forest officials it is reveled that most of these initiatives were not going to generate revenue as they have certain inherent problems. FD officials themselves are not aware of some of the market mechanisms. For instance, FD invested on *Bodha* oil machine in SR Palem in Kadapa district. But, FGD with MC members informs that, they were not given information of market of the *Bodha* oil and its marketing is exclusively done by the FD. With regard to honey hives, our FGD with MC members of Pandrludi informs that FD officials did not give them training on how to protect the hives and extract honey. As result of it, honey hives are getting spoiled. Thus, the initiatives taken in the CFM to generate income have not rooted in deep understanding of local conditions.

Table 10
Employment or Income Generating Initiatives Undertaken in CFM

District/VSS	*Nature of Initiative*	*Results*
Kadapa		
MR Pelly	Amala processing	Failure due to lack of yield
SR Palem	*Bodha* processing machine	Rs. 2000 loses to MC in 2005
RC Puram	–	–
Adilabad		
H. Pur	Biodiseal plantation	Result not yet known.
S.N. Tanda	–	–
P. Luddi	Honey bees hives	Processing not yet started
Visakapatnam		
S. Kota	Leaf plates machine	Failure
G. Veedi	Honey hives	Result not yet known
N. Valasa	Leaf plate machine	Failure

Source: Field study.

OUT COME OF THE COMMUNITY FOREST MANAGEMENT PROGRAMME

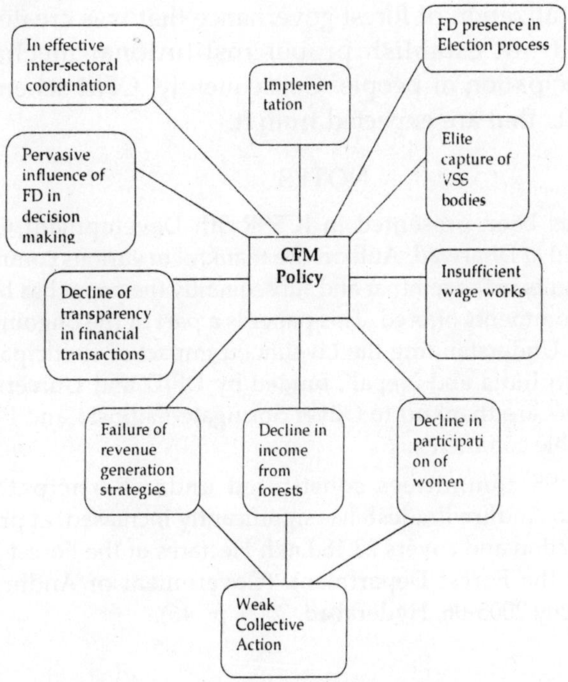

The out comes which were shown in the above flow chart, shows the set of factors, which had undermined the positive outcomes decentralization in forest management. The authoritarian attitude of FD on the one had and socio-economic disparities within the local communities on the other hand, are reasonable for ineffective functioning of local institutions for the management of VSS.

CONCLUSION

Participatory forest management system in AP was introduced to create the local institutions, which would channelise the collective action of different stakeholders in managing forest resources. In this paper, it is shown the elite capture and FD dominance in VSS management are found pervasively in CFM programme. Instead of fission of decentralization, fusion decision-making mechanisms have taken place in CFM. The benefits envisaged in the CFM programme are mostly appropriated by elite sections leaving poor people away from the access to benefits. The main reason for this is, Government only recognised usufructory rights, which could not generate adequate accountability and responsibility among VSS members. Undoubtedly, decentralization of forest management under CFM brought about attitudinal change in FD Officials and improved the relation between people and FD, but this change remained superficial. Most of the lower level bureaucracy was not receptive to this scheme and they complain that this programme increased their duties and they need to write records, sanction of funds, identify and supervise the VSS works. Thus, the decentralization of forest governance that was created through JFM/CFM could not establish proper institutional mechanism for wholesome participation of people. Consequently, CFM scheme did not achieve the results that are expected from it.

NOTES

This paper has been presented in ICSSR 5th Development Convention Conference held at Dharwad. Authors are thankful to various comments made by the participants in the seminar and subsequently the paper has been revised based on the comments offered. This paper is a part of the ongoing project in CESS entitled 'Understanding the Livelihood impact of Participatory Forest Management in India and Nepal', funded by DFID and University of East Anglia. Authors are thankful to Oliver Springate-Baginski and Piers Blaikie for their valuable comments.

Number of VSS committees constituted under Participatory Forest Management in Andhra Pradesh has significantly increased, at present 8,343 VSS are in function and covers 23.18 Lakh Hectares of the Forest land under the control of the Forest Department. (Government of Andhra Pradesh, Economic Survey 2005-06, Hyderabad, 2006, p. 46).

REFERENCES

Andhra Pradesh Government (2002), *Andhra Pradesh Community Forest Management Project: Project Implementation Plain*, Vol. I & II, Hyderabad.

Agrwal Arun and Gupta Krishna (2005), 'Decentralization and Participation: The Governance of Common Pool Resources in Nepal's Terai', *World Development*, Vol. 33, pp. 1101-1114.

Baker Dustin and Ostrom Elinor (1995), 'Human Ecology and Resource Sustainability: The Importance of Institutional Diversity', *Annual Review of Ecology and Systematics*, Vol. 26, pp. 113-133.

Bauamm, P. and Farringtron (2003), 'Decentralising Natural Resource Management: Lessons From Local Government Reform in India', ODI Working Paper on 'Natural Resources Prescriptive', No. 86, 2003.

Correa Mariette (1996), 'No Role for Women: Karnataka's Joint Forest Management Programmes', *Economic and Political Weekly*, June 8th 1996, pp. 1382-1384.

Emel L. Jacque and Brooks Elizabeth (1988), 'Changes in Form and Function of Property Rights Institutions under Threatened Resource Scarcity', *Annals of the Association of American Geographers*, Vol. 78, No. 2, pp. 241-252.

Gadgil Madhav (1989), 'Forest Management Deforestation and People's Improvishment', *Social Action*, Vol. 39, October–December, pp. 357-383.

Grafton Quention (2000), 'Governance of the Commons: A Role for the State?' *Land Economics*, Vol. 76, No. 4, pp. 504-517.

Hechter Michael, Friedman and Appelbaum (1982), 'A theory of Ethnic Collective Action', *International Migration Review*, Vol. 16, No. 2, pp. 412-434.

Jaffery Rojer and Sundar Nandini (1999), *Moral Economy for India's Forests: Discourse of Community and Participation New Discourse on the Community Management in India*, Sage, Publications, New Delhi.

Jodha, N.S. (2000), 'Joint Management of Forests: Small Gains', Economic and Political Weekly, Dec. 9th, Vol. ?, pp. 4396-4399.

Jonshon Craig and Forsyth Timothy (2002), "In the Eyes of the State: Negotiating a "Right-Based Approach" to Forest Conservation in Thailand", *World Development Review*, Vol. 30, No. 9, pp. 1591-1603.

Kameswari. V.L.V. (2002), 'Gendered Communication and Access to Social Space: Issues in Forest Management', *Economic and Political Weekly*, February 23, pp. 797-801.

Kulkarani, K. and Hiremath, S.R. (ed.) (1995), *All About Forest Bill and Forest Lands: Towards Policies and Practices as If People Mattered*, Third Edition, Samaj Parivatran Samudaya, Dharwad, 1995, p. 16.

Kumar Sanjay (2002), 'Does "Participation" in Common Pool Resource Management Help the Poor? A Social Cost-Benefit Analysis of Joint Forest Management in Jharkhand, India', *World Development*, pp. 763-782.

Menon Ajit (1995), 'Construction of Local: Decentralization of Forest Management, Economic and Political Weekly, Vol. 30, Issue 34.

Nicholas, K.M. (2000), 'Communities and their Partners: Governance and Community-based Forest Management', *Conservation and Society*, Vol. 2, No. 2, pp. 450-456.

Poffenberger, M., McGreen (Eds.) (1996), *Village, Voice, Forest Choices: Joint Forest Management in India,* OUP, New Delhi.

Reddy, V., Reddy, M.G., V. Saravanan, M. Bandhi Oliver Springate (2004), 'Understanding Livelihoods Impact of Participatory Forest Management Implementation Strategies in India': The Policy Issue and Impacts of Joint Forest Management in India with Particular Reference to Andhra Pradesh: A Review, CESS, Hyderabad, Working Paper, 62.

Ravindranath, N.H., K.S. Murali and Malhotra (2000), *Joint Forest Management and Community Forestry in India: An Ecological and Institutional Assessment,* Oxford and IBH, New Delhi.

Saberwal, Vasant, and Sharachchandra Lele (2004), 'Locating Local Elite Negotiating Access to Forests: Havik Brahmins and the Colonial State, 1860-1920', *Studies in History,* 20, 2, n.s. pp. 273-303.

Samatha (2005), *Andhra Pradesh Community Forest Management Project: A Preliminary independent evaluation of a World Bank Forestry Project,* Hyderabad.

Sharma, C.H. (2006), 'Decentralization Dilemma: Measuring the Degree and Evaluating the Outcomes', The Indian Journal of Political Science, Vol. LXVII, No. 1, Jan-Mar., 2006, 49-64.

Singh, Chatrapathi (1986), *Common Property and Common Poverty: Indian Forests, Forest Dwellers and the Law,* Oxford University Press, New Delhi.

Sundar Nandini (2001), "Is Devolution Decentralization?" *World Development,* Vol. 29, No. 12, pp. 2007-2023.

——, Roger Jaffery and Neil Thin (ed) (2001), *Branching Out: Joint Forest Management in India,* Oxford University Press, New Delhi.

Tang Yan Shui (1991), "Institutional Arrangements and Management of Common-Pool Resources", Public Administration Review, Vol. 51, No. 1, pp. 42-51.

Twyman Chasca (2000), "Livelihood Opportunity and Diversity in Kalhari Wild life Management Areas, Botswana: Rethinking Community Resource Management", *Journal of Southern African Studies,* Vol. 26, No. 4, Special Issue, pp. 783-806.

Vyrastekova Jana and Soest. van Dean (2003), 'Centralized Common-Pool Management and Local Community Participation', *Land Economics,* Vol. 79, No. 4, pp. 500-514.

GLOSSARY

AP	-	Andhra Pradesh
GB	-	General Body
BC	-	Backward Caste
CFM	-	Community Forest Management
CP	-	Chairperson
FD	-	Forest Department
FGD	-	Focused Group Discussion
HH	-	House Holders
JFM	-	Joint Forest Management
MC	-	Management Committee
MP	-	Micro Plain
NGO	-	Non-Governmental Organisation
NTFP	-	Non Timber Forest Products
PFM	-	Participatory Forest Management
PRA	-	Participatory Rural Appraisal
SC	-	Schedule Castes
ST	-	Schedule Tribes
VCP	-	Vice Chairperson
VSS	-	Vana Samrakshna Samithi

Chapter - 6

Urbanisation in an IT Prominent State of India: Patterns, Issues and Policy

G.S. Sastry

INTRODUCTION

It has been projected that the 21st century will be the urban century with almost 60 per cent of the world population living in urban area by 2030, the highest share of population ever lived in urban areas. This is mainly because unlike previous centuries, current and future centuries are likely to experience rapid shift in the nature of human activities from primary to non-primary mainly due to changing resource base and environmental conditions, and rapid progress in human endeavors in science, technology, management and development. Such a shift would obviously enhance human affordability and capabilities to achieve improved standard of living through better access to infrastructure and services. However, all these achievements are possible provided the rapid urbanization is managed in a sustainable way. The rapid urbanization process which was set-in in the 20th century at the global level has initiated the process first in Europe followed by North America, Oceania and Latin America, has resulted in almost a similar levels of urbanization. The existing and proposed patterns of urbanization identified at various continental levels on the basis of their current as well as future potentialities, and on-going trends have revealed that (i) North America as the highest urbanized continent followed by Latin America, (ii) by future potentials while Europe and Latin America would be more prominent in the level of urbanization, (iii) the future potential candidates for rapid urbanization are Asia and Africa (Table 1).

The projected urbanization pattern by regional economies has indicated that urbanization in developing countries as a whole is more rapid and massive as the share of urban population by 2020 will increase by more than double the current share thus touching the share of almost 54 per cent. from just 17 per cent in 1950. In particular, it has been proposed that now it is the Asia's turn to take over the rapid urbanization process from Latin America which had experienced spectacular urbanization process by reaching urban population from 44 per cent to the level of 75 per cent during the second half of the last century (Mathur, 1992 and Mohan, 2005). The main reason for such a proposal is that Asia has almost fifty per cent of the global urban population and it is going to house a major share of global urban population (Asia 2.7 billion and all other regions put together 2.3 billion) in the near future. Secondly, Asian region has been dynamic as revealed by rapid and diversified levels of urbanization (high level: Singapore, Hong Kong, Japan, Newzealand, Australia; medium level: China, India, Pakistan; low level: Bhutan, Nepal, Maldives) and emergence of primate cities and primate regions (Bangkok city and its region; Seoul city and its region; Bombay city and its region, Bangalore and its region etc.) (Mathur,1992). This process although has led to higher levels of urbanization, but are concentrated in certain pockets thus, promoting city-regional disparities in their levels of development. The problem of city-regional disparities would be further accentuated on account of location pattern of cities as out of 21 cities which are expected to reach 10 million plus population by 2015, seventeen cities will be in developing countries, and more significantly 11 out of 17 cities will be in the Asian region (Mohan, 2005).

Table 1
World Urbanization Pattern

Region	Level of Urbanization (per cent to total population)	
	2000	2030
Africa	37.2	52.9
Asia	37.5	54.1
Latin America	75.4	84.0
Oceania	74.1	77.3
North America	77.4	80.5
Europe	73.4	84.5
World	47.2	60.2

Source: United Nations, 2002.

Urbanization and economic growth are strongly associated, and hence, urban areas in general and cities in particular have been identified as the 'engines of economic growth', and 'agents of change' (Mohan, 2005). Hence, rapid urbanization brings significant economic growth and prosperity to the region through trickle-down hypothesis. This means massive improvement in the accessibility to basic services like primary education, health, water supply and sanitation, and other infrastructures. Another advantage of rapid and higher level of urbanization is the integration of developing economics into global economics and markets, an essential criterion for national development (Mathur, 1992). In the context of the on-going disparity based urbanization in Asia, the proposed rapid and higher level of urbanization along with efficient policy measures would most probably promote uniform urban development and prosperity in the Asian region. However, in addition to prosperity, rapid urbanization also imposes innumerable problems of city management like environment and pollution, land-use, water, energy, transport, slums, demographic and social etc which need to be addressed effectively for sustainable urbanization. Added to this, unlike developed countries, rapid urbanization in developing countries is taking place at a much lower GDP levels which would aggravate the emerging problems due to financial constraints in implementing various environment and development programmes. This obviously calls for adoption of comprehensive urbanization policy in the Asian region by incorporating the concepts of resource conservation and mobilization, environmental management, appropriate policy instruments and associated institutional structure for implementation and monitoring and people participation. Hence, Asian region as a whole has to make all out efforts to mobilize the resources to meet the challenges of proposed rapid urbanization. This paper attempts to demonstrate the problems and prospects of rapid urbanization in the Asian region based on the rapidly urbanizing state of India-Karnataka-and its capital city-Bagalore and its region-which has been identified as a globally known primate city for its information technology development and services, and draws policy directions for a balanced urban development.

URBANIZATION PATTERN: INDIA AND KARNATAKA

Karnataka, one of the frontline states of India ranks 6th by per capita net state domestic product, per cent share of urban population, life expectancy, infant mortality and maternal mortality rates, 7th by literacy, and 9th by population size (Heitzman, 2001 and Census, 2001). Karnataka accounts for almost 6.3 per cent of national urban population and 5.4 per cent of total number of towns in the country. By share of urban population, Karnataka (33.98) stands much above the national average (27.78%) in 2001. With its conducive location characteristics for industrial and commercial development, the two engines of economic growth and urbanization, Karnataka's urbanization has been consistently progressive with gradual increase in urban population from 12.59 per cent to 33.98 per cent during 1901 and 2001. In particular, during 1901-2001, the state's urban population has increased almost eleven times with annual growth of 9.91 per cent. As a result, the share of Karnataka's urban population has been on the much higher side as compared to the national pattern during 1901-2001. As per the projected urban population, the same higher growth trend of urban population would continue in Karnataka till 2016 by reaching urban population share as high as 39.3 per cent while, at the national level, it will be just 33.7 per cent (Fig. 1). By per cent annual urban population growth, Karnataka is on the higher growth range along with the other prominent states, while north –eastern states, Tamil Nadu and Haryana have recorded the highest growth pattern (Table 2). All these characteristics have made Karnataka as a forward looking state in the country.

Figure 1
Per cent Urban Population : 1901-2016

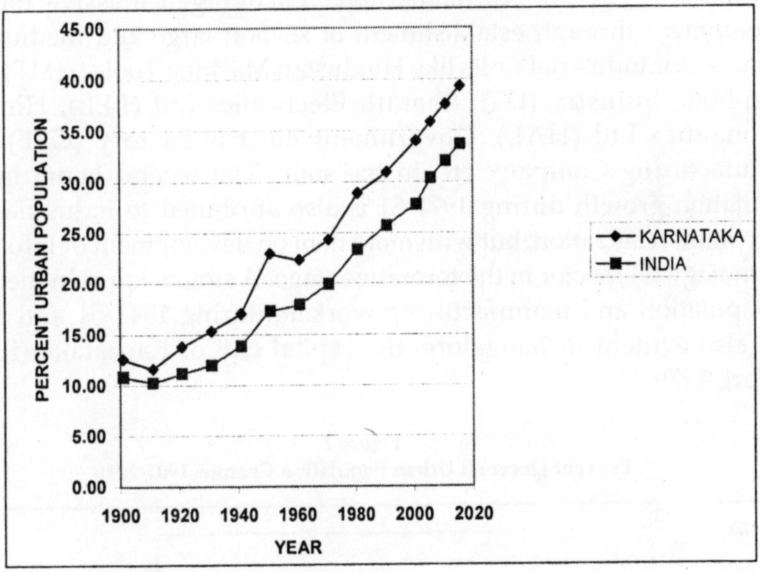

Table 2
Per cent Annual urban population growth by States of India: 1991-2001

Population growth	*States*
Negative	Punjab
0 - 2	Andhra Pradesh, Kerala, Manipur
2 - 4	Bihar, Karnataka, Orissa, West Bengal, Assam, Goa, Gujarat, Himachal Pradesh, Madhya Pradesh, Maharastra, Meghalaya, Mizoram, Rajasthan, Uttar Pradesh
More than 4	Sikkim, Nagaland, Arunachal Pradesh, Tamil Nadu, Haryana

Source: Census, 1991 & 2001.

The on-going urbanization pattern in Karnataka has revealed that its urban population growth trend has been, by and large study and smooth, and very close to the national trend (Fig.1). While, decenial urban population change pattern has revealed a criss-cross pattern by hovering around the national pattern. In particular, urban population change trend of Karnataka has exhibited bimodal pattern with two peaks, a much steeper one at 1951 and a moderate one at 1981. The national trend has also exhibited almost a similar bimodal pattern, but with moderate peaks. However, as per the projected urban population trends, by 2016 Karnatak's growth trend would be on the lower side as compared to the national pattern (Fig. 2). The main implication of projected higher urban population share and lower growth is that there will be higher concentration of population in cities and towns in Karnataka as compared to the national pattern. This has obvious implications on the city and town management in terms of infrastructure and services. The main reason for such high urban population growth peak during 1941-51 in Karnataka is the state's initiative towards industrialization. This is the period in which both govt. of India and govt. of Karnataka have encouraged massive industrial development through establishment of several large and medium scale public sector industrial units like Hindustan Machine Tools (HMT), Indian Telephone Industry (ITI), Bharath Electronics Ltd (BEL), Hindustan Aeronautics Ltd (HAL), Government Electric Factory (GEF), Radio Manufacturing Company etc. in the state. The second boom in urban population growth during 1971-81 is also attributed to industrialization and commercialization, but with more dent on development of Information Technology (IT) sector in the formative stage. A similar spurt in the growth of population and manufacturing workers during 1941-51 and 1971-81 was also evident in Bangalore, the capital city of Karnataka (Rao and Tewari, 1979).

Figure 2
Per cent Decenial Urban Population Change: 1901-2016

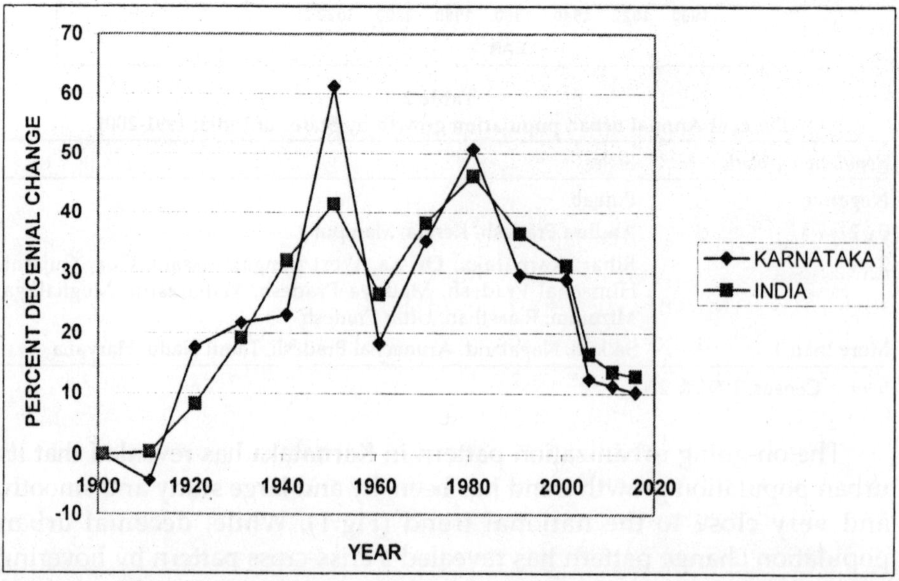

The urbanization pattern in Karnataka may be reinterpreted in terms of different time periods such as pre-independence, post- independence but pre-reform and post reform. From Fig. 1 it is evident that urbanization in terms of share of urban population to total population has shown an increasing trend in all the identified time periods thus indicating a positive influence on the urbanization trend in all the specified time period. However, in terms of decadal growth, during pre-independence and just after the independence, high thrust on industrialisation and urbanisation has revealed an increasing growth of urban population with a crest culminating in the reorganization of state of Karnatakain 1956. During reorganization, in addition to its own urban population, Karnataka also got urban areas from its neighbouring states of Andra Pradesh and Tamil Nadu which has added to the urban population and hence, resulted in higher decadal per cent growth of urban population (Fig. 2). Again a similar phenomenon was evident during post- independence but some part of pre-reform period. This second high growth peak is attributed to migration, continued phase of industrialisation and initial stages of IT development. Interestingly, though urban population growth had slackened up to reform period, but gained some momentum immediately after reform with sustained growth pattern till 2000 and such a pattern is likely to be repeated from 2004 on wards as per the projections. In fact, the rapid developments in IT sector in the state has been passing through the stage of higher urban population growth, especially in the Karnataka state. Such a growth pattern is also due to the policy thrust on urbanization and industrialization by the state.

The characteristics of urbanization explained in terms of GDP/SNDP composition and primacy is that while industry led urbanization may be characterized as (a) high concentration of workforce engaged in the manufacturing sector, (b) higher share of workforce with technical specialization, (c) growth of small scale sector as ancillaries to feed the production requirements of large scale industrial units, (d) more organized labour with less disparity in income, and (e) demand for better landuse planning for organized location of labour and associated economic and service activities. On the other hand, if the urbanization is based on tertiarisation, the broad implications are (a) higher concentration of unorganized labour, (b) heterogeneous educational attainment of population, (c) higher income disparity among the workforce, (d) more chances of development of slums to meet the demands of the unorganized sector, (e) landuse planning will be a complex for the reasons of location of various tertiary based urban activities. Obviously, higher primacy would lead to more of city-region disparities in urbanization pattern. In Karnataka, Bangalore has maintained its primacy and, it has increased significantly from 2.4 to 7.2.

In Karnataka, number of towns have increased marginally by 8.2 per cent while, population has increased by 990.7 per cent during 1901-2001. The marginal increase in number of towns as compared to a big leap in the population growth, clearly implies that additional urban population that had accrued in the state through migration and natural growth during 1901-2001 has by and large followed the process of infilling into the existing urban areas. This process has obviously lead to rapid increase in city and town sizes in the state. While, country has experienced both diffusion as well as infilling process of additional urban population accrued in the country during 1901-2001 (1003.7%) into existing as well as new towns and cities which has recorded 172.3 per cent growth during the said period. Similarly, to begin with, the distribution of towns in Karnataka by size class has revealed a well balanced typical pyramidal shape with strong base, with highest concentration of class VI (less than 5,000 population) and least share of class I towns (more than 1,00,000 population) at the top. However, subsequent urban development policies which encouraged higher size towns has led to redistribution in concentration of towns by eroding the pyramidal base. A similar growth pattern is evident at the national level as well. While, the concentration of urban population by size class is concerned, the issue has been more serious as the population distribution has assumed a perfect inverted pyramid with highest and least concentration of population in class I and VI towns respectively in Karnataka as well at the national level during 1901-2001. This implies that both state and national urban development policies have consistently reinforced each other to encourage highest concentration of population in class I cities (Karnataka: 67%; India: 70%).thus highlighting the' top heavy' character of Indian urbanization. This urbanization pattern in turn has encouraged primate cities and primate city regions in the country which has resulted in urban-regional disparities.

By economic characterization of urbanization through its associated sectors of the economy (secondary, tertiary), tertiary sector's contribution at both national and state levels is prominent. During 1950-2001, the increase in the share of territory sector in the GDP/NSDP is much faster at the state level as compared to the national pattern. In Karnataka, the development of the IT sector has been very prominent and more so during the last decade which has promoted the state in general and Bangalore in particular to a global scale. This in turn has multiplied the tertiary sector related activities on a massive scale which in turn has contributed significantly to the state's economy. Interestingly, secondary sector's contribution ranks third, next to the primary sector at both state and national levels. This is in spite of well designed industrial development policies since independence at both national and state levels for its over all development in the country. The share of secondary sector in the GDP/SNDP has increased at a much faster rate at the national level than at the Karnataka. The main implication of this is that at the national level industrialization has still remained as the prominent sector for its contribution to the national economy. This is because industrial activities by and large makes sustained contribution to the economy than the IT sector which is most unpredictable in terms of growth and development. This has been experienced globally in the recent days. On the other hand, the primary sector's share has reduced at a much faster rate at the national level than at the Karnataka level (Table 3). In this context, Karnataka's urbanization may be characterized with more of rural attributes than at the national level. As a result, urban–regional disparity in Karnataka has been much sharper than at the national level. For instance, the rapid urbanization of the globally known primate city-Bangalore, has led to more pronounced city–region disparity as revealed by various socio-economic and environmental characteristics like education level, income, type of occupation, piped water supply, toilet facility and solid waste disposal (Table 4). As a result, instead of the city–region symbiosis, the region has been experiencing acute problems of environment and under development.

Table 3
GDP/SNDP, share by Sectors and per cent Urban Population, India and Karnataka : 1950-51/1960-61 to 2000–01

Sector	*1950-51*	*1960-61*	*1970-71*	*1980-81*	*1990-91*	*2000-01*
India						
GDP (in crores)	9547	16220	42222	130176	510954	1902999
% Primary	59.20	54.75	48.12	41.82	34.93	26.25
% Secondary	13.29	16.61	19.91	21.59	24.49	24.90
% Tertiary	27.51	28.63	31.96	36.59	40.58	48.85
% Urban pop	17.29	17.90	19.91	23.34	25.71	27.78
Percapita GDP (Rs.)	264	369	770	1906	6061	18530
Karnataka						
SNDP (in crores)		692	1763	5587	20550	93333
% Primary		61.27	57.86	46.05	37.11	30.61
% Secondary		15.17	18.38	20.76	24.04	20.92
% Tertiary		23.55	23.77	33.18	39.85	48.47
% Urban pop		23.33	24.31	28.89	30.92	33.98
Percapita SNDPP (Rs.)		296	622	1527	4608	17808

Source: Economic Survey, 1994-95 & 2003-04, Government of Karnataka.
Economic Survey, 2004-05, Government of India.

REGIONAL PATTERN OF URBANISATION

Physiographyically Karnataka has been divided into coast, malnad, southern maidan and northern maidan regions. As a result, the development policies have been encouraged according to the location characteristics and hence, the pattern of urbanization. In Karnataka, southern maidan region is the highest urbanized region (50.6%) while, coastal region (7.4%) is least urbanized. Both Malnad (21.4%) and northern Maidan (20.6%) for obvious constraints have revealed medium levels of urbanisation. Southern Maidan (34.7%), for its location advantages and infrastructure facility has also recorded the highest urban population growth in the state. Southern maidan being the hard core region of the erstwhile princely state of Mysore has cornered all special privilege since beginning for its well planned development in terms of the location of industrial and commercial activities and development of infrastructure and services. Although Malnad (22.8%) has recorded the least increase, it is significant in terms of its magnitude which is of very great concern as it an ecologically fragile forest resource region and hence, the region has been identified as one of the twelve biodiversity hot spots of the world (Sengupta, 2001). Malnad regional has emerged as having very strong urban characteristics (Sastry, 2005).

Table 4
Percentage Distribution of Household by Various Socio-economic and Environmental Characteristics in Bangalore city and its Region

Variable	*City*	*Conurbation*	*Greenbelt*
Education			
Illiterates	13	21	30
Primary	4	5	9
Higher primary	23	25	34
secondary	32	33	19
intermediate	7	6	2
Graduation and post graduation	15	9	6
Professionals	7	1	0
Workers			
Unskilled	12	23	50
Skilled	32	40	12
Monthly Household Income (Rs.)			
Less than 2000	10	13	19
2000 - 6000	56	70	68
More than 6000	29	8	7
Piped water supply	73	8	6
Toilet facility	66	47	26
Open defection	1	35	70
Solid waste disposal			
House collection	34	0	0
Dustbin	53	29	2
Open space	7	64	72

Source: Sastry (2004a)and AusIndia (2002).
Note: Conurbation: city fringe area; Greenbelt: beyond the city fringe.

By regional concentration of towns, northern maidan has the highest concentration followed by malnad region. For obvious constraints, coastal region has the least concentration of towns. Surprisingly, Malnad, the ecologically fragile region, due to high concentration of various development activities (industrial, infrastructure, and irrigation projects) had the highest concentration of towns and particularly smaller size towns (town sizes IV, V and VI) in 1991and have been reduced drastically due to declassification of towns in 2001 (Table 5). By size class while, southern maidan has the highest concentration of the most significant size class, the class I town and class three III towns, northern maidan has the highest concentration of class II town (Table 5). Malnad has the second highest concentration of class I towns next to the southern maidan. This is because the major towns like Hubli-Dharwaḍ, Mysore, Shimoga, Hassan are located in this region. Malnad is a resource rich region (forest, agriculture, industry and services). Hence, in addition to major cities various town sizes are also concentrated (I, III, IV, V) to provide both higher and lower level urban functions and services to the large rural hinterlands of the region. In an another study by the author on the western ghats region of Karnataka, Malnad region has been identified as urban and industrial dominant region with higher level of development (Sastry and Rao, 2002). Interestingly, the number of towns under size class 20,00-50,000 have increased significantly during 1991-01 and this increase is again concentrated in southern maidan region. It appears that both southern maidan and malnad regions have been experiencing greater urban population pressure on account of higher concentration of class I towns thus, demanding efficient urban development policy interventions for balanced urban development.

Table 5
Percentage Distribution of Towns by Size Class and Region: 1991 & 2001

Town size	*Coast*		*Malnad*		*Southern Maidan*		*Northern Maidan*		*Karnataka*	
	1991	*2001*	*1991*	*2001*	*1991*	*2001*	*1991*	*2001*	*1991*	*2001*
100,000 and more	6.7	6.7	7.4	10.1	11.4	13.4	6.8	8.4	8.3	10.1
500,000-100,000	10.0	10.0	2.5	7.3	8.6	11.9	8.2	15.5	6.7	11.4
20000-50000	20.0	30.0	28.4	39.2	32.9	50.8	41.1	43.7	32.3	42.6
10000-20000	33.3	26.7	27.2	24.6	27.1	13.5	27.4	26.8	28.0	22.4
5000-10000	16.7	20.0	22.2	17.4	15.7	8.9	6.8	4.2	15.4	11.4
Less than 5000	13.3	6.6	12.3	1.4	4.3	1.5	9.6	1.4	9.4	2.1
Total	100.0 (30)	100.0 (30)	100.0 (81)	100.0 (69)	100.0 (70)	100.0 (67)	100.0 (73)	100.0 (71)	100.0 (254)	100.0 (237)

Source: Town Directory, Karnataka, Census of India,1991.
Provisional Population Total, Karnataka, Census of India, 2001.

As explained before, Karnataka's cities and towns have been experiencing rapid population growth on account of infilling of additional urban population accrued in the state. As a result, almost 28.8 per cent of towns have experienced more than 3 per cent annual growth followed by 55.7 per cent of the towns with 1-3 per cent growth thus, contributing significantly to rapid urbanization process in Karnataka. By regional concentration of growth performance of towns, again southern Maidan has the highest concentration of towns with annual growth of 1-3 per cent and more than 3 per cent followed by northern Maidan (Table 6).

Historically, southern maidan being the hard core of erstwhile princely state of Mysore has been the concentration for almost all development activities like location of industries and commerce, infrastructure and services etc. In addition, Bangalore, the capital city of the state is located in this region. Hence, by and large, individual growth performance of towns is much faster and prominent in southern Maidan. Interestingly, malnad region in spite of its location constraints has also recorded comparatively higher growth performance of towns (Table 6). Malnad is a resource rich region. Hence, innumerable towns of various sizes have emerged as growth centers to provide urban functions and services to the large rural hinterlands. Obviously, with the intensification of the urban related activities, these towns have attracted more population to record higher growth. Interestingly, majority of towns have recorded 1-3 per cent annual growth during 1981-91 and 1991-01 and such high growth performance is concentrated in malnad, northern maidan and southern maidan regions. In particular, coastal zone has more than doubled the share of towns which have recorded more that 3 per cent annual growth during 1981-91 and 1991-01. The rapid growth performance of towns and cities, in addition to location advantages, depend on their functional specialization.

Table 6
Percentage Distribution of Towns by Annual per cent Population Growth by Regions, Karnataka

Population Growth	*Coast*		*Malnad*		*Southern Maidan*		*Northern Maidan*		*Karnataka*	
	1991	*2001*	*1991*	*2001*	*1991*	*2001*	*1991*	*2001*	*1991*	*2001*
Negative	13.0	4.8	10.4	3.0	0	1.7	4.9	7.7	5.8	4.2
Less than or equal to 1	26.1	33.3	18.2	15.1	3.1	8..3	14.7	3.1	13.4	11.3
1-3	47.8	33.3	55.8	66.7	62.5	53.3	52.4	53.8	56.2	55.7
More than 3	13.0	28.6	15.6	15.1	34.4	36.7	27.9	35.4	24.5	28.8
Total	100 (23)	100 (21)	100 (77)	100 (66)	100 (65)	100 (60)	100 (65)	100 (65)	100 (226)	100 (212)

Source: Town Directory, Karnataka, Census of India, 1991.
Provisional Population Total, Karnataka, Census of India, 2001.

The functional specialization of towns and cities have been derived on the basis of the number of workers employed in various sectors of urban activities. Accordingly, the quality of urbanization in Karnataka is still in the primitive stage as highest share of towns (31.1%) are specialized in primary activities followed by tertiary sector (27.2%). This might be the reason for the more prominent share of the primary sector to the state economy contributed through the highest number of towns with primary sector specialization. In spite of rapid industrialization process introduced in the state for a very long time, only 14.2 per cent of the towns are specialized in manufacturing sector. Interestingly, due to dominance of more number of functions in a single town, quite a significant share of towns (26.4%) have been identified as multi-function towns (Table 7). The emergence of functional specialization of towns would also depend on the development policy interventions by the state on the various sectors of the economy. As of now greater policy boost is being given to the IT sector in the state for its overall development and such growth boot is restricted to class I cities only.

By physiographic regions, coastal zone has the highest concentration of towns,. which are specialized in tertiary sector (40%) followed by secondary sector (26.7%). The coastal region for its rich resource base and location advantages has attracted large number of industries and associated service sector. Similarly, Malnad region for its obvious location specificity and rich natural resource endowment has also encouraged larger share of towns (40.7%) which are specialized in tertiary activities followed by the towns specialized in primary activities (32.1%). Surprisingly, malnad, the well-known forest region has encouraged large-scale agriculture (Sastry and Rao, 2002), which in turn has contributed significantly to functional specialization of towns in primary sector. Southern maidan with its locational advantages for industrial, commercial and service activities along with better infrastructure facilities has encouraged the highest concentration of multi-functional towns (towns which are specialized in more than one function) (32.9%). In addition, its location specificity has also encouraged the towns which are specialized in secondary (24.3%) and primary sector (24.3%) as well. While, northern maidan for its obvious high agriculture and irrigation potentials and associated infrastructure has the highest concentration of towns with specialization in primary sector (43.8%) followed by tertiary sector (19.2%). In addition, northern maidan has the second highest concentration of multi-functional towns (27.4%) (Table 7).

Table 7
Percentage Distribution of Towns by Functions and Region

Functional Category	*Coast*	*Malnad*	*Southern Maidan*	*Northern Maidan*	*Karnataka*
Primary	13.3	32.1	24.3	43.8	31.1
Secondary	26.7	4.9	24.3	9.6	14.2
Tertiary	40.0	40.7	18.6	19.2	28.3
Multi-functions	20.0	22.2	32.9	27.4	26.4
All Towns	11.8	31.9	27.5	28.7	100.0

Source: Census, 1991.

An integrated analysis of towns by size, growth and functional specialization by region has enabled to identify a few typologies of towns and their potential growth performances. In coastal region, cities and large towns like Mangalore, Udupi, Sirasi and Puttur, which are multifunctional are growing rapidly as compared to other functional towns. While Mangalore and Udapi are coastal towns, Puttur and Sirasi are in the midst of forest resource base and all of them are located in an ecologically sensitive coastal zone. Hence, their growth process and pattern need to be regulated to maintain both forest and coastal ecology. In particular, Udapi has recorded very high growth (97.1%) during 1981-91, thus attracting administrators and policy makers to take special care in the growth process of Udapi town. Incidentally, in recognition of the high growth performance and historical importance of Udapi, which was a part of Dakshina Kannada district till 1995 has been recently carved out as a separate district along with a set of villages and towns. In fact, both Mangalore and Udapi with their rapid growth and associated urban environmental problems of industrial pollution, solid waste and sewerage disposal have been posing serious threat to the coastal ecology. In addition, the other coastal zone towns Karwar, Bantval, Dandeli, Putter, Bhatkal, Yellapur, Honnaver and Karkala with multifunctional specialization and higher population growth have emerged as potential growth centers for future investments and development. Hence, these potential growth centers need adequate growth regulations under the coastal zone management for their sustainable development. Similarly, several new towns were added, and several project towns have recorded significant population decline mostly due to decline in the project activities.

In malnad region, which has higher concentration of towns specialized in primary and tertiary sector activities due to difficult terrain needs adequate care in promotion of urbanisation in the region. As a result, towns like Arakalagud, Heggaddadevanakote, Mundargi, Hangal and Navalgund which are specialized in primary sector, and CR Patna, Haveri, Kushalnagar and Hubli-Dharwar, which have multifunctional specialization, have recorded high population growth, thus emerging as potential growth centers. While, Hubli-Dharwar, the second largest city in the state and Mysore, the most prominent city of the state, require greater infrastructure facilities to manage their growth performance. The remaining towns need to be encouraged by making use of the available regional or local resource base. Like coastal region, malnad with its strong forest resource base is also an ecologically sensitive region. Hence, adequate care is required while development of these towns.

Southern maidan with its multifunctional infrastructure facilities has encouraged the towns which are specialised in all the three sector viz; primary, secondary and tertiary sectors. In particular, southern maidan has accommodated Bangalore, the capital city of Karnataka which has accounted for almost 31 per cent of state's urban population and the entire state depends on it for various functions and services. The main concern of the southern maidan is increasing concentration of population in

Bangalore, which needs to be discouraged in order to encourage balanced regional development in the state. In this context, several towns of this region like KR Pet, Holalkera, Siriguppa, Hadagali specialized in primary sector; Maddur, Mulibagal, Anekal, Harihar, Kanakapura and Vijayapura specialized in secondary sector; Hosadurga, Tumkur, Kolar, Bagepalli, Bangarpet, Challakere, Chintamani, Chitradurga, Davanagere, Hiriyur, Koratagere, Kunigal, Malur, Pavagada and Srinivaspura. have emerged as potential growth centers with higher population growth performance. Hence, these potential centers need adequate encouragement in accordance with the regional growth perspective as well as the available local resource base.

Similarly, Northern maidan due to high irrigation potentials has accounted for major share of towns with specialisation in primary sector and in particular agriculture based activities followed by multi-functions. In particular, the region has concentration of major cities like Belgaum, Gulbarga, Bidar, Bijapur. and Raichur which are specialised in multi-functions. In addition. several towns like Indi, Mudhol, Gangavathi, Manvi, Sindhanur, Hatti, Mudebihal, Badami, Bhalki, Mahalingapur, Sadem, with higher population growth have emerged as potential growth centers which need to be encouraged with appropriate regional perspective along with the available regional resource base. Hence, by proper choice of potential growth centres across the state would induce balanced urbanization process in Karnataka.

As mentioned before, rapid urbanization has been sharpening the regional disparities. This has been demonstrated in the case of Bangalore city region. A similar disparity is evident at the regional levels as well. In the Southern maidan, Bangalore urban district for its obvious rapid urbanization has cornered all the infrastructure facilities along with very high per capita SNDP.While, other districts in the region are still lagging behind in terms of urban population, literacy and specially toilet facilities. A similar pattern has emerged in the Malnad region where Dhrwad district has gained prominence followed by the Mysore district. Where as the other districts of the region have remained low due to lower level of urbanization and associated services and per capita income. In particular, the higher levels of urbanization has reconfirmed its close association predominantly with the higher share of the tertiary sector's contribution to the district GDP followed by the secondary sector as clearly revealed by Bangalore Urban, Dharwad, Mysore and Uttara Kannada districts which have recorded higher level of urbanization with least trickle-down effect (Table 8). Surprisingly, irrespective of the level of urbanization there has been a higher share of households with access to safe drinking water and very low access to toilet facility. This is mainly because, to begin with greater attention was given to water supply alone by various development programmes concentrating on water supply alone, however, with the

Table 8
Urban, Service and Economic Indicators by Regions of Karnataka:1991 & 2001

Region	% Uurban Population		Literacy		% Households with Safe Drinking Water*		% Households with Toilet		% Primary		% Secondary		% Tertiary		Per capita SNDP	
	1991	2001	1991	2001	1991	2001	1991	2001	1991	2001	1991	2001	1991	2001	1991	2001
Southern Maidan																
Bangalore. U	86.2	88.1	76.3	83.9	82.1	96.2	72.9	85.3	3.1	4.8	48.9	38.8	48.0	56.4	14127	32083
Bangalore. R	18.1	21.7	50.2	65.0	86.5	97.4	16.8	33.8	37.2	32.3	25.0	24.6	37.7	43.0	8639	17270
Bellary	32.0	34.9	45.9	58.0	84.2	93.7	12.9	27.2	47.1	33.2	16.2	26.4	36.6	40.4	7232	17822
Chitradurga	16.6	18.1	52.3	64.9	88.1	97.1	17.0	27.7	45.4	42.1	19.1	16.9	35.5	40.9	7734	12841
Kolar	23.3	24.7	50.5	63.1	89.8	97.2	19.8	33.3	49.3	47.5	14.6	13.8	36.0	38.6	6739	13802
Mandya	16.2	16.0	48.1	61.2	71.2	93.2	14.3	25.4	48.1	47.0	18.9	15.1	33.0	37.9	7840	15258
Tumkur	16.6	19.6	54.5	67.2	80.8	96.9	14.0	26.0	46.5	37.6	18.8	23.6	34.7	38.7	7013	13881
Northern Maidan																
Belgaum	23.5	24.1	53.0	64.4	64.2	75.0	14.4	26.7	43.3	40.4	24.2	22.3	32.4	37.4	8953	16439
Bidar	19.6	64.4	45.1	62.0	60.5	79.6	10.3	19.5	44.6	38.0	16.2	16.3	39.1	45.7	5944	10892
Bijapur	19.5	62.0	56.5	57.5	73.3	83.0	6.9	12.7	48.8	43.2	17.8	14.6	33.3	42.1	7207	14885
Gulbarga	2.6	57.5	38.5	50.6	63.0	80.5	12.2	18.6	40.5	37.9	23.3	20.4	36.2	41.6	7115	13446
Raichur	24.6	50.6	34.3	49.5	65.4	83.2	7.3	14.8	48.6	48.2	13.7	12.4	37.6	39.4	6275	11344
Malnad																
Chikmagalur	16.9	19.5	61	72.6	69.5	81.8	23.1	42.0	58.5	54.9	8.6	8.4	32.9	36.7	11918	21387
Dharwad	52.5	55	62.7	71.9	81.5	90.6	21.6	31.5	37.7	25.4	22.1	22.3	40.1	52.3	7512	17915
Hasan	17.4	17.7	56.9	68.7	79.5	93.0	16.1	27.8	50.5	47.0	13.9	12.9	35.6	40.1	7519	14697
Kodagu	16.0	13.8	68.3	78.2	44.8	53.1	32.1	52.1	63.5	58.4	6.3	7.2	30.2	34.4	14826	29608
Mysore	35.8	36.9	50.9	63.7	82.7	94.6	24.9	37.0	35.3	27.2	28.2	26.3	36.4	46.5	8886	19560
Shimoga	32.4	34.8	63.9	74.9	66.5	72.6	25.5	48.2	47.1	39.4	19.6	19.3	33.3	41.4	9204	19349
Coast																
U. Kannada	24.1	28.7	66.7	76.6	20.0	33.5	34.1	34.6	36.4	29.3	23.8	25.7	39.8	45.0	8137	17689
D. Kannada	31.7	38.4.7	76.7	83.5	30.2	31.5	22.8	60.2	29.4	12.9	27.4	43.5	43.2	43.5	10252	39817

Source: State Domestic Product, Karnataka, 1980-81, 1990-91 to 1997-98;1993-94 to 2000-Directorate of Economics and Statistics, Govt. of Karnataka; 2001, Census 2001.

recently emerged holistic concept of 'water supply and environmental sanitation' has begun to improve the sanitation facility as well. The government of Karnataka in particular has taken up several rural sanitation programmes to improve the sanitation facility at the rural level. With the emergence of several potential growth centres and functionally specialized cities and towns, unless proper urban development policy is implemented, the revealed disparities would be further would be further sharpened to promote lopsided urbanization in the state. These disparities have already resulted in innumerable urban environmental problems like high population density, air and water pollution, and solid waste disposal problems. The high vehicular concentration in cities have led to higher emission load of pollutants to the atmosphere. Similarly, inefficient solid waste management has also contributed significantly to urban environmental problems of major cities in the state (Table 9). These environmental problems has been further accentuated with improper disposal of untreated urban sewage water in most of the cities of the state. As on date, only 37 out of 208 cities and towns have been provided with under ground sewerage and of them only 14 towns and cities have waste water treatment facility (Website: kuwsdb). Hence, a thorough mismanagement of urban sewerage by letting into water bodies has resulted in serious water pollution problems both in up stream and down stream stretches of almost all the prominent rivers in the state (Table 10).

Table 9
Some Indicators of Environmental Problems

City	*Population density*	*Pollution load (tonnes/day)*	*Solid waste generated (tons/day)*	*Solid waste cleared (tons/day)*	*No. of Vehicles*
Bangalore	14943	2856.7	2500	1400	1934761
Mysore	5087	243.0	230	183	306418
Dharwad	3395	159.9	250	200	184896
Mangalore	2747	153.4	250	200	171940
Belgaum	2597	137.9	120	100	168392
Gulbarga	7204	96.7	120	100	112477
Bijapur	2562	75.7	80	50	81918
Bellary	3724	65.5	70	40	78201
Bidar	2814	28.5	60	30	33610

Source: Census,1991; Karnataka,2004; Sastry (2004b).

GROWTH PATTERN OF BANGALORE

Bangalore, the globally known software city and capital of Karnataka is known for its trade and commerce and industrial development since its inception. As a result, it has become one among the million cities of India as early as 1961 and whose growth and development is comparable with the seven 'million' and capital cities of India. As per 2001 census, Bangalore ranks fifth, next to Chennai by population size. Population size trend of Bangalore has been smooth all along and very close to the baseline unlike Greater Bombay, Calcutta and Delhi (Fig. 3). All the seven 'million' cities have revealed the growth trend of bi-model pattern with growth peaks at 1951 and 1981(Fig. 4). In particular, the main reason for such high population growth of Bangalore during 1941-51 is large scale industrial development encouraged by both govt. of India and Karnataka and area expansion. While, 1971-81 growth is also attributed to industrial development especially the IT sector in its formative stage and area expansion (Heitzman,2004 and Sastry,1986).

Table 10
Highly Polluted River Stretches in Karnataka

Sl. No.	River stretch	
1.	**Bhadra River Shimoga:**	Upstream of MPM and VISL, Bhadravati; Downstream of MPM, Bhadravathi
2.	**Tungabhadra River, Davanagere:**	Upstream of Harihar Polifiber; Downstream of Harihar Polifiber;
3.	**Kali River, Uttara Kannada:**	Upstream of West Coast Paper Mills Downstream of West Coast Paper Mills
4.	**Hebbala River, Mandya:**	Hebbala village, near Mandya
5.	**Kabini River, Mysore District:**	Intake of KIADB, Nanjanagud; Bathing Ghat, Nanjanagud
6.	**Tungabhadra River:**	Haralahalli bridge
7.	**Arkavathi River:**	Downstream of Kanakapura
8.	**Krishna River:**	Downstream of Devasagara bridge
9.	**Bhima River:**	Downstream of road bridge ghanagapura village

Source: KSPCB, 1996-97 to 2002-03 Annual Report.

The area of the city has recorded significant increase by 92.1 per cent and the population by 37.8 per cent during 1991-01.As per the projected estimate, the population of Bangalore would reach 9.8 million by 2016. While, IT development has been in progress, the corresponding infrastructure and services required for smooth functioning of IT sector was not geared up. The main victim of such expansion is the peripheral areas of the city as it has experienced uneven development and sever environmental problems with unique 'rurban' characteristics which is quite different from the city. Some of the characteristics are higher concentration of households with large household size, higher illiteracy rate, higher share of unskilled and primary sector workers, higher share of medical expenses as compare to city, larger share of kacha or semi-pacca house structure, least water and sanitation facility, and almost no solid waste disposal provision and high concentration of slums and uneven city- peripheral transport facility (AusIndia, 2002; Sastry, 2004).

Figure 3
Population Size of Million Cities of India: 1901-2001

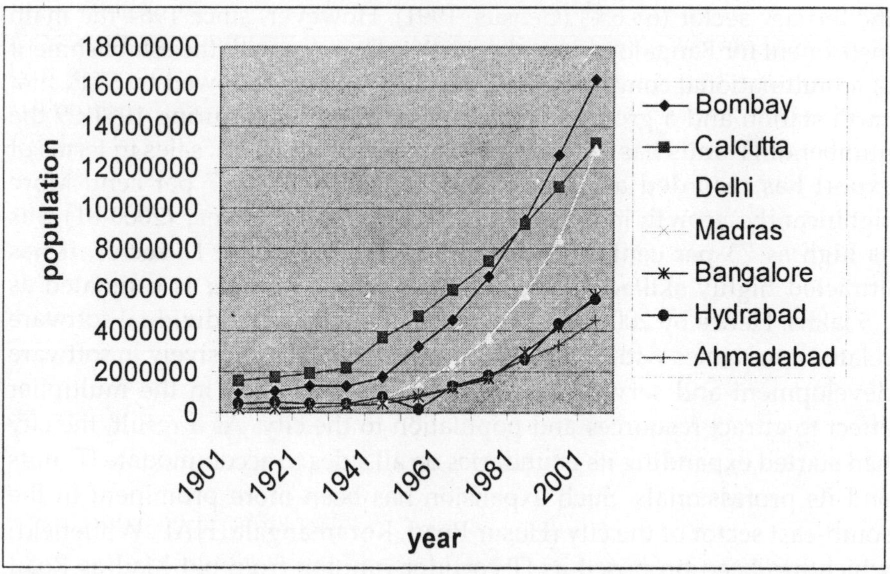

Figure 4
Population Growth of Million Cities of India : 1901-2001

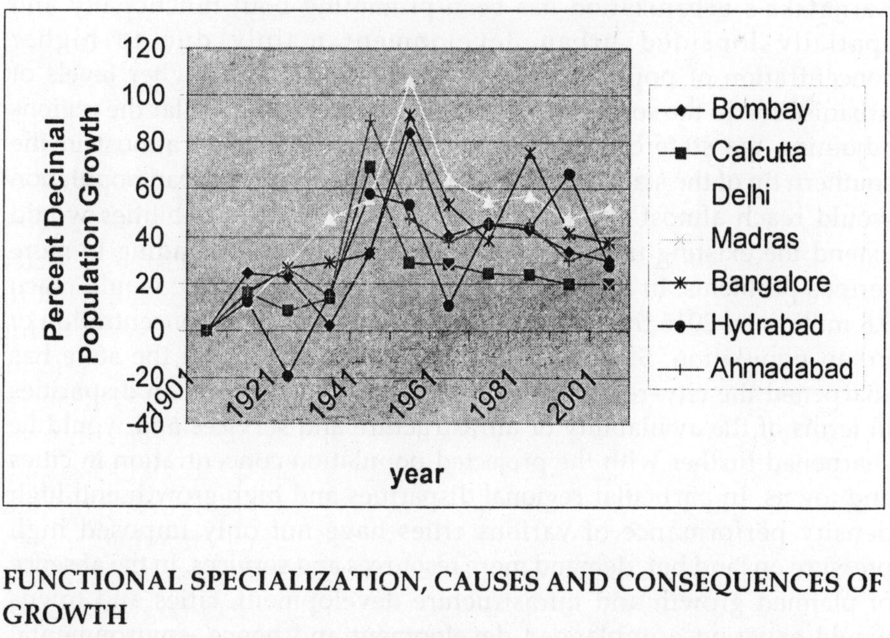

FUNCTIONAL SPECIALIZATION, CAUSES AND CONSEQUENCES OF GROWTH

By functional specialization, Bangalore has consistently emerged as a bi-functional city with specialization in manufacturing and service sectors. In addition, trade and commerce for obvious location specificity has acquired grater significance. As a result, almost 97.5 per cent of the total work force were employed in non-primary sector with a major share in the tertiary sector (63.6%) (Census, 1991). However, since 1984 the main instrument for Bangalore's rapid growth is IT sector with the establishment of a multinational company, the Texas Instruments followed by STPI first earth station and a group of 13 company. Especially, during 1991-99 the number of IT units has increased by 361.5 per cent while, sales in terms of export has recorded an unparallel increase by 22566.7 per cent. More significantly, growth in export of software in a single year (2000-01) was as high as 73 per cent. For smooth functioning of the IT sector, it has attracted highly skilled IT professionals whose number is estimated as 1.5 lakhs. Hence by 2000, the Bangalore city had 2020 individual software related companies with 765 companies specialized exclusively in software development and service This has obviously resulted in the multiplier effect to attract resources and population to the city. As a result, the city had started expanding its boundaries on all sides to accommodate IT units and its professionals. Such expansion has been more prominent in the south-east sector of the city (Hosur Road, Koramangala, HAL, Whitefield) which has been proposed as IT corridor running from old Madras Road to New Madras Road (Karnataka, Undated).

CONCLUSION AND STATE URBAN DEVELOPMENT POLICY

Karnataka's urbanization has been promoting both functionally and spatially lopsided urban development mainly due to higher concentration of population in the Class I cities and higher levels of urbanisation in the southern maidan region, and in particular the regions adjoining the state capital, Bangalore which is located almost in the southern tip of the state boundary. By 2016, the share of urban population would reach almost 40 per cent which may in all possibilities would extend the existing uneven urbanization pattern thus, leading to more serious problems. In addition, the population of Bangalore would reach 9.8 million by 2016 thus adding to the problem of high concentration of urban population. Such uneven urbanization pattern in the state has sharpened the city–region disparities as well as inter region disparities in terms of the availability of infrastructure and services and would be sharpened further with the projected population concentration in cities and towns. In particular regional disparities and high growth and high density performance of various cities have not only imposed high pressure on land but, demand more resources and services. In the absence of planned growth and infrastructure development, cities and towns would experience unplanned development and hence, environmental degradation. Regional disparities in urban development has also been identified in the recently commissioned study by the government of Karnataka (Karnataka, 2002).

There is a need for policy direction to encourage balanced urban development in the state through diverting the population concentration especially from the megha city region to the emerging potential growth centres or regions. This uneven urban development has been well recognized by the state planners and policy makers and corrective measures have been proposed as early as in the state's eight five year plan document. Accordingly, the state level urban development strategy, 1994 has focused on dispersal of urbanization and equitable distribution of urban benefits; development of counter magnets to slow down the growth of megha cities; development of areas of special potentials like west coast, growth areas and administrative towns; establishment of proper hierarchy of small, medium and large towns; and development of urban - rural linkages (Karnataka, 2002: 544).

Of late, rapid infrastructure development along the major corridors of the state have encouraged rapid urbanization, along these developing corridors and in particular along the Bangalore–Belgaum corridor which is a part of the golden quadrilateral national road network, Bangalore-Mysore corridor, a miniature of the golden quadrilateral being exclusively developed by the state, and Mangalore-Karwar corridor as a part of the west coast corridor. While, self induced urban corridor development is a very good sign towards balanced urban development in the state, but state has to regulate it properly to achieve the main goals. It has been identified that almost 84 per cent of the state urban population and 74 per cent of the total urban investment are concentrated in these rapidly urbanizing corridors (Shivaramkrishna, 2001).

By population size and associated functions, the following more conspicuous six tier hierarchy of urban centers has emerged in the state (Table 11). Spatially, one can find both gaps and overlaps in the existing hierarchic structure of towns. Especially, the second order centres are only just two (Hubli-Dharwad and Mysore) which are suppose to serve the entire Karnataka with the required functions.Though each one of this centre is located ideally in northern and southern Karnataka, however, because of infrstructural constraints, they can not take the entire load. Similarly, third and fourth order centres are not spatially well distributed to encourage balanced urban development in the state. Hence, for balanced urban development in the state, reordering in the existing hierarchic order is very much essential especially at the second and third levels. In order to achieve this objective, the proposed hierarchy of urban centers has been discussed as below (Table 12).

The importance of Bangalore as the capital city and globally known software center need to be maintained by encouraging its sustained growth in the state as the first order urban center and also as an important national metro in the southern India along with four other metros of the country. In particular, with the increasing city-region disparities, Bangalore's

Table 11
Existing Hierarchy of Urban Centers in Karnataka: City and Population

Hierarchic Order	*Town and Population*
I (1)	1. Bangalore: 5686844
II (2)	1. Hubli-Dharwad: 786018; 2. Mysore: 785800
III (8)	1. Mangalore: 538560; 2. Belgaum: 506235; 3.Gulbarga: 435631; 4. Davanagere: 363780; 5. Bellary: 317000; 6. Shimoga: 274105; 7. Bijapur: 253307; 8. Tumkur: 248592
IV (13)	1. Raichur: 205634; 2.Bidar: 173678; 3.Hospet: 163284; 4. Bhadravathi: 160392; 5. Robersonpet: 156961; 6. Gadag-Betigeri: 154849; 7. Mandya: 131211; 8. Chitradurga: 125060; 9.Udapi u a: 112706; 10. Hassan: 113331; 11. Kolar: 113299; 12. Gangavathi: 101397; 13. Chikamagalur: 101022
V	Towns with populations: 100,000-50,000.
VI	Towns with populations: Less than 50,000

Table 12
Proposed Hierarchy of Urban Centers in Karnataka

HierarchicOrder	*Town*
I (1)	1. Bangalore
II (6)	1. Mysore, 2. Hubli-Dharwad, 3. Mangalore, 4. Belgaum, 5. Gulbarga, 6. Davanagere-Hariher
III (17)	1. Bellary, 2. Bijapur, 3. Shimoga–Bhadravati, 4. Tumukur, 5. Raichur, 6. Koalr Gold Fields, 7. Hospet, 8. Gadag-Betigeri, 9. Bidar, 10. Mandya, 11. Hassan, 12. Chitradurga, 13. Gangawati, 14. Bagalkot, 15. Marcara, 16. Udapi, 17. Sirasi
IV	Other Towns

growth should be integrated with its region to encourage an integrated development of the city and its region with proper symbiosis. This can be achieved mainly by reducing the existing functional gaps between Bangalore and other four national metros with appropriate development vision for the city and its region. At the second hierarchic order, only five cities: Mysore, Hubli-Dharwad, Mangalore, Belgaum and Gulbarga have emerged with spatial gaps and overlaps. Hubli-Dharwad and Belgaum are almost adjacent centres with several overlapping regions, and similarly, the central part of the state is left with huge unsaved area with out having any second order centre. Hence, to rectify the spatial gap and overlap, instead of Belgaum, it is preferable to upgrade Davngere-Harihar to the second order level to serve the central area of the state. However, Belgaum with its location advantages as a border city of Karnataka and Maharastra will develop as a second order centre in spite of little planning push which should be carefully monitored for its overall development.. Hence, with the readjustments in the spatial pattern of location of second order centres, the proposed six second order centers with spatially well balanced locations would reduce both functional and spatial gaps in serving the urban functions in the state (Fig. 5). In this, context, in addition to

Davangere -Harihar, the second order cities of Mangalore, Bulgaum and Gulbarga have to be brought to the levels of Mysore and Hubli-Dharward through appropriate development policies to function as second order centres. Similarly, it is preferable to have spatially interspersed fifteen "third order" urban centers which would further reduce both functional and spatial gaps. These towns and cities are Bagalkot, Bellary, Bijapur, Bhadravati-Shimoga, Bidar, Chitradurga, Chikamagalur, Gadag-Betigeri, Hassan, Hospet, Kolar Gold Fields, Maracara, Mandya, Raichur, and Tumkur. Meanwhile, the coastal zone, with its rich resource base and dynamic economy, is being served only by the second order centre Mangalore thus looking for some lower order centres to facilitate the urban related activities of the region. Though potential growth centres like Udapi and Sirasi have not come up to the level of higher order centre, need to be developed as third order centres, in order to bridge the spatial gap. However, since coastal zone is ecologically fragile, extra care is needed in promoting urban development activities in the region. Hence, totally seventeen third order centre need to be developed for balanced urban development (Fig. 5).

Figure 5

Proposed Hierarchy of Urban Centres in Karnataka

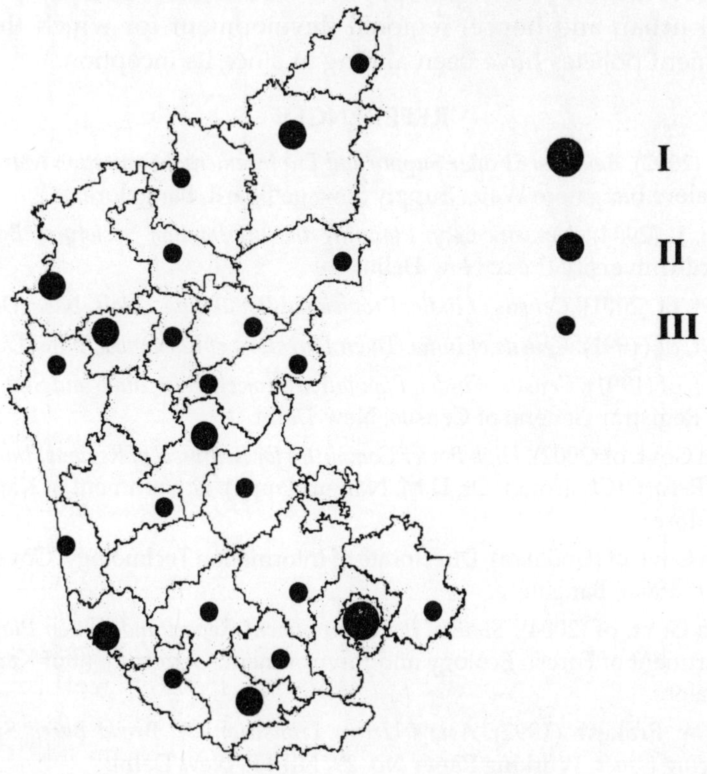

By size, growth and functional typology, both large and medium towns that are specialized in tertiary, secondary and multifunction with their rapid growth process have emerged as potential growth centers in all the four regions (coast, malnad, southern and northern maidan). Incidentally, many of them are located in the well-known west coast corridor between Mangalore–Karwar, all along the Bangalore-Mysore Infrastructure Corridor and Bangalore- Belgaum golden quadrilateral corridor. In addition, many of these potential towns are the part of the proposed hierarchic model to be encouraged with their strong local resource base or induced functional specialization for balanced urban development in the state. While, higher order urban centres need to be encouraged as per the proposed hierarchic order, at the lower levels, the interspersed urban development need to be induced preferable by identifying several strategic potential growth centres emerged during both function and growth performances to achieve balanced urban development in the state. However, while Karnataka's urban development need to be encouraged under the regional urban system perspective, Bangalore growth according to both regional and national perspective. Hence, it is essential that Karnataka's urban development policy need to be integrated with national urban development policy to achieve the development objectives of the state. All these reoriented urbanization processes if encouraged with appropriate development perspective would undoubtedly promote balanced urban and hence, regional development for which the state development policies have been aiming at since its inception.

REFERENCES

AusIndia (2002), *Bangalore Water Supply and Environmental Sanitation Master Plan,* Bangalore.Bangalore Water Supply Sewage Board, Bangalore.

Heitzman, J. (2004), *Network City: Planning the Information Society in Bangalore,* Oxford University Press: New Delhi.

India Govt. of (2001), *Census of India, Provisional Population Totals,* New Delhi.

India Govt. of (1991), *Census of India, Town Directory of Karnataka,* New Delhi.

India Govt. of (1991), *Census of India, Population Projection for India and States, 1996-2016,* Registrar General of Census, New Delhi.

Karnataka Govt. of (2002), *High Power Committee for Redressal of Regional Imbalances, Final Report,* (Chairman: Dr. D.M. Nanjundappa), Government of Karnatana, Bangalore.

Karnataka Govt. of (Undated), Directorate of Information Technology, Government of Karnataka, Bangalore.

Karnataka Govt. of (2004), *State of the Environment Report and Action Plan- 2003,* Department of Forest, Ecology and Environment, Government of Karnataka, Bangalore.

Mathur Om Prakesh (1992), *Asia's Urban Transition: A Broad Based Survey of Emerging Issues,* Working Paper No. 29, NIPFP, New Delhi.

Mohan Rakesh and Shubhagato Dasgupta (2005), The 21st Century: Asia Becomes Urban, Special Articles, *Economic and Political Weekly,* January 15, 2005.

Ramachandran H. and G.S. Sastry (2001), 'An Inventory and Typology of Slums in Bangalore' in *Living in India's Slums* (ed.) Hans Schenk, New Delhi: Manohar Publisher and Distributor.

Rao V.L.S. Prakasa and V.K., Tewari (1979), *A Structure of An Indian Metropolis: Bangalore,* Bombay: allied.

Sastry G.S. (2004a), *Socio-Economic and Ecological Characteristics of Peri-Urban Region: Bangalore,* International Workshop on Energy and Transport in Peri-Urban Interface, 12-14 July, 2004, TERI, Southern Center, Bangalore.

Sastry G.S. (2004b), *Karnataka-Environment,* Institute for Social and Economic Change, Bangalore.

Sastry G.S. and Janarthan Rao (2002), Emerging Development Issues in a Hill-Forest Region, *Social Science Review,* 4 (2): 58-78.

Sengupta Ramaprasad (2001), *Ecology and Economics;* New Delhi: Oxford University Press.

Shivaramakrishan K.C. (2002), Seminar Presentation on *Future of Urbanisation.*

United Nations (2002), *World Urbanization Prospects,* New York.

Chapter - 7

Productivity Growth, Technical Progress and Efficiency Change in the Unorganised Manufacturing Sector During Reforms Period: Insights from major States in India

Rajesh Raj S.N. &
Malathy Duraisamy

INTRODUCTION

Liberalization, Privatization and Globalization (LPG) policies that started in early 1980s in India and strengthened in the 1990s, opened the Indian manufacturing sector to greater competition from within as well as from outside. One of the major components of the economic reforms package has been the deregulation and delicensing in the manufacturing sector. The justification provided for this often centers on the reason of encouraging competition, which, in turn, is expected to enhance the efficiency and productivity performance of the manufacturing sector. Given that the main objective of the reforms was to enhance the efficiency and productivity performance of the Indian industry, especially the manufacturing sector, it would be appropriate to investigate how far the reforms have succeeded in achieving the objective.

In the last few years several studies have examined the productivity performance of the Indian manufacturing sector (Brahmananda, 1982; Balakrishnan and Pushpangadhan, 1994; Dholakia and Dholakia, 1994; Goldar, 2002, 2004). The influence of economic reforms on manufacturing productivity has also been studied and the findings are mixed. Whereas some studies point to improvement in total factor productivity (TFP) growth in the reforms period (Krishna and Mitra, 1998; Pattnayak and Thangavelu, 2003; Unel, 2003) others show that economic reforms have adversely affected productivity (Goldar and Kumari, 2003 and Balakrishnan, Pushpangadan, and Suresh Babu, 2000). The productivity performance of the manufacturing sector across the Indian states has been the subject of inquiry in Ray (1997, 2002), Aghion et.al (2003) and Kumar (2004) among others and there is evidence of a tendency towards convergence in total factor productivity (TFP) growth rate among Indian states in the reform years (Ray, 2002; Kumar, 2004). A common thread in most of these studies is that they have considered only the organized segment of the manufacturing sector[1]. Only a small number of studies have analysed productivity trends in the unorganized manufacturing sector (Unni et al, 2000; Mukherjee, 2004). The impact of reforms on TFP growth has been addressed in the work by Unni et al (2000) and it was found that TFP growth in the unorganized manufacturing sector declined in the reforms period. To our knowledge, the productivity performance of the unorganized manufacturing sector in the Indian states before and after the reform has not been subject to rigorous analysis. This paper attempts to fill this gap.

The main purpose of this study is to analyze productivity growth, technical efficiency and technical change in the unorganized manufacturing sector in fifteen major Indian states for the years 1978-79 to 2000-01[2]. The study also compares the performance of the sector across the Indian states in the reforms period with that in the pre-reforms period. The period up to 1989-90 is considered as pre-reforms period and the subsequent period is regarded as reforms period[3]. Data for the study come from the nationwide surveys of the unorganized manufacturing sector conducted by the National Sample Survey Organization (NSSO). To measure levels of technical efficiency of the sector in each state for each of the sample years, a non-parametric approach called Data Envelopment Analysis (DEA) is used. Further, we use the Malmquist multi-factor productivity indexes to compare the performance of the sector in each state in terms of multi-factor productivity growth before and after the reforms. It may be noted that the non-parametric approach has used to examine the effect of reforms on the organized manufacturing productivity in India (see Ray, 2002 and Kumar, 2004). We are not aware of any study that has used a non-parametric approach such as DEA to analyze productivity growth in the Indian unorganized manufacturing sector, especially at the sub-national level.

The scheme of the paper is as follows: section 2 discusses the relevant literature on the trends in productivity in the unorganized manufacturing sector in India. Section 3 discusses the methodology, database and variables used for the study. The relative position of the selected states in the Indian economy and in the unorganized manufacturing sector is explained in section 4. In section 5, we discuss the empirical results. Section 6 provides the summary and concluding remarks.

SELECTIVE REVIEW OF LITERATURE

As mentioned above, there are very few studies that have analyzed the trends in productivity in the unorganized manufacturing sector in India. Goldar and Mitra (1999), using the 45th and 51st rounds of NSSO data, estimated the total factor productivity (TFP) growth for the unorganized manufacturing sector between 1989-90 and 1994-95. However, they have confined their analysis to own-account manufacturing enterprises (OAMEs) and non-directory manufacturing enterprises (NDMEs) in the rural and urban areas[4]. The study did not find any growth in TFP either in OAMEs or NDMEs in the rural areas whereas the TFP reported a moderate growth in the OAMEs and a decline in the NDMEs in urban areas. Unni *et. al.* (2000) compared the productivity performance of the organized and unorganized manufacturing sectors in India before and after the introduction of economic reforms. They observed that the unorganized sector has witnessed positive labour and capital productivity only during the late 1980s. According to the study, the total factor productivity grew at a faster rate in the organized manufacturing sector compared with the unorganized manufacturing sector during the period 1978-95. The TFP growth in the unorganized manufacturing sector peaked in the initial phase of the pre-reforms period (1978-85) and tapered off in the reforms period. Bhalla (2001) computed TFP growth in the unorganized manufacturing sector for two periods, 1984-85 to 1989-90 and 1989-90 to 1994-95. The study reported a positive TFP growth in NDMEs in the rural areas and a high negative TFP growth in DMEs in the urban areas in the first period. The growth in TFP in the second period was negative in both types of enterprises in urban and rural areas. Mukherjee (2004) made an attempt to identify the important determinants of productivity level in unorganized manufacturing enterprises. The study argued that technological upgradation, better access to resources and inputs, and general structure of the economy play an important role in determining the productivity level of the enterprises. The study by Raj and Duraisamy (2005), using partial factor productivity ratios, examined the productivity performance of the sector for the period 1984-85 to 1994-95. The study found that the enterprises in the sector have utilized the resources more efficiently despite a fall in the number of enterprises, employment and fixed capital stock.

The main reason for the dearth of studies on productivity in the unorganized manufacturing sector is perhaps the inadequacy of data on this sector. Despite this limitation, a number of studies have emerged in the recent times as is evident from the literature reviewed above. However, these studies have examined the unorganized manufacturing productivity either at the sectoral or industry levels. To our knowledge, the productivity performance of the unorganized manufacturing sector at the sub-national level in the reforms period has not been examined except for a study by Unni et.al, (2000) which is, however, confined to the all-India level and for the state of Gujarat. Hence, in this study, we have made an attempt to look at the productivity performance of the sector in 13 major Indian states. It is also important to know how the sector has been performing in these states in the reforms years in comparison with the pre-reforms years. Further, the study also identifies the possible source of total factor productivity growth (TFPG) in the unorganized manufacturing sector of Indian states by decomposing TFPG into efficiency change and technical change.

METHODOLOGY AND DATA SOURCES

Technical efficiency has received considerable attention in the economic literature in recent years. Technical efficiency is concerned with how closely the production unit operates to the frontier of the production possibility set. The historical roots of a rigorous approach to efficiency measurement can be traced to the works of Koopmans (1951), Debreu (1951) and Farrell (1957) who used the concepts of isoquant frontiers and production functions to define relative technical efficiency as the firm's (any unit of observation) "distance" from a production frontier built with observed data from input-output combinations.

A variety of approaches, parametric and non-parametric, have been developed in literature to measure efficiency (see Kalirajan and Shand, 1999 for detailed survey). In parametric models, one specifies an explicit functional form for the frontier and econometrically estimates the parameters using sample data for inputs and output, and hence the accuracy of the derived technical efficiency estimates is sensitive to the functional form specified. In contrast, the method of Data Envelopment Analysis (DEA) introduced by Charnes, Cooper and Rhodes (CCR) (1978) and further generalized by Banker, Charnes and Copper (BCC) (1984) offers a non-parametric alternative to parametric frontier production function analysis. The advantage of the method is that it is parameter free, and it envelops observed input-output data without requiring apriori specification of functional forms. A production frontier is empirically constructed using linear programming methods from observed input-output data of sample firms. Efficiency of firms is then measured in terms of how far they are from the frontier.

DEA can be either input-orientated or output-orientated. In the input-orientated case, the DEA method defines the frontier by seeking the maximum possible proportional reduction in input usage, with output levels held constant, for each state while in the output-orientated case, the DEA method seeks the maximum proportional increase in output production, with input levels held fixed. The output-and input-oriented measures provide equivalent measures of technical efficiency when constant returns to scale exist (Fare and Lovell, 1978). In this paper, we have subscribed to the output-oriented measure.

Frontier functions and technical-efficiency measures can be compared over time by means of the Malmquist index. Malmquist productivity indexes were first introduced into the literature by Caves, Christensen, and Diewert (1982) and were empirically applied by Fare, Grosskopf, Norris and Zhang (FGNZ) (1994). FGNZ developed a non-parametric approach for estimating the Malmquist indexes, and showed that the component distance function could be derived using a DEA-like linear program method. They also decomposed total factor productivity indexes into efficiency change and technical change components. According to them, the total factor productivity may grow by more efficient utilization of resources or by technical change. Nishimizu and Page (1982) in their paper argued that it is very important to study the distinction between technical change and efficiency change particularly in the context of developing countries. Following FGNZ, the output-oriented Malmquist TFP change index between period *s* (the base period) and period *t* (the terminal period) is given by

$$m_0(y_s, x_s, y_t, x_t) = \frac{d_0^s(y_t, x_t)}{d_0^s(y_s, x_s)} \left[\frac{d_0^s(y_t, x_t)}{d_0^t(y_t, x_t)} \frac{d_0^s(y_s, x_s)}{d_0^t(y_s, x_s)} \right]^{1/2} \quad (1)$$

where the notation $d_0^s(y_t, x_t)$ represents the distance from the period *t* observation to the period *s* technology. A value of m_0 greater than one will indicate positive TFP growth from period *s* to period *t* while a value less than one indicates a TFP growth decline. In equation (1), the term outside the square bracket measures the output-oriented measure of Farrell technical efficiency between period *s* and period *t* and the term inside measures technical change, which is the geometric mean of the shift in the technology between the two periods. In other words, TFP growth can be decomposed as,

TFP Growth = Technical Efficiency Change (Catching up Effect) × Technical Change (Frontier Effect)

This study assumes constant returns to scale (CRS) technology to estimate the above distance functions so as to obtain accurate measure of TFP index (Grifell-Tatje and Lovell, 1995)[5]. In any case, the assumption of CRS seems to be appropaiate when applying the Malmquist index at state level, while in the case of plants such an assumption could be problematic. We have used the linear programming (LP) technique called DEA to calculate the distance functions[6]. This requires solving of four LPs for each DMU. Overall, for 13 states and 5 time periods, 260 LPs are solved. The four LPs to be solved for each DMU are:

$$\left[d_0^t(y_t, x_t)\right]^{-1} = \max_{\phi\lambda} \phi,$$
$$st \quad -\phi y_{it} + Y_t\lambda \geq 0,$$
$$x_{it} - X_t\lambda \geq 0,$$
$$\lambda \geq 0,$$

$$\left[d_0^s(y_s, x_s)\right]^{-1} = \max_{\phi\lambda} \phi,$$
$$st \quad -\phi y_{is} + Y_s\lambda \geq 0,$$
$$x_{is} - X_s\lambda \geq 0,$$
$$\lambda \geq 0,$$

$$\left[d_0^t(y_s, x_s)\right]^{-1} = \max_{\phi\lambda} \phi,$$
$$st \quad -\phi y_{is} + Y_t\lambda \geq 0,$$
$$x_{is} - X_t\lambda \geq 0,$$
$$\lambda \geq 0,$$

and

$$\left[d_0^s(y_t, x_t)\right]^{-1} = \max_{\phi\lambda} \phi,$$
$$st \quad -\phi y_{it} + Y_s\lambda \geq 0,$$
$$x_{it} - X_s\lambda \geq 0,$$
$$\lambda \geq 0,$$

where y_{it} is a MXI vector of output quantities for the *i*-th industry in the *t*-th year;

x_{it} is a KXI vector of input quantities for the *i*-th industry in the *t*-th year;

Y_t is a NXM matrix of output quantities for all N industries in the *t*-th year;

X_t is a NXK matrix of input quantities for all N industries in the *t*-th year;

λ is a NXI vector of weights and ϕ is a scalar.

The efficiency scores and Malmquist indexes are computed based on National Sample Survey data for 15 states pertaining to five time periods, 1978-79, 1984-85, 1989-90, 1994-95 and 2000-01. In this paper, the unorganized manufacturing sector is modeled as an industry producing a scalar output measured by the gross value added at constant prices by employing the factor inputs, labour and capital. Using gross value added at constant prices to represent output is a common practice in the Indian empirical literature (Ray, 2002; Unel, 2003; Goldar, 2004; Kumar, 2004). Data on gross fixed assets from the NSSO reports are used to measure capital input[7]. Employment refers to the number of workers in the sector including full-time and part-time, hired and other workers. The data on value added and value of fixed assets are deflated by constructing price deflators using net state domestic product (NSDP) figures pertaining to the unregistered manufacturing sector with 1993-94 as the base[8].

Before proceeding to the analysis, it is important to mention some of the limitations of the study. The present study suffers from various data limitations such as the lack of time series data for the sector and related problems with the price deflators and the measurement of capital stock. The focus of the study has been exclusively on efficiency and productivity. The paper could not address the welfare consequences of the reforms within the limited scope of this paper.

INDIAN STATES: WHERE DO THEY STAND?

In this section, we present some stylized facts about the selected states in the Indian economy and Indian unorganized manufacturing sector.

In the Indian Economy

As mentioned earlier, our analysis is based on 13 major Indian states and they together account for 91 per cent of India's population and around 87 per cent of industrial output in the country. The basic characteristics of these states in terms of selected indicators such as share in GDP, per capita state income, annual average growth of state income, share in Indian manufacturing, share of manufacturing to GDP, and annual average growth of real manufacturing value added are given in Table 1. We observe marked differentials across the states in per capita income, share in Indian manufacturing value added and share or manufacturing to state income. Real per capita income of the rich or high income state (Punjab) is around five times higher than the poorest state, Bihar. Similarly, in the richer states of Maharashtra, Gujarat, and Tamil Nadu, the manufacturing sector's contribution to Indian manufacturing sector is high with the notable exception of Punjab, where the agricultural sector is relatively well developed compared to the other states. The former three states are the most industrialized as revealed by the share of manufacturing to state income. Further, they have registered the fastest growth in real manufacturing value added in the 1990s. The states such as Orissa and Bihar recorded a poor performance in all the indicators considered here for the analysis.

Table 1
Select Characteristics of some Selected Indian States

States	*Share of GSDP to GDP in 2001(%)*	*Per capita real GSDP in 2001 (1993-94 prices) in '000*	*Annual average growth of real GSDP (%) in the 90s (1993-94 to 2000-01)*	*Share of manufacturing to Indian manufacturing in 2000-01(%)*	*Share of manufacturing to GSDP in 2000-01 (%)*	*Annual average growth of real manufacturing value added (%) in the 90s (1993-94 to 2000-01)*
Andhra Pradesh	7.10	11.1	5.3	6.41	15.51	6.2
Bihar	2.53	3.6	4.05	0.77	5.19	5.4
Gujarat	6.42	15.1	5.98	12.80	34.27	8.32
Karnataka	5.86	13.2	7.92	5.93	17.38	7.03
Kerala	3.22	12.1	5.14	2.24	11.94	4.61
Madhya Pradesh	3.97	7.8	4.2	4.25	18.39	7.67
Maharashtra	13.99	17.2	5.75	22.04	27.07	6.64
Orissa	1.89	6.1	3.22	1.04	9.47	-0.53
Punjab	3.55	17.4	4.95	3.30	15.99	5.68
Rajasthan	4.24	9.0	6.58	3.31	13.42	7.74
Tamil Nadu	7.46	14.3	6.04	10.31	23.75	3.71
Uttar Pradesh	9.12	6.5	4.17	7.77	14.65	4.29
West Bengal	7.20	10.7	6.88	6.70	16.00	6.45

Note: Growth rates are estimated using semi-log regression equation, $\ln Y = b_1 + b_0 X$
Source: National Account Statistics, EPW Research Foundation, 2002.

In the Indian Unorganized Manufacturing Sector

This sub-section provides a discussion on the relative positions of selected Indian states in the unorganized manufacturing sector in terms of gross value added, fixed capital stock, employment and number of enterprises (Table 2). In 2000-01, the combined share of 13 selected states (in all India totals) in gross value added and fixed capital stock was about 80 per cent. In terms of number of enterprises and workers, they together occupied a share of around 88 per cent. Maharashtra was the leading contributor to value added and fixed capital stock followed by Uttar Pradesh and Tamil Nadu. The largest contribution to employment and enterprises came from West Bengal. Other states that followed West Bengal were Uttar Pradesh and Tamil Nadu. It is interesting to note here that the share of Maharashtra in gross value added and fixed capital stock is more than that of the share enjoyed by West Bengal and Uttar Pradesh but the latter states accommodate approximately twice the number of workers and enterprises in the sector of Maharashtra.

EMPIRICAL RESULTS

Given the importance of productivity growth for improvements in the standard of living and quality of life, aggregate labour productivity trends are closely monitored by economists and policy makers. It is the most commonly reported as well as the most widely understood measure of

Table 2
Relative Importance of the Major States in Indian Unorganized Manufacturing: 2000-01

State	*Expressed as a percentage of all India total*			
	Gross Value Added	*Fixed Capital Stock*	*Employment*	*Enterprises*
Andhra Pradesh	6.5	4.9	8.9	9.4
Tamil Nadu	10.2	10.4	9.3	9.0
Karnataka	5.0	5.1	5.5	6.1
Kerala	2.9	3.1	2.9	3.0
Maharashtra	12.8	12.9	8.0	7.3
Gujarat	7.7	8.5	4.0	3.2
Madhya Pradesh	2.6	2.8	4.0	4.4
Orissa	1.9	1.4	5.9	5.8
Punjab	3.8	6.0	2.0	2.0
Rajasthan	3.8	4.2	3.1	3.7
Uttar Pradesh	10.5	10.4	14.6	13.5
West Bengal	10.7	6.6	15.8	16.3
Bihar	4.0	2.6	4.1	4.8
Total of the above states	82.4	78.9	88.1	88.5
All India	4116123*	4951686*	37081#	17024#

Note: '*'indicates that figures are in Rs. Lakhs and '#' indicates that the figures are in thousands.
Source: NSSO survey on the Unorganized Manufacturing Sector, 2000-01.

productivity (Ray, 2004). Balakrishnan (2004) argues that ignoring changes in labour productivity reflects an inadequate concern for potential increase in consumption. In the present study, we first report the trends in levels of labour productivity (at constant 1993-94 prices) for the period 1978 to 2001. The productivity of labour increased from Rs. 4,728 in 1978-79 to Rs 11,100 in 2000-01 (Figure 1). In the pre-reforms period (average of three rounds, 1978-79, 1984-85 and 1989-90), it was Rs. 6549 and increased to Rs. 9200 in the reforms period (average of three rounds, 1989-90, 1994-95 and 2000-01). Considering the movement of these figures over the period under study, one may be tempted to conclude that the reform process has positively contributed to the productivity performance of the sector, measured using output per worker. An alternative question to ask would be whether the growth in labour productivity has accelerated after the reforms[9]. Therefore, we computed the per annum growth in labor productivity, which is reported in Table 3. Labour productivity showed considerable fluctuation in year-to-year rate of growth but the growth rate registered in the reforms period (3.3 per cent per annum) was lower than that registered in the pre-reforms period (4.6 per cent per annum). Yet again, based on the measure of labour productivity growth, it would be incorrect to conclude that the reforms have had an adverse impact on the productivity performance of the sector. Following Ray (2002), it may be merely due to the fact that when the *productivity level* becomes larger the *proportionate rate* of growth slows down.

Figure 1
Average Labour Productivity Levels

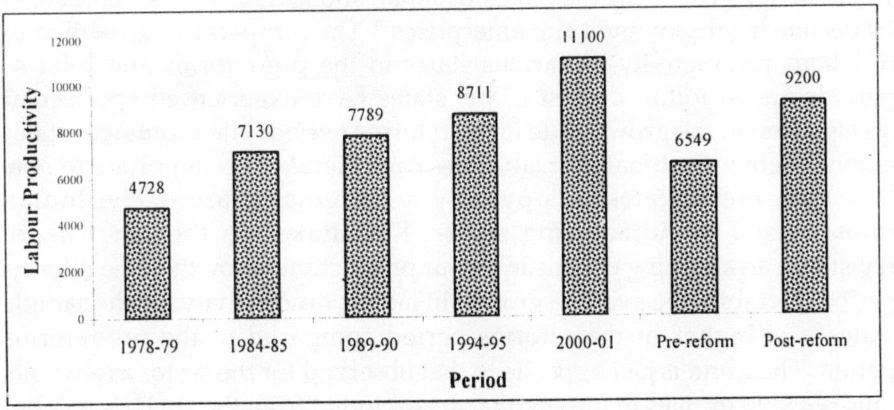

Table 3
Labour Productivity Growth: All India

Period	*Growth inLabour Productivity*
1978-85	7.1
1985-90	1.8
1990-95	2.3
1995-01	4.1
Pre-reforms	4.6
Reforms	3.3

Note: Pre-reforms corresponds to the period, 1978-79 to 1989-90, and reforms corresponds to the period, 1989-90 to 2000-01.

Table 4 shows the levels and changes in labour productivity for individual states; levels are reported for two time points, 1978-79 and 2000-01, and changes in labour productivity are estimated for the periods before and after the reforms. It is found that all the states except Orissa and Rajasthan have registered an increase in labour productivity levels. In 2000-01, the output per worker was higher in the states of Gujarat, Punjab and Maharashtra whereas Orissa, Madhya Pradesh, West Bengal and Uttar Pradesh registered the lowest labour productivity levels. Turning to the growth in labour productivity, it exhibited considerable variation across the states. Excepting Rajasthan, all the states have registered a positive growth in labour productivity in the reforms period. Comparison of the growth rates across the states should be made keeping in mind the large differences in the base period level of labour productivity in the states. Growth rates are generally found high in states that start with relatively low levels of labour productivity at the beginning of the period and vice versa. Thus, states like Bihar, Punjab, Orissa, Kerala and Andhra Pradesh, which all had low levels of labour productivity to start with, reported relatively higher growth rates. The study also found that the labour productivity growth in the states of Bihar and Orissa was accompanied by decline in employment and enterprises[10]. The comparative growth rates of labour productivity of various states in the pre-reforms and reforms periods are as follows. Most of the states have experienced spectacular acceleration in the growth rate in the reforms period. The prominent states among them were Bihar, Punjab, Orissa and Kerala. It is important to note here that these states occupy only a marginal share in the Indian unorganized manufacturing sector. Karnataka, on the other hand, registered an alarming decline in labour productivity growth in the reforms period. Notably, the average growth in labour productivity for the sample states was higher in the reforms period compared to the pre-reforms period. The trend is just opposite to that observed for the sector as a whole. This possibly implies that states that are excluded from the analysis account for the observed decline in labour productivity growth in the reforms period.

Table 4
Levels and Growth of Labour Productivity

States	*APL (in rupees)*		*Growth in APL*	
	1978-79	*2000-01*	*Pre-reforms*	*Reforms*
Andhra Pradesh	3416	8087	2.0	6.0
Bihar	3566	10708	-3.6	14.7
Gujarat	15457	21234	1.4	1.5
Karnataka	4979	10072	6.0	0.6
Kerala	4969	11029	0.4	7.1
Madhya Pradesh	5404	7089	-0.6	3.1
Maharashtra	10970	17740	3.2	1.2
Orissa	4406	3583	-8.7	7.5
Punjab	4976	21024	4.3	9.3
Rajasthan	19347	13596	-3.0	-0.1
Tamil Nadu	11025	12152	-1.5	2.4
Uttar Pradesh	4644	7985	3.0	2.0
West Bengal	11152	7536	-5.5	2.1
Average for the sample states	8024	11680	0.06	3.41
India	4728	11100	4.64	3.27

Note: Pre-reforms corresponds to the period, 1978-79 to 1989-90, and reforms corresponds to the period, 1989-90 to 2000-01.

One problem with a partial productivity measure like output per worker is that it fails to incorporate the contribution from other inputs such as capital and material inputs used in the production process. According to Farrell (1957: 11), labour productivity is a patently unsatisfactory measure and may indeed have unfortunate effects on economic policy. It is also argued that a rapid growth in a partial factor productivity measure could be due to a rapid growth in an omitted input category and thus could be quite misleading (Diewert, 2003). Similarly, these measures are incapable of identifying the causal factor accounting for observed productivity growth. This problem could be resolved by analyzing total factor productivity growth, which encompasses the effect not only of technical progress but also of better utilization of capacities, learning-by-doing, and improved skills of labour (Ahluwalia, 1991). Therefore, a measure of total or multi-factor productivity change is much more useful and informative. The study has calculated the change in total factor productivity using the Malmquist productivity index. The results are reported in Table 5. Unlike the measure of output per labour, the Malmquist index did not show a steady upward trend period after period. In fact, there was a productivity decline during the period 1978-85 followed by a growth in productivity during 1985-90. The productivity growth decelerated again in 1990-95 and rose in the late 1990s. Notwithstanding such ups and downs, the average annual rate of productivity growth, however, was higher during the reforms years than in the pre-reforms years. The Malmquist total factor productivity increased from a negative growth rate of 1 per cent per year in the pre-reforms years to 0.7 per cent per year in the reforms era.

Table 5
Malmquist Total Factor Productivity Growth: All India

Period	*Growth in TFP per annum*
1978-85	-6.3
1985-90	7.8
1990-95	0.4
1995-01	1.7
Pre-reforms	-1.0
Reforms	0.7

Note: Pre-reforms corresponds to the period, 1978-79 to 1989-90, and Reforms corresponds to the period, 1989-90 to 2000-01

Table 6 presents the TFP growth rates of the Indian states measured using the Malmquist multifactor productivity index. Compared with the pre-reforms period, 8 out of 13 states have reported acceleration in the rate of productivity change in the reforms period. In Karnataka and Maharashtra, the direction of productivity change reversed from increase to decline after the reforms. For Andhra Pradesh, the growth rate declined but remained positive. Madhya Pradesh and West Bengal recorded a further decline in TFP in the reforms period compared with the pre-reforms period. On the other hand, Tamil Nadu, Kerala, Gujarat, Orissa, Punjab, Rajasthan, Uttar Pradesh and Bihar switched from productivity decline to productivity growth. Growth rates were generally found higher in those states that start with relatively low levels of TFP at the beginning of the period and vice versa. Thus, states like Bihar, Punjab, Orissa, Andhra Pradesh, and Kerala, which all had low TFP levels to start with, showed relatively high growth rate. In sum, the overall evidence from the Malmquist indexes was that in most of the states the rate of productivity growth had improved after the reforms.

Table 6
Average Annual Rates of Malmquist Multi-Factor Productivity Growth

States	*Pre-reforms*	*Reforms*	*Overall*
Andhra Pradesh	1.8	1.3	1.3
Tamil Nadu	-1.9	0.0	1.5
Karnataka	3.8	-0.9	-0.8
Kerala	-2.1	0.6	-0.8
Maharashtra	1.1	-0.9	0.3
Gujarat	-0.6	0.2	-0.3
Madhya Pradesh	-0.3	-0.6	-0.3
Orissa	-2.6	1.0	-1.0
Punjab	-1.9	6.1	1.2
Rajasthan	-2.6	0.1	-1.3
Uttar Pradesh	-1.0	0.0	-0.7
West Bengal	-0.9	-1.7	-1.2
Bihar	-3.1	6.4	0.2
Mean	-1.0	0.7	-0.2

Note: Pre-reforms corresponds to the period, 1978-79 to 1989-90, and Reforms corresponds to the period, 1989-90 to 2000-01.

Table 7
Average Level of Technical Efficiency (State-Wise)

States	*Pre-reforms*	*Reforms*	*Overall*
Andhra Pradesh	0.576	0.735	0.659
Bihar	0.452	0.752	0.624
Gujarat	1.000	1.000	1.000
Karnataka	0.697	0.768	0.729
Kerala	0.634	0.747	0.700
Madhya Pradesh	0.692	0.743	0.740
Maharashtra	0.831	1.000	0.899
Orissa	0.567	0.678	0.634
Punjab	0.612	0.867	0.765
Rajasthan	0.771	0.823	0.804
Tamil Nadu	0.779	0.858	0.830
Uttar Pradesh	0.689	0.737	0.726
West Bengal	1.000	1.000	1.000
Mean	0.715	0.824	0.778

Note: Pre-reforms corresponds to the period, 1978-79 to 1989-90, and Reforms corresponds to the period, 1989-90 to 2000-01.

An important factor contributing to productivity growth (decline) is improvement (decrease) in the level of technical efficiency. If a firm becomes more efficient over time, its average productivity rises. Table 7 reports average levels of technical efficiency for the pre-reforms and reforms years. Means are given for the "all" as well as for each of the 13 states. If we report that the average efficiency score in the pre-reforms period is 0.715, we mean that these states in the Indian unorganized manufacturing sector are producing, on average, 71.5 per cent of the output that could be potentially produced using the same input quantities[11]. Our results show that Gujarat and West Bengal are consistently defining the frontier in all the periods. Maharashtra entered into the set of frontier states in the reforms period. A look at the technical efficiency scores reveals that all the states except Gujarat and West Bengal have reported an increase in technical efficiency. For the states, Gujarat and West Bengal, there was no evidence of technical efficiency either before or after the reforms. On the whole, Bihar recorded the lowest average level of technical efficiency in the pre-reforms period while it was the lowest in Orissa in the reforms period.

Table 8
Decomposition of Malmquist Productivity Growth: Annual Average Growth Rates

States	*Pre-reforms Period*			*Reforms Period*		
	Technical Change	*Efficiency Change*	*MALM*	*Technical Change.*	*Efficiency Change*	*MALM*
Andhra Pradesh	-0.5	2.4	1.8	-1.2	2.8	1.3
Tamil Nadu	-1.1	-0.9	-1.9	-1.0	1.1	0.0
Karnataka	-1.4	6.1	3.8	-1.1	0.3	-0.9
Kerala	-0.9	-1.3	-2.1	-1.2	2.1	0.6
Maharashtra	-0.7	2.0	1.1	-0.9	0.0	-0.9
Gujarat	-0.6	0.0	-0.6	0.2	0.0	0.2
Madhya Pradesh	-1.6	1.5	-0.3	-0.8	0.3	-0.6
Orissa	0.1	-2.7	-2.6	-2.4	4.6	1.0
Punjab	-0.7	-1.3	-1.9	0.3	5.7	6.1
Rajasthan	-0.6	-2.2	-2.6	-0.9	1.1	0.1
Uttar Pradesh	-1.1	0.1	-1.0	-0.6	0.7	0.0
West Bengal	-0.9	0.0	-0.9	-1.7	0.0	-1.7
Bihar	0.1	-3.2	-3.1	-1.4	9.3	6.4
Mean	-0.8	-0.2	-1.0	-1.0	1.9	0.7

Note: Pre-reforms corresponds to the period, 1978-79 to 1989-90, and Reforms corresponds to the period, 1989-90 to 2000-01.
MALM implies Malmquist total factor productivity growth.

Having examined the direction of productivity change in the pre-reforms and reforms periods, it is essential to find out the main cause of the increase in productivity in the reforms period. The unorganized manufacturing sector can improve the level of total factor productivity either by improving technical efficiency (catching-up) and/or by improving the level of technology (shift in the production frontier). The component measures of total factor productivity, efficiency change and technical change, show that efficiency has been the main contributor to the success of total factor productivity in the reforms period (Table 8). The average technical efficiency change was 1.9 per cent per year, while the technical change registered a negative growth (-1.0 per cent per year).

This implies that the conversion of productivity decline, recorded in the pre-reforms period, to productivity growth in the reforms period was achieved mainly through the improvement in technical efficiency. On the other hand, technological regress has further accelerated in the reforms period. This suggests that, for the sample states, absence of technical progress has been the main constraint to the achievement of high levels of total factor productivity during 1990-2001. Our analysis across the Indian states shows that in 12 out of the 13 states efficiency change has outperformed technical change. In fact, technical change was positive only in the state of Gujarat. This suggests that there is a growing urgency for sustained improvements in technology, which can create an overwhelming effect on productivity growth in the future.

CONCLUSION

One of the major problems confronting the Indian unorganized manufacturing sector is to increase the level of production through improvement in productivity, leaving the employment generating capacity of the sector untouched. In this paper, the efficiency and productivity performance of the unorganized manufacturing sector in the Indian states was gauged using Data Envelopment Analysis during both the pre-reforms and reforms periods. The findings of the study reflect that the annual rate of productivity growth has been higher in the reforms period as compared to the pre-reforms period. The decomposition of productivity growth into technical change and efficiency change reveals that the latter has played a major role in the reforms period. At the other end, the technological regress has been pronounced during the said period. Further, in productivity growth and efficiency aspects, a wide gap is noticed across the states. Therefore, it suggests that technological upgradation needs to be prioritized so as to improve growth in output of the unorganized sector. However, as argued by Mukherjee (2004), any technological up-gradation programme for the sector must keep in mind that the stress should not be on transformation to a capital-intensive technology, but towards evolution of innovative and adaptive technology for the enterprises in the sector.

ACKNOWLEDGEMENTS

The authors are grateful to P R Panchamukhi, and Mihir Kumar Mahapatra for comments on an earlier draft of this paper.

MAJOR DATA SOURCES

1. Domestic Product of States of India: 1960-61 to 2000-01, Economic and Political Weekly Research Foundation, Mumbai, June 2003.
2. Handbook of Statistics on Indian Economy, Reserve Bank of India, Mumbai (Various Issues).

3. National Account Statistics, 1950-51 to 2002-03, Economic and Political Weekly Research Foundation, Mumbai, December 2004.

4. Survey on the Unorganized Manufacturing Sector, National Sample Survey Organization, Ministry of Statistics and Programme Implementation, Government of India (Various Issues).

NOTES

1. Indian manufacturing sector is broadly classified into organized and unorganized sectors. Unorganized manufacturing sector comprises of units with less than 10 employees and units with 10 to 19 employees that do not use electric power. All other manufacturing activities are classified under organized manufacturing sector.

2. The states are Kerala, Tamil Nadu, Andhra Pradesh, Karnataka, Maharashtra, Gujarat, Madhya Pradesh, Orissa, Punjab, Rajasthan, Uttar Pradesh, West Bengal and Bihar. For the purpose of comparison, figures for some of the newly formed states have been merged with their parent states (undivided state).

3. These cut-off years were selected based on the availability of data in the unorganized manufacturing sector. However, 1989-90 can be considered as the last year of the pre-reforms period.

4. The unorganised manufacturing sector is comprised of three types of enterprises, Own Account Manufacturing Enterprises (OAMEs), Non-Directory Manufacturing Enterprises (NDMEs), and Directory Manufacturing Enterprises (DMEs). The distinction between these is that where as the OAMEs employ only family labour, the NDMEs and the DMEs employ hired labourers–the number of workers being less than six in the case of NDMEs and six or more in the case of DMEs.

5. Grifell-Tatje and Lovell (1995) showed that the traditional definition of the Malmquist productivity index incorrectly measures productivity change in the presence of variable returns to scale..... "in our judgment a new productivity index is required, one which scales the Malmquist productivity index by a term which accounts for returns to scale" (p. 174).

6. For estimation, we have used DEAP 2.1, a program for data envelopment analysis developed by Coelli (1996).

7. Following Salim and Kalirajan (1999) and Hossain and Karunaratne (2004), we argue that the use of gross figures to represent the capital stock can be justified in the case of developing countries such as India in general and unorganized manufacturing sector in particular on the ground that capital stocks are more often used at approximately constant levels of efficiency for a period far beyond the accounting life measured by normal depreciation until it is eventually discarded or sold for scrap. Thus even though the value of old machine declines, it need not lead to any decline in the current services of the capital equipment. In addition, we believe that if there is any distortion in the capital input, it would be distorted uniformly in all the states. Therefore, the relative performance of states should not be seriously affected by this shortcoming.

8. At the state level, we were not able to obtain a series of the state's fixed capital formation. Hence we have used the state domestic product for the unorganized manufacturing sector to deflate fixed capital stock. The NSDP figures for the unorganized manufacturing sector of Indian states are taken from the report on Domestic Products of States of India: 1960-61 to 2000-01 (EPWRF, 2003).
9. Labour productivity implies the average productivity of labour, computed by dividing gross value added by number of workers.
10. Study by Trivedi (2004) on the inter-state differences in productivity movements in the organized manufacturing sector reported a high productivity growth of the sector in Bihar. However, the study found that the high growth has been mainly achieved by joblessness. Due to shortage of space, we have not reported the growth rates of enterprises and employment in the paper. However, detailed tables of growth rate of output and employment can be obtained from the authors on request.
11. As we have not adjusted the data for difference in labour quality, depreciation in the capital stock and so on, the figure should be approached with caution.

REFERENCES

Aghion, P., Burgess, R., Redding, S. and Zilibotti, **F.** (2003), "The Unequal Effects of Liberalisation: Theory and Evidence from India" *(http://econ.lse.ac.uk/staff/rburgess/wp/abrz031002.pdf)*.

Ahluwalia, I.J. (1991), Productivity Growth in Indian Manufacturing, Oxford University Press, New Delhi, India.

Balakrishnan, Pulapre (2004), "Measuring Productivity in Manufacturing Sector," *Economic and Political Weekly*, 39, ?: 1465-71.

Balakrishnan, Pulapre, K. Pushpangadan, and M. Suresh Babu (2000), "Trade Liberalisation and Productivity Growth in Manufacturing: Evidence from Firm-Level Panel Data," Economic and Political Weekly, 35, No. 41: 3679–82.

Banker, R., A. Charnes and W.W. Cooper (1984), Some models for Estimating Technical and Scale Inefficiencies in Data Envelopment Analysis, Management Science 30, No. 9: 1078-1092.

Bhalla, S. (2001), "Assessing the Quality of Employment Growth Using National Sample Survey Data", paper presented to a Conference on 'Understanding Human Development through National Surveys' at Pune, India.

Brahmananda, P.R. (1982), Productivity in the Indian Economy: Rising Inputs for Falling Outputs, Himalaya Publishing House, Mumbai.

Caves, D.W., L.R. Christensen, and W.E. Diewert (1982), The Economic Theory of Index Numbers and the Measurement of Input, Output and Productivity, Econometrica, 50, No. 6: 1393-1414.

Charnes, A., W.W. Cooper, and E. Rhodes (1978), Measuring the Efficiency of Decision making units, European Journal of Operational Research 2, No. 6: 429-444.

Coelli, T. (1996), "A Guide to DEAP Version 2.1: A Data Envelopment Analysis (Computer) Program," Working Paper No. 96/08, Centre for Efficiency and Productivity Analysis (CEPA), University of New England, Australia.

Debreu, G. (1951), "The Coefficient of Resource Utilization," Econometrica, 19, No. 3: 273–292.

Dholakia, R.H. and B.H. Dholakia (1994), 'Total Factor Productivity Growth in Indian Manufacturing', *Economic and Political Weekly*, 29 , No. ?: 342-344.

Diewert, W.E. (2003), "Services and the New Economy: Data Needs and Challenges", Discussion Paper No. 03-09, Department of Economics, University of British Columbia (UBC), Vancouver, Canada.

Fare R., Grosskopf S., Norris M., Zhang Z. (1994), "Productivity Growth, Technical Progress, and Efficiency Change in Industrialized Countries," American Economic Review, 84, No.1: 66-83.

Fare R. and Lovell C.A. Knox (1978), "Measuring the Technical Efficiency of Production," Journal of Economic Theory, 19, 150-162.

Farrell, M.J. (1957), "The Measurement of Productive Efficiency," Journal of the Royal Statistical Society, 120, No. 3: 253-290.

Goldar, Bishwanath (2004), "Productivity Trends in Indian Manufacturing in the Pre-and Post-Reform Periods," Working Paper No. 137, Indian Council for Research on International Economic Relations (ICRIER), New Delhi, India.

Goldar, Biswanath and Kumari, Anitha (2003), "Import Liberalization and Productivity Growth in the Indian Manufacturing Industries in the 1990s," The Developing Economies, 41, No. 4: 436-60.

Goldar, Biswanath and Arup Mitra (1999), 'Productivity Growth in Informal Manufacturing Sector in India', presented to a Workshop on 'Measurement of Productivity in India', at New Delhi, India.

Grifell-Tatje, E. and C.A.K. Lovell (1995), "A Note on the Malmquist Productivity Index," Economic Letters, 47, No. 2: 169-175.

Hossain M.A. and Karunaratne N.D. (2004), "Trade Liberalization and Technical Efficiency: Evidence from Bangladesh Manufacturing Industries," The Journal of Development Studies, 40, No. 3: 87-114.

Kalirajan K.P. and Shand R.T. (1999), Frontier Production Functions and Technical Efficiency Measures, Journal of Economic Surveys, 13, No. 2: 149–172.

Koopmans, T.C. (1951), "An analysis of Production as an Efficient Combination of Activities," in T.C. Koopmans, ed., *Activity Analysis of Production and Allocation, Cowles Commission for Research in Economics*, Monograph No. 13, John-Wiley and Sons, New York.

Krishna, Pravin, and Devashish Mitra (1998), "Trade Liberalization, Market Discipline and Productivity Growth: New Evidence from India," Journal of Development Economics, 56, No. 2: 447–62.

Kumar, Surender (2004), "A Decomposition of Total Factor Productivity Growth: A Regional Analysis of Indian Industrial Manufacturing Growth," Working Paper No. 22, National Institute of Public Finance and Policy (NIPFP), New Delhi, India.

Mukherjee, Dipa (2004), "Productivity in the Small Manufacturing Enterprises: Determinants and Policy Issues", The Indian Journal of Labour Economics, 47, No. 4: 913-927.

Nishimizu M. and J.M. Page Jr. (1982), "Total Factor Productivity Growth, Technological Progress and Technical Efficiency Change: Dimensions of Productivity Change in Yugoslavia, 1965-1978", The Economic Journal, 92, No. 368: 920-936.

Pattnayak, Sanja S. and S.M. Thangavelu (2003), "Economic Reform and Productivity Growth in Indian Manufacturing Industries: An Interaction of Technical Change and Scale Economies," Working Paper No. 0307, Department of Economics, National University of Singapore (NUS), Singapore.

Raj, Rajesh S.N. and Duraisamy, Malathy (2005), "Structure, Employment and Productivity Growth: Evidence from the Unorganised Manufacturing Sector in India, 1984/5-1994/5", Journal of International Business and Entrepreneurship, 11, No. 1:?,

Ray, Subash C. (1997), Regional Variations in Productivity Growth in Indian Manufacturing: A Nonparametric Analysis, *Journal of Quantitative Economics*, 13, No. 1: 73-94.

Ray, Subash C. (2002), Did India's Economic Reforms Improve Efficiency and Productivity? A Nonparametric Analysis of the Initial Evidence from Manufacturing, Indian Economic Review, 37, No. 1:23-57.

Salim, R.A. and Kalirajan, K.P. (1999), "Sources of Output Growth in Bangladesh food Processing Industries: A Decomposition Analysis", *The Developing Economies*, 37, No. 3: 247-269.

Trivedi, Pushpa (2004), An Inter-State Perspective on Manufacturing Productivity in India: 1980-81 to 2000-01, Indian Economic Review, 39, No. 1: 203-237.

Unel, Bulent (2003), "Productivity Trends in India's Manufacturing Sectors in the Last Two Decades," Working Paper No. 03/22, International Monetary Fund (IMF), USA.

Unni, Jeemol, Lalitha, N. and Rani, Uma (2000), "Economic Reforms and Productivity Trends in Indian Manufacturing," Working Paper No.119, Gujarat Institute of Development Research (GIDR), Ahmedabad, India.

Chapter - 8

Regulation of Power Sector in Orissa: An Evaluation

Md. Zakaria Siddiqui

INTRODUCTION

Orissa was one of the first states to bring in compressive reforms in the power sector. The objective of this paper is to analyse the impact of power sector reforms on the incentives for the firms involved in distribution of electricity. After the reform various studies have come up but none of them have tried to see the impact of power sector reforms in such objective manner. After the initiation of the reform there has been significant increase in the tariffs of electricity. Our purpose here is to see whether the tariff orders issued by the Orissa Electricity Regulatory Commission (OERC) have been able to restrict the opportunistic behaviour of the stakeholders.

The three important exogenous channels through which the cost of supply of electricity has experienced manifold increase in Orissa are:

- Increase in the required rate of return that utility can earn, from 3 per cent to 16 per cent.
- Artificial revaluation of assets of power sector by two times and
- Withdrawal of subsidy by the government.

These changes presumably have led to tariff hikes that have considerably affected the access to and affordability of electricity to households. It was thought that efficiency gains in the operation after initiation of reform would offset such increase in costs. But this could not be materialised as there were some endogenous factor within the reform model itself which led to increased cost of supply of power. The reform model was unable to target the serious ailments of the power sector in Orissa. The complex web of perverse incentives that existed in pre-reform era is still intact. Because of this, the generic problem of the power sector that is high T and D losses and low cash collection efficiency by the utility still persists (Siddiqui 2004 chapter 4 and 5).

What is Power Sector Reforms?

Power sector reforms in developing with initially having vertically integrated structure generally denotes three things:

1. The deintegration of publicly owned vertically integrated structures separate entities e.g.,
   - Generation
   - Transmission and
   - Distribution

   Initially the three segments are separated and then horizontal deintegration of potentially competitive segments i.e., Generation and Distribution are done to foster competition.
2. Privatisation of these separated units.
3. Appointment of independent regulatory body which sets the tariff and monitors the performance of the private operators.
4. Gradually introducing competition in potentially competitive segment, mainly generation

In Orissa first three steps have been completed, in the name competition, reform document stated that grant of generating plants will be based on competitive bidding. Orissa Electrcity Board was fragmented in the following manner (see Appendix for chronology of implemtation).

Figure 1
Process of Restructuring of Assets of OSEB

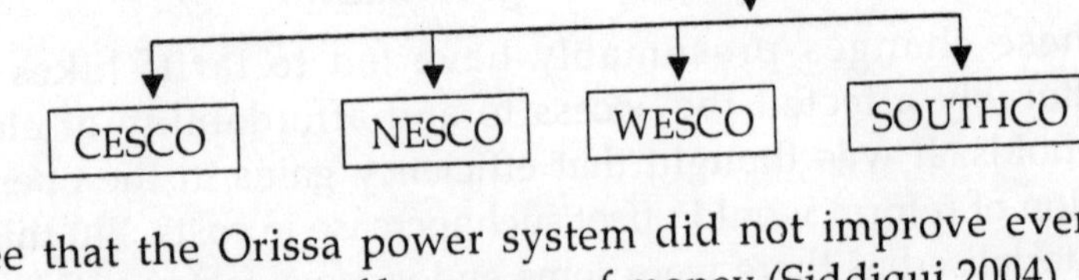

We see that the Orissa power system did not improve even after restructuring and injection of huge sum of money (Siddiqui 2004). One of the most important document through which most of the regulation comes out from the Orissa Electricity Regulatory Commission (OERC) like any other state level regulatory commission is tariff orders. In the process of making a tariff order the OERC goes through several complications. Main job of the regulators is to make the realistic assessment of cost and demand data provided by the licensees or companies under their jurisdiction. In this paper we examine the issues underlying such regulatory process.

In pre reform era the method of regulation was usually the Rate of Return Regulation (RORR) or 'cost plus' regulation as envisaged by the Electricity (supply) Act 1948 and the tariff was decided by the OSEB. In post reform scenario also the method of regulation has remained broadly RORR but it is the OERC which decides about the tariff through their tariff orders. The OERC for its regulatory activities was earlier guided by the Orissa Electricity Reform Act (OERA), 1995. But now it is guided by the Electricity Act 2003 along with OERA 1995. Based on the above law, the commission may change its method of regulation, if it feels that other forms of regulation may be more conducive to the ESI. Over the time we have seen that there is significant amount of variation in the method of regulation (from a pure RORR model to a mixture of Performance Based Regulation (PBR) and RORR).

This paper has five sections including introduction. The next section describes the process of tariff order, and third section discusses various issues underlying the tariff order while the fourth section provides some of the suggestions to improve the regulatory practice. Fifth section concludes.

MAKING OF TARIFF ORDER

Initially licensees are notified to produce an annual revenue requirement (ARR) proposal in front of the OERC. After licensee submits the ARR, the OERC notifies publicly in leading newspapers of the state inviting objections on the said ARR. If ARR does not have the required information, the OERC may again notify the licensee to provide such information. After the OERC has received the objections on ARR, it fixes a date of hearing when the objecting parties, the OERC members, and licensee or any other interested person can attend the proceedings. In hearing the objectors register their objections and the licensee is supposed to clarify or reply to those objections. After hearing all this, OERC finally gives the approval to what it feels justified on the basis of certain pre-decided norms. The document detailing the approval is called the Tariff Order. This process of finalisation of the Tariff Order generally takes around three months of time. The whole process may be summarised in the figure 2.

Figure 2
Process of Tariff order

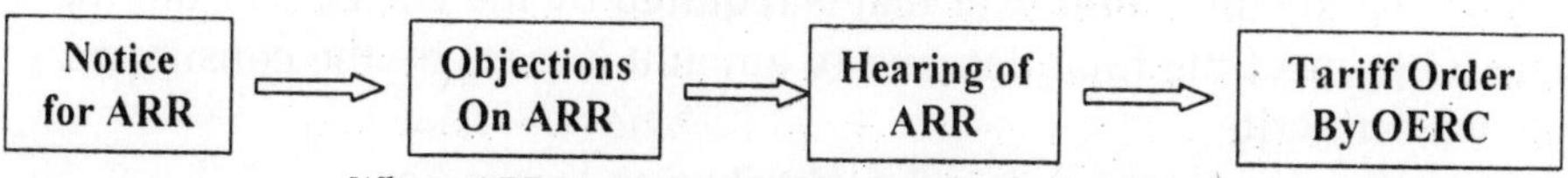

Where ARR is annual revenue requirement proposal

The experience of hearing process shows that the parties attending the hearing are interested in maximising their gain or minimising their loss. Though there is emphasis on penalising the inefficiency we may not be able to see, during eight years of regulatory experience any objector giving specific suggestions to reduce the overall cost of the system. The process of hearing by the OERC provides different interest group a platform to list their stakes. This could be a breeding ground for the public action. But till now we have never seen such happenings.

ISSUES UNDERLYING TARIFF ORDERS

Here our analysis is based on the Tariff orders given by the OERC for various years. This helps us to identify if there is any regulatory effectiveness. We try to address the major issues involved in tariff orders of bulk supply tariff (BST) and retail supply tariff (RST) order. For initial three years starting from 1996-97, the GRIDCO was responsible for both transmission and distribution of power. Except for the first year, it has always operated under the regulation of the OERC till date. Here we will examine the major changes, which occurred primarily due to regulations. Issues, which are central to discussion during hearings, are mainly to question the GRIDCO's and DISTCOs' proposal and suggestions to the OERC for better regulation, basically to reduce cost and thus tariff in the short run. What seems to be lacking in the process of hearing is that no individual or group came up with suggestion on improving the internal corporate structure of the GRIDCO and DISTCOs in such a way that employees at all levels of corporate functioning have incentives to perform better than their erstwhile organisation, the OSEB. This question is at the heart of the problem. Literature relating to efficiency and ownership has concluded that efficiency of an organisation does not depend on public or private ownership but on the level of competition. But, if competition is not feasible then the only way to reduce inefficiency is to improve the incentive structure of the organisation so that the whole corporate practise is characterised by transparency, accountability and participation (TAP).

Cost of Purchase of Power

The power is purchased by the GRIDCO from various state-dedicated sources and central utilities like the NTPC and the NHPC. The GRIDCO has to buy power to meet the demands of the DISTCOs. The DISTCOs' requirements are determined by final demand of consumers plus the distribution losses. Here we propose a power purchase multiplier to facilitate the understanding of this mechanism.

Let Y be the units of power that is required by the DISTCOs from the GRIDCO to meet the final demand of amount X (say) by the consumers. Then we can write

$(Y - bY) = X$ where $b < 1$, is the distribution loss factor

$$Y(1 - b) = X$$

Therefore, $Y = \dfrac{X}{1-b}$

Now differentiating Y with respect to X, we get Power purchase multiplier as

$$\frac{dY}{dX} = \frac{1}{1-b}$$

Power purchase Multiplier $= \dfrac{1}{1-b}$

Now if *b*, that is loss factor is 42 per cent then the value of the multiplier is 1.72. This implies that to satisfy one unit of final demand of the consumers DISTCOs will have buy 1.72 units of power from the GRIDCO. Power purchase multiplier is expected be higher for those DISTCOs, which have higher loads in LT category. Table 1 gives the calculation made on the basis of multiplier.

Table 1
Power Purchase Requirements with Actual and Normative Multiplier

	Final demand (MUs)	*Distribution Loss (%)*		*Power Purchase Multiplier*		*Power Purchase (MUs)*		*Energy Savings (MUs)*	*Money Savings* (Rs. Million)*
		Actual	*Norma-tive*	*Actual*	*Norma-tive*	*Actual*	*Norma-tive*		
1999-2000	5602.83	43.9	15	1.78	1.18	9987.22	6591.56	3395.65	39.23
2000-01	6081.32	43.95	15	1.78	1.18	10849.81	7154.49	3695.32	42.69
2001-02	5772.87	47.47	15	1.90	1.18	10989.66	6791.61	4198.05	48.50
2002-03	6731.779	40.75	15	1.69	1.18	11361.65	7919.74	3441.91	39.76

Note: *we have calculated this by assuming power purchase cost of 115.52 paise per unit for all the years as approved by OERC for GRIDCO's purchase cost.
Source: OERC (2002g)

From the above table simple view at value of multiplier gives good insight which we generally do not get while reporting distribution loss as such. We also give an estimate of money that could have been saved, if ystem operated at normative level (15 per cent) of distribution loss.

The cost of power purchase has risen to significantly high levels. The OERC has been continuously making changes in the purchase plan of the GRIDCO in order to minimise the cost of power purchase. OERC is always emphasising that it should draw maximum power from the cheapest plants so that the revenue requirements are lowest thus leading to lower tariffs. But after the introduction of the Avaiability Based Tariff (ABT) this problem has got further aggravated.

The power is procured under the power purchase agreements (PPA). The PPA between the generator (e.g., NTPC and the GRIDCO is signed under the supervision of the Central Electricity Regulatory Commission

(CERC). Initially the two parties of the PPA are supposed to negotiate and reach an agreement but in case of failure of such negotiations the CERC will dictate the terms and condition of purchase which should finally be acceptable to the two parties. Previously we discussed that various high powered incentives are concentrated in the generation sub-sector of the industry. The PPA typically depicts those incentives. The generating companies are generally assured of the returns with virtually no risk as the minimum mandated performance level (62 per cent of PLF) is not that difficult to achieve for any generating company. 'Cost plus' agreements along with condition of performance indicator induce the generation companies to be less bothered about cost minimising exercises and generally tend to be capital intensive. This kind of contract is prone to gold plating as the RORR is based on capital base. The impact of the PPA is very well reflected in the financial results of the NTPC and the buying utilities. It should be noted that the NTPC is a well performing profit making corporation. But on the other hand the buying utilities have been continuously suffering losses. This is not to say that all the losses of buying utilities or the SEBs are attributable to the PPAs but this certainly is one of the major factors contributing to losses. Several experts claim that one of the major reasons of financial erosion of the SEBs' are PPAs with either the IPPs or the NTPC (Grutoo and Pandey 2001, Kannan and Pillai 2002 and Morris 2000).

The major contention of the reform was to remove the inefficiencies in the wire segment of the business, which has not yet been addressed. In the absence of these efficiency improvements the purchase requirements are impossible to decline. Therefore these losses of GRIDCO will continue till efficiency improvements are realised by the GRIDCO and the other 4 DISTCOs.

A typical PPA consists mainly of three parts. One is about the determination of fixed charges, second is standard of physical operation and the third is regarding the variable charges mainly depending upon fuel usage and prices of the fuel. Fixed charges have various components. The PPA discusses the justification of these components.

Components of Fixed Charges: capital base, rate of interest on loan, return on equity, depreciation, O and M (operation and maintenance) expenses, interest on working capital, income tax, etc.

Components of Physical Operation: plant load factor, target availability, satiation heat rate[1], auxiliary consumption, specific fuel oil consumption.

Problem with such take or pay PPA is that the utility will be charged for full capacity it has contracted irrespective of the utilisation of capacity. One way to solve this problem is that contracted generation capacity should be tradable. In cases where a buying utility is not in a position to utilise her contracted capacity fully for a particular time period she should be free to trade the unutilised capacity with any other utility, which is in need of capacity. Objectors of proposal of the GRIDCO have argued that the GRIDCO should buy all the power and export it so that the burden of capacity cost could be minimised. But such solution may not be the best thing to do as it requires administrative complexity and involves risk. But the earlier solution may lead to significant amount of administrative ease and reduction in the risk of the utilities and efficient allocation of generating capacities.

GRIDCO's Risk in Revenue

GRIDCO is charging the DISTCOs on the basis of two-part tariff as said earlier. But the notable point is that they do so just to maintain the tradition of two-part tariff. The fixed charges in reality never represent the actual fixed costs incurred by the GRIDCO on transmission network and procurement of power. In, all tariff orders the demand charges (fixed charges) are quite lower than the required levels (around 25 per cent of the actual fixed cost). The remaining part of the fixed expenditures is added with variable expenses to arrive at energy charges. The problem with such arrangement is that the projected sale of GRIDCO might be more than what actually GRIDCO sells to DISTCOs while the energy charges are determined by the projected sale. Therefore GRIDCO in actuality may not be able to realise its required revenue. This is how the demand risk, imposed by the DISTCOs, is borne by the GRIDCO. On the other hand GRIDCO has to pay the fixed charges equal to the actual fixed cost incurred by the generating utilities. This particular arrangement of tariff reveals that publicly owned GRIDCO is being used as shock absorbing organisation for Orissa's power sector. The similar case can be seen from table 2.

Table 2
Normative and Actual Tariff Structures

Structuring Option	*Demand Charges Rs./kVA/Month*	*Energy Charges Paisa/unit*
Structuring Demand Charges to cover full cost of transmission and all the fixed cost of power purchase. Energy Charges will cover only the variable costs of generation or normative tariff structure.	1057.58	62.07
Actual as approved by the OERC	200	91*

* Actual energy charge for each DISTCO is different depending upon the projection of purchase of energy units by a particular DISTCO. This is the average of energy charges of all DISTCOs.
Source: OERC (2002g).

In the above case what happens at the end of the financial year is dependent on the following difference, viz., (Y- Y^*), where Y is actual units bought by the DISTCOs and Y^* is expected units of electricity to be bought by DISTCOs. If the above difference is positive the GRIDCO will earn profit but if the difference is negative the GRIDCO will run into loss. In addition, this pricing structure has an in built perverse incentive for the DISTCOs to show high-expected purchase of power from GRIDCO while filing ARR so that the energy charges are low because the formula for arriving at energy charge is

$$EC = \frac{(FE - FC) + VE}{ES}$$

Where EC = Energy Charge, FE = total fixed expenses, FC = total revenue earning through demand charges, VE = Variable expenses and ES= expected units of sale to DISTCOs,

Thus there is an inversely proportionate relationship between energy charge and the projected purchase by DISTCOs, i.e., higher the projected units of sale, lower will be the energy charge. Therefore, it will be in DISTCOs' interest to buy less units of power than actually it has projected to buy so that it escapes from paying the capacity or fixed charges. In such case the GRIDCO would not be able to cover its required revenue. Therefore the GRIDCO lives with a risk of demand uncertainties. One may argue here that the DISTCOs should be charged according to their projected energy purchase rather than actual purchase. The problem in this solution is that the GRIDCO will have little incentive to be efficient and responsive to the demands of the DISTCOs because it has already ensured its revenue. Table 3 helps us understand the case more clearly.

Table 3
Power Purchase of the DISTCOs for the year 2002-03

DISTCOs	*Projected*	*Approved (y*)*	*Actual (Y)*	*Y-Y**
CESCO	4321	4321	4055.75	(-)265.25
NESCO	3023	2291.2	2395.38	104.18
WESCO	3066.54	3066.54	3353.78	287.24
SOUTHCO	1713.71	1682.39	1556.7	(-)125.69
Total	12124.25	11361.13	11361.61	0.48

Source: OERC(2002 all Tariff Orders).

We can see from table 3 that the WESCO is actually drawing more than its projected purchase. But we must be aware of the fact that the WESCO, owned by the BSES, might operate in collusion with the SOUTHCO, and the NESCO, which also owned the BSES to misguide the regulators. Putting all the BSES companies together, their projected energy purchase was 7803.25 MUs but they actually have drawn only 7305.86 MUs. A difference of around 500 MUs i.e *Y-Y**= (-) 500 MUs. In case the regulator had calculated energy charges based on projected energy purchase by the DISTCOs, then the GRIDCO might have suffered a loss of Rs. 69.40 crores. It might be true that regulators can correctly estimate the purchase which can be seen from table 2 that approved purchase units are nearly similar to actual purchase units in aggregate but there is significant error in estimation of company wise purchase which is shown in the last column. This means that distribution of revenue required by the GRIDCO might be covered but the burden of revenue shared by the DISTCOs is not justified, i.e., some of the DISTCOs are gaining out of this process; for example, the CESCO and the SOUTHCO and others may loose like the NESCO and the WESCO. In aggregate the GRIDCO is running into little bit of surplus out of this process. But the point here is that the GRIDCO's fate is highly dependent on actual purchase of power by the DISTCOs which at sometimes might be quite different from what was expected.

One more possibility that there may be deliberate attempt to over project the purchase of power by the DISTCOs in cases when regulators and the DISTCOs collude. In other words the DISTCOs might influence the regulators through kickbacks to allow their higher projected purchase for tariff calculation. Therefor the demand charge should be able to cover the total fixed costs; otherwise there is a possibility of opportunistic behaviour by the purchaser and seller of the power including the regulator.

Dealing with Depreciation

The allowed rate of depreciation can have significant impact on the tariff. For the initial years the OERC simply adopted the rates which were followed earlier. It was a well-known fact that the assets values were simply revalued without any physical addition to the capital stock. For example if an asset of Rs. 500 is just revalued to Rs. 1000 without any addition to capital on the discretion of the government but depreciation rates remain constant, then in that case the value of depreciation will be quite high because the base was revalued. Let us take deprecation rate as 5 per cent; then the depreciation amount in the earlier case would be Rs. 25 but in post revaluation scenario it will be Rs. 50.This is much higher than the previous one. Such a situation emerged with the 1997-98 tariff order of the GRIDCO. The OERC could have mitigated a part, if not full, impact of revaluation of assets by heavily reducing the depreciation rates. This came to the wisdom of the OERC only after a few years of operation. For the financial year 2003-04, the OERC gave the above reason and calculated the depreciation amount based on quite low rates than the earlier ones.

Liquidity Crisis in the ESI

The GRIDCO faces huge liquidity crisis because the DISTCOs are not able to pay money on time; but at the same time the GRIDCO has to pay its dues to generating companies on time. Disproportionate distribution of opportunities and challenges or responsibilities of the Orissa ESI will ultimately turn out to be unsustainable in the long run. So far there is no attempt from the regulator's side to ensure that the liquidity problem is solved. Liquidity problem emerges out of inability of the DISTCOs to collect money with high efficiency levels as mandated by the OERC. Initial ARR filings were based on the assumption that immediately after the DISTCOs are in operation, billing to collection efficiency will be 100 per cent as envisaged by the SAR. Failure of this led to the non-payment of dues to the GRIDCO, which in turn could not pay its dues to the generating companies on time. On the suggestion of the Kanungo Committee Report, the OERC from the year 2003 started basing its regulatory activity on aggregate commercial and technical (AC and T) losses, which includes distribution losses collection inefficiency, rather than just distribution (T and D) losses (see Siddiqui 2004,Chapter 3 for details of AT and C loss).

Issue of Distribution Losses

This is one of the most important and bewildering parameters concerning the Indian power sector. With the introduction of the restructuring process in some of the states the actual amount of distribution losses have been revealed to be much higher than generally shown by their erstwhile SEBs. The SEBs usually concealed their losses by dumping them as consumption of the unmetered consumers, usually agricultural and domestic consumers. The elements comprising distribution losses are commercial losses and technical losses. The phenomenon of wide spread theft has also been emphasised in the literature. But here we are going to focus on the issue of regulatory effectiveness. There was huge gap in proposed and approved loss levels. The regulators were usually adamant on keeping the approved loss levels at 35 per cent level. The OERC also provided the DISTCOs with incentive that benefit of any cost savings beyond 35 per cent level would be the profit of the firm. For example, even if a particular DISTCO is able to operate at lower than 35 per cent say 32 per cent loss levels the OERC will calculate revenue requirement of the DISTCO assuming 35 per cent of distribution loss. Thus cost saving due to 3 per cent less loss will be the profit of the DISTCO. But the DISTCOs could not respond to this incentive scheme. Their actual losses are still very high. Ultimately the World Bank in 1998 resolved the issue by stating that 35 per cent loss level benchmarked by their study was an unachievable target in the given condition. Therefore the OERC raised its target of loss levels to around 42 per cent for all the DISTCOs. But even then the DISTCOs' distribution loss levels remained quite high compared to the 42 per cent mark (see figure 3).

Issues of Information Asymmetry

For an effective regulation, a regulatory body—no matter how expert and independent—needs access to reliable information to make sound

Figure 3
Distribution losses of the DISTCOs

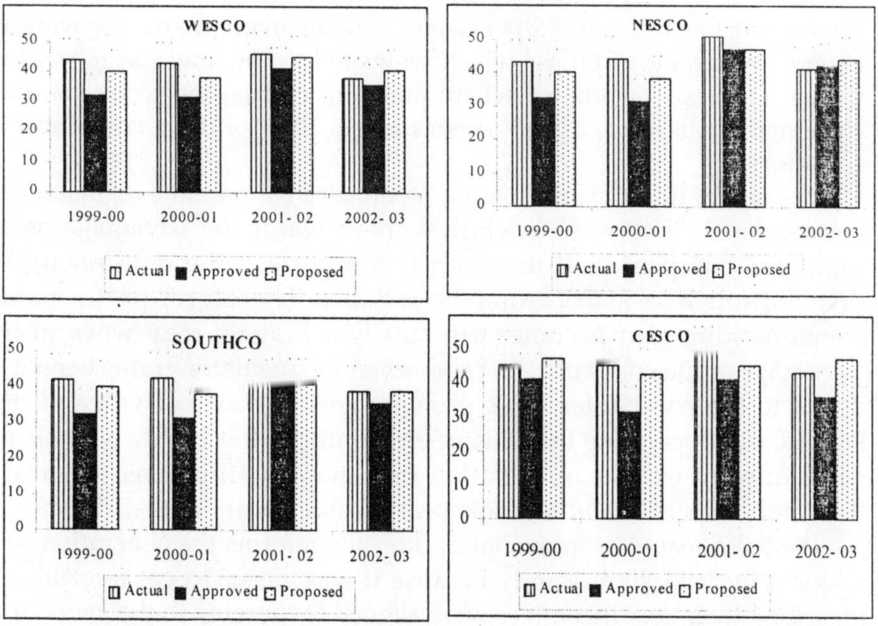

decisions. This includes information about the needs and priorities of consumers, firms and other stakeholders, as well as about the performance of the regulated firms—alternatively demand and cost information. We know, to get reliable information regarding the demand we need 100 per cent metering at all feeder levels and consumer points. But in Orissa large number of consumers are still either unmeterd or are having defective meters (see Table 4).

Table 4
Metering status of the DISTCOs (%)

		CESCO	*NESCO*	*WESCO*	*SOUTHCO*
Working meters	1999-01	39.78	47.09	60.90	68.22
	2001-02	57.15	46.04	69.40	72.11
	2002-03	53.47	52.08	67.77	78.62
Defective meters	1999-01	40.14	31.83	17.12	25.03
	2001-02	28.38	26.45	12.03	20.97
	2002-03	30.90	24.74	11.76	16.11
Unmetered	1999-01	20.07	21.07	21.98	6.75
	2001-02	14.47	27.51	18.57	6.92
	2002-03	15.62	23.18	20.47	5.27

Source: OERC, all the tariff orders of DISTCOs from 1999 onwards.

Share of the consumers with working meters is quite lower than expected. In fact the share of the consumers with working meters have declined after improvement from the initial year of operation except for SOUTHCO. A large number of consumers in LT category are still unmetered. Overall, only 62 per cent of the consumers are having working meters in the state of Orissa which seems to be quite low specially when the agricultural consumers, where metering is expected to be the most challenging job, forms only 3.13 per cent (in 2001) of the total number of consumers.

Because of this, the information asymmetry between the regulator and the regulated firms widens which works towards the advantage of the regulated companies. If metering is not perfect, the data regarding distribution loss also cannot be reliable. Therefore, performance benchmarking also becomes difficult which again may work to the advantage of the companies in cases when the regulator grants benefit of doubt to the companies. This problem gets aggravated when all the DISTCOs are operating in collusive environment. It is highly possible for companies to extract information rent in such situations, when the regulatory expertise and technological capabilities are in their infancy.

We have seen that immediately after the reforms the generation sub-sector improved significantly because it was easier to get information regarding them and incentives were aligned favourably to the generation companies but similar dramatic improvement did not take place in distribution side. It was because of the possibility of severe information rent extraction and incentives were not aligned in the ways where companies could narrow down the information asymmetry. A part of the information asymmetry is maintained because of lack of incentives provided by the regulators to bring about technological innovation. For example if proper incentives were designed to introduce computerised reading meters, then easier and accurate forecast for the demand was possible. Therefore, the regulators have to be careful about the innovations which can make process more transparent and they can get reliable information. Though tariff orders direct DISTCOs to achieve 100 per cent metering till now the OERC has not enforced any financial penalty in case of not doing so.

One of the important factors, which help the DISTCOs to misreport the consumption data by different categories, is non-existence of 100 per cent metering at consumers' level. It is easy for the DISTCOs to dump the consumption of one category as the other categories' consumption. DISTCOs have incentive to do this because if they report higher consumption at low tension (LT) categories then they may be granted to operate at higher AT and C loss. In addition to this, they may earn unreasonable revenue (rent) out of this process. Suppose a consumption of industrial consumers of quantity Q was dumped as consumption of domestic consumers, then the following will be the unreasonable profit or rent that can be earned by any of the participant in the process of sale of power, i.e., company, employee, consumer or all of them together if they do it in a collusive environment.

Rent = (Pi-Pd) × Q where P_i is industrial consumers tariff and P_d is the tariff for domestic consumers.

Earning such a rent is possible only when the price differences among different categories exists (necessary condition). Enabling factor for this process to happen is the absence of metering (sufficient condition). If these price differences disappear there will be no incentive for them to delay in metering. But as long as this price difference (cross-subsidy) exists, companies will have incentive to delay metering. In near future it is highly unlikely that these price differences will disappear. Therefore only option for the regulators is to provide enough incentive to the DISTCOs to implement metering in 100 per cent so that the enabling factor of dumping disappears.

Pandey and Morris (2004) has shown that after metering of some of the distribution circles in the case of Madhya Pradesh, there was dramatic improvement in the distribution loss and collection efficiency, reduction in power purchase requirements and ultimately the financial performance of the circles improved. This was all possible because of the aggressive metering campaign conducted by the determined officers coupled with support from the top political offices. It was also argued that a public owned organisation has comparative advantage over the private organisation for implementation of such reforms. Privately operated DISTCOs may not be an efficient agent to implement this reform because this cannot be done by the DISTCOs alone but needs the help of several other supportive institutions, e.g., police administration, political offices and society at large. Therefore it would easier for publicly owned distribution companies to seek co-operation from other public institutions compared to a private DISTCO.

Therefore, the first step of the regulators should be to make sure that necessary infrastructure needed to reduce the information asymmetry is implemented at the fastest possible rate because each moment lost entails loss of money. For this regulators need to increase the intensity of incentive on metering. Currently incentives intensity is applied on distribution loss but not on metering and voltage of wires which help to reduce the T and losses.

Discrimination Against Publicly Owned Company

When reforms were initiated, it was agreed in principle that all the companies involved in the Orissa's power sector would get the same rate of return irrespective of its ownership. But the manifold increase in the price of power compelled the Kanungo committee to look at the sources for reducing the tariff. In order to do that it recommended that the GRIDCO and the OHPC, that is publicly owned companies, should not be allowed to earn any rate of return. They should just be covering their fixed and variable cost. This will reduce the revenue requirements of the two companies, which ultimately will translate into lower tariffs at retail level. Thus commercial principle was compromised to keep the prices low. Therefore apparently we do not see any perceptible difference in the mode of thinking of the policy makers in post reform scenario. Since the hope of deriving benefits from the efficiency improvement is far from realisation, we look at pseudo ways of reducing cost, i.e., through financial manipulations.

AN ALTERNATIVE STRATEGY TO REGULATE IN THE CURRENT SCENARIO

As already explained the regulatory strategy to promote efficiency and to rectify the misallocation of resources has been based on the advice of the World Bank. The structure was established with the Orissa Electricity Reform Act 1995, which based its basics on the earlier laws like the Electricity Supply Act 1948 and Indian Electricity Act 1910. Electricity Act 2003 became the OERC's guiding principles after its advent. There may be significant changes because of this. The regulation broadly is RORR at all levels, i.e., generation, transmission, distribution along with some element of Performance Based Regulation (PBR). The major advantage of the PBR is that it may be tailored to suit the parameters of performance that the regulators choose to impose on the regulated utilities (Shankar and Ramachandran 2000). This form of regulation is well suited to the Indian conditions as PBR can help the regulators to target the specific matters of performance well judged from costs and benefits of the improvement in a particular parameter. In other words, intensity of incentives to improve a particular parameter can be designed on the basis of the perceived benefits that can be derived from the improvement.

What regulators are doing in India is quite non-conventional in nature. Their efforts are directed towards making the utilities run on commercial grounds rather than introduce competition into the sector. Most of the utilities in India are near financial bankruptcy and the first and the foremost challenge that the regulators face is to convert the financial deficit into reasonable surplus. The regulators have also learnt that changing the structure is not going to help much as it was quite evident from the Orissa experience. It has also been experienced that regulating the utilities on the basis of broad parameters like distribution losses only has not helped till now. From the experiences of the Dhabol Power project and California energy crisis we have learnt that the private sector has will never miss the chance to make use of the weaknesses of the rules of the game(Kannan and Pillai 2002, Dubash and Rajan 2001, and Phadke and Rajan 2003). It should also be borne in mind that incentive might not work in the cases where the individual or parties affected under the incentive scheme is not in the capacity to respond to the incentives, i.e., the incentive will work provided the selection of the companies are not adverse. Experience till now suggests that both government and private sectors have failed to bring about the desired change. The answer to problems of electricity supply industry (ESI) therefore has to be very cautious henceforth. What seem to work are the targeted improvement programs for different performance indicators. This kind of philosophy is currently in use through the Accelerated Power Development and Reform Programme (APDRP) initiated by Ministry of Power (MoP) where they plan to reduce the aggregate technical and commercial losses (AT and C losses). What we propose here is to take such philosophy to broader level. Below we discuss some of the issues to be addressed by the above measures.

Maintaining Reliability

Reliability is one of the important parameters from the consumer's point of view. This issue is continuously being raised in public and legislative assembly of Orissa. Here there is a big role to be played by the regulators whose job would be to assign the distributor with a particular level of reliability at which it has to supply power to particular region or circle of distribution. Different categories of consumers are generally connected to the same wires, so regulator may resort to differential pricing mechanism for different categories of consumer enjoying same level of reliability. For example, in urban areas the commercial consumers and household consumers are connected to the same wires therefore they enjoy the same level of reliability. In other words reliability is a non-excludable commodity for all the consumers connected to a given wire.

Regulators can also prioritise hours of the day at which different categories need the highest reliability in case of shortages. In urban areas consumers at HT and EHT end are industries which require highest reliability during the office hours of the day (say, from 0900 hours to 1700 hours); on the other hand consumers at LT end, i.e., commercial and households, may require highest reliability during non-office hours. It is needless to say that the commercial sector will need power at all points of time more desperately than any other classes. But given a choice that whether they would like to have high reliability at immediately before and after office hours or at other points of time then they may prefer the first choice. Nothing can be said concretely about such prioritisation of reliability in absence of a comprehensive survey, which is beyond the scope of the present study. For our purpose what is important is that such prioritisation is possible and can be adopted by the regulators after comprehensive survey to mitigate the problem of shortages in the short run.

The cost of system reliability is dependent on tensions at which power is provided. There can be some kind of cross subsidy mechanism among the different classes served at the same tension as well as other tensions. The literature in the west regarding the ESI suggests that the tariff should be based on not only the amount of electricity consumed but also on the reliability level which consumer enjoys (Moorhouse 2001). The tariff level should have a component of reliability at which the consumers demand power. But providing different reliability levels to individual consumers according to their demand may not be possible in current technology of metering. All the consumers connected to a particular feeder will enjoy the same level of reliability. One should keep in mind that such pricing regime is possible only when the metering is also capable of rationing the electricity. This is not immediately possible in India where even simple meters which just reads the number of electricity units consumed are not installed and even if installed a large proportion of them are not in working condition. A noteworthy point here is that not only the cost of supply of electricity is inversely related to the voltage at which electricity is supplied but also the reliability, i.e., additional cost of providing an additional unit of reliability at high voltage end is low when compared to lower voltages. On the other hand, the categories that demand higher reliability generally consume electricity at high voltage end. Therefor these categories can be charged higher than the actual cost of reliability. So there is a possibility of extracting surplus from such consumers which can be transferred to the other consumer groups, which has low capacity to pay mainly agricultural and domestic consumers. At this level regulators can play a major role. They can regulate the reliability of the supply through the code of supply (as by the Electricity Act 2003).

The high demand for reliability from the industrial consumers can be confirmed from the emergence of the Captive Power Producers (CPPs) in the states in Gujarat and Orissa. The industrial sector appears to be deprived of high reliability because of the political pressure on utility to supply the power to households without controlling the huge Transmission and Distribution losses. Ramesh, Thukral and Kaul (1990) show that the usage of captive power generation facilities by industries is at the maximum level during the agricultural seasons. This has led to the vicious circle of the higher tariff for subsidising category of consumers (Figure 4). The falling reliability in supply has forced the industrial consumers to seek alternative sources of power. As a result, the demand for electricity by the consumers groups, which cross-subsidise the other classes of consumers, has reduced. This has led to the need for further increase in the price of electricity for subsidising classes, so that enough revenue is generated to subsidise the increasing number of consumers in subsidised category. Low reliability coupled with the high prices has further induced the subsidising consumers to opt for other sources of power. So this cycle goes on until the picture becomes totally unbearable. Figure 4 gives the Vicious Circle.

Figure 4
Vicious Circle of low Quality of Power Supply

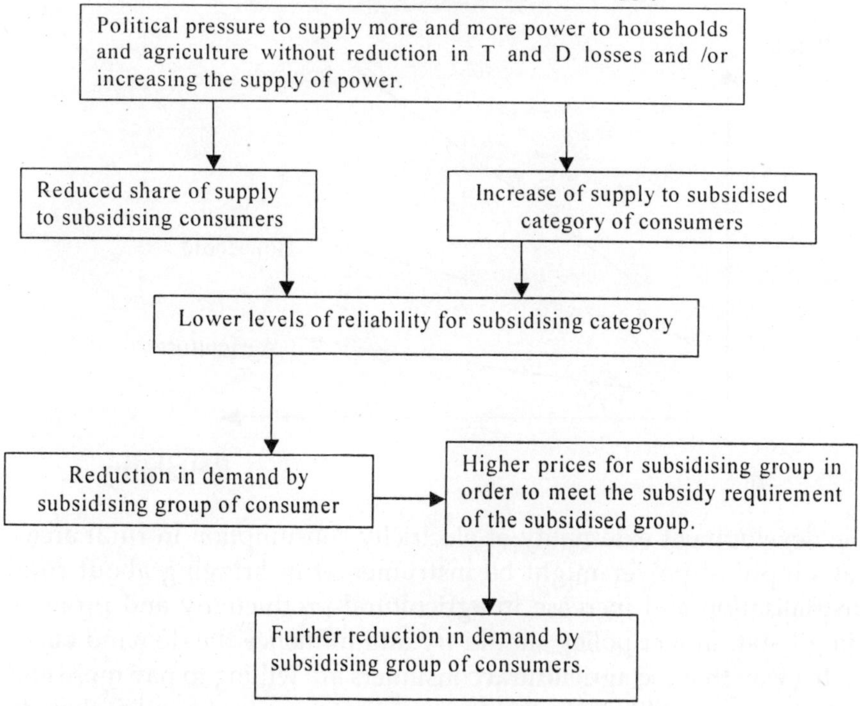

Demand for Reliability

Cost of having higher reliability than the one provided by the incumbent utility is extraordinarily high. Here we take a category of consumer as one consumer group, i.e., the domestic, agricultural, commercial and industrial consumers. If we assume that all consumers of one group has common preference for the reliability, it is possible for one to perceive the likely shapes of the demand curves for the reliability (figure 5). We can very well imagine that consumers would like to bid higher prices for the higher level of reliability, i.e., positively sloping demand curve. But different categories will have different willingness to pay. Thus the price elasticity of demand and the area under the demand curve, i.e., the utility, will be different for different categories of the consumers.

From intuition it is clear that higher reliability is preferred by different categories of the consumers at different intervals of the time of the day. We see that the industry values reliability the highest. Thus its willingness to pay is the highest along with highest price elasticity of demand such that it is ready to accept a higher price in order to have an additional unit of reliability. On the other hand, agricultural consumers have the lowest willingness to pay as a whole as well as for any additional unit of reliability. This does not mean that we can ignore such consumer. We must be aware

Figure 5
The Demand for Reliability for Different Categories

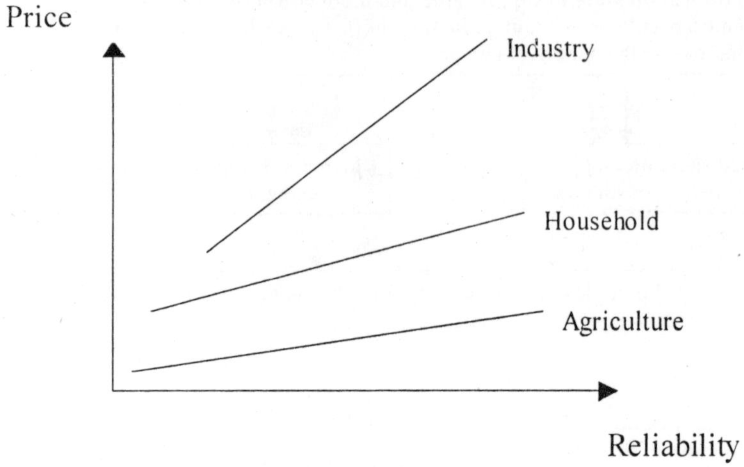

of the development externality of electricity consumption in rural areas. Rural supply of power might be instrumental in bringing about rural industrialisation and increase in agricultural productivity and promote reading habit. In fact policy should try and influence the demand curve in such a way that the agricultural consumers are willing to pay more and they derive more utility from the consumption compared to what they do now. This can happen if rural population become aware of the potential benefit that can be derived from increased reliability of power. The story for household consumer lies in the middle of the two extremes.

Reducing the Distribution Losses

In the case of Orissa, the companies have not been able to stand up to the expectation of the regulators. Companies have not been able to find ways through which it could reduce losses as per the regulator's order. Now in such situation regulators' role becomes more of executive director rather than just regulators. This means that the regulators need to focus on the disaggregated parameters, which are crucial in minimising distrbution losses rather than just that. For example, technological improvements in metering, computerised billing, transformer capacities may help in reducing commercial losses along with increasing the transparency of the system; by regulating the low voltage (LV) and medium voltage (MV) ratios in the netwrok of distribution wire regulators can check the technical part of the T and D losses. The Ministry of Power has already adopted this approach under the Accelerated Power Development and Reform Programme (APDRP) which presently focuses on reducing T and D losses by closely monitoring the above parameters (MoP 2002). Under this programme, utilities are provided with financial assistance based on their achievements relative to the target fixed in previous period. In the last chapter we saw that the major components of cost are power purchase and interest payments. One of the major reasons for very high cost of purchase is the huge T and D loss. Here we propose some ways to regulate the sector so that the chaotic state of affairs prevailing in the sector could be arrested.

Strategy of controlling the distribution losses should be well spelt out. One of the major sources of the high distribution loss is theft of electricity. If we take account of the non-payment of the power sold, i.e., collection inefficiency, then this figure is much higher. The revenue recovery of even the recorded electricity sold is not 100 per cent.

Controlling the Theft

(a) **Educating the Masses:** Educating the masses may be one of the important factors, which can lead to reduction in theft in the long run. Simple estimates by the regulatory commission about possible reductions in the tariff in absence of theft can be publicised through various mechanisms like taking help of school children to convey the massage to the parents, using electronic media etc. The basic idea here is to make people realise about how much of resources are being wasted.

(b) **Political willingness:** Improvement in the quality of power seems to be an impossible dream unless theft is arrested. Hooking is social phenomena in Orissa while industry steals power with greater amount of sophistication (Parayas 2002 and Mahalingam 2002). Control of theft of electricity is highly dependent on the level of political willingness. Kannan and Pillai (2002:82) have highlighted that the culture of theft enjoys the patronage of the SEBs officials and the government. In fact the non-payment of the utility bills is not only because of inability of the consumers to pay but largely because of their attitude. We see most of the defaulting consumers are public organisations and people having political influence. On the other hand, most of the time utility employees are also not very serious to collect the bills. Surprisingly even after defaulting, these consumers continue to get power. This is possible only because of political pressure on the SEBs to continue the supply for electoral mileage. This kind of informal pressures from the people having political influence to supply power to commercially unattractive sections of consumers results in worsening quality of supply to categories which cross-subsidises the other categories. This induces them to go for CPP as shown in figure 3.

(c) **Individual Incentives for Reporting Theft at Various Levels:** The regulators may provide incentive by offering a reduction in the electricity bill of the individual who helps to trace the theft of the electricity. It may be a fixed amount linked to each reporting or fixed percentage of the bill or fixed as some faraction of the magnitude of power theft controlled with the help of that person. The last one is the most incentive intensive scheme as this is directly linked to amout of energy saved. On the other hand, the first incentive will not give any inducement for reporting the theft according to the priority; i.e., amount of theft. In this incentive scheme, people will be interested only in reporting the theft and they will not be interested in giving importance to the magnitude of theft. The second scheme has perverse incentive for consumer who has higher bill amounts. This means that if the discount is 10 per cent of the bill amount, a person with electricity bill of Rs 1000 will have more incentive to report a theft than that of a person who has to pay only Rs 100 as his electricity bill. On the hand the third scheme can be applicable all individual or groups whoever reports (irrespective of whether he is a consumer or not) the theft of electricity should be entitled to cash payment after the confirmation of theft. One may think that there is no incentive for employee who is supposed to be responsible for tracing the thieves. One must be aware of the fact that currently most of the theft takes place with collusion of such employees and the consumer and that is why we need a third party intervention so that transparency is maintained. When third party (the reporter of theft) is interested in getting the discounts in electricity bill or cash prize he will make it sure that the case of the theft moves fast and judiciously and also that the employees and thief do not collude. We may have such incentive schemes for the employees (particularly line mans) also where his payment (wage) is two-part. One is fixed amount, which should be based on basic amenity expenditure, and the other part should be based on the performance of the employees in handling the cases of theft and detecting the theft themselves.

Incentives for the Employees

The incentive for employees to perform better can be designed at various levels of activity. Lack of employees' accountability has been a major factor responsible for the huge losses in power utilities in India. The low productivity of the employees as well as their collusion with thieves of power has been the main source of the AT and C losses. The employees can behave in contrast to the motive of the organisation only when they are sure that the terms of the employment cannot be enforced. The employees have this perception that they cannot be fired so easily even if they are caught in helping somebody to get rid of their electricity bills or in stealing of power. On the other hand, the perceived probability of being caught is extraordinary low. Hence the expected cost of being caught, the product of these two factors, seems to be still lower.

Another important factor responsible for low productivity of the employees in SEBs including the OSEB is the centralised decision making process. Ruet (2001a) gives a detailed account of how rigid these boards are. There is no or lack of budgetary allocation for employees at even high levels, which can be instrumental in cost minimisation exercise. Further there exists a long chain of approval list prior to the execution of a field officer's recommendation for change or repair of equipment. These kind of cumbersome process demoralises even the dutiful individuals. Therefore, organisational rigidities, flaws in employment contract along with very low cost of being not loyal to the organisation make employees inefficient.

The alternative design of the employment contract should be such that incentives are in line with the goal of the organisation. First thing is to link the remuneration of the employees with their productivity (Kannan and Pillai 2002:41-42). The current fixed level of payment gives little incentive to put in more effort. Going to office would be enough to entitle the employee to the payment. One of the reasons why private firms have more labour productivity than the government companies is because incentive intensity is higher in private firms. And there is nothing, which can stop public firm to introduce incentive intensity similar to that of private firms' (Corneo and Rob 2003 and Kannan and Pillai 2002). On the other hand, if the employees are to be more responsible they have to be given decisional as well as financial autonomy. If this is done then they do not have to go through the long list of approvals in order to implement a change in which he or she is the best person to decide.

CONCLUSION

We see that the practice of regulation has been in its infancy as regulators have not been able to allocate the risk, costs and benefits in a judicious way among different stakeholders of the power sector in Orissa. The risks and costs are heavily loaded with the GRIDCO. Regulators need continuos research support, which is lacking at the moment. They need to be careful about the parameters on which they choose to apply incentive intensity, i.e., incentive intesisty should applied be according the marginal benefit principle. They need to be more proactive to minimise the information asymmetry. We have also indicated that there are several things that can be done by just changing the rules of the game, i.e., reallocating the incentive intensity specially in case of metering.

NOTE

1. Heat Rate is defined, as heat required per unit of generation of power (e.g kcals/kWh). It serves the purpose of conversion (of fuel to electricity) efficiency parameter in a generating utility.

REFERENCES

Corneo G. and R. Rob (2003), "Working in Public and Private Firms" *Journal of Public Economics*, Vol. 87, p. 1335-1352.

Dubash N.K. and S.C. Rajan (2001), "Power Politics: Process of Power Sector Reform in India" *Economic and Political Weekly*, January 9.

Kannan K.P. and V.M. Pillai (2002), "*Plight of Power Sector in India: Inefficiency, Reform and Political Economy*" Centre for Development Studies, Trivandrum.

Mahalingam S. (2002), "The Great Power Robbery" *Frontline*, Vol. 19 No. 6, Mar. 16–29.

Moorhouse (1991), "Competitive Markets for Electricity Generation" The Cato Journal, Vol. 14, No. 3.

MoP (2002), "Structuring of APDRP, Reform Framework and Principles of Financial Restructuring of SEBs" *Report of The Expert Committee on State Specific Reforms, Ministry of Power*, Government of India, September.

Pandey A. and S. Morris (2004), "The Beginning of Distribution Reforms in West Madhya Pradesh: A Report" in Morris, S. (ed) "*India Infrastructure Report 2004*" Oxford University Press, New Delhi.

Parayas (2002), "HT Energy Audit:The Crucial Starting Point for Curbing Revenue Loss" *Prayas Occasional Report, Energy Group, Prayas*, Pune, February 2002.

Phadke A. and R.C. Rajan (2003), "Electricity Reforms in India: Not too Late to go Back to the Drawing Board" *Economic and Political Weekly*, July 19.

Ruet J. (2001a), "Winners and losers of the SEB Reforms: An Organisational Analysis", *Occasional Paper, French Research Institute in India*, New Delhi.

Sankar T.L. and Ramachandran U. (2000), "Electricity Tariff Regulators: The Orissa Experience" *Economic and Political Weekly*, May 27, p. 1825-1834.

Thukral and Kaul (1990), "Integration of Short and Medium/Long Term Planning in the Indian Power Sector" *The Energy Journal*, Vol. 11, No. 1.

APPENDIX

- The Talcher Thermal power station of the OSEB has been transferred to NTPC (3rd june 1995).
- The OSEB was Corporatised into the Grid Corporation of Orissa (GRIDCO) with wiring and distribution functions and the Orissa Hydro Power Corporation (OHPC) in charge of the hydropower projects (1 April 1996).
- The Orissa Electricity Regulatory Commission (OERC) established (August 1996).
  - (a) Issued seven tariff orders till date.
  - (b) Level of cross subsidy is being reduced.
  - (c) Tariff has experienced a huge hike
- The Orissa Power generation corporation (OPGC) which was established in 1984 got privatised in 1998 with transfer of 49 per cent of stake to the private operator, AES consortium, for Rs. 603 Crore.
- The distribution and retail supply of electricity was vested in four distribution companies initially as wholly owned subsidiary companies of the GRIDCO, namely the Central Electricity Supply Company of Orissa limited (CESCO), the North Eastern Electricity Supply Company of Orissa limited (NESCO), the Southern Electricity Supply Company of Orissa limited (SOUTHCO) and the Western Electricity Supply Company of Orissa limited (WESCO). Three of these distribution companies i.e., except the CESCO were privatised on 1st April 1999 (acquired by BSES) and the CESCO on 1st September 1999 after dis-investment of its 51 per cent share (Acquired by AES consortium, a global Power company from US but now the CESCO is administered by a government official as it backed AES backed out from managerial responsibility of the company). The GRIDCO received Rs. 1.6 billion for 51 per cent of the stake of the distribution companies (DISTCOS). While the GRIDCO retains only high voltage wiring business under single buyer model. Figure 1 depicts the process of restructuring of the Orissa Electricity board (OSEB).

Chapter - 9

Use of Anti dumping Measures Against Developing Countries: The Indian Experience

Nandana Baruah

INTRODUCTION

The alarming rise in the use of anti dumping measures has drawn the attention of economists as well as policy makers in the recent times. Till 1880s use of anti dumping measure was confined to a few traditional users like the USA, the EU, Canada and Australia. But during the 1990s a set of new countries started using anti dumping measures extensively. Many of these new users are developing countries such as Brazil, Mexico, and India. However, these developing countries are not only initiating anti dumping cases, but most of the time they are the targets of such initiations. More than 70 per cent of the cases were initiated against the developing countries during 1995 to 2005. Moreover, the numbers of developing countries against which cases have been initiated are much higher than the countries initiating anti dumping cases. This will have serious implications for the exports from these countries, as they already have very low shares in the world trade. In this context we look at the anti dumping cases initiated against India. No doubt India has initiated large number of anti dumping cases, but the cases initiated against India are also fairly high. Though a few studies[1] have tried to analyse the use of anti dumping by India, none have tried to look at India's situation from the receiving end. Therefore here our attempt is to analyse India's situation as a target of anti dumping initiations. We proceed in the following way. The 2nd section discusses general trend in the use of anti dumping measures by the WTO member countries. In the 3rd section we discuss the trends in the use of anti dumping cases against India. In the 4th section we try to examine the rationale behind the use of anti dumping measures against India as well as the possible implication for India's exports. Section 5 concludes the study.

ANTI DUMPING MEASURES AND DEVELOPING COUNTRIES

WTO has reported anti dumping initiations by 41 countries for the period covering 1995 to 2005 (Jan-June). Among them, 29 are developing countries and remaining 12 are developed countries.[2] But if we look at the other side of the picture we can see that the numbers of countries getting affected by these initiations are much larger. All these cases have been aimed against 98 countries, out of which 66 are developing countries and the rest 32 are developed countries. Thus the number of developing countries getting affected by anti dumping use is more than two times the number of countries initiating these cases. The following table presents the number of anti dumping cases initiated as well as the number anti dumping measures in force by user nations for the period 1995 to 2005 (Jan-June).

Table 1
Anti dumping Cases by Developed and Developing Countries (1995-2005)

Year	*Developing Countries*		*Developed Countries*		*Total*	
	Anti dumping initiations	*Anti dumping measures*	*Anti dumping initiations*	*Anti dumping measures*	*Anti dumping initiations*	*Anti dumping measures*
1995	79 (50.32)	47 (39.50)	78 (49.68)	72 (60.50)	157	119
1996	146 (64.89)	33 (35.87)	79 (35.11)	59 (64.13)	225	92
1997	122 (50.21)	64 (15.20)	121 (49.79)	61 (48.80)	243	125
1998	167 (65.23)	100 (58.82)	89 (34.77)	70 (41.18)	256	170
1999	186 (52.54)	119 (64.67)	168 (47.46)	65 (35.33)	354	184
2000	161 (55.14)	124 (53.45)	131 (44.86)	108 (46.55)	292	232
2001	205 (56.32)	76 (45.78)	159 (43.68)	90 (54.22)	364	166
2002	225 (72.12)	138 (63.89)	87 (27.88)	78 (36.11)	312	216
2003	159 (68.53)	181 (81.90)	73 (31.47)	40 (18.10)	232	221
2004	130 (61.32)	115 (76.16)	82 (38.68)	36 (23.84)	212	151
2005 (Jan-June)	72 (75)	30 (56.60)	24 (25)	23 (43.40)	96	53
Total	1652 (60.23)	1027 (59.40)	1091 (39.77)	702 (40.60)	2743	1729

Source: WTO Anti dumping database.

During this time period a total of 2743 cases have been initiated by all the reporting members. More than 63 per cent of these cases have been resulted in duty. The share of developing countries has remained higher than the developed countries not only in initiation of cases but also in the cases resulting in duty. They initiated 79 cases (50.32 per cent) in 1995, which increase to 146 cases (64.89 per cent) in the next year. Thus, at the end of 2005 (Jan-June), the developing countries account for 60.23 per cent of total initiations and 59.40 per cent in the total measures in force. However, if we look at the share of cases resulting in duty, we see that developed countries have a higher share. Of all the initiations, 64.34 per cent of cases resulted in duty for the developed countries, while the corresponding share of the developing countries is 62.17 per cent.

As we have already noted developing countries are most often are the targets of these initiations. This can be seen from the following table 2. It reports the number of anti dumping cases initiated against developing as well as the developed countries.

Table 2
Anti dumping Cases against Developed and Developing Countries (1995-2005)

Year	*Developing Countries*		*Developed Countries*		*Total*	
	Anti dumping initiations	*Anti dumping measures*	*Anti dumping initiations*	*Anti dumping measures*	*Anti dumping initiations*	*Anti dumping measures*
1995	102 (64.97)	85 (71.43)	55 (35.03)	34 (28.57)	157	119
1996	151(67.11)	72 (78.26)	74 (32.89)	20 (21.74)	225	92
1997	144 (59.26)	96 (76.80)	99 (40.74)	29 (23.20)	243	125
1998	164 (64.06)	104 (61.18)	92 (35.94)	66 (38.82)	256	170
1999	255 (72.03)	116 (63.04)	99 (27.97)	68 (36.96)	354	184
2000	207 (70.89)	165 (71.12)	85 (2911)	67 (28.88)	292	232
2001	261(71.70)	121 (72.89)	103 (28.30)	45 (27.11)	364	166
2002	239 (76.60)	158 (73.83)	73 (23.40)	58 (26.85)	312	216
2003	156 (67.24)	172 (77.83)	76 (32.76)	49 (22.17)	232	221
2004	169 (79.72)	120 (79.47)	43 (20.28)	31 (20.53)	212	151
2005 (Jan-June)	82 (85.42)	40 (75.47)	14 (14.58)	13 (24.53)	96	53
Total	1930 (70.36)	1249 (72.24)	813 (29.64)	480 (27.76)	2743	1729

Source: WTO Anti dumping database.

In 1995 around 65 per cent of the cases were initiated against the developing countries which increased to 67 per cent in the next year. By the end of 2005 (Jan-June), the share increased to more than 85 per cent. More than 64 per cent the all the cases initiated against developing resulted in duty, while the corresponding figure for the developed countries is 59 per cent. Some of these developing countries facing large number of anti dumping cases are China, Taiwan, India, Korea, Thailand, and Brazil.

It will be also interesting to find out where developing countries are facing more anti dumping cases. From table 3 we can see that developed countries have initiated 310 (28.41 per cent) cases against other developed countries, while 781 (71.59 per cent) cases against developing countries. At the same time, developing countries have initiated 503 (30.45 per cent) cases against developed countries but have initiated 1149 (69.55 per cent) cases against other developing countries, which is more than 2 times the cases against developed countries. This shows that not only developed countries are targeting developing countries but many developing countries have filed cases against other such countries. As a result while for the developed countries no of cases initiated against them (813) is much smaller than the cases initiated by them (1091), the reverse is the case with developing countries. There are 1652 cases initiated by them as against 1930 cases against them. There are a few countries like Honk Kong, Singapore, Bangladesh, Nepal etc that are facing anti dumping cases in other countries but have not initiated any anti dumping case yet.

Table 3
Anti dumping Initiations: Exporting Vs Initiating Countries (1995-2005)
Exporting Countries

Initiating Countries ↓	*Developed Countries*		*Developing Countries*		*Total*	
	Anti dumping initiation	*Anti dumping measures*	*Anti dumping initiation*	*Anti dumping measures*	*Anti dumping initiation*	*Anti dumping measures*
developed countries	310 (28.41)	163 (25.83)	781 (71.59)	468 (74.17)	1091	631
developing countries	503 (30.45)	317 (28.87)	1149 (69.55)	781 (71.13)	1652	1098
Total	813 (29.64)	785 (45.40)	1930 (70.36)	944 (54.60)	2743	1729

Source: WTO Anti dumping database.
Note: Figures in parenthesis presents the percentage share.

Table 4
Distribution Across the Product Groups

Product Groups	*Developing countries*	*per cent share*	*Developed countries*	*per cent share*	*Total*	*per cent share*
Live Animals; Animal Products	25	53.19	22	46.81	47	1.71
Vegetable Products	30	75.00	10	25.00	40	1.46
Prepared Foodstuffs, Beverages	24	58.54	17	41.46	41	1.49
Mineral Products	48	76.19	15	23.81	63	2.30
Products of the Chemical or Allied Industries	321	58.79	225	41.21	546	19.91
Plastics and Articles Thereof; Rubber and Articles Thereof	254	70.17	108	29.83	362	13.20
Wood and Articles of Wood	23	50.00	23	50.00	46	1.68
Pulp of Wood or of other Fibrous Cellulosic; Paper or Paperboard; Paper and Paperboard and Articles Thereof	62	51.24	59	48.76	121	4.41
Textiles and Textile Articles	165	87.77	23	12.23	188	6.85
Articles of Stone, Plaster Ceramic Products; Glass and Glassware	72	77.42	21	22.58	93	3.39
Base Metals and Articles of Base Metal	621	77.33	182	22.67	803	29.27
Machinery and Mechanical Appliances; Electrical Equipment; Parts Thereof;	154	68.44	71	31.56	225	8.20
Miscellaneous Manufactured Articles	55	82.09	12	17.91	67	2.44
Total	1930	70.36	813	29.64	2743	100.00

Source: WTO Anti dumping database.

All the anti dumping cases involve a broad range of product groups, the most prominent among them being chemicals (19.91 per cent), base metals (29.27 per cent), and plastic and rubber articles (13.20 per cent). The developing countries have bigger share in the total initiations for almost all the products. Table 4 presents some of the product groups attracting large number of anti dumping cases.

Thus we can see that, use of anti dumping measures have shown many fold increase in the last decade. The increase is evident in the number of cases as well as in the number of user countries. But the numbers of countries getting affected are much higher, majority of them being developing countries.

ANTI DUMPING CASES AGAINST INDIA

India faced its first anti dumping case in 1990, initiated by the EU for the exports of synthetic fibre of polyester. Since then there has been a gradual rise in the number of anti dumping cases against India and it reached a two-digit level (11 cases) in 1996. By the end of the first half of 2005 a total of 123 cases have been initiated against India by its trading partners.

Figure 1
Distribution of the Cases against India (1990-2005)

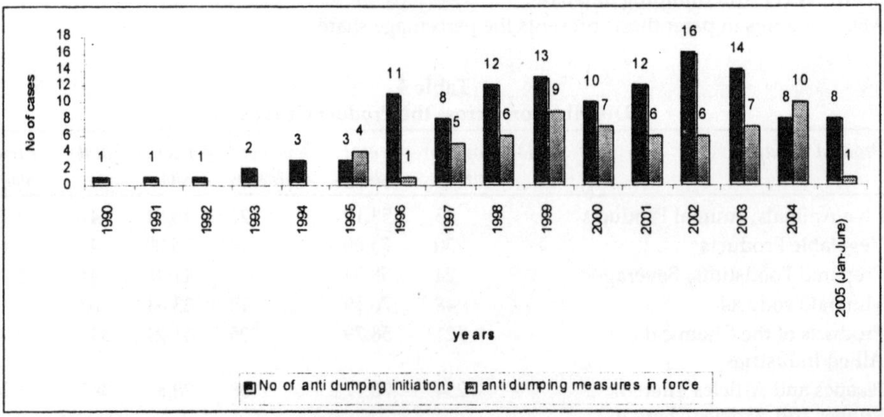

Source: WTO Anti dumping database & Annual Report, Directorate General of anti dumping and Allied Duties, GoI 2002-03.

Note: Cases prior to 1995 are reported from Annual Report, Directorate General of anti dumping and Allied Duties, GoI 2003. It doesn't report measures in force.

As many as 18 countries have filed anti dumping cases against India. The EU have initiated maximum number of cases against India (29 cases), followed by the USA (21 cases) and South Africa (20 cases). These three countries together account for almost 56 per cent of the total anti dumping cases against India (table 5).

Among the countries initiating anti dumping cases against India, 13 are developing countries.

Table 5
Countries initiating Anti Dumping Cases against India (1990-2005)

Countries	*No of Cases*	*per cent Share of Cases*
Argentina	5	4.07
Australia	4	3.25
Brazil	4	3.25
Canada	6	4.88
China PR	2	1.63
Egypt	4	3.25
EU	29	23.58
Indonesia	10	8.13
Korea RP	3	2.44
Malaysia	1	0.81
Mexico	1	0.81
Peru	1	0.81
Poland	1	0.81
South Africa	20	16.26
Thailand	2	1.63
Trinidad and Tobago	2	1.63
Turkey	7	5.69
USA	21	17.07
Total	123	100.00

Source: WTO Anti dumping database and Annual Report, Directorate General of Anti dumping and Allied Duties, GoI 2002-03.

They have initiated around 62 cases while the developed countries have initiated 61 cases.

Table 6
Distribution of Anti Dumping cases Against India Across the Product Groups

Product Groups	*Cases*	*Per cent Share of Cases*
Live Animals; Animal Products	1	0.87
Vegetable Products	3	2.61
Products of the Chemical or Allied Industries	29	25.22
Plastics and Articles Thereof; Rubber and Articles Thereof	17	14.78
Pulp Of Wood or of Other Fibrous Cellulosic Material; Paper and Paperboard and Articles Thereof	2	1.74
Textiles and Textile Articles	13	11.30
Footwear, and other related products	2	1.74
Articles of Stone, Plaster Ceramic Products; Glass and Glassware	3	2.61
Base Metals and Articles of Base Metal	35	30.43
Machinery and Mechanical Appliances;	9	7.83
Miscellaneous Manufactured Articles	1	0.87
Total	115	100.00

Source: Same as table 5.

Looking at the products, at appears that that a wide range of Indian exports are attracting anti dumping cases (table 6). The most prominent among them is Base metal and articles made of it accounting for 35 cases.

Chemical products are attracting another 29 initiations. Export of products made of plastic, rubber, glass are facing 17 initiations. Textile products occupy the next place with 13 cases. Together these four product groups account for more than 80 pecent of the total anti dumping cases against india.

Thus we can see that Indian exports to large number of countries are facing considerable number of anti dumping cases involving a wide range of products.

Rationale behind Anti Dumping Cases Against India

Possibility of Predation

According to the provisions of WTO anti dumping agreement and national legislations, anti dumping protection should be given to those domestic industries which get injured due dumping from foreign countries. Thus as per law, dumping and resulting injury to the domestic producers is the major justification for imposition of duty. However in the mainstream economic theory anti dumping duty is considered as a rational policy choice only if dumping is strategic or predatory in nature. Strategic dumping describes the situation when the foreign seller experiences significant economies of scale through investment in R & D and learning by doing. Now, if the exporter's home market is foreclosed from foreign competition and the exporter enjoy a substantial share in the home market, they will have a cost advantage over rivals. This enables the exporter to dump in other country's market (Willing, 1998). However with opening up of economies through reduced tariffs as well as other initiatives taken by the nations, the possibility of maintaining a closed home market is coming down. Predatory dumping on the other hand refers to 'an act of setting prices in the home market by a foreign rival with the intent of driving home firms out of business leaving all the home market to the foreign rival and allowing the rival to recoup its losses, and thus injure competition. (Clarida, 1996). Thus there are three necessary elements for price cutting to be predatory (Ordever, 1998):

1. It must involve deliberately reducing profits (or even making losses) for a period of time.
2. It must have as its objective the elimination of one or more competitors or at least be designed to weaken them to such a degree that they can no longer offer strong competition or otherwise discourage competition.
3. It is essential that the predator earns supra-normal profit in future for predation being worthwhile, and this in turn requires the existence of barriers to entry. Otherwise attempts to raise prices following predation will be undermined by new entry.

Thus charging low prices in the foreign market is not an offence in itself, if the exporter has no intention of driving the domestic producers out of the market. Successful predation clearly requires fulfillment of strict conditions. For example the firm who has predatory motive should have a dominant position not only in the importing country's market but also at the global level. In that case it will be possible for the firm to compensate for the losses it will incur in the importing country's market due to predatory attempt with the profits from other markets. Again, there is a chance the monopoly position of the firm may attract the other firms into that market. So the predator must be in a position to check entry of other firms to that market (Tharakan, 1995). Moreover, for some products, a number of foreign exporters may be charging low prices. So after the domestic firms are eliminated, these exporters may get engaged in aggressive competition among themselves (Deardorff, 1989). Given such stringent conditions, it was felt by many that, confining the use of anti dumping measures to only to predatory cases will reduce its misuse.

However, identifying such predatory dumping attempts has remained a major challenge for national authorities. Any investigation on predatory behaviour should ideally be based on cost price comparison. However, even at national level application of cost-based rules invite problem. Therefore straight application of such rules in international context brings in further complications. Tharakan (2000) argued that two-tier approach as proposed by Joskow & Klevorick (1979) might be used, with the necessary adaptation for the international context. The first tier involves market structure analysis and the second tier will involve cost based test.

He grouped the structural characteristics into three groups:

1. Factors indicative of short-run monopoly power.
2. Conditions of entry into the market.
3. The dynamic effects of competition or entrants on the cost of production and quality of products offered to consumers.

Based on this two-tier rule a few empirical studies have been undertaken. Bourgeois and Messerlin (1998) for example, examined the likelihood of the existence of 'monopolising behaviour' in the EC anti dumping cases initiated during 1980-89. They used a detailed screening process with five rounds of screening to examine if the marker structure conditions are favorable for predation. These included examining the market share of all the exporting countries in the EU, number of countries and number of firms involved etc. At the end of this five-stage screening they were left only 12 cases i.e. 2% of the total cases which were 'possible candidate for a closer examination of predatory behaviour'.

A similar attempt to identify predatory dumping in the context of the USA made by Hyun Ja Shin (1998). She examined anti dumping investigations completed in the USA during 1980 to 1989. Besides looking at the number of exporting firms and exporting countries she also considered the concentration in the domestic producers. A highly concentrated domestic market makes predation easier as it will involve eliminating only a few producers from the market. Again instead of import share, the study considered import penetration. This is obviously more representative of the market power of the foreign sellers. Examining such structural conditions suitable for successful predation, this study also found that only a few cases can actually qualify as possible candidate for predation. In the Indian context also possibility of predatory dumping was examined by Aggarwal (2002) and Singh (2005). They used mainly four criteria to identify the possibility of predation. Firstly, import penetration should be high, indicating considerable market power for the exporters. Secondly, the predator should be a large supplier at the global level. To approximate this both the studies considered the share of the foreign supplier in the total exports to India. They argued that, if there are large numbers of exporters and consequently the share of particular country is less, then possibility of predation in limited. Thirdly, export market should be concentrated, i.e. the number of foreign sellers should be small. Lastly, exporters should have a dominant position in its home market. In the absence reliable information in this regard both studies used the number of known producers reported in the anti dumping investigation by the authority as a proxy for this. Examining on these four criteria both the studies found that, only for a very few cases the structural conditions were suitable for any predatory attempt.

Given the limited information available on anti dumping cases against India, examining all these aspects is difficult. However, we look at few indicators to get some general idea about the possibility of Indian exporters behaving as predators. High import penetration is one of the important pre-condition for successful predation. However, information on import penetration ratio for these products could not be found. Therefore, as a close approximation, we have considered India's share in the total import of the allegedly dumped product in the anti dumping case initiating country. Countries having high share in the imports of the particular product are likely to have high import penetration in the importing country's domestic market. For this analysis we could consider 64 cases. Data for the rest of the cases could not be acquired.

Table 7 presents the percentage share of India's exports in the total import of the products, in which they are facing anti dumping charges, in the respective countries. The table shows that, for 31 cases (more than 48 per cent), the share of Indian exporters in the total imports to the country is lower than 5 per cent. For 10 products (15.63 per cent), the share ranges between 5 to 10 per cent. For another 14 products (21.88 per cent) the share lies between, 10 to 20 per cent. In fact, there is only one case where we found India's share in the total imports to be more than 50 per cent.

Table 7

India's Share in the Total Imports of 'Dumped' Product

Percentage Share in the Total Imports	*Cases*	*Per cent*
0-5	31	48.44
5-10	10	15.63
10-20	14	21.88
20 - 30	6	9.38
30 - 40	1	1.56
40 - 50	1	1.56
More than 50	1	1.56
Total	64	100.00

Source: UN COMTRADE.

Table 8

India's Share in the Total Imports of Dumped Products: Country-wise Distribution

Country	*Percentage Share of India in the total Import of the allegedly dumped product*							
	0-5	*5-10*	*10-20*	*20 - 30*	*30 - 40*	*40 - 50*	*more than 50*	*Total*
Argentina			1					1
Australia	1							1
Brazil	1		1			1		3
Canada	2	2	1					5
China			1					1
EU	15	6	2					23
Indonesia	1		1	1	1			4
Mexico				1				1
Trinidad &Tobago	1							1
Russian Federation	1							1
South Africa	2		2	1			1	6
Thailand			1					1
Turkey			2	2				4
USA	7	2	2	1				12
Total	31	10	14	6	1	1	1	64

Source: UN COMTRADE.

Table 8 gives the country wise details of the export share. In the EU, India is facing 23 cases, out of which in 15 products India's share in their imports is less than 5 per cent. Only two of these products have a share, which is more than 10 per cent. In case of the USA also, which is having the second highest number of cases, 9 products (out of 12) are having a share of less than 10 per cent. The picture is not different for other countries.

Another condition necessary for successful predation is that, the exporters should have global dominance in the product, which they are selling at a lower price in the foreign market. Then only it will be possible for the firm to sell the product at a lower price in some markets with a predatory motive. Table 9 reports India's share in the global export of some of allegedly dumped commodities.

Table 9
India's share in Total World Exports of the Dumped product

Percentshare	*Cases*	*Per cent*
0 to 5	43	69.35
5 to 10	5	8.06
10 to 15	12	19.35
20 to 25	1	1.61
30to 35	1	1.61
Total	62	100.00

Source: UN COMTRADE.

It appears that out 62 products considered here, for 43 products India's share is less than 5 per cent.

For another 5 products the share lies between 5 to 10 per cent. There are however 12 products for which the share is between 10 to 15 per cent. These products include jute bags to Brazil, bicycle tires and tubes to Argentina, bed linen to the EU etc.

Lastly, for the products where India enjoys more than 10 per cent share in the total exports, we looked at the number of countries exporting to the country which has initiated the case. If the number of exporting countries is high, then it will not be possible to practice predation for a single country; because, even if the domestic producers leave the market, other exporting countries may fill the gap. Here we found that the number of exporter countries is more than 10 for al the products where India has a share of more than 10 per cent in exports.

Thus we can see that, in case of many of the products for which India is facing anti dumping cases, India's share in total import of initiating country is very small. Moreover, for most of these products India does not have high share at the global level also, so that losses incurred due to predatory pricing in the initial phase can be compensated by high earnings from other markets. Again, most of the exports destinations are characterised by the presence of exporters from other countries. Hence, in such situations the possibility of any Indian exporter behaving as a predator is negligible.

Possibility of Retaliation

Studies discussing the motives behind the increased use of anti dumping measures in the recent years, also point out the fact that anti dumping measures may be used by countries in a strategic way to retaliate against the cases it faces in other countries.[3] To see whether that line of argument can explain the case of India, we looked at the number cases initiated by India against the countries where it is facing anti dumping initiations (table 10).

Table 10
Anti Dumping Case Against India and cases Filed in India

Countries	*No of Cases against India*	*No of Cases by India*
Argentina	5	0
Australia	4	1
Brazil	4	7
Canada	6	5
China PR	2	81
Egypt	4	0
EU	29	36
Indonesia	10	16
Korea RP	3	29
Malaysia	1	8
Mexico	1	2
Peru	1	0
Poland	1	4
South Africa	20	6
Thailand	2	16
Trinidad and Tobago	2	0
Turkey	7	4
USA	21	22

Here we see that, the EU and the USA which initiated the maximum number of anti dumping cases against India are also facing large number of anti dumping initiations in India. But South Africa which is another major user of anti dumping cases against India is facing 6 anti dumping initiations in India against 20 cases initiated against India. Similarly for countries like Australia, Canada and Turkey the number of cases initiated against India is much higher than the cases initiated by it. But at the same time there are quite a few countries against which India has initiated large number of anti dumping cases, though it is facing much fewer anti dumping initiations in those countries. They include China, Korea RP, Malaysia, Thailand etc.[4] Given such a situation we can say that retaliation may explain large-scale anti dumping initiations to some extent, though not fully.

Implication for Indian Exports

Given the large number of anti dumping cases that India is facing, the next important question is what will be the impact of such behaviour on India's exports. India's share in total world trade is very low. It accounts for even less than 1 per cent of the total world trade. India's exports as a percentage of world exports remained at around 0.5 per cent in the first half of 1990s. Though, it has improved to 0.61 per cent during 1998 and further to 0.65 per cent during 1999 and 0.7 per cent in 2000-01, its share in the world exports is still considerably low (WTO, 2002). However, trade policy reform measures has been initiated over the last decade aiming at creating an environment for achieving rapid increase in exports and making exports an engine for achieving higher economic growth. Over the years EXIM policy have been formulated in such a way so as to 'strengthen export production base, remove procedural irritants, facilitate input availability besides focusing on quality and technological upgradation and improving competitiveness. Steps have also bee taken to promote exports through multilateral and bilateral initiatives, identification of thrust areas and focus regions'.[5] But, increasing use of disguised protectionist measures such as anti dumping may appear as serious hurdles in achieving higher growths in exports.

Looking at the export pattern of India, we find that manufactured items constitute the biggest share. The share of various product groups in the export of India during the 1990s has been shown in the table 11.

Table 11
Export from India (1995-96 and 2001-02)

Product groups	*Percentage share (1995-96)*	*Percentage share (2001-02)*
A. Agricultural & Allied products	16.00	13.3
B. Ores & Minerals	4.00	2.6
C. Manufactures	77.7	76.1
(i) Leather Manufacturers	3.7	
(ii) Gems & Jewellary	16.8	16.0
(iii) Drugs/Pharmaceuticals	3.00	4.5
(iv) Manufactures of Metals	2.6	3.8
(v) Iron & Steel (Primary & Semi Finished)	1.7	1.7
(vi) Cotton yarn, Fabrics, Made ups	8.2	7.4
(vii) Readymade garments	12.0	11.3
D. Crude & Petroleum products	1.6	5.3

Source: Economic Survey 1995-96 and 2001-02.

We have already seen that majority of the anti dumping cases against India involve base metal products, which is followed by chemicals, textiles products etc. The table shows that though the share of manufactured metal was 2.6 per cent in 1995-96, it increased to 3.8 per cent in 2001-02. Textile and the articles of textile account for a substantial share of the total manufacturing exports. Its share was 20.2 per cent in 1995-96, which however has gone down to 18.7 per cent by 2001-02. Drugs and pharmaceuticals are also showing a considerable increase in its share in total exports from 3 per cent in 1995-96 to 4.5 per cent in 2001-02. These three sectors together accounted for nearly 30 per cent of the India's total exports by 2001-02. Thus, it may be a matter of concern that, the major sectors in which India is facing anti dumping charges accounts for a substantial portion of India's total exports.

Given this, the next point of query would be whether the initiating countries are major destinations for India's exports. If these countries are the major destinations for India's exports, anti dumping cases initiated by them will have higher distortionary effect on our exports. The EU is the biggest destination for our exports. Its share was 17.5 per cent during 1980-85, which further increased to 23 per cent during the later part of 1980's. North America held the second position, whose share increased from 17.5 per cent in 1980-85 to 19 per cent during 1985-90.[6] However, during 1990s we notice a few significant changes (table 12).

Table 12
Destination of India's Exports (1995-96 and 2001-02)

Countries	*Percentage share (1995-96)*	*Percentage share (2001-02)*
1. EU	27.39	22.47
2. North America	18.32	20.76
3. OPEC	9.68	11.92
4. Eastern Europe	4.20	2.86
5. Developing Countries	28.93	30.88
5.1. Asia	22.98	23.58
5.1.1. SAARC	5.41	4.62
5.2 Africa	4.76	5.16
5.3 Latin America	1.19	2.15

Source: RBI Handbook of Statistics, 2003.

Though the EU is still the major destinations of India's exports, its share has come down to 22.47 per cent in 2001-02. The share of the USA however increased to 18.32 per cent in 1995-95, which further increased to 20.76 per cent by 2001-02. The share of Eastern European countries registered heavy decline in their share in the total exports. On the other hand, there has been a significant rise in India's exports to the destinations like OPEC and developing countries in Asia, Africa and Latin America. Economic survey, 2001-02, reported that, the main countries contributing to increased share in India's exports includes, Thailand, Malaysia, China, Sri Lanka, Singapore, Bangladesh, Egypt, Kenya, Nigeria, Brazil, Mexico and Chile.

Looking at the countries which have initiated anti dumping cases against India, we can see that the EU and the USA who are biggest trading partners of India, are the two regions who have initiated maximum number of anti dumping cases against India. However, in the recent years developing countries like China, Thailand, Malaysia, Brazil etc, who have emerged as new destinations for our exports have also started initiating anti dumping cases against India.

To assess the possible implication for India's exports, we report the share of the country initiating anti dumping case against India, in the total export of that commodity from India. Higher the share of these countries in the total exports from India of that particular product, more serious will be the impact on the exports.

Table 13
Share of the Anti dumping case Initiating country in the total Export of the Allegedly Dumped Product from India

Percentage share	*Cases*	*Percentage of cases*
0 to 10	28	40.58
10 to 20	11	15.94
20 to 30	8	11.59
30 to 40	6	8.70
40 to 50	7	10.14
50 to 60	3	4.35
60 to 70	1	1.45
above 70	5	7.25
Total	69	100.00

Source: Commerce Ministry database and UN COMTRADE.

Table 13 shows that for 28 cases (40.58 per cent) the anti dumping case initiating country account for less than 10 per cent of the total export of that commodity from India. For another 11 cases the share lies anywhere

Table 14
Country wise Distribution of the Share of the Anti dumping case Initiating country in the total Export of the Allegedly Dumped Product from India

Country	*Percentage share of the products facing dumping charge in the total exports from India*								*Total*
	0 to 10	*10 to 20*	*20 to 30*	*30 to 40*	*40 to 50*	*50 to 60*	*60 to 70*	*above 70*	
Argentina	1								1
Australia	1								1
Brazil	3								3
Canada	4	1							5
China			1						1
EU	1	2	4	4	6	3		4	24
Indonesia	4	1			1				6
Mexico		1							1
Trinidad & Tobago	1								1
South Africa	7	1						1	9
Thailand	2								2
Turkey	2	1	1						4
USA	2	4	2	2			1		11
Total	28	11	8	6	7	3	1	5	69

Source: Commerce Ministry database and UN COMTRADE.

between 10 to 20 per cent. For the rest 30 cases the share in more than 20 per cent. In fact there are 9 products where the export to the particular country accounts for more than 50 per cent of India's exports of that product.

Looking at the country wise distribution, in case of the EU, we can see that, most of the cases involve products in which EU accounts for a major share in the total exports from India (Table 14).

For 17 of these products the EU's share in the total export is more than 30 per cent. For USA, which has initiated 11-cases, 6 of the products have a share of less than 20 per cent and the rest of the products have more 20 per cent of share in the total exports of that particular commodity. Thus we can see that the major export destinations of India are initiating maximum number of anti dumping cases against India. Practice of such disguised protectionism will seriously hamper the growth of Indian exports.

CONCLUSION

As we have stated in the beginning, there has been unprecedented rise in the use of anti dumping measures in the recent times. Besides the traditional users, many developing countries have also started using it very frequently. However, the number of developing countries facing anti dumping cases is much higher that the number of countries initiating them. This will have grave implication for these countries as they already have low share in the world trade. In this context we examined India's situation. India has been active in using anti dumping measures in the recent time, but the number of case it is facing in other countries is also very high. Our analysis shows that all these initiations against India can not be justified on predatory ground. First of all, India's share in the world market for most of the subject commodities was found to be too low to exercise any significant market power. More importantly, in the countries where they are facing anti dumping cases, they account for very small share in the total import of the allegedly dumped product. Therefore, the possibility of these exporters acting as predators is remote. We also saw that retaliatory motive behind initiation of anti dumping cases can not be ignored.

High number of anti dumping cases against India may have serious implication for its exports. Because the countries initiating anti dumping cases against India are the major trading partners of India to where considerable portions of our exports are directed. Moreover, in the case of many of the products, the countries, which have initiated the anti dumping cases, account for a major share in the total export of that commodity from India.

Thus the rampant use of anti dumping measures has appeared as a new menace in the arena of international trade. Frequent use of such contingent measures of protection will substantially reduce the benefit, which is expected to be realised from lowering the tariff rates. This is more applicable for the developing countries. This calls for revisiting the WTO anti dumping agreement and also the national laws. Here we must remember that in case anti dumping measures there is already a legal text reached at after rounds of multilateral negotiations. However, the WTO anti dumping agreement gives only the broad guidelines for the nations to frame their own anti dumping legislation. This gives the nations ample opportunity to interpret the different clauses of the agreement in a way that serve their protectionist objectives. Thus, the ambiguity of the WTO anti dumping agreement has caused widespread misuse of the law by the countries to protect their domestic industry. Many studies are of the view that the dynamics of national trade policies have led inexorably to creeping 'procedural protectionism' in anti dumping laws, as administrating authorities and legislatures develop rules and practices that increasingly tilt decision making process in favour of domestic interest.[7] They have pointed out a number of shortcomings of the anti dumping measure at the operational level.[8] Therefore what is required at this point is further clarification and improvement in the various provisions of the law. Initiations have been started in this regard. WTO requested the member nations to submit proposals identifying the issues which require further clarification. As many as 141 submissions were received from different countries. Important issues raised include process of determining the dumping margin (many argued for the prohibition of the practice of zeroing), determination of injury, standardizing the questionnaire, mandatory application of lesser duty rules etc. It is expected that current rounds of negotiations will help in further clarifying the legal issues and facilitate judicious use of the anti dumping law.

NOTES

1. See Agarwal A (2002), Baruah (2005), Singh S. (2005).
2. We have used UNCTAD classification of Developing and Developed countries. Refer to UNCTAD Handbook of Statistics for the same.
3. See Prusa and Skeath (2001).
4. Here we should however remember that year of adopting anti dumping legislations varies from one country to another. For example China started having an anti dumping law only from 2001.
5. Economic Survey, 2001-02.
6. Economic Survey, 1990-91.
7. Matsumoto K. and Finlayson G. (1990).
8. For detailed discussion on legal loopholes of the anti dumping law, refer to Jackson and Vermulst (1990).

REFERENCES

Aggarwal A. (2002), "Anti Dumping Law and Practice: An Indian Perspective", *Indian Council Research on International Economic Relations (ICRIER) Working Paper,* No. 85.

Baruah N. (2005), "Anti Dumping as a Measure of Contingent Protection: An Analysis of Indian Experience" *Centre for Development Studies (CDS) Working Paper,* No. 377.

Bourgeois J.H.J. and P. Messerlin (1998), "*The European Community's Experience'* in R.Z. Lawrence (ed.) *'Brooking Trade Forum'* The Brooking Institution.

Clarida R.H. (1996), "Dumping in Theory, in Policy and Practice' in Bhagwati (ed.) *Fair trade and Harmonization :Pre-equisites for free trade?* MIT Press.

Deandroff A.V. (1989) "Economic Perspective on Anti dumping Law", in Jackson J.H. and Vermulst E.A. (ed.) *Anti dumping: Law and Practice,* The University of Michigan.

Government of India (2003), Annual Report, 'Directorate *General of Anti dumping and Allied Duties'* .

Government of India "Economic *Survey*", Various Issues in R.Z. Lawrence (ed.) *'Brooking Trade Forum'* The Brooking Institution.

Jackson J.H. and E.A. Vermulst (ed.) (1990) "*Antidumping Law and Practice: A Comparative Study*" University of Michigan Press, USA.

Joskow P.L. and A.K. Klevorick (1979), '*A Framework for Analyzing Predatory Pricing Policy'* Yale Law Journal Vol. 89, pp. 213-270.

Krugman P. (1986), "Introduction: New Thinking About Trade Policy" in Krugman P. (ed.) "*Strategic Trade Policy and the New International Economics*" MIT.

Matsumoto K. and G. Finlayson (1990), "Dumping and Anti Dumping: Growing Problems in World Trade", *Journal of World Trade* Vol. 24, No. 4.

Ordever J. (1998), 'Predatory Pricing' in P Newman (ed.) '*The New Palgrive Dictionary of Economics and Law*', Vol. 3, Macmillan, London.

Prusa T. and S. Skeath (2001), "The Economic and Strategic Motives for Antidumping Filings", *NBER Working Paper,* No. 8424.

Reserve Bank of India (2003) "*Handbook of Statistics, 2003*".

Shin J.S. (1998), "*Possible Instances of Predatory Pricing in Recent US Antidumping Cases*".

Singh S.K. (2005), 'An Analysis of Anti Dumping Cases in India' *Economic and Political Weekly* March 12.

Tharakan P.K.M. (1995), "Japan-EC Drams Anti dumping Undertaking" *Centre for Development Studies, University of Antwerp - UFSIA, Publication* No. 5.

Tharakan P.K.M. (2000), "Predatory Pricing and Anti-dumping" in G. Norman and J.F. Thisse (ed.) '*Market Structure and Competition Policy*' Cambridge University Press.

Willig R.D. (1998), "Economic Effects of Antidumping Policy" in R.Z. Lawrence (ed.) '*Brooking Trade Forum*' The Brooking Institution.

WTO (2002), "Trade *Policy Review: India*".

Chapter - 10

The Economic and Health Insecurity of the Elderly in the India

Syam Parasad

INTRODUCTION

Ageing can generally be described as the process of growing old and is an intricate part of the life cycle. Basically it is a multi-dimensional process and affects almost every aspect of human life. Introduction to the study of human ageing have typically emphasised changes in demography focusing on the 'ageing of population'-a trend, which has characterized industrial societies throughout the twentieth century but in recent decades, has become a worldwide phenomenon. Ageing is basically the result of a two dimensional demographic transformation which is explained by overall declines in mortality and fertility.

This is a dynamic process and was first observed in post-industrial European societies in the nineteenth century. The United Nations Conference of Ageing Populations in the context of the family held in Japan in1994 observed that all developed countries at least one demographic issue in common: population aging which was the inevitable consequence of fertility decline. But although fertility decline is usually the driving force behind changing population age structures, changes in mortality assume greater importance as countries reach lower levels of fertility. Ageing of the population is a major phenomenon in the present day world as a result of the changing demographic transition. Though the phenomenon has a universal character, it occurs in various countries at different points of time. The ageing is a phenomenon already occurred in the developed countries in the later half of the twentieth century. The similar situation is emerging in the developing countries in the recent periods. Although the proportion of elderly in the age of 60 years and above is considered to be relatively low in the case of the developing countries such as India and China, they have a larger population base. Developed countries have aged with high social and economic development, the socio economic condition of the elderly in the developing world is a cause for concern as most of them end up in living below poverty line in old age due to inefficient social security (Rajan 2004).

GLOBAL AGEING

The projected size and growth of elderly population is of major concern among the demographers and policy makers throughout the world. Table 1 outlines the global aging scenario for the next 150 years as per the United Nations projections.

Table 1
Global Ageing Scenario: UN Estimates

Year	*Population (billion)*	*% aged 60+*	*% aged 65+*	*% aged 80+*
2000	6.0	9.9	6.8	1.1
2025	8.0	14.6	10.8	1.7
2050	9.4	20.7	15.1	3.4
2075	10.1	24.8	19.1	5.3
2100	10.4	27.7	22.0	7.1
2125	10.6	29.2	23.6	8.6
2150	10.8	30.5	24.9	9.8

Source: United Nations. 2003.

The population of the world stood at around 6.1 billion in the early 21st century and projected to increase to 9.4 billion in 2050 and 10.4 billion in 2100. If we compare the global population, it is doubled between 1950 and 2000 and likely to add another 4.4 billion in the next 100 years. However, the growth of the elderly population is much higher than that of general population (please put a reference) The proportion of elderly aged 60 and above is expected to grow from 9.9 per cent in 2000 to 14.6 per cent in 2025 and 21.1 per cent in 2050 respectively. Among the elderly, the oldest old (80+) is likely to increase its proportion from just 1.1 per cent in 2000 to 3.4 per cent in 2050 and 7.1 in 2100. Overall, the female elderly outnumber the male elderly. This is a clear indication of feminization of ageing (Bhat 1992).

The long-term estimates presented in Table 1 are an indicative that the 21st century will witness a gradual transition from a young nation to an ageing society the world over. The process of aging, which was first witnessed in low fertility western societies and in Japan, is now experienced in the developing countries of Asia, Africa and Latin America. Countries like China and India will not only are at the forefront in terms of absolute number of total population in the world, but also in terms of absolute number of elderly population. In brief, the long-term impact of decline in fertility will lead to a decrease in the population of children (0-14 years), which in turn will push up the population in the working age group and finally ends up with population ageing.

AGEING IN INDIA

Population ageing is the most significant consequence of the process known as demographic transition. Reduction in fertility leads to a decline in the proportion of young in the population. Coupled with fertility decline, reduction in mortality enhances the life span of individuals leading to higher life expectancy at older ages. In other words, population ageing involves a shift from high mortality/high fertility to low mortality/low fertility.

In the beginning of 20th century, the life expectancy for India was just 23 years for both sexes (Davis, 1951). In 1947, when India became independent from the British rule, life expectancy was around 32 years-added 9 years during the first half of the twentieth century. Improvements in public health and medical services have led to substantial control of specific infectious diseases and eradicated few more diseases, which translated into significant decreases in mortality rates among all ages. Government sponsored sanitation and maternal and child immunization programs have improved maternal health and reduced infant mortality. The infant mortality in 2002 for India is 63 of which it is 62 for males and 65 for females (Registrar General, 2004). This has enhanced the life expectancy at birth to 61 years for males and 63 years for females–30 years increase during the second half of the twentieth century (Registrar General, 2003).

The level of fertility is also equally high during the last 100 years and it still continues to be high; however, the process of decline is already being initiated. In 1901, the crude birth rate was around 50 per thousand populations, declined to 40 in 1951 and 24 in 2001 (see Table 2). Government sponsored family planning programs made initial impact in urban areas and later diffused to rural India. The total fertility rate for India is now around 3.1 per woman (Guilmoto and Rajan, 2005) and the Government of India aims to reach to 2.1 by 2010 (Government of India, 2000).

Table 2
Fertility, Morality and Life Expectancy in India

Year	*CBR*	*CDR*	*e60 males*	*E60 females*
1961	41.7	22.6	11.2	13.0
1971	41.2	19.0	13.6	13.6
1981	33.9	12.5	13.8	14.7
1991	29.7	10.7	14.5	15.4
2001	23.9	8.4	15.2	16.7

Source: Registrar General, Government of India, 2001.

The Indian aged population is currently the second largest in the world after China (100 million). The absolute number of 60 and over in India will likely to increase from 77 million in 2001 to 137 million by 2021 (United Nations, 2003). The decadal growth rate among elderly population during 1991-2001 is about 40 per cent–double than the general population growth of 21 per cent. The per centage of elderly in India has increased from 5.4 per cent in 1951 to 6.4 per cent in 1981 and further to 7.4 in 2001. If the per centage of elderly population is above seven per cent in any country, as per the UN criterion that country is ageing. In other words, India has emerged as "aging India" in the beginning of the 21st century. Thus twenty first century is the century of old (Leibig and Rajan, 2003).

Table 3
Aged in India, 1901-2001

Year	*Total*		*Males*		*Females*	
	Millions	*Per cent*	*Millions*	*Per cent*	*Millions*	*Per cent*
1901	12.06	5.06	5.50	4.55	6.56	5.59
1911	13.17	5.22	6.18	4.81	6.99	5.65
1921	13.48	5.37	6.48	5.04	7.00	5.70
1931	14.21	5.09	6.94	4.86	7.27	5.35
1941	18.04	5.66	8.89	5.43	9.15	5.91
1951	19.61	5.43	9.67	5.21	9.94	5.66
1961	24.71	5.63	12.36	5.46	12.35	5.80
1971	32.70	5.97	16.87	5.94	15.83	5.99
1981	43.98	6.42	22.49	6.35	21.49	6.50
1991	55.30	6.55	28.23	6.45	27.07	6.66
2001	76.62	7.44	37.7	7.11	38.88	7.85

Source: Sharma and Xenos, 1992; Updated by the researcher.

In 1991 census, the elderly population in India (excluding Jammu and Kashmir where no Census could be undertaken because of disturbed conditions) was 57 million compared to 20 million in 1951 (when the first Census after Independence was conducted) and that of 12 million as per the first census in the twentieth century. The 2001 census of India enumerated 76.6 million elderly persons (aged 60 and above), including the population of Jammu and Kashmir. Among them, 29 million are above 70 years and 8 million are above 80 years.

The different demographic regimes with in the country provide different stages of demographic development vary across states and union territories. Due to this divergence, we provide detail discussion on the elderly in India by states and territories as documented by the Registrar General of India with various indices of population ageing (Table 4).

Ageing of population has regional dimensions in India depends upon its stages of demographic transition. Among the states, Uttar Pradesh led with 11 million elderly, followed by Maharashtra (8.5 Million), Andhra Pradesh and West Bengal (5.7 million each) and Bihar and Tamil Nadu with 5.5 Million each. The smallest number of elderly is found in the union territory of Lakshadweep. The low fertility state of Kerala ranks as number one with the highest proportion of elderly in the country with 10.5 in 2001. Punjab and Himachal Pradesh occupy the second largest position in terms of per centage of elderly, followed by states of Tamil Nadu (8.9) and Maharashtra (8.7). Dadra Nagar Haveli registered the lowest proportion (4). The highest per centage of 80 years and above is seen in Himachal Pradesh (1.3 Per cent), followed by Kerala (1.2 Per cent).

Table 4
Demographic profile of aged in India 1991-2001

States/union territories	*2001*		*1991*	
	Number in '000	*Per cent to total population*	*population in '000*	*percentage of elderly*
India	76622	7.44	55606	6.58
A & N Islands	17	4.87	10	3.55
Andhra Pradesh	5788	7.64	4306	6.47
Arunachal Prad.	50	4.57	37	4.33
Assam	1560	5.86	1186	4.25
Bihar	5501	6.64	5227	6.05
Chandigarh	45	4.99	29	4.52
Chhatisgarh	1504	7.23	NA	
D. & N. Haveli	9	4.00	6	4.4
Daman & Diu	8	5.09	6	6.32
Delhi	720	5.22	444	4.72
Goa	112	8.35	74	6.34
Gujarat	3499	6.92	2540	6.15
Haryana	1584	7.51	1230	7.42
Himachal Pradesh	548	9.01	402	7.79
Jammu & Kashmir	675	6.71	432	5.78
Jharkhand	1579	5.87	NA	
Karnataka	4062	7.70	3041	6.78
Kerala	3336	10.48	2549	8.77
Lakshadweep	4	6.15	3	5.22
Madhya Pradesh	4281	7.09	4254	6.43
Maharashtra	8455	8.74	5453	6.91
Manipur	145	6.09	109	5.94
Meghalaya	106	4.58	82	4.62
Mizoram	49	5.50	34	4.93
Nagaland	90	4.54	65	5.4
Orissa	3039	8.28	2217	6.98
Pondicherry	81	8.32	56	6.9
Punjab	2192	9.02	1532	7.56
Rajasthan	3810	6.75	2666	6.06
Sikkim	29	5.37	19	4.66
Tamil Nadu	5507	8.87	4073	7.29
Tripura	233	7.29	192	6.96
Uttar Pradesh	11649	7.02	9250	6.65
Uttaranchal	584	6.89	NA	
West Bengal	5700	7.11	4087	6

Note: Calculation by the researcher based on the 1991 and 2001 censuses.

In 1991 census Uttar Pradesh had more than nine million elderly followed Maharashtra and Bihar with more than five million elderly in total population. The lowest number of elderly of three thousand was recorded in lakshadeep. In 1991, Kerala had the highest proportion (8.8%) of elderly population, followed by Punjab (7.8%), Haryana (7.7%) and Tamil Nadu (7.5%). Among major states, the lowest proportion was in Assam (5.3%) followed by West Bengal (6.1%), Bihar (6.3%), Rajasthan (6.3%), Gujarat (6.4%), Madhya Pradesh (6.6%), Andhra Pradesh (6.8%) and Uttar Pradesh (6.9%). All states and union territories in India have shown an increase in absolute numbers and per centages of elderly indicating that all states have undergoing both fertility and mortality transition at various stages.

Population ageing as a result of fast demographic changes in fertility and mortality in India is witnessing a phenomenon of fast ageing in rural areas with relatively larger proportion of elderly falling in the rural areas. Though the onset of fertility-mortality decline first occurred in the urban areas due to improvement in the health care and thus extended life but in India proportion of the elderly population is high in the rural areas.

More than three fourth of the elderly in India is living in the rural areas. This per centage is relatively large in the states of north and northeast where the rural elderly constitute more than eighty per centages. In the south Indian states and relatively industrialized states the proportion of the rural elderly is more. One of the underlying features of the increased rural elderly is that return migration by the elderly to the villages at the last stages of the life due to economic insecurity and cultural sentiments (Irudaya Rajan, Mishra and Sarma, 1999).

SOCIO ECONOMIC CONDITION OF ELDERLY IN INDIA

It is important to assess the socio economic conditions of the elderly in the context of current ageing population. Though census provides some basic data on economic activity among elderly, it does not provide other characteristics such as dependency status, unmet needs, ownership of property and financial assets. We have extensively used the 50th and 55th rounds of National Sample Surveys (NSS).

WORK PARTICIPATION AMONG AGED

As per the 2001 census, the work participation (both main and marginal workers) among the aged persons is forty per cent with sixty per cent among males and twenty one per cent among females. Work participation in rural areas is as high as forty five per cent while it is just twenty six per cent among the urban areas that reveals that elderly in the rural India is being compelled to work to an extended period of life cycle.

The NSS data is giving freedom so that we can manipulate with the raw data and improve the work participation rate among elderly men and women. This is what attempted in this analysis.

Table 5 gives details about work participation among elderly based on the two rounds of NSS. Here the activities such as household duties and domestic activity as considered as work and included in work participation rate.

Table 5
Work Participation Among Elderly
52nd round (1993-94)

Age	RURAL			URBAN			TOTAL		
	Male	Female	Total	Male	Female	Total	Male	Female	Total
60+	70.8	59.4	65.6	45.9	55.3	51.1	62.6	58.0	60.3
70+	48.8	33.4	42.0	30.8	31.3	31.0	42.7	32.6	37.7
80+	24.7	17.5	22.1	15.68	15.5	15.5	21.8	16.2	16.2

55th round (1999-2000)

Age	RURAL			URBAN			TOTAL		
	Male	Female	Total	Male	Female	Total	Male	Female	Total
60+	64.4	56.0	60.3	40.9	52.7	47.0	56.2	54.0	55.5
70+	43.0	29.5	36.5	26.8	30.3	28.3	37.3	29.7	33.6
80+	23.7	12.5	18.2	13.4	12.9	13.1	2.7	12.1	16.3

Calculated by researcher by using NSSO raw data (52nd and 55th rounds).

The 55th round of the NSS shows that nearly 56 per cent of elderly continue to work to earn a livelihood for themselves and their families. As the age advances, the work force participation rate declines–34 per cent at ages 70 and above and 16 per cent among aged 80 and above. The work participation of the elderly is much more visible in the rural areas where the deprivation is more acute due to changing family and social relations (Bose 2001, Bose and Shankardass, 2004) The increased participation of women in the work force is another noted findings of the NSS surveys. While in the NSS 52nd round also notes similar trend; however, there is a slight increase in the work force participation between two rounds of NSS. The analysis also indicates a need for enhanced social safety nets for elderly to provide a relief at the advanced ages of life. The high work participation among the elderly is also a sign of dependency as they are struggling to make a livelihood.

DEPENDENCY OF AGED

The sign of greater dependency among the elderly with their children and grand children is visible from the fifty second NSSO round. The data addresses the issues of fully, partially dependent or fully independent based on the questions answered by the elderly themselves. This is also an indication how the elderly perceive their socioeconomic status in the respective family.

In India, about fifty-five per cent of elderly persons reported themselves as fully dependent. As expected, the dependency ratio of among elderly females is much higher (61 per cent) compared to their male counterparts (45 per cent). Again, the dependency ratio is found to be higher in urban areas compared to rural areas, as most of the elderly continue to work in rural areas for extended years of life. In rural areas, 58 per cent females and 48 per cent of males were reported as fully dependant. The same ratios for urban areas are 54 and 45 respectively. As stated earlier, women are in the receiving end and their dependency ratios are much higher than males. Interestingly, one-third of elderly reported as fully independent.

Table 6
Dependency status of the Elderly

Status	*Rural*			*Urban*			*Total*		
	M	*F*	*T*	*M*	*F*	*T*	*M*	*F*	*T*
Non dependent	35.4	25.7	30.7	38.6	22.4	30.4	37.2	23.8	30.6
Partly dependent	18.6	17.1	17.8	16	13.5	14.5	17.5	15.5	16.5
Dependent	48	58.2	51.5	45.5	64	55	45.2	60.5	54

Note: Calculated by the researcher using NSSO raw data (55th round).

The states like Punjab, Kerala, Karnataka and west Bangal are on the top based on the fully dependency status. In most of the states, the fully dependency is more than half in the case of women. In general, except in the case of West Bangal, more urban elderly are fully dependent. In Kerala, more than sixty per cent of urban elderly are dependent. The condition of the urban women elderly is more volatile with higher dependency. The condition of the elderly discussed above is making a case for comprehensive social and economic safety nets.

The basic notion about the dependency of the elderly depends on which way they are dependant? It is crucial to assess the fact that whether they are deprived of the basic needs such as food, clothing, and medicines? The NSSO 52nd round addresses the above questions and the results derived from the survey are presented in Table 7. Our analysis indicates that three per cent of the rural elderly deprived of basic food needs in rural areas but it is 4.5 per cent in the case of clothing and it is ten per cent in the case of medicine. Ten per cent of them are deprived of at least one of the basic needs. This shows aged in the rural areas is subject to more vulnerability in terms of access of basic needs of Food, clothing and medicines.

THE OWNERSHIP OF ASSETS BY ELDERLY

The deprivation of the elderly mainly depends up on the lifetime earning of the individual as per the life cycle income. The assets owned are the best available savings of lifetime income (Modigliani 1952) .The ownership of the asset is an important indicator of the economic well being of the elderly. As a part of existing social practice of inheritance (Gosami 2001) most of the elderly person in India finds shortage of property in the upper end of the life. As per 52nd round of NSSO, sixty per cent and thirty per cent of rural and urban elderly are with out assets.

Table 7
Basic needs unmet by the Elderly in percentage

Basic Needs Unmet	*Rural*			*Urban*			*Total*		
	M	*F*	*T*	*M*	*F*	*T*	*M*	*F*	*T*
Food	2.9	3.3	3.1	1.4	1.6	1.5	2.3	2.7	2.5
Clothing	4.1	4.9	4.5	1.9	2.3	2.1	3.3	3.9	3.6
Medicine	8.9	10.2	9.5	3.8	4.6	4.2	7.0	8.0	7.5
At Least one	9.2	10.6	9.9	4.1	4.8	4.5	7.3	8.3	7.8

Calculated by researcher using NSSO raw data (55th round)

Around forty three per cent of the elderly do not own the financial assets while it is thirty five per cent in the case of property other than financial assets. A very signified finding is that rural urban divide is more visible in the case of non-financial assets in favour of the rural aged population with two third of them owns the assets. In general in India the denial of ownership is more acute among aged women.

In Kerala the deprivation is found to more acute with around sixty five per cent is denied off the financial assets when they are old with more than seventy five per cent in the case of women. Kerala is followed by other southern states Andhra Pradesh (62%) and Tamil Nadu (57%) of the aged population are denied of financial assets. On the issue of property ownership despite urban rural divide more than 50% of the elderly women have no ownership as per 52nd round of the NSSO. More interestingly there is a phenomenon that of a gender bias is visible in the property ownership of the elderly. The gender bias is very sharp in southern states with Kerala tops with more than seventy per centages of rural elderly in Kerala.

HEALTH CONCERNS OF ELDERLY

Demographic change or process that results in the process of ageing can have long run impact on the health of the elderly. A decline in the mortality with a fast ageing population can have higher incidence of morbidity among elderly (WHO 2004). In India health condition of the elderly in the extended life period is more vulnerable and majority of the elderly are ailing from chronic diseases such as cardiovascular diseases, cancer, diabetes etc. as per NSSO 52nd round more than fifty per cent of the elderly population in the rural areas are in the high incidence of the chronic diseases. Nearly forty per centage of aged in the rural India is having joint pain. Around 10% is having heart diseases and related blood pressure. Aged are also suffering from other diseases such as of cancer and diabetes.

Table 8
Disease Pattern among Elderly in India

Disease	*Male*	*Female*	*Total*
Cough	25.0	19.5	22.2
Piles	0.3	0.2	0.2
Problem of Joints	36.3	40.4	38.4
Blood pressure	10.8	10.5	10.6
Heart disease	0.3	0.3	0.3
Urinary problem	0.4	0.2	0.3
Diabetics	0.4	0.3	0.3
Cancer	0.02	0.03	0.03

More over elderly in India are mostly suffering from different forms of hearing, visual, speaking and locomotive disability. Table 9 shows India is having larger number of disabled aged in India. Among elderly there is a high prelavance of visual disability, which is almost as double as of hearing disability. Other forms of disabilities also there exist largely among aged in India.

Table 9
Disability Among Elderly in Millions

Type of Impairment	*1991*			*2001*		
	Males	*Females*	*Total*	*Males*	*Females*	*Total*
Visual disability						
Rural	1.00	1.48	2.48	1.29	1.93	3.22
Urban	0.20	0.31	0.51	0.34	0.53	0.88
Hearing disability						
Rural	0.51	0.54	1.11	0.74	0.70	1.44
Urban	0.15	0.10	0.29	0.25	0.25	0.50
Speech disability						
Rural	0.70	0.05	0.12	0.10	0.06	0.16
Urban	0.02	0.01	0.03	0.04	0.02	0.06
Locomotor disability						
Rural	0.67	0.44	1.11	0.86	0.58	1.44
Urban	0.15	0.13	0.28	0.25	0.22	0.47

In general aged in India is in a condition of vulnerability and living long in midst of various type and dimensions of insecurity. This detracting condition of aged in the extended years of life makes them more uncomfortable in the life.

AGEING IN KERALA

Due to an offshoot of the Kerala model of development by which the State has reached what demographers call the final stage of demographic transition. This is the stage at which there are fewer births and deaths in a population. From a demographic point of view, Kerala is about 25 years ahead of the rest of the country. A child born in the State today can expect to live over 70 years. A girl child fares even better - she can hope to live to 76.

Kerala is in the highest level of demographic transition appears as the most aged state in India with a total of 3.3 million aged persons, which is about 10.5% of total population. More than one per cent of the state's population is in the oldest old. The state also has high sex ratio in favour of women and also followed by around women above sixty suffering from widowhood and are more dependent on others to earn a living.

Breaking down of family ties and formation of the small and nuclear family had led to a negligence of the aged (Achenbaum 1978). As the family size cuts down as a result of demographic process, the belief that children will take care of the parents in old age is eroding in India (Dandelkar 1996). The situation in the urban areas shows of a rejection of the older people by the next generation and is spreading to rural areas (Desai 1985). In the nuclear family regime, the position of the aged became more vulnerable and treated as a burden to the family (Nayar 1992). Changing social and economic relations with a change in the family and non-family relations within the society had resulted in the social exclusion among aged in India.

In Kerala due to a shrinking family size as a result of low fertility resulted in a change in the intergenerational balance within the society. As a result of small family size and a decline in the number of children, the dependency of the aged is acute and thus led to a state of exclusion of the aged in the state. The transition from joint family to that of nuclear families has resulted in a family relation that creates a negligence of the elderly.

The migratory tendency among the population, as is evident in Kerala, leads to several implications on the living of elderly as the migration of the younger population will hamper the old age care system and return migration of the aged will hamper intergenerational balance (Wiseman, 1980). In Kerala increased stress on migration by the younger workers have created a condition of aged being left alone (Zachariah, Mathew and Rajan, 2003).

In Asian condition with the modernization of the society there is complete paradigm shift in the old age care there is a widespread expectation that the elderly will be taken care of by their children and that at least one child will co-reside with them (Cowgill, 1972; Knodel, Havanon and Pramualratana, 1984; Pramualratana, 1990; Tuchrello, 1989) but with a change in the perception with old age care was separated from familial relationship. Traditional Indian system had a legacy of treating elderly as head of the family and were taken care of the family itself in the later years (Jai Prakash 2001). A multiplicity of factors contribute to the changing status of elderly and thus vulnerability among elderly.

Studies have shown that a large proportion of this aged population live under conditions of deprivation and poverty which may be the result of relative deprivation in terms of income and social negligence (Rajan 2004). Though the data provides a brief idea about vulnerable condition of elderly in Kerala in the same pattern as in the Indian states.

ELDERLY IN KERALA: SOME CASE STUDIES

With this background here an attempt has been made to look this social reality from a micro prospective to understand the dynamics of socio economic deprivation and other concerns experienced by the elderly in Kerala from a micro level prospective. To conceive and reflect on the varied dimensions of such deprivation, we adopt an individual based enquiry on a case study basis. This case study method of enquiry is designed to account for varied situation and circumstances giving rise to vulnerability in old age, which is quite different from the prevailing perceptions. Here the study is carried out in Mattannur municipality of Kannur district of Kerala.

Mattannur like any other semiurban area of the state is having 15 per cent of total population that·constitute to an estimated number of 11500 as per 2001 census. The composition of the population is very much like other parts of the state with relatively dominance of agriculture sector that constitute nearly thirty per cent of population and followed by service and trading. Area is also having a significant migratory component in their total population.

Following section is documenting case specific narration of the living condition of elderly based on case studies.

C-I

Mr. Das* is 68 years old. He is a widower for the past 10 years and has no children. While in service, he lost his eyesight on account of a severe illness. But he says that even after his illness, he managed to continue working and earning a living without depending much on others. Now his health has deteriorated and he has become very weak. He gets a pension of Rs. 200 per month but he is hardly able to survive with that. He does not have any relatives and since his wife died several years ago, his only support is his friends with whom he stays. Some kind hearted and philanthropic people help him by proving financial assistance for which he is very grateful. He gets a bus travel concession on account of his physical handicap. He does not have any serious health problems, but is very weak and frail, and fully depends on people to help him.

C-II

Ms. Prema* is 71 years old and is a resident of an old age home for the past four years.. She is from a well -educated and rich family and has three brothers. Teaching was her only interest so she did not marry, as she was more involved with her career. At the age of 63, she had a very serious fire accident, which made her totally bedridden for the next two years. After a lot of medical care she is now able to move about slowly with a walker. As all her brothers are very busy people with no time to care for her, she was put in an old age home. The home takes care of most of her needs and also her daily necessities. She feels that she gets better care here than at home. She is totally independent economically and has absolutely no problem with money. However she is forced to adjust to the conditions of the old age home in Kannur, and she has no privacy or independence. Though most of her needs are satisfied, she sometimes feels very depressed and lonely.

C-III

Mr. Manikandan* is a retired railway employee and is presently 84 years old. He has four sons and a daughter. His wife died 23 years ago. He is now staying in a city with one of his sons. He finds his retired life quite enjoyable. He spends his time taking walks and reading religious books and is also currently involved in writing a book. He has studied unto high school and joined the railways as a clerk. He now gets a pension of about Rs.4300 and also free railway concession and medical facilities. He suffers from high blood pressure and also has problems with his teeth due to which he cannot eat his favourite food sometimes. He greatly enjoys being with his grandchildren and feels loved and cared for by his family, his children and grandchildren. He is very happy with life.

C-IV

Ms.Gita* is about 75 years old. She is a spinster who lives alone with her servant in an independent house. Ms.Gita began to feel old when she entered her seventies. Physical debilities and the lessening of faculties made her feel that old age had come. Earlier she could do everything herself, specially gardening which is her main hobby, but she began to develop osteoporosis (fragility of the bones). Three years ago she had a fall in a hospital where she had gone to visit a friend, which caused a fracture of the leg primarily due to osteoporosis. She counts herself lucky not to have fallen at home. But she had a lot of trouble due to this and had to undergo physiotherapy. She has a servant who is very efficient. Her nephews and nieces are always there to help her. She gets pension of Rs.4500 from the telephone department where she worked as a supervisor. She says that her pension is enough as long as she is not hospitalised. Loneliness is terrible problem. She gets few visitors. Who would come to see me she asks. She is a graduate in philosophy and is informally trained in music. Ms. Gita says that she has nothing to look forward to, no joys, no sorrows, but adds that she much better off than many others. The only thing she regrets is being a spinster. But her cheerful nature and her view of life and the joy of listening to music keep her going.

C-V

Mr. Sankaran* is 65 years old, and works as a shop assistant in a stationary shop. His son-in-law owns the shop. He did not have any fixed employment any time in his life, but for the past seven years has been working in the same shop. He is married with one son and one daughter both of whom are currently well settled. He says that his children stay close by and that he is "very happy" with them. Basically he lives on the income that he gets from the shop. Otherwise he does not get any kind of benefits from the government. He suffers from acute arthritis. But this does not prevent him from carrying out his daily activities and his work. He is quite happy with his life and does not feel the strain in anyway.

CS-VI

Ms. Leelamma* is 84 years old and a widow. She has one son who is working as a peon in an institution. Ms. Leelamma is uneducated and was an 'ayah' in an institution for almost fifty years. Recently the institution where she was working decided to send her away as she is too old to work. They also decided to give her a good sum of money for her loyalty. However, her son took matters into his own hands and insisted that the money be put in his name. At this point Leelamma was give the choice of living in an old age home, but she prefers to stay with her son in spite of his shabby treatment. She says that her daughter-in–law ill-treats her, but she prefers to live with her son rather than live in an old age home.

The case studies presented here are presented as a qualitative tool of analysis. Each case study shows the specific problems that a particular category of the aged may face. There are different categories of elderly. We see that there are three factors that affect the well being of the elderly:

Physical security
Emotional satisfaction
Financial security

Physical security: physical security relates to the satisfaction of physical needs such as food, shelter and clothing. It can be seen from the given case studies that though this is an important factor, it is not necessarily the most important factor.

Emotional security on the other hand seems to play a more important role since the lack of physical needs is compromised by the attitude to life, which plays a very important role in the overall satisfaction of the elderly.

Financial security on the other hand seems to be the least important of the three.

Though we see the importance of certain factors over others, it can be noted that the socio economic conditions of the aged to a great extent affects the conditions of the aged. With changes in technology and science, there have been changes in the traditional family set-up. The breakdown of the joint family, migration, changes in the attitude towards parents, changes in lifestyle and work environment have all affected the way people view the elderly and how the elderly view themselves. Fewer and fewer families stick on to the traditional joint family system. The concept of a one-child nuclear family where both parents go to work is a familiar norm in most modern societies. In many developing countries, this norm is slowly changing the traditional family network, where the joint family was the best social net for the elderly in terms of care and support. While the joint family network took care of all the needs of the elderly, the changes that have occurred in the social and economic dimensions have greatly altered the care and support given to the aged.

The case studies described here are presented as a qualitative tool of analysis. Each case study shows the specific problems a particular category of the aged may face. While some factors like loneliness, emotional stress or mental satisfaction cannot be measured in real quantitative terms, we can see how important these qualitative factors are in shaping measurable factors like marital status etc. and hence in the analysis in the socio economic profile of the aged. One point that can be observed about the three factor influences the aged. It can be seen that emotional security is neither influenced by physical well-being or economic factors but is completely independent in determining the well being or the level of satisfaction of the aged. Specific rural-urban differences and also gender differences can be seen even at the micro level. While we see that the level of education to some extent influences the financial status of the elderly what is more important is how the elderly view themselves. Differences with gender also can be seen from the micro level which itself is influenced by various economic end social factors like education, marital status and financial factors.

CONCLUSION

The process of ageing that was result of demographic events of decline in the mortality and fertility is having implication in the social and demographic spectrum. The socio economic and health condition of the aged in the rural India have shown a grim picture as they are acquainted with economic, health and social deprivation that resulting in vulnerability among elderly.

The condition of the most aged state of Kerala is also not much different from the India as per the case studies among the rural elderly; it is evident that they are suffering from Increased stress when they are old from economic, emotional and social isolation from the general population. The migratory tendency among the population, as is evident in Kerala, leads to several implications on the living of elderly as the migration of the younger population will hamper the old age care system and return migration of the aged will hamper intergenerational balance. In Kerala increased stress on migration by the younger workers have created a condition of aged being left alone. This along with demographic structural shift such as decline in the family size and changing role of family and break down of the joint family has resulted in the isolation among the aged.

The social and economic deprivation of the elderly in India is evident from the surveys mentioned above. The poverty and economic deprivation make the elderly in a state of misery and negligence. So the concept of the social security is having a crucial role to play in providing "well being" for the elderly. So to improve condition of elderly in the rural areas India requires a comprehensive insurance system to cut shot the risk of the aged in the period of extended life.

REFERENCES

Achenbaum, W.A. (1978), Old Age in the New Land: The American Experience since 1790 Baltimore: The Johns Hopkins University Press. (Paper edition).

Bose A. (2000), Demographic Transition, Seminar Paper in a Symposium on the Greying of Our Society, New Delhi.

Christaphe G.Z. and S. Irudaya Rajan (2001), Half a Century of Fertility Transition in the Indian Districts 1951-2001, Population and Development Review, New Delhi.

Christophe Gulimoto and S. Irudaya Rajan (eds.) (2005), Fertility Transition in South India, Sage publications London/Thousand Oaks/New Delhi.

Cowgill, Donald O. (1972), "The Role and Status of the Aged in Thailand", in: D.O. Cowgill and L.D. Holmes (eds.), *Aging and Modernization* (New York, Appleton-Century-Crofts), pp. 91-101.

Indrani Gupta and Deepa Sankar (2003), "Health of the Elderly in India: A Multivariate Analyis" in Journal of Health & Population in Developing Countries, 24 June.

K.C. Holden, R.V. Burkhauser, and D.A. Myers (1986), Income Transitions at Older Stages of Life: the Dynamics of Poverty, the Gerontologist 26: 292-297.

Knodel, John, Napaporn Havanon and Anthony Pramualratana (1984), "Fertility Transition in Thailand: A Qualitative Analysis", *Population and Development Review* 10, pp. 297-328.

Mari Bhat P.N. (1992), 'Changing Demography of Elderly in India' Current Science 63 (8) October 25.

Nayar P.K.B. (1992), Needs and Problems of the Aged, a Case Study of Kerala ICSSR 1992.

Raghavaiah Radhika (2005), Ageing in India: Micro Perceptive (Unpublished Paper).

S. Irudaya Rajan (2004), Chronic Poverty Among the Elderly WP 17 Chronic Poverty Research Centre IIPA.

S. Irudaya Rajan, U.S. Misra, P.S. Sharma (1996) India National Ageing Trends, Life Long Preparation for Old Age in the Asia and the Pacific United Nations.

The Population Year Book 2001 and 2003 United Nations.

Zachariah, Mathew and Rajan (2003), Dynamics of Migration in Kerala: Determinants, Differentials and Consequences, Oriental Longman.

Chapter - 11

State's Health Expenditure in India: An Analysis of Pre and Post Reform Period

Sandeep Sharma

INTRODUCTION

Health expenditure is one of the prime mechanisms to enable higher levels of health achievement as well as increasing overall access to health service. Health sector was placed in directive principle in the constitution of India and with a vision for creating a welfare state, much of the initial initiative for development of this sector was by the government specially till 70s. Banerjee (2001) has termed this period as golden period for health sector in this country, it witnessed rapid growth of public institutions. With this rapid increase in public institutions the health sector in India followed a mixed economy with significant growth in private health care system. Economic reforms initiated in 1990's was another benchmark in health care sector in the country with surge for stabilising the economy and boost economic growth, the focus was on productive sector and less stress on already lacking social sector.

Economic reforms initiated in our country from 1991, had a multiple agenda of correcting fiscal situation as well as creating investment friendly environment, to boost economic growth. Structural Adjustment Programme (SAP) in one such corrective mechanism, it refers to a set of policy advice given to developing countries by international agencies, mainly the World Bank and the International Monetary Fund (IMF), but also other donor agencies like USAID. The objective of SAP has been to enhance economic growth through macroeconomic stability and elimination of market distortions. These adjustment policies from the perspective of health sector development have raised numerous debates.

Structural adjustment meant overall fiscal squeeze with lesser amount of money left for the social sectors, health sector like other social sector has to reduce its sectoral allocation. Also greater deregulation was accompanied with privatization. All these aspect bears a negative implication for health care delivery as it means the state has to withdraw from playing an active role and there is shift in perceiving health as need to demand defined by consumers willingness and ability to pay (Baru, R. 1999). Another important aspect related to this adjustment policy is the reform in the health sector of the public health institution, wherein the public institution will mobilize their own resources through mechanism like user fees on the basis of ability to pay by the people or we can say that taking money from those who can pay for the service while the service remaining accessible for the poor.

Health falls in the concurrent list, which means that both centre as well as state has a responsibility towards health sector allocation. Kaur et al (2002) points out the share of state is more then 80% of the total allocation, which means that state has a major responsibility in health development of this country. With economic reform states were free to take their stance on reform policies, but with the existing centre state fiscal relationship on revenue sharing and already deteriorating state finances, the social sector was facing strain at the state level. Mahendra Dev (2002) while analysing social sector expenditure found better performance of centre compared to state. In fact in the states the share of social sector has been less during the post reform period. Author concludes that although social sector expenditure is related to centre state fiscal relationship, the centre's better performance is in the cost of state by withholding money to state. Prabhu (1999) observes that there was a sharp decline in allocation of centre for health moreover the pattern of allocation has been mostly disease specific with public health being neglected at large (Baru 2001).

With this background, this study to look at how health sector expenditure have changed with the initiation of the reform process This analyses role of state in terms of health expenditure and what is the direction it has taken from pre reform to post reform period. Whether reform process has affected the allocation process or state has been able to maintain its stance.

Data source for the paper are Reserve Bank of India (RBI) Bulletins various issues for expenditure, Central Statistical Organisation (CSO) government of India for Net State Domestic Product (NSDP), and National Sample Survey 52nd Round on Health. Both the expenditure data as well as the NSDP data are at the constant 1993-94 prices. Health expenditure includes expenditure on Medical and Public health and Family welfare and it includes both revenue and capital expenditure. The period of analysis is from 1980-81 to 2002-03.16 major states are taken for analysis.

This paper is divided into 8 sections, the 1st section gives the introduction and in the 2nd section we look at the theoretical underpinning behind health sector financing. The 3rd section looks at significant development in health sector in India. The 4th part looks at the broad trends in health sector expenditure across states, 5th section looks the relationship between income and health expenditure across states. 6th section looks at the within public expenditure of states how health have fared and lastly the 7th section looks at the desegregation of health expenditure and utilisation pattern of government services. The last section concludes the discussion.

STATE AND HEALTH CARE: THE ALTERNATIVE APPROACHES.

There are two approaches to understand the investment in health. The human development and human capital approach. Human capital approach views investment in health as an investment in capital goods required for economic growth. Whereas in human development approach the thrust is on enabling basic human capabilities, both these approaches have been in limelight in recent decades.

In human capital approach the thrust is on investment in health, which will lead to productive life. It considers investment in education, health, nutrition and health as leading to formation of human capital, a critical mass of which is a means to higher productivity and higher economic growth. In this framework role of state is that of mere facilitator. Direct state investment is limited and confined to expenditure on 'merit goods' that yield large positive externalities. Following this viewpoint, public finance is mostly limited to areas of control of communicable disease, immunisation and other specific programmes that has large positive externalities .The overall delivery of health services or the promotion of basic health care is not necessarily being the focus of the government. A significant thing to be noted that such human capital formation is expected to take place at an individual level; individuals invest in themselves in expectation of higher private earning in the future (Prabhu 1998). In case of human development approach[1] the importance is given to health as an end of a development process. In assessing well being of people in developing countries human development approach asks questions such as do people live long? Do they escape preventable morbidity? Do they avoid mortality during infancy and childhood? Do they avoid under nourishment and hunger? Do they enjoy freedom and personal liberty? In this framework fulfilling the health needs of the people becomes one of the important goal of development process. Human development approach becomes relevant if we target overall health improvement of the people and in this context state's role in providing health care as a public good becomes pertinent.

HEALTH SECTOR DEVELOPMENT IN INDIA

In India although there has not been direct dent on reducing inequalities in health but the need of underprivileged were recognised right from the time of independence. Health was included in directive principle of our country so it acted as an impetus for the health sector development.

There have been various milestones in health sector development, where state had a proactive role. Alma atta declaration of 1978 paved the way for increase of health infrastructure, national policy of 1983 clearly laid focus on increasing the primary health care in the country along with well developed tertiary level health care. But there has been resentment in implementation of these programmes, for instance primary health care for all was viewed as selective primary health care and the focus was to identify SOME diseases on the basis of mortality and morbidity, and it replaced comprehensive primary health care. The concept of selective primary health care rapidly gained popularity in official international circle despite its major problem in its conceptualisation. For example, disaggregating some diseases undermine the issue of interlinkages between diseases, which are responsible for mutual exacerbation as in case of diarrhoea and malnutrition (Qadeer 1999).

Although there has been various criticism on implementation of selective disease programme in the country question were also raised at the functioning of health facilities in general. Ineffective health delivery by state has been documented to a large extent in India. Several reasons have been identified in the literature for the problems that India's health care system faces. These vary from misallocation of resources to inefficiencies in delivery system (Tulasidhar, 1996). World Bank report explains the inefficiency of public system can be related to the low resources and low capability for effective intervention (World Development Report 1997). These aspects act as a background for another shift in health care towards health sector reforms across the developing countries of the world. As the cost aspect of health gained momentum and the dream of state led free health for all movement gradually stagnated. The focus shifted to efficiency of the health care system, following the appearance of the World Bank's influential financing health services in developing countries.

Banerji (2001) evaluating the health sector of the country regards the first two decades after independence as the period of public health care system development aimed at increasing access in health and improving overall health. He observes that in the last three decades, the quality of health service has declined to a great extent, and he identifies three forces behind it, preoccupation with family welfare programmes, the imposition of so called international initiative in health (Development aids determines the health programme) and considerable involvement of western countries in shaping social sectors (including health), economic and political policies of the country in the form of pressure for privatisation in SAP from the late eighties onwards. So, even with rapid growth of health care system in the country 75% of hospitals are in private hands. The dominance of the private sector not only denies access to poorer sections of society, but also skews the balance towards urban-biased, tertiary level health services with profitability overriding equality, and rationality of care often taking a back seat (Deogaonkar 2004)..

TREND IN HEALTH EXPENDITURE ACROSS STATES

In this section we will look at the trends in health expenditure across states from 1980 to 2003.The main focus will be on the broad pattern of health expenditure across states and how it has changed from pre reform to post reform period.

Figure 1 shows the average of all states in per capita health expenditure along with variation across states. Overall there has been increase in health expenditure, although the increase has not been uniform. There is a dip from period 1984-85 to 1986-87. From 1986 to 1991-92 there is a rise in health expenditure, in the next periods we don't see much increase till 1996-97. In the last part of 90's we see again the rise in health expenditure. In case of variation across states we see overall decline, but it is sharpest for the period 1980 to 1984.Variation shows increasing trend 1983-84 to 1998-99, although with fluctuations. Again it falls back till 2001 and again increases in 2002-2003.

Figure 1
Average and Coefficient of Variation of Per Capita Heath Expenditure (PCHE) of the States at 1993-94 Constant Prices

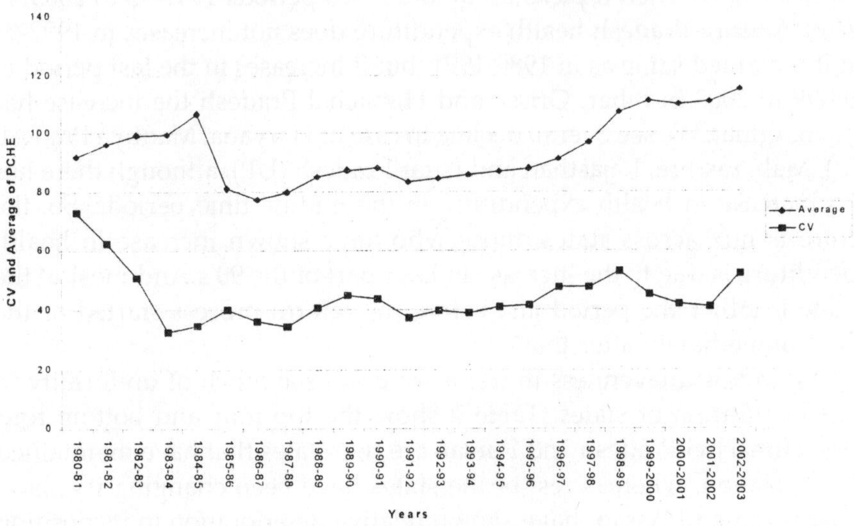

To get the better picture of the individual states, Table 1. shows the state wise per capita health expenditure.

Table 1
Per Capita Health Expenditure Across States in Different Time Periods
(At Constant 1993-94 Prices)

States	*1980-85*	*1986-91*	*1992-97*	*1998-2003*
Andhra Pradesh	82	72	72	99
Assam	80	78	74	68
Bihar	50	47	52	58
Gujarat	93	85	88	161
Haryana	118	79	76	93
Himachal Pradesh	255	192	209	257
Karnataka	69	80	87	123
Kerala	107	92	98	120
MP	80	57	59	75
Maharasthra	105	86	86	104
Orissa	76	61	59	80
Punjab	112	119	107	152
Rajasthan	124	74	94	108
Tamil Nadu	104	84	103	124
UP	56	61	61	51
West Bengal	68	68	72	103

Source: RBI Bulletin various issues. The population figures has been taken from CSO.

Assam is the only state that has shown constant decline with time, whereas West Bengal and Karnataka are the only states that have shown increasing trend with time. In case of Andhra Pradesh, Bihar, Himachal Pradesh, Kerala, Maharasthra, Orissa, Punjab and Tamil Nadu we see overall increase in health expenditure although there is a decline from 1980 to 1990-91. Then it picks up in latter two periods 1992-93 to 2003, in case of Andhra Pradesh health expenditure does not increases in 1992-93 and it remained same as in 1986-1991, but it increases in the last period of 1998-99 to 2003.In Bihar, Orissa and Himachal Pradesh the increase has been marginal. We see overall decline in case of Haryana, Madhya Pradesh (MP), Maharasthra, Rajasthan and Uttar Pradesh (UP), although there has been increase in health expenditure in the middle time periods. So, the picture is mix across states, those who have shown increase in health expenditure is due to the increase in later part of the 90's.And most of the decline is either the period just before the reform process started or the period immediately after that.

Due to this unevenness in trend we don't see much of uniformity in terms of position of states. Table 2 show the top four and bottom four states. Himachal Pradesh and Punjab are two states that have maintained its top position, whereas rest of the states have been changing its place. Maharasthra and Assam have shown relative deterioration in its position whereas Karnataka and West Bengal have shown improvement in its position. Kerala is among top four for two periods. Interestingly, among poor states we see some degree of commonality with states such as Bihar, UP, MP, Orissa and Assam.

Table 2
Performance of State in Allocation to Health Sector in Different Time Periods

Relative Position of Sates	*1980-85*	*1986-1991*	*1992-97*	*1998-2003*
Top Four States	Punjab	Maharasthra	Kerala	Tamil Nadu
	Haryana	Kerala	Tamil Nadu	Punjab
	Rajasthan	Punjab	Punjab	Gujarat
	Himachal Pradesh	Himachal Pradesh	Himachal Pradesh	Himachal Pradesh
	Bihar	Bihar	Bihar	UP
Bottom Four states	UP	MP	Orissa	Bihar
	West Bengal	UP	MP	Assam
	Karnataka	Orissa	UP	MP

INCOME AND HEALTH EXPENDITURE

Income both at household level as well as at the state level influences the level of health expenditure. In fact this route of economic growth leading to higher allocation of health expenditure is one of the main arguments in favour of growth leading to positive health outcome (Human Development Report1996). This route seems to fit the ideas of believer of globalisation process, better economic progress leading to better health outcome. At the same time we know about the achievements of country like Sri Lanka where it was proved that economic growth is not a sufficient condition and strong public action can be a better policy option.

In this section we look at the relationship between NSDP and health expenditure. We will look at the relationship between the two both in absolute level and also we will look at the share of health expenditure from the NSDP. Figure 2 show the scatter between the two for 1980-85 and 1998-2003.

Scatter in figure 2 between per capita NSDP and per capita health expenditure across the states does not show strong positive relationship. The correlation coefficients for two periods are 0.35 and 0.54 between these two variables. Himachal is an outlier in both the time periods, with very high health expenditure. Bihar, UP, Orissa, Assam and MP not only have low-income levels but also relatively lower health expenditure. At the higher income level Punjab and Haryana had higher health expenditure in 1980-85 and in 1998-2003 it is Gujarat and Punjab. In the second period health expenditure of Haryana has reduced a great deal, Maharasthra another state with high level of income with relatively high health expenditure in 1980-85 showing decline in 1998-2003. Rajasthan, Karnataka, Kerala, Tamil Nadu and West Bengal fall in middle category

Figure 2
Per Capita NSDP and Per Capita Health Expenditure in 1980-85 and 1998-2003

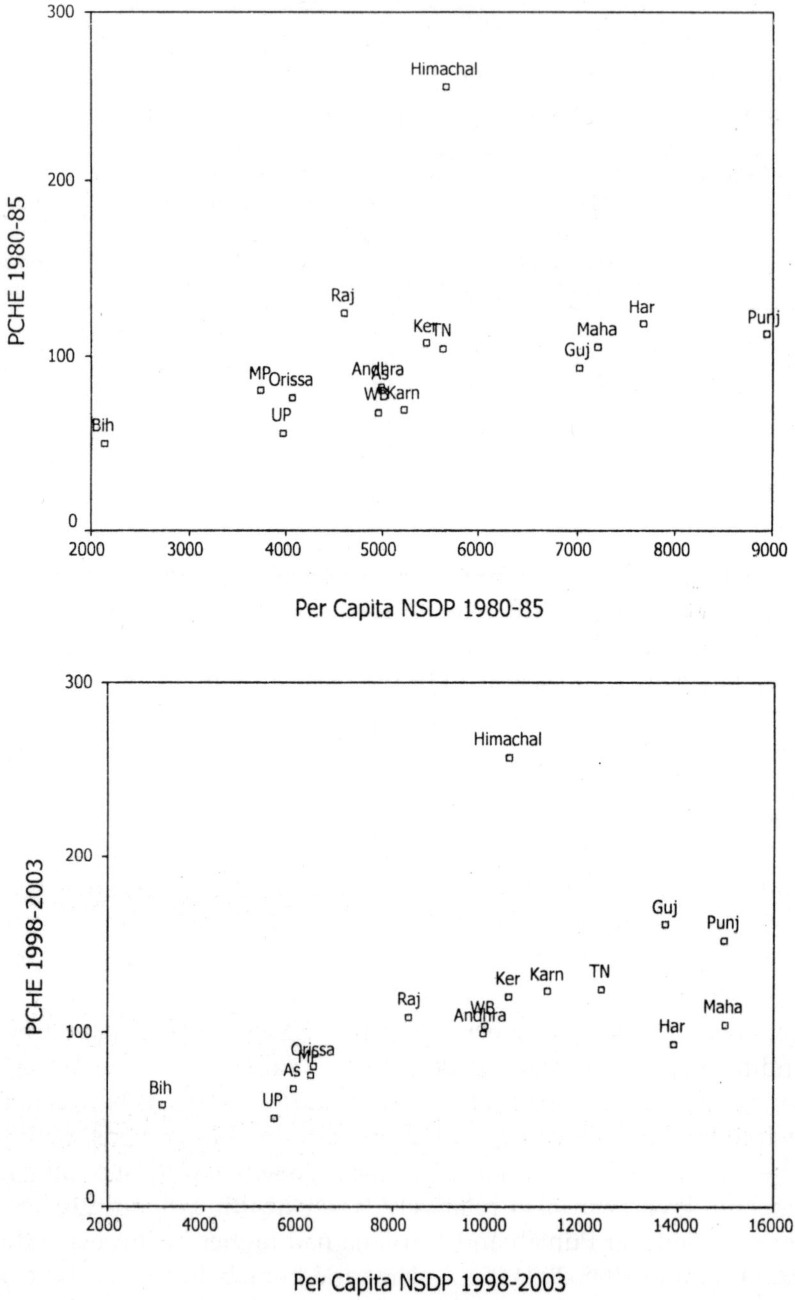

Andhra = Andhra Pradesh, AS = Assam, Bih = Bihar, Guj = Gujarat, Har=Haryana, Karn= Karnataka, Ker = Kerala, MP = Madhya Pradesh, Mah = Maharasthra, Punj = Punjab, Raj= Rajasthan, TN = Tamil nadu, UP = Uttar Pradesh, WB = West Bengal.

although in some cases say in 1980-85 the health expenditure of Rajasthan exceeded that of Punjab or the health expenditure of West Bengal in the same period was lower then Orissa. The grouping of middle category becomes clear in 1998-2003.

These scatter diagram helps us to get the broad pattern and it definitely suggests that the poorer states are relatively worse off in terms of health expenditure. To see relationship between income and health expenditure within states we have looked at health expenditure as a percentage of NSDP (Figure 3). The four vertical blocks represents different time period starting with the first time at the left.

Figure 3
State wise Health Expenditure as Percentage of NSDP in 1980-85, 1986-91, 1992-97 and 1998-2003

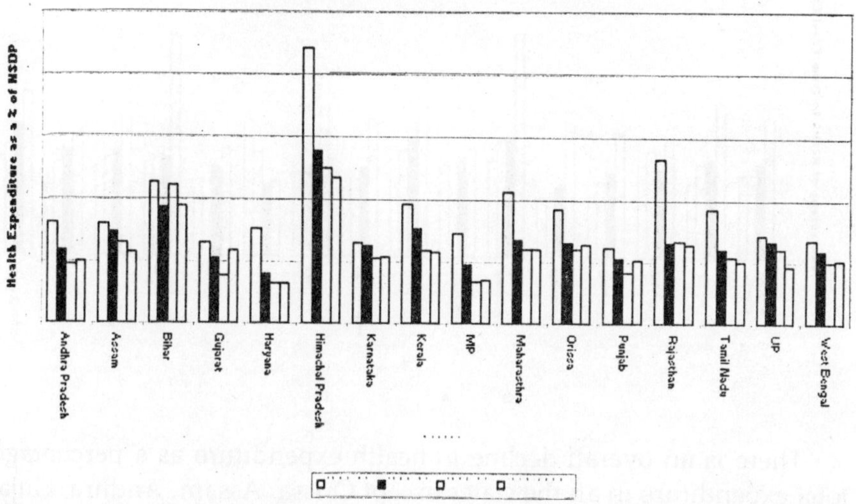

There is overall decline in all the states from 1980-81 to 2002-03 in the share of health expenditure from the NSDP. In case of Assam, Himachal Pradesh, Maharasthra, Kerela, and Tamil Nadu and UP there has been a constant decline in all the time periods. In Gujarat, Haryana, Karnataka, Orissa and West Bengal overall decline is accompanied by slight increase from periods 1992-97 to 1998-2003.Whereas for Rajasthan, Punjab and Bihar there is slight increase from 1986-91 to 1992-97. At an average the expenditure has been less then 2% across states with Himachal Pradesh being at the top and Haryana being at the lower end in all the time period. In the 80's Himachal Pradesh, Bihar, Maharasthra, Rajasthan, Kerala and Assam (in 1986-91) are the higher spender whereas Punjab, Gujarat, West Bengal (in 1980-85), UP (in 1980-85), Haryana (in 1986-91), MP (in 1986-91) and Andhra (in 1986-91) are at the lower side. In 90's the states with higher allocation are Maharasthra, Himachal Pradesh, Bihar, Rajasthan, Assam (in 1992-97) and Orissa (in 1998- 2003). At the lower side we have

Haryana, Punjab (in 1992-97), MP, UP, Gujarat, Andhra and Tamil Nadu (in 1998- 2003).

HEALTH EXPENDITURE AND TOTAL EXPENDITURE

In the previous section we have seen that health expenditure as a share of income has shown decline in the post reform period. Share of health expenditure out of total expenditure will enable us to understand the health expenditure performance and whether there has been any provision to protect this sector. Health expenditure comes under development expenditure as a broad category and it is listed under social sector.

Figure 4

State wise Health Expenditure as Percentage of Total Expenditure in 1980-85, 1986-91, 1992-97 and 1998-2003

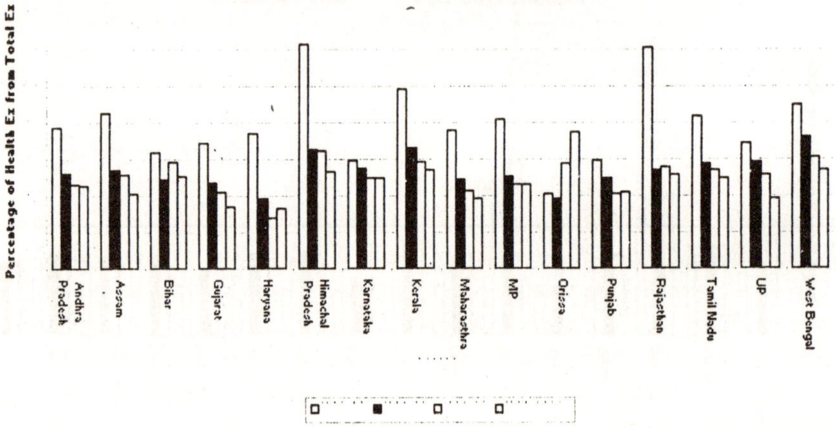

There is an overall decline in health expenditure as a percentage of total expenditure in all the states except Orissa. Assam, Andhra, Gujarat, Gujarat, Himachal Pradesh, Kerala, Maharasthra, Tamil Nadu and West Bengal have shown absolute decline with time. In case of Karnataka, MP and Punjab there is a decline in the share of health expenditure from 80's to 90,s although in both time period of 90's there is no change in allocation in these states. In case of Bihar, Rajasthan and Orissa there is an increase from period 1986-1991 to 1992-97 and again it goes down in the last period. In case of Haryana there is an increase from 1992-97 to 1998-2003, but overall there is a decline.

In the 80's the top states are more or less common with West Bengal, Kerala, Rajasthan, Himachal Pradesh and UP (Only in 1986-91). Whereas at the lower side we see Orissa, Punjab, Karnataka and Bihar in 1980-85. Haryana, Gujarat, Orissa and Maharasthra in 1986-91. In 90's again we see West Bengal, Kerala and Himachal Pradesh with higher share on health in both the time periods, also there are Bihar (in 1992-97) and Orissa (in 1998-2003) under this category. At the lower side we have Haryana, Maharasthra, Gujarat, Punjab in 1992-97 and UP in 1998-2003.

Figure 5
Share of Health Expenditure from Social Expenditure in 1980-85, 1986-91, 1992-97 and 1998-2003

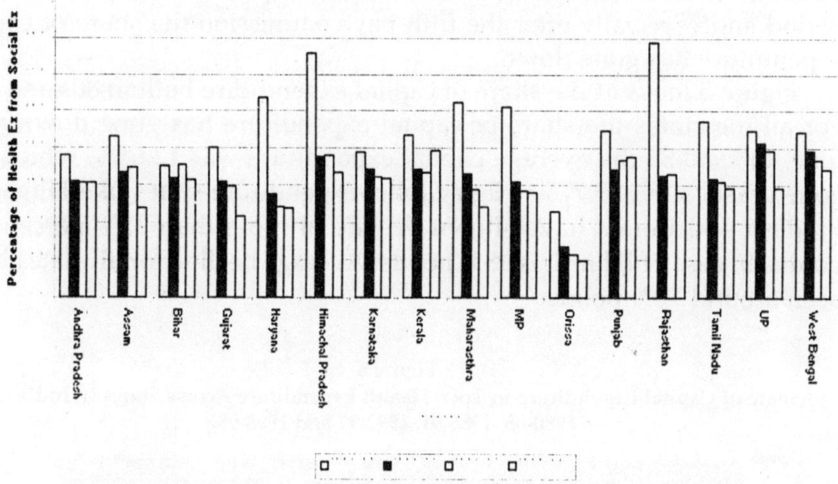

Even in case of share of health expenditure from social expenditure we see the same pattern, as there is an overall decline in all the states (Figure 5). As it was seen in the preceding section this decline has not been even across all the states, same pattern we see here. In case of Bihar Gujarat, Haryana, Karnataka, Maharasthra, MP, Orissa, Tamil Nadu, UP and West Bengal there has been an absolute decline with time. In Andhra and Kerala we see an increase in health sector share from1992-97 to 1998-2003. Assam, Himachal Pradesh and Rajasthan show an increase from 1986-91 to 1992-97. In Punjab with a decline from 1980-85 to 1986-91 it show an increasing trend.

States with higher shares in 80s are Maharasthra, Himachal Pradesh, Rajasthan in 1980-85 and Himachal Pradesh, Kerala, West Bengal and UP in 1986-91. At lower side there is Andhra, Orissa, Bihar and Karnataka in 1980-85 and Orissa, Haryana, Andhra and Gujarat in 1986-91.In the 90s, we see some commonalities with few exceptions West Bengal, Punjab, Himachal Pradesh, UP (in1992-97) and Kerala (in1998-2003) at the higher side. At the lower side we see Maharasthra (in1992-97), Haryana, MP, Gujarat (in 1998-2003) and Assam (in 1998-2003).

DISAGGREGATING HEALTH EXPENDITURE AND UTILISATION OF HEALTH SERVICES

Expenditure in health just like any other government's expenditure is divided into capital and revenue account. Capital expenditure is meant for building up of the health infrastructure and the revenue expenditure deals with effective functioning of the system. Together these components ensure quality of health care services. Reform process can have an offsetting affect if there is a cutback in capital expenditure, in other words it means higher participation of private players in health delivery. Duggal (2000) points out that the declining trend in capital expenditure after the reform period and especially after the fifth pay commission the share of capital expenditure has gone down.

Figure 5 looks at the share of capital expenditure both in 80s and 90s. For all the states the share of capital expenditure has gone down with time. In 1980-85 the average capital expenditure was 12.61%, which has gone drastically to 3.77%. High capital expenditure states like Himachal Pradesh and Kerala have shown decline of more than 75% percentage points. In case of Bihar it is 98% points. Average decline for all states have been around 70% points.

Figure 6

Share of Capital Expenditure in Total Health Expenditure Across States in India in 1980-85, 1986-91, 1992-97 and 1998-03

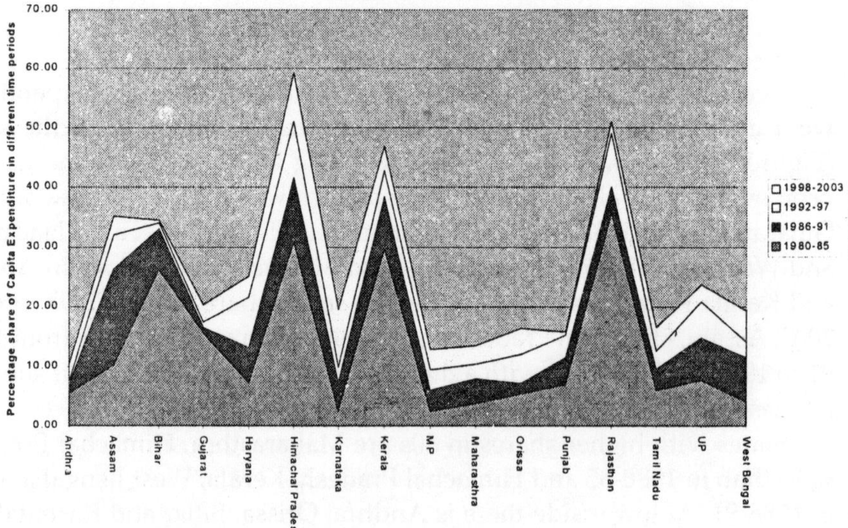

With this drastic cut in capital expenditure will have an impact on the avaibility of public health services. Table 3 below clearly shows the decline in reliance on public health institutions from 1986-87 to 1995-96 for inpatient care. In case of outpatient care reliance on private facilities across all the states have been high but we have not reported them here as it is the tertiary level of care which is going to be most affected due to adjustment policies of the government. World development Report on Health (1993) basically talks about cut back in tertiary level of care and to enable hospitals to raise their own resources (Baru, 1999).

Total reliance on government hospitals of all type have come down from 60% to 45% in rural areas whereas in urban areas it has declined from 60% to 43% (Table 3). In case of non-governmental sector it has shown growth both in rural and urban areas. The highest proportions of those going for private care are going to private hospitals. This clearly indicates the growth of private service in the country.

Table 3
Percentage Distribution of per 1000 Distribution of Hospitalised Treatments by Type of Hospital During 1986-87 and 1995-96 According to NSSO Survey

Source of Treatment	*Rural*		*Urban*	
	1995-96 (52nd Rd.)	*1986-87 (42nd Rd)*	*1995-96 (52nd Rd)*	*1986-87 (42nd Rd)*
Public hospital	39.9	55.4	41.8	59.5
P.H.C./C.H.C.	4.8	4.3	0.9	0.8
Public dispensary.	0.5	0.0	0.4	0.0
All govt. sources	45.2	59.7	43.1	60.3
Private hospital	41.9	32.0	41.0	29.6
Nursing home	8.0	4.9	11.1	7.0
Charitable inst.	4.0	1.7	4.2	1.9
Others	0.8	1.7	0.6	1.2
All non-govt. sources	54.8	40.3	56.9	39.7

Source: NSSO (1998): Report No 441 on Morbidity and Treatment of Ailments.

With the existing socio economic inequality the gradual withdrawl of the state will affect the poor most as the table 4 reveals high percentage of population in the lower income group still depend on public facilities.

Table 4
Distribution of Inpatient Care Across the States (1995-96)

	Share of Bottom quintile	*Share of top quintile*
Andhra	61.9	28.5
Bihar	19.3	39.2
Gujarat	43.3	25.4
Haryana	63.5	21.6
Himachal Pradesh	100	89.6
Karnataka	70.1	44.2
Kerala	58.5	41.5
Maharasthra	69.7	22.3
MP	44.8	63.1
Orissa	94.9	85
Punjab	26.5	28.6
Rajasthan	83.8	76.5
Tamil Nadu	72.3	27.1
UP	64.2	49.7
West Bengal	93.6	67.3

Source: Ajay Mahal, (2002), Who benefits from Public health Spending, National Council of Applied Economic Research.

In most of the cases it is seen relatively higher share of poor people resort to public facilities only exception in the table above is Bihar. With the increase in privatisation it is the poor who are going to be affected the most. In case of higher income groups we see high reliance on government hospitals both in case of developing states such as Orissa, UP and MP, but also in case of their better counterparts such as Kerala, Himachal Pradesh, Rajasthan, Karnataka and West Bengal. This reliance of higher income group on public facility is the basic reason or justification for initiating health sector reforms. But at the same time it is important quite a large number of poor are dependent on public facilities.

Few states[2] in India have gone for Health sector reform as part of obligation to World Bank loan for the state. But the evidence so far on health sector reforms have not been very positive. Creese (1990) looking at the experience of user charge across countries observed that the whole mechanism tend to be concentrated on cost recovery objective with little importance on improving quality and health outcome. In low-income countries the rationale for discouraging user fees in the public sectors falls into two categories. The first is one of equity: this financing mechanism increases the financial barriers disproportionately faced by the poor when seeking health care. The second is financial: user fees lack the potential to secure increased private contributions to publicly provided health services needed for quality of care improvements. Arhin-Tenkorang, (2000) on the basis of African countries experience observes that user fees are administratively and institutionally difficult to implement and therefore, in practice, user charges price the poor out of the market with potentially dire consequences for their health status. Closer home there has been criticism with respect to user charge as initiated in Punjab after the health sector reform. Dr. Vinita Gupta (2002) observes that user fees have resulted in denial of right to health and undermining state responsibility in providing basic health care to its citizens. Moreover the introduction process was accompanied with existing corruption in the system and it also lead to administrative confusions.

CONCLUSION

This paper looked at the State's performance in health expenditure across major 16 states both in pre reform and post reform period. It was seen that at the absolute level there has been increase in health expenditure across states although it has not been uniform with time and also 5 states have shown decline in health expenditure in the post reform period. In terms of state variation across states it has come down with time.

There is a positive relationship between health expenditure and state income, but it is not very strong. The states with lower level of income have relatively lower expenditure on health. Health expenditure as a share of income as well as total expenditure have shown decline from pre reform period to post reform period clearly indicating that the reform process has acted as an impediment in the growth of health care sector in the country. The most affected is the capital expenditure, it has come down drastically with time. The utilisation pattern showed the greater dependence on private health care service in the country.

The reform process initiated in the country with main aim of globalisation with the world economy do have some trade offs, as it was seen in this paper as the health sector development which is so much dependent on the state's initiative has to take a step backward. With this shift from need based approach to efficiency of public good like health it is the vulnerable sections of the society who are going to be worst hit, as it was seen from limited evidence of health sector reform, poor have very high chances of getting out of the health care market.

ACKNOWLEDGEMENT

This paper focuses on health sector expenditure in the pre reform and post reform periods and looks at what are the trends in health sector allocation from pre and post reform period at the state level. The levels of health sector allocation, health expenditure as a share of total expenditure and income are analysed for both the periods. Health expenditure as a proportion of income as well as expenditure has declined during the post reform period .At the same time the utilization pattern of health services reveals that economically backward section of the society still rely on public services.

NOTES

1. Human development approach is based on the capability approach as postulated by Sen (Anand, S. and Ravallion, M. 1997). Sen in his argument is critical of "opulence"(Income, wealth or material possession) and utility (whether interpreted as happiness , desire fulfilment or simply fulfilment of choice) as a measure of well being. Instead he argues that "well being" has to do with being well, which in most elementary term is about being able to live long, being well nourished, being healthy, being literate and so on. What should be valued intrinsically are people's achievements their being and doing or their capabilities to function.
2. According to Baru (2001), Punjab, Andhra, West Bengal and Karnataka have gone for health sector reform.

BIBLIOGRAPHY

Anand, S. and Ravallion, M. (1997), "Human Development in Poor Countries: On the Role of Private Income and Public Services", *Journal of Economic Perspectives*, 7 (1): 133-50.

Arhin-Tenkorang, D. (2000), "Mobilizing Resources for Health: The Case for User Fees Revisited", Commission on Macroeconomics and Health Working paper Series.

Baru, R. (1999), "The Structure and Utilisation of Health Services", in Disinvesting in Health, The World Bank Prescription to Health, edited by Mohan Rao, SAGE Publication New Delhi.

Baru, R. (2001),"Health Sector Reform and Structural Adjustment: A State Level Analysis", in Public Health and the Poverty of Reforms: The South Asian Predicament, ed by Qadeer, I, et al, Sage Publication, New Delhi.

Banerjee, D. (2001), "Landmark in Heath Sector Development in India", in Public Health and the Poverty of Reforms: The South Asian Predicament, ed. by Qadeer, I, et al, Sage Publication, New Delhi.

Creese, A. (1990),"User Charges For Health Care: A Review of Recent Experience", WHO SHS, Paper No 1.

CSO, Government of India.

Deogaonkar, M. (2004), "Socio-economic Inequality and its Effect on Healthcare Delivery in India: Inequality and Health Care", *Electronic Journal of Sociology* ISSN: 1198 3655.

Dev, M. and Moij, J. (2002)), "Social Sector Expenditures in the 1990s Analysis of Central and State Budgets", *Economic and Political Weekly* March 2: 853-866.

Dreze, J. and Sen, A. (1989), Hunger and Public Action, Clerendon Press. Oxford.

Duggal, R. (2000), "Utilisation of Health Care Services in India" in Sharma A., et al. edited Health Securities in India: Policies and Prespectives, Institute for Human Development, New Delhi.

Gupta Vineeta (2002), Punjab Govt. Commission for Closure of World Bank Funded Health Care Projects, PUCL Bulletin.

Kaur, B. and Misra, S. (2003), "Social Sector Expenditure and Attainments: An Analysis of Indian States", *Reserve Bank of India Occasional Papers*, 24.

Mahal, A. (2002), "Who benefits from Public Health Spending", National Council of Applied Economic Research.

NSSO, 52nd Round. National Sample Survey Organisation, Department of Statistics, Government of India.

Prabhu, K. Seeta (1999), "Structural Adjustment and the Health Sector in India", in Disinvesting in Health, The World Bank Prescription to Health, edited by Mohan Rao, SAGE Publication New Delhi.

Prabhu, K. Seeta, (1998), "Social Sectors in Economic Development", *Journal of Social and Economic Development*, I (2), 268-87.

Schultz, T.W. (1961), "Investment in Human Capital", *American Economic Review*, 51 (1): 1-17.

Tulasidhar, V.B. (1993), 'Expenditure Compression and Health Sector Outlays" *Economic and Political Weekly*, November 6.

UNDP (1996), Human Development Report, Oxford University Press.

Qadeer, I. (2001), "Impact of Structural Adjustment Programme on Concepts of Public Health" in Public Health and the Poverty of Reforms: The South Asian Predicament ed by Qadeer, I, et al, Sage Publication, New Delhi.

RBI Bulletin, Various Years. Reserve Bank of India.

World Bank (1997), World Development Report, Oxford University Press, Washington.

Chapter - 12

Sculpting for a Global Market: Indian Ayurvedic Manufacturing Sector in the Open Regime

Harilal M.S.

PROLOGUE

This paper is an attempt towards understanding the growth, dimensions, initiatives and issues of Ayurvedic sector, which has a huge potential in the context of newly awakened consumer preference for herbal medicines and products. *Ayurveda,* the knowledge of life and longevity, is the oldest, most comprehensive scientific discipline, a complete health care system or healing system that was preached, practiced and documented in the ancient times by omniscient sages. The system of Ayurvedic medicine evolved over thousands of years through processes of experience, observation, experimentation and intuition. This development has many facets of embeddedness - political, social, cultural and moreover economic. While looking back to the recent history, the contemporary status of ayurveda is a culmination of the events over the last 200 years of colonial rule, pre-independence policies of the Indian National Congress, the post-independence policies of the government of India and role played by industrial stakeholders and civil society (Banerjee, 2002). The politics of nationalism in the pre and post Independence periods, however, has ensured a permanent place for indigenous systems of medicine in Indian society, thus rescuing them from ignominy and restoring a certain measure of state patronage, which was completely absent during colonial rule. Despite this, Indian system of Medicine (ISM), especially ayurveda has not flourished in Independent India. This is possibly because of two reasons: first, the Indian allopathic community has played a major role in discrediting ISM, and second, the ISM community itself has remained inert, not rising to the contemporary challenges of health care despite a favorable political climate.

The often contradictory and changing scientific and moral attitudes towards the knowledge systems like ayurveda is linked to a history in which Western science has by turns absorbed local knowledge (both non western and folk European) in to its own, and rejected it as inferior only to rediscover its practical benefits (Grove, 1998). The importance given by the Dutch and Portuguese governments of the 16th century to these systems and later negligence of the same shows this. While considering the addition to the global biological knowledge, the contribution of the knowledge systems remains on top. And it is to be noted that at that time, as a part of the exploitation of traditional knowledge, Western government popularized the system. But in the course of time it was left unrecognized though in some parts of the third world region, like Kerala it got attention. The resurgence of this system at present is to be viewed as the resurgence of the same in the West, especially in the modern era with the glamour of globalization and modernization. The story should be read along with the new market strategies and the market extension ideologies of the West. In short, it seems to be pertinent to look into what kind of transformation this system undergoes as a consequence of changing world scenario of consumption and marketing strategies. This forms a background to analyze the potentials and problems of the sector.

The *first section* of the paper talks about the transformation and recent developments in Indian Ayurvedic sector along with an understanding of its current status and major efforts for institutionalization. *Second section* portrays two examples from Kerala as an evident for the current innovation and supplementary tools led growth. This is followed by *third section,* details on major hurdles that India face in the promotion of Ayurvedic sector and gives a brief picture about the policies pursue by the importing countries and finally we conclude with some possible forwards.

I

STATUS AND DIMENSIONS

The Modernization Alias Transformation

The sum and substance of ayurveda is undergoing a complete revamp in the modern context. This transformation can be seen as a process, with a recognizable pattern in its change. The 'modernized' form of ayurveda has travelled a long way in form and appearance, from what were practiced hundreds of years back largely by physicians, who had colossal knowledge in the various formulations depicted in the classical texts. Currently the global market for herbal products, which includes medicines, food supplements, herbal beauty and toiletry products is estimated at around

US$ 62 billion. Out of this, the market for herbal medicine alone is estimated at around US$ 5 Billion (EXIM bank, 2002) and now it may be around US $ 12 Billion.

The transformation of the system is multi faceted: from being dispensed to individual patients to becoming available off the shelf, from being made by a Vaidya in a small *rasashala* to being mass manufactured by a manufacturing company, from being identified with a region or a school to becoming positioned as brands, from *Sukthas* being learned from the classical texts to being administered and taught professionally and above all from being a medical epistemology to an industry with diversified products in the global market (Banerjee, 2002). It might be an outcome of the interplay of consumption and production techniques. Now ayurveda, with an increased demand for botanical medicine, is making inroads in the world market. This move has been backed by the increasing 'beauty business' and hence diversified demand for Ayurvedic cosmetics and food supplements because of rising health consciousness. And sometimes it can be argued that the capitalist imperative for accumulation (generally through innovation techniques like new products, new markets, new organizational form etc.) can shape consumption patterns. Even the modernization and development were supplanted by the transnational flows and the institutional forms, fashions and commodities have transformed by the context, by which they moved. This seems to have worked in the case of ayurveda too.

Table 1
Sales Turnover of Major Ayurvedic Firms in India
(in Rs. Crores)

Companies	*1995*	*1996*	*1997*	*1998*	*1999*	*2000*	*2001*	*2002*	*2003*	*CGR*
Dabur India Ltd.	405.58	563.93	707.52	813.17	918.27	1046.29	1172.61	1167.6	1236.3	13.18
Zandu Pharma Works Ltd.	59.37	76.35	91.35	99.32	115.58	109.68	103.06	113.67	113.38	7.45
Arya Vaidya sala	31.72	36.98	40.79	45.02	48.31	56.2	58.54	72.5	76.56	10.29
Kerala Ayurveda Pharmacy Ltd.	2.03	2.38	3.5	5.42	6.7	8.52	11.59	12.59	13.26	23.19
Shree Dhoota-papeshwar Ltd.	NA	6.06	6.62	7.47	5.91	4.46	5.77	7.12	7.47	2.65

Source: Compiled from CMIE and annual reports of the companies, 2005.

Table 1 gives a picture of the major companies' turnover in Ayurvedic sector; where the industry has been very much concentrated in India. The industrial scene in Ayurvedic sector is of an oligopolistic structure, where a small number of firms dominate the market share, while thousands of small firms adding up to very meager portion. While these large firms are adopting different kind of modern techniques and drug discovery, small/tiny firms are still serving the healthcare needs of a large section of people. The leading companies have achieved a significant growth in the last few years. Dabur, Zandu, Himalaya, AVS are examples. Out of the 9000 Ayurvedic firms, merely 2% constitute more than 80% of the market shares while the rest of the firms (small/tiny/household) constitute very meager share.

Features of Present Global Demand for Ayurvedic Products

The growth of Ayurvedic industry, especially of the major vendors is mainly in three different, but mutually complementing, directions:

1. The pure classical traditions as followed by Arya Vaidya Sala Kottakkal (AVS), Arya Vaidya pharmacy, Coimbatore, which revolve around a physician and his/her prescription. The growth of this sector is very slow but steady.
2. The growth pattern using classical as well as patent and proprietary medicines (PP) and OTC (Over the Counter) products. Probably Dabur is the best example. Their classical side is rather slow in growth and expansion where as their PP products are popular.
3. The growth pattern of PP and OTC alone with a focus on the modern medicine practitioners as well as new ayurvedic generation physicians. Himalaya Drug Company makes such preparations and perhaps its fast growth in the last few decades is an indicative of this trend.

In short, Ayurvedic and Unani health and beauty products can be broadly divided into three categories: classical formulations, bio-medical providers and consumer brands. The consumer brands are advertised directly to consumers through public media such as television, radio, newspapers, magazines etc. in contrast the bio-medical provides are marketed to physicians, pharmacists and the whole chemists and the term ethical marketing is used to describe this. This route of marketing not necessarily implies that these drugs can be bought only with the prescription of a physician. On the contrary a large number of drugs have been purchased in this category without any prescription and about 80 per cent of them are now getting without any prescription. But generally there is a very thin line between these three categories and quite often manufacturers vary their products between these three categories. A case for this is *pudin hara,* a remedy for gripping, stomach aches, gas and indigestion has recently converted by Dabur into the consumer good category, because of its huge production costs and now it is widely advertised through popular media (Bode, 2002). Marketing strategies for the classical products are similar, and often the known classical formulations like cyavanapras, dasamularisht, triphala are purchased by the public without the prescription of the physicians, while some of the lesser known formulations like praval bhasm, candraprabha vatika only according to the prescriptions. Generally the proprietary medicines and the beauty products fall into the category of consumer brands and seem to be fast moving in the world market (FMCG category). For example, as Bode explains, the cyavanpras, which is used by different companies as different category products, i.e. for Himalaya it is consumer good category, for Dabur it is bio-medical provider and for Kottakkal it is classical medicine.

Table 2
Break-up of the Sales of the four Large Ayurvedic Manufacturers in India[1]

Categories	*Share*
Consumer brands	70%
Bio-medical brands	18%
Classical medicines	12%

Source: Bode, 2002.

In the financial year 1998 (till March 1999) the turnover of Dabur, Himalaya, Zandu and Arya Vaidya Sala are calculated to be Rs. 982 crores. In that as the above table shows the striking finding is that about 88% of the total production is branded products, while the classical formulations constitute only 12%. The domestic market is fast growing for traditional medicine and the potential is not properly exploited by this sector yet. But they are now mainly concentrating on export market. Further break up is given in the following table:

Table 3
Break-up of the Sales of the Four Large firms According to Product Sales

Manufacturers	*Dabur*	*Himalaya*	*Zandu*	*AVS*
Branded products	97%	100%	80%	None
Classical products	3%	None	20%	100%

Source: Same as above.

With the AVS as an important exception, branded products dominate the sales of other firms. Within the firms there are some products, which can be considered as the leading products, in the form of highest income creator for the firm. For example, 70% of the Dabur sales value is through four products: *Dabur Amla Hair oil* (160 crores), *Dabur cyavanapras* (120 crores) *toothpowder Lal danthmanjan* (110 crores) and *hajmola* (60 crores). In the case of Zandu, *Zandu balm, cyavanapras, Keasari jeevan* and *Pancarishta* forms the fifty-per cent of the turnover. Similar is the case of Himalaya too. Only in AVS, the major income source is from classical products like *cyavanapras, dasamularisht* and *triphala ghrita* and it make 20% of the total sales.

Now most of the companies target the external market than the domestic market and they are finding newer and newer marketing techniques and this has resulted in considerable shift in product pattern to suit the Western demands. Notable example is the leading ayurvedic firm, Dabur. Dabur attributes its growth over the last decade to the sale of its products via the route of wholesalers dominating in specific markets in the areas as large as the Netherlands and Greece. In line with the new policy, the earlier version of selling the medicines directly to the patients, after consultation with the traditional physicians has disappeared, and Dabur has started large scale production of the fast moving consumer goods to become the largest company in India in 1884. Diversification of products and huge advertisement campaign for its branded products led Dabur to the turnover of 200 million US dollars. And now the company is very much away from the traditional Ayurvedic status and the structure looks like this:

Dabur hair oil, Lal danthamanjan tooth powder are the major items (provides 67 million US dollars) of the family products and the *cyawanapras* and *hajmola*, digestive *pudin hara* include in the health care products (60 million US $) and the ayurvedic specialties are the minor category of the product sections of Dabur and unwittingly, they all are branded products. Indeed apart from being symbolic devices, Indian medicines have become instrumental in profit making and curing. In this respect as Leslie points out it is no way different from the modern drugs and cosmetics (Leslie, 1999). Ayurvedic and Unani beauty products are part of modernity and are therefore shaped by the market dynamics and the production of modern pharmacological evidence. This is true for manufacturers of medical products and Indian therapeutic substance alike.

In short, the change in the pattern can be seen in two ways: one, as the strategic response of the manufacturers as of ayurveda to the historical conditions of disempowerment and hence the effort to make their own space in the era of globalization or secondly, ayurveda simply as a helpless victim of modern science and westernization. The transformation of ayurveda was as much as a response to the consumer choices as to the choices of technologies of production (Banerjee, 2002). This modern emergence and appearance; with a different suit, to an extent supplemented by the institutionalization efforts from government and industry. This is been evident from efforts of Kavirajas in Bengal and AVS in Kerala (Panikkar, 1995).Recently, with the wake of herbal awareness, these institutionalization efforts have been improved at different facets. A brief look on the same will be ideal.

Efforts for Institutionalization

A complementary institutionalization from both civil society and the state is very much fruitful in spreading ayurveda overseas. An economic consideration was in the forefront as a basis of this approach. Though in the initial period, the efforts were mainly made from the civil society later this has been substantially supplemented with government policies. It is quite visible in the establishment of education centres, research and standardization institutes allover India. The institutionalization efforts from the part of Indian government are very much active in the last decade or even recently. This is first reflected in the formation of the Department for Indian System of Medicine in 1995 for managing the problems solely related to Indian Indigenous medicine. Though the budget allocation for the Department of AYUSH (otherwise known) is very much minimal, this was a welcome move. Priorities of this department include, education, standardization of drugs, enhancing the availability of raw materials, research and development, information, communication and larger involvement in the national system for delivering health care. Next step was establishing the Central Medicinal Plant Board and other State Boards. CMPB is a national level body of the GOI, "constituted to look after formulation, coordination with ministries/departments, ensuring sustainable availability of medicinal plants and to coordinate all matters relating to their development and sustainable use" (MOHFW, 2000). Another very important move from government was the effort put in for the establishment of a Traditional Knowledge Digital Library (TKDL). This will serve the purpose of bringing the Traditional knowledge of various communities under one umbrella or to a particular data base and hence can work as resistant of the large number of bio-piracies. Lot of doubts was being mentioned from different sections of thinkers about its ability as official referendum and to tackle the piracy effectively. On the other hand, there are arguments that this will help for easy piracy or cumulative innovation and which will put India in a worst edge. But this has been considered as a positive move.

Many interdisciplinary researches on drug discovery and new combinations have been promoted with the formation of Central Council for Research in Ayurveda and Siddha. Government has established 10 new drug testing laboratories and initiated efforts for upgrading the existing laboratories to comply the evidence based drug development and standardization testing. One of the major Research and Development activities at Central Drugs Research Institute (CDRI) is the exploration of terrestrial plants, including Indian traditional remedies for novel molecules for drug development. Several Regional Research Laboratories (RRL) are also involved in the regional Medicinal and Aromatic Plant (MAP) conservation and proper utilization through R & D. RRL-Thiruvananthapuram is involved in search for bioactive/polymer compounds from natural resources and development of new synthetic systems of technological interest; agro-processing of and value addition to spices, coconut, oil palm, cassava, etc. In short, a separate Ayurveda, Siddha and Unani Technical Advisory Board (ASUDTAB), an Ayurveda, Siddha and Unani Drugs Consultative Committee (ASUDCC) Pharmacopoeial Laboratory of Indian Medicine (PLIM) are some of the government initiatives. Pharmacopoeial Committees have been constituted separately for ASU systems. It is the responsibility of these Committees to lay down standards of quality, purity and strength of drugs and approve drug formularies. So far, 326 monographs of Ayurveda drugs in 4 volumes, 45 of Unani drugs, 916 of Homeopathic drugs have been published. Another 98 monographs on Ayurveda drugs are in the pipeline.

The institutionalization of manufacturing might have started from the Kavirajas of Bengal and which, has been followed by Kottakkal P.S. Varier with a large scale manufacturing unit (Kumar, 1998). This is followed by many manufacturing units at different parts of the country like Dabur, Zandu etc. Understanding the nature and forms of institutionalization in the case of manufacturing and education it self is an area to be thoroughly studied. As noted by Banerjee, the institutionalization efforts by the domestic authorities would have definitely influenced by the pressure and guidelines of international agencies like WTO, WHO etc for accepting ayurveda all over the globe (Banerjee, 2002). On the other hand, the process of institutionalization was already begun in the educational sector of ayurveda. Today this is an industry with 8533 licensed pharmacies and more than 8000 manufacturing units and 427504 Ayurvedic practitioners. The Government of India regulates the teaching and practice of ayurveda in India. There are hundreds of colleges nationwide which teach the Bachelor of Ayurvedic Medical Science (BAMS) and higher degrees.

Table 4
Number of Ayurveda Colleges in India

State/UTs	*No. of Colleges*	*Capacity (UG&PG)*	*State/UTs*	*No. of Colleges*	*Capacity (UG&PG)*
Andhra	4	150	Karnataka	50	3180
Assam	1	50	Kerala	11	530
Bihar	11	330	MP	14	615
Chandigarh	1	50	Maharashtra	56	3125
Chattisgarh	2	95	Orissa	6	160
Delhi	1	40	Punjab	11	510
Goa	1	40	Rajasthan	6	160
Gujarat	10	420	Tamil Nadu	7	260
Haryana	3	50	Uttaranchal	3	160
HP	1	74	UP	1[illegible]	400
J&K	1	50	West Bengal	3	116
Jharkhand	1	40	Total	218	10605

Source: compiled from *www.cciminindia.org*, excerpted on: 4th January 4, 2006.

This system of college based Ayurvedic education is mainly a post-independence development, modelled on Western medical education. Its establishment was highly controversial, and for good reasons. In pre-colonial times, education in ayurveda was principally conducted in traditional Sanskrit schools, in which students started very young (10 or less), and were grounded for over 12 years in the Sanskrit language and in the medical literature. Apprenticeship to a practicing physician was also essential. Unlike China, pre-modern Indian did not develop a system of medical licensing.

An early institutionalization started from 1920s onwards. Prior to that generally *gurukula* education was followed. Prior to 1900, there were three ayurveda *patasalas* in Kerala, Punjab and in Uttar Pradesh. The first formal one was established in Thiruvananthapuram in 1886. Now government has monopoly of Ayurvedic education in Madhya Pradesh, Assam, Himachal and West Bengal. In Kerala, Andhra Pradesh, Orissa and UP the public sector has the upper hand. Not only state the initiatives from Private sector also very much visible in the case of states like Karnataka, Maharashtra and Kerala. 32 colleges in Karnataka and 20 colleges in Maharashtra were started in the last 20 years and all were in the private sector. In 2003 there were 7 colleges came in to being in the sector. In the case of Ayurvedic research, there are new initiatives and the number of colleges offering post graduate courses is going up. Thus the manufacturing and educational institutionalization is a combined outcome of the efforts from the side of government and private to promote the system in a much more comprehensive and acceptable manner (*for details see the end note*). In the case of a centralized standardization procedure government has started efforts for an official formulary and pharmacopeal standards. Till now three volumes have come out. With the completion of this, a uniform formulation code will be established for the items produced in different parts of the country. For example, the *dasamularishtam,* which is produced by different companies, has to base on these formulations. Then the major efforts should proceed to external front, to make the importing country to convince the same formulary. Institutionalization is very important because this set the background for further growth of Ayurvedic sector.

Export front-destinations and Dimensions

An estimate[2] shows that about 84% of the domestic market for Indian system of Medicine is dominated by ayurveda. Unani and Siddha have a very negligible share (around 3%) in the domestic market. The same can be assumed in the case of export market also. Indian Ayurvedic industry is now considered to be at the amount of Rs. 4000-5000 crores, but as meager as 2% of the world herbal market. The unorganized nature and the lack of availability of data remain as a major bottle neck in the sector to understand the world wide demand for Ayurvedic products. The wide acceptability of natural medicines and increased use of the derived products, prima facie opens a wide range of possibilities for this sector. The data available from DGCIS (8 digit level) has been used below to understand the quantum and other dimensions of export of Ayurvedic and Unani products from India. If we follow the same assumption, in the export market also around 97%[3] will be constituted by Ayurvedic products.

Below given figure shows that the exports are mainly under three heads. They are *Code 1211*: Plants and parts of plants including seeds and fruits used for perfumery pharmacy or similar purposes. *30039001*: Ayurvedic and Unani medicines (under the head-medicaments consisting of two or more constituents, which have been mixed together for therapeutic uses or prophylactic uses, not put up for retail sale) *300449001*: Ayurvedic and Unani medicines for retail sale.

Figure 1
Export of Ayurvedic and Unani Products

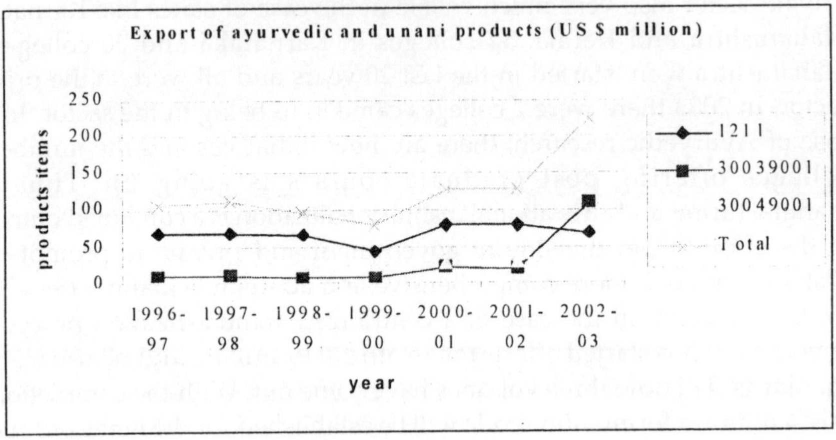

Source: DGCIS, Ministry of Commerce, GOI.

The figure, in which data have been furnished for the last seven years, shows that the Ayurvedic and Unani products for bulk sales (i.e., 30039001) have been going up in a substantial scale. It has projected a growth of 39% in the last 7 years, more than 5% annually. But actually the higher growth occurred in the last year, in 2002-03. This is due to the acceptance of Ayurvedic products in the USA. The export under this head to USA has gone up from merely 2 million US$ in 2001-02 to 71 million US$ in 2002-03, which hiked the share of USA in total export under this head from 10% to more than 65% in a year. This put USA as a major trade partner of India in the traditional medicine export front. Recently, Nepal is also emerging as a major destination with more than 5 million US$ under this code. This all helped the total Ayurvedic and Unani exports (including all the categories) to make a substantial improvement of 11.29% secular growth in the concerned years and reached a 223million US$. Medicines exported for retail sale also added significantly to this growth with an average growth of 7%.

In the case of plants and plant materials, the growth of export is not much promising. This should be read along with the difficulty of many firms to get the adequate and non-adulterated plant material for the production of medicines and products. While enormous demand on the one hand, there was great concern for the depletion of biological diversity as a result of over harvesting and many known reasons on the other. In the case of plants too, USA is the major export destination, with around more than 40% of the exports. Recently the import of plant materials also going up, though the data is not been furnished here. Another point to be noted here is that Saudi Arabia is increasingly emerging as an export destination though there is a small decline in the last year. This sector doesn't show much potential in the case of future prospects. But efforts are to be made to avoid dependency on imported raw materials and to become self sufficient.

Table 5
Export Destinations under Code 1211 (in US$ Million)

	1996-97	*1997-98*	*1998-99*	*1999-00*	*2000-01*	*2001-02*	*2002-03*	*2003-04*	*CGR*
Total	66.87	68.52	63.88	44.18	78.24	77.78	69.05	65.75	-0.21
USA	28.25	37.97	27.85	17.69	31.02	37.19	27.1	24.39	-1.82
UK	4.07	3.21	3.61	1.67	3.93	2.7	3.5	2.46	-6.10
Germany	5.91	4.15	3.21	2.48	3.26	2.1	2.76	2.96	-8.28
Spain	4.58	3.43	2.4	0.94	1.04	1.55	0.84	0.87	-18.75
Saudi	1.03	0.69	1.26	0.49	1.95	0.95	2.16	1.46	4.46
Pakistan	1.57	1.33	1.37	1.66	1.78	1.06	1.17	1.24	-2.91
Japan	4.32	6.21	5.46	4.34	3.58	2.36	3.32	2.6	-6.15

Source: DGCIS, Ministry of Commerce, GOI

Table 6
The major Export Destinations under 30049001 at Two time Points

	Export in 1996-97 (US$M)	*Share*	*Export in 2002-03 (US$M)*	*Share*
Total	27.75		45.13	
USA	2.51	9.05	3.17	7.02
Russia	7.97	28.72	4.85	10.75
UK	0.54	1.95	2.56	5.67
Nepal	5.53	19.92	0.64	1.42
Germany	0.76	2.74	1.66	3.68

Source: DGCIS, Ministry of Commerce, GOI.

Ayurvedic medicines exported for retail sale is another area where, more focus should be given. In the last few years it is shown a substantial growth and shift in the export destinations. UK and USA are replacing Russia and Nepal in the case of retail Ayurvedic products. But still Russia remains the single largest importer. Now it accounts to more than US$ 45 million in the international market.

The world demand for medicinal plants also looks very healthy. It is estimated that Europe imports about 400,000 tons of medicinal plants per annum, with an average market value of US$ 1 billion from Africa and Asia. Germany is by far the largest market and within Europe, largest consumer of medicinal plants, spending £ 1.4 billion (US$ 2.2 billion) annually. France is second (£ 116 million) and the United Kingdom stands third (£ 88 million) (Masood, 1997). Among the importers of botanical drugs, Hong Kong is at the top followed by Japan, Germany and USA. Germany and the USA are among the top four countries in import as well as export, expressing their policies can be much influential for medicinal plant trade worldwide. While analyzing this export market, from UK and Canada made their domestic policy very stringent. This has larger implications in the international market. So an understanding of the policies of these major existing export markets is very important. An effort in this concern is made in the fourth section of the paper.

II

INNOVATION AS A STRATEGY FOR CREATING/EXPANDING MARKETS-CASE OF TWO FIRMS

As mentioned earlier, Ayurvedic industry in India is of a more concentrated one, though highly fragmented, than the general pharmaceutical market (major 10 firms occupy around 70-80 percentage share, while the rest 9000 constitute the small left over). Modern Ayurvedic firms need to pursue a strategy of technological innovation based on R&D investment and technological alliances that help product development, modern manufacturing and marketing and thereby to compete in the newer regime. This is why the modern firms are forced to go for innovation and invest more and more money on R&D. Return on this investment seems to be very high when it is supplemented with a similar share of expenditure in the marketing and product promotion. This investment on innovation can be either from the part of firms or from the part of government institutions. In the case of ayurveda, most of the R&D coming in is mainly from the private firms.

The effort for research and innovation is very much evident in the case of herbal medicines world wide. What is important that how much the Indian companies are able to withstand the technologies and develop more and more proprietary and patented drugs. An analysis of the international scene in terms of the patents cited and granted makes it clear that Indian Traditional medicine lag far behind the Chinese medicine. The patent citation can be considered as an outcome of efficient drug innovation. This seems to be low in the case of Traditional Indian Medicine, as far as compared to Traditional Chinese Medicine. This can be due to low expenditure on R&D in India.

This table is a self explanatory, which says that drug discovery is very much minimal in Ayurvedic medicine, and the proportion of granted patents as a share of filed also higher in the case of Traditional Chinese Medicine. At present, for many diseases especially like Asthma, rheumatics, diabetes etc, most of the people depend on Ayurvedic treatment. In the same way the unexplored wealth of Indian flora might be used for getting the extracts for the current dangerous diseases like AIDS, cancer etc. For this, extensive research is on at different parts of the country and the world is looking eagerly for the remedy of these killing diseases from traditional medicine. This necessarily points to the fact that drug discovery and new extracts from plant sources are going to be very crucial along various kinds of traditionally practiced, existing systems. Botanical immunodrugs from traditional medicine can provide newer opportunities to bio-prospect diverse and synergistic chemical moieties, which in combination act on multiple targets and improve the therapeutic spectrum. In this case also the example of Chinese traditional medicine set example with wide variety of new drugs in the international market. Starting with the ephedrine, an amphetamine like stimulant, now they have around 1141 different traditional plant drugs, registered for their therapeutic activities including several new single compounds from plants and many of which have a monopoly power in the European market and in many other countries like Japan and Korea.

Table 7
Citations and Patent Data for Indian and Chinese Medicine
(as on September 2005)

Database	*Keywords: TIM*	*Citations/ patents*	*Keywords: TCM*	*Citations/ patents*
PubMed	Ayurvedic Medicine	1045	Chinese Medicine	10278
	TIM	361	TCM	6847
Science Direct	Ayurvedic Medicine	87	Chinese Medicine	990
	TIM	77	TCM	612
Google Scholar	Ayurvedic Medicine	4220	Chinese Medicine	476000
	TIM	32900	TCM	68300
US Patent granted	Ayurvedic Medicine/ TIM	3	Chinese Medicine/ TCM	195
US Patent filed	Ayurvedic Medicine/ TIM	26	Chinese Medicine/ TCM	259

Source: Patwardhan et al. (2005).

In India also this kind of drug developing procedures are active at firm level and state level. Central drug Research Institute, Botanical research institute, various regional Research Laboratories and the institutes like Indian Council for Medical Research are giving immense support for this. But a close understanding shows that many effective drugs in the market are developed by different manufacturing groups of the country, like Dabur, Zandu, Himalaya etc. These Ayurvedic companies, seemingly, not much differ from the modern pharmaceutical firms, in the sense that, they are also looking for Schumpeterian innovations like new products, new markets, newer appearance, and organizational shift. It is mentioned that the pharmaceutical MNCs spent around 40-45% for marketing, they incur only 8 to 10% each for R&D and manufacturing cost (Dadha, 1992). This is increasingly becoming the tendency among modern Ayurvedic companies also (Dabur, Himalaya and Pankajakasthuri spent more than 30% as selling cost). Since raw material remains to be the major expenditure, it generally falls into the second highest category. The expenditure on R&D has to be improved among the medium firms also, in Kerala most of the mediocre firms spend less than 1% for R&D. Kerala Ayurvedic Pharmaceuticals Limited (KAPL), Nagarjuna are evident for this (0.6 and 0.9 respectively) (Harilal, 2004). The major research is concentrated under three heads in these companies, clinical research, process related research and medicinal plant research and most of the expenditure under this heads are actually diverted to the standardization process.

Here we are trying to understand how the modern firms are innovating on tradition to achieve the gains in global market. Though mainly they aim at modernization, many products have been emerged through constant innovation and trial and error experiments in their laboratories, which are supplemented by modern promotional and marketing strategies. Here two examples from Kerala, one private company and another public enterprise have been picked to see how and what kind of innovative activities are generally firms adopt on traditional Ayurvedic knowledge for creating their own market in the herbal world.

Case one: Pankajakasthuri Herbal India Limited

Unlike other systems of medicine, the diagnosing methods used in Ayurveda impose a high degree of restriction on the day to day habits[4] of those who seek treatment. On the other hand, the prevalence of alternative systems of medicine especially Allopathy, enables patients to get relief in short span of time, without any change in their lifestyle and moreover unlike Ayurveda, the formulations are in the form of pills, tonics etc. This necessitated a kind of shift in the form and appearance of medicine, prescribed in Ayurveda. As mentioned earlier, in due course of time Ayurvedic firms developed mechanisms for blending the age-old traditional knowledge and the modern techniques of production. Here Pankajakasthuri Herbals India Ltd (PKHIL) is setting an example.

Understanding the pulse of consumers and without losing the basics of the traditional knowledge, Pankajakasthuri Herbals India Ltd., started mass production and established an overwhelming presence across the globe with a vast range of products and services in Ayurvedic sector. It also is a multi division entity with interests in Manufacturing, Research & Development, Education, Hospitals, Panchakarma Centers, Health Tourism etc. Pankajakasthuri is a South Kerala based Ayurvedic Company, established in 1986 (then named as Sree Dhanwanthari Ayurvedics) as a small Ayurvedic dispensary with a very few products especially to treat asthma, bronchitis and other common ailments rechristened when it became a private limited company in 1996. Now PKHIL, founded by Dr. J. Hareendran Nair, has grown from a local outfit to a company with a reach outside India. And it is set to mark its entry into the Kingdom of Saudi Arabia (KSA) with the export order it has acquired, enabling it to ship its products for diabetes and blood pressure in to the Kingdom. The Company has recorded a phenomenal growth rate during the past few years while totaling up revenues of over Rs 250 million in 2004. Moreover sound marketing sense and techniques, employed by a talent pool of professionals has seen to the increasing presence of the company's products in the shop shelves around the world.

Breakthrough via innovation–Pankajakasthuri Breath EC: Initially Dr. Nair (professional Ayurvedic doctor) began practicing Ayurveda in the traditional form, but over time he began to experiment with new Ayurvedic formulation for respiratory ailments, as he was getting more and more patients with respiratory ailments. The basic idea needed for developing the formulation was available in age-old Ayurvedic texts. Dr. Hareendran began his experiments on a trial and error basis by testing various combinations and began to collect the impact of each of them. The efficiency and effectiveness of each one of them was also looked into. After 4 years his experiments began to yield fruits. Starting with small-scale, but intensive research at his clinic, Dr. Nair made a breakthrough with his Ayurvedic cure for asthma and launched a drug under the name Pankajakasthuri, with the financial backing from State government. Pankajakasthuri proved to be the most effective remedy for asthma and all types of breathing disorders and soon gained immense popularity. Even now 'Pankajakasthuri granules', which is promoted with the help of the modern packing and labeling techniques, holds the monopoly power in the granule market and forms 70 per cent of the turnover of the company. The innovative aspect of the product (Pankajakasthuri/Breathe EC) was that unlike the other traditional Ayurvedic drugs, which are administered in the form of Lehyams or Kashayams this is in granule form and could easily be consumed by the patient. Moreover it also retained all the traditional characteristics. In 1999, the department came out with two more wonder drugs; Ilogen excel Tablets for diabetes and Somatone Capsules for hypertension. And since then, the progress has been consistent and continuous. Innovation of *Pankajakasthuri* is considered to be the major breakthrough and this was followed by a series of innovations.

Stepping to cosmeceuticals and outreach to external markets: Three major factors which made Dr. Nair to diversify his company into cosmeceutical market are: increasing beauty consciousness of consumers, a large chunk of Ayurvedic research papers regarding properties of Ayurvedic substances to enhance beauty and the size and potential of Indian cosmetics industry of Rs. 840 crores. His initial aim was to acquire a market, which extends at least one- per cent of the total cosmeceutical market. The firm has developed various Ayurvedic cosmetic products to capture the beauty market like *Kaveri fairness cream, Kaveri milk cream, Pankajakasthuri dandruff oil* etc.

Backing on the knowledge base of Ayurveda, research projects undertaken by him have led to the formulation of drugs for the treatment of diseases like asthma, diabetes and hepatitis B, on which the effect of allopathic medicine has been limited. The company has also diversified and marked an entry into the competitive soap market with four herbal soaps, apart from making inroads into foreign markets. It is marketing the *Breathe EC* (Pankajakasthuri) in Malaysia through *Oze* Marketing agency and their herbal soaps are available in the Gulf countries. Now the company has different category products diversified in to the sections like OTC, FMCG and ethical products. A new-found and surging interest in the cures offered by Ayurveda and awards[5] won for pioneering work in this field has helped to grow and strengthen PKHIL's hold in the herbal drug sector. According to him even the allopathic doctors prescribe Pankajakasthuri products for Asthma and other bronchitis disorders. "It would have been easy for us to export all our products under the edible food category, as they all are nothing but herbal formulations. But we waited as we are particular to export a capsule or even a granule of our products only under the drugs category license from the respective governments", says Dr. J. Hareendran Nair. The clinical trials and the toxicological study are done in KEM hospital Mumbai and some of the laboratory quality test is done in Tropical Botanical Garden and Research Institute of Thiruvananthapuram.

The below table reaffirm the fact that there is a shift in demand from herbal medicines to more of nutraceuticals and cosmetic categories, and hence the production.

Table 8
An analysis of product wise sales of Pankajakasthuri
(in Rs Lakhs)

Name of the Product	*2000*	*Share to total*	*2002*	*Share to total*
Pankajakasthuri Granules	271.90	45.03	292.35	47.22
Illogen Excel	298.97	49.52	132.93	21.47
Somatone	11.85	1.96	2.89	0.47
Peekay Tablet	.342	0.06	.906	0.15
Herbal soaps	17.49	2.90	12.10	1.95
Sandal soaps	3.22	0.53	1.86	0.30
General medicine			3.27	0.53
Brahmi capsule			2.24	0.36
Kaveri fairness milk cream			170.26	27.50
Kasturi cough mix			.033	0.01
Kasturi hair tonic			.291	0.05
TOTAL	603.78	100.00	619.12	100

Source: Primary survey, 2003.

Illogen excel and somatone has helped PKHIL to achieve a turnover of Rs. 6.52 crores in the past financial year (1999-2000), as against Rs. 3.25 crores the year before. In 2004 it stands around 25 crores of rupees (detailed data could not get) with 18 panchakarma centers all over the world and with 23 different products, other than the classical category. Though a wide range of classical formulations like *Aristas, Lahyas, thailas, oils, choornas,* capsules, tablets and traditional *gulikas* are being produced, company mainly concentrate on the FMCG and OTC products. PKHIL believes that advertisement has a major role to play in sales maximization as its spends around 25% of its turnover to advertisement. The feed back is phenomenal. A close look in the product pattern of PKHIL shows, there is a shift from actual ayurvedic medicine to nutraceuticals and recently a shift again from nutraceuticals to concentrate the cosmeceutical market or more of consumer brand goods. This actually represents the nature of the industry as a whole due to the change in the demand pattern. The company already has a presence in Malaysia, Singapore and other Middle Eastern Countries. Now around 15 per cent of the company's turnover is from the exports. It is all set to start Panchakarma hospital in St. Petersburg in Moscow and in UAE. *Harmony*[6] and *Panacea*[7] are the other innovative efforts from the part of Pankajakasthuri to find the world market.

This example is cited to show that how a small dispensary, which initially had very few traditional medicines, diverted its products in such a fashion, gained monopoly in many of its products with a 100 per cent growth in recent years. This is a success story of skillful application of innovation on traditional knowledge, innovation of drug discovery, finding new markets and presenting the products in different forms. Without any institutional help, by mostly concentrating on export market, with quality products and expert marketing methods, Pankajakasthuri set a success story for the emerging herbal firms.

Case Two: Pharmaceutical Corporation of Kerala (Oushadhi)

Pharmaceutical Corporation of Kerala (PCK), popularly known as Oushadhi, is a success story of a public company, with its constant effort to understand the consumer demand in the modern world and successfully shifting its product pattern towards the same. Efficiently incorporating the innovation and modernization in the traditional Ayurvedic sector, this company is remaining as a model for the public enterprises and more surprisingly, not entering into the cosmetic market/not targeting the external market. The company aims domestic market, mostly the government demand and unlike Pankajakasthuri, it concentrates mainly on ethical Ayurvedic products.

Oushadhi was established in 1941, by the then Maharaja of Kochi for supplying medicines to Government Ayurvedic Hospitals. In 1959, it is converted and registered as a co-operative society and in 1975 incorporated as a company under the Companies act 1956 and renamed as Pharmaceutical Corporation of Kerala (PCK). Interestingly the company was making loss till 1994; thereafter there has been a continuous growth in the surplus generated. The importance and success of Oushadhi can be summarized as : one, manufactures more than 450 Ayurvedic formulations as per ancient classical texts, rare combinations of expert, experienced Keralite authorities and special combinations developed in the Research wing. Two, upholds ancient traditional methods of manufacturing along with series of innovations in the traditional formulations with modern machinery and technology under strict quality control measures. Three, quality medicines are made available to the public at reasonable prices. Four, meets the entire medicine requirements of Government Ayurvedic Hospitals and Dispensaries under the Department of Indian Systems of Medicines. Five, meets public demands through a network of 500 exclusive Oushadhi dealers and Agents.

In the year 2000, the total profit rose to Rs. 56 lakhs and in the last year (2004) it has become Rs. 1.01 crores. The improvement in the financial performance can be attributed to mainly the innovation of introducing new products and marketing network. Though the company has restrained in its purpose of producing the medicine for the government hospitals till recently, the huge push factor from the consumer side made company to get into the OTC market and now, the major OTC product remain as the major income earner for the company. The product diversification especially the new product for the treatment of diabetes and its popularity within and outside Kerala and wider marketing promotion boosted this surplus. This medicine known as *Pramehoushadhi* is the major income earner of Oushadhi.

Concentration on Traditional Ayurvedic medicines and financial performance: The state government itself buys medicines worth more than Rs 3 crore every year from Oushadhi for its Ayurvedic hospitals. Pramehoushadhi, a highly demanded medicine for the treatment of diabetes, the major innovation of the company, alone contributes more than 60 lakhs rupees to the turnover. The table 9 gives the picture that in the general category of Ayurvedic medicines, arishtasavams account for a value of Rs. 7.17 lakhs in 1999. Except Kashaya choornams and ghruthams, the sale for all other category of medicines is increasing. Kashayams and the medicated oil growth are promising (with the compound growth rate of 11.61 and 7.23 from 1992 to 1999).

Since Oushadhi started producing Over the Counter (OTC) drugs, expenditure on advertisement also increased from Rs.2 lakhs to 20 lakhs. Cyavanaprasam, Pramehoushadhi and herbal oil consumes a major share of this advertisement cost. As mentioned earlier, Oushadhi adopted two strategies for product marketing. The employment of sales representatives to contact Ayurvedic consultants for promotion of sales, and second is the setting up of different consultant agencies at different parts with all the facilities. The first option is less favoured because, in this case all medicines have to be made available in the locality, maintaining a large team is costly in terms of their salaries and emoluments etc. The second option is preferred because of the advantages that the company will have in terms of better control and feedback. Capital employed (net fixed assets including capital work in progress plus working capital) has been improved from Rs. 470.84 lakhs in 2001 to Rs. 672.28 lakhs in 2003 and net worth (paid up capital plus reserves and samples less intangible assets) has grown from 470.84 lakhs to 664.13 lakhs in 2003. Oushadhi paid the state Government a dividend of Rs. 17.43 Lakhs for 2001-02 (Web site, Govt. of Kerala). Oushadhi had distributed ayurveda medicines to the tune of Rs. 1.75 crores to Government ayurveda hospitals in Chattisgarh, Orissa, and Madhya Pradesh, Rajasthan, Delhi, Himachal Pradesh and Pondicherry during in 2003. Overall the company achieved a compound annual growth of 14.8 per cent in the sales turnover in the last decade. This is higher than that of Ayurvedic companies in Kerala. The PBT as a per centage to the capital employed increased from 15 per cent in 1995-96 to 38 per cent at the close of this decade and as the data shows the profit margin is on a consistent rise.

Table 9
Product-wise Trends in the Oushadhi Sales (sales in lakhs)

Year	*Arishta-savams (ltr)*	*Kasha-yams (ltr)*	*Ghru-thams*	*Gulikas (kg)*	*Choor-nams*	*Kashaya choornams*	*Lehyams*	*Med. oils*
1992	4.94	–	0.32	0.27	0.38	2.8	0.5	1.65
1994	6.12	1.08	0.27	0.33	0.71	2.53	1.12	1.81
1995	7.05	1.58	0.2	0.52	0.28	3.21	0.67	2.24
1996	7.09	1.48	0.16	0.63	0.28	4.02	0.71	2.15
1999	7.17	1.87	0.22	0.67	0.53	2.78	0.69	2.69
CGR	5.47	11.61	-5.21	13.87	4.87	-0.10	4.71	7.23

Source: Compiled from annual reports

Oushadhi spends around Rs. 5 crores for the raw materials and which forms the major cost of the firm. But the less expenditure on R&D (around 1%), as of other Ayurvedic firms is a major concern. They use around 450 medicinal plants. More than 50% of the raw materials are medicinal plants and of which, 60-65% collected from the wild and 15 per cent is indigenously available, 15% coming from outside the state and 5-10 per cent is from cultivation. Some medicinal plants like *gulgul* and *Kottam* are getting from states like Himachal Pradesh and Uttar Pradesh. The main sources are from local suppliers and traders and the Oushadhi has an extensive linkage with the SC/ST federations, which supplies medicinal plants collecting from tribal collectors (Harilal, 2004). Through this phenomenon, it is giving employment to a large number of individuals.

Now there are 417 employees in the unit. If the employment through linkages is added, this will constitute thousands.

The example of Oushadhi is setting a totally different model showing that without entering into the export market or cosmeceutical market also, a firm can succeed by innovating on the classical formulations with a disciplined marketing and production networks. Comparing Pankajakasthuri, Oushadhi is spending only 2% of its turnover to advertisement. But still it is able to achieve a substantial profit, and is able to achieve a brand name in the case of disease like diabetes. This is to be understood along with the fact that this firm is facing all the constraints of a public enterprise, but at the same time set a model by innovating on traditional drugs and OTC drugs as Pramehoushadhi, at the same time serving the needs of most of the government owned hospitals in India. The above two example shows, though innovations of non technological types are more in the case of Ayurvedic products, recently, product innovations also gaining importance.

III

INDUSTRY SPECIFIC CHALLENGES

While the industry is very much receptive to innovation and product pattern shift, the major challenges faced by the sector are many. Other than the general problems like competition from other countries (in the case of ayurveda, it is China), cost competitiveness and demand enrichment, investing on innovation and technology etc. it face some unique problems like (a) Availability of right and quality raw material, especially medicinal plants (b) standardization, and validation of Ayurvedic products as per the modern trials for selling larger market outside and (c) Problems regarding the protection under IPR regimes. That means upgrading the domestic market or strengthening industry from within alone will not be sufficient, but an effort should be there to solve major external problems. The common feature of these issues is state has a crucial role in assuaging all these issues. Now we will analyse these issues one by one.

Depletion of Medicinal and Aromatic Plants

'Right and timely availability of raw material' is going to be a crucial factor if not, one of the biggest problems that this industry is going to face in the coming future. 'Right' here means of right kind and right quality. Depletion of the same due to ruthless cultivation and forest destruction is of major concern. Since the demand for medicinal plants is a derived demand from the demand for Ayurvedic medicines and related products, and mainly 80% of the Ayurvedic raw material consists of medicinal plants, the growth of Ayurvedic industry will result in consequently a same increase in the medicinal plant demand. An estimate shows that Ayurvedic industry is growing at a rate of 12 to 15% in Kerala (Harilal, 2004). A same growth can be expected in other parts of the country also. This will put an additional compulsion on the medicinal plant sector to provide matured and specific quality raw material for the growing industry. This problem has been addressed in international arena through various conservation activities and cultivation promoting programmes. Many studies (MAPPA 1998, Suneetha and Chandrakanth 2001, Devi and Joseph 2003) have addressed the problem of economic scarcity of medicinal plants in relation to the demand from the pharmacies in and outside Kerala.

Table 10
Market Analysis of the Major Medicinal Plants[8]

Name of the plant	*Quantity demanded (in tons)*	*Price elasticity of demand*	*Scarcity ratio (ratio of availability to needed)*
Sida spp.	608	0.54	2.79
Tinospora cordifolia	282	0.35	0.00
Terminalia chibula	164	3.31	-3.20
Withania somnifera	149	0.60	-4.02
Adathoda sp	141	1.46	-1.60
Cedrus deodara	138	1.98	-3.80
Woodfordia frutisoca	123	0.42	-5.16

Source: Devi and Joseph (2003).

A study by Suneetha and Chandrakanth (2002), using the real price increase as a proxy of relative scarcity, also reach the conclusion that many plants are getting extinct in Indian forests. There are various medicinal plants which the firms in the country are getting from outside, since it is no longer available in the country. At the same time, India is supplying around 14% of the medicinal plant needed in the European Union herbal market. This shows that, we have comparative advantage in the collection and cultivation of some of the plants while we have disadvantage in some others. So the promotion of both in-situ and ex-situ cultivation and various other methods like gene banks and herbal parks should be encouraged nation wide. This conservation issues are hitting the headings at present especially after the Convention on Biological Diversity (1992), in which the first declaration regarding the rights of indigenous community and equal sharing is being made and need for conservation also emphasized. Direct ways of protection and indirect methods through incentive policies should be pursued. Since a large literature on this issue is available, here we will concentrate more on other concerns.

Standardizing the Products/process for the World Market[9]

The main issues the industry faces in terms of quality and standardization are:

Lack of Product and process validation: Once a product is conceived the efficiency of the product has to be proved authentically. For which internationally accepted non-clinical trials to prove the efficacy of the product in animals abiding OECD guidelines, toxicity studies, pharmacokinetics, pharmacodynamics, bio-equivalence etc. should be used. As far as Ayurvedic medicines are concerned no such validation methodology has been used for generations together. Since the toxicity of the product is not known, the action of the product in human body cannot be known and thus the modern medical community will not accept Ayurvedic product as a medicine. There should be uniform process techniques for each product and this should not be changed from batch to batch so as to get uniform products from each batch. There should be a Standard Operating Procedure for each product and this should be clearly followed and the standard operating procedure should start right form the selection of raw materials and continues till the final product gets packed. There should be a uniform procedure for each product manufacturing, which is called process validation. Till date nothing has been developed in the field of Ayurveda for Process Validation (Varghese, 2005).

Lack of Quality Control and quality assurance: Quality Control refers to the processes involved in maintaining the quality of validity of a manufactured product. Regardless of the form of herbal preparation, some degree of quality control is necessary. Currently, there is no organization or government body that certifies a product is 'labeled correctly'. Without proper QC, there is no assurance that the herb contained in the bottle is the same as what is stated on its outside label. The solution to this is for manufacturers and suppliers of herbal products to adhere to QC standards and good manufacturing practices. With improvements in the identification of plants by laboratory analysis, consumers should at least be guaranteed that the right plant is being used. Currently, only a few manufacturers in India adhere to complete QC and good manufacturing procedures including microscopic, physical, chemical and biological analysis. In general, it is believed that if the active components of a particular herb are known, whatever forms the herb product is, the herb should be analyzed to ensure that it contains these components at an acceptable/standardized level. More accurate dosages can then be given for optimal use of the herb. Currently, in many countries, numerous standardized extracts fulfill requirements for marketing as drugs. During the production process, there shouid be a continuous monitoring of a quality assurance department to see that all quality parameters were strictly followed during manufacturing. If we go through the specifications of international standards like USFDA, TGA etc., they have definite standards for each and every activity, which gives better performance during the manufacturing stage. If we can develop such guidelines and evolve specific procedure, our entry to the international herbal pharmaceutical market will be much easier and we can take the advantages of WTO, by patenting our processes and products.

Lack of GLP and GMP: GLP regulations were intended for toxicity testing only. It was reserved for labs undertaking animal studies for pre-clinical work. Some laboratories follow GLP's whenever the studies are to be used to support applications for research or marketing studies to be submitted to the FDA. GLP regulates all non-clinical safety studies that support or are intended to support applications for research or marketing permits for products regulated by the FDA or other similar national legislation. Good Manufacturing Practice (GMP) regulates manufacturing and its associated quality control (in contrast to GLP which covers more drug development activities). GMP predates GLP. GMP regulations have been developed to ensure that medicinal (pharmaceutical) products are consistently produced and controlled to the quality standards appropriate to their intended use. GAPs stress the selection of correct germ plasm with high content of stable active components. GAPs also establish standards for noxious and harmful contaminants like heavy metals, pesticide residues and microbes in plants. Chinese success story should work for India as a model[10].

Lack of Toxicological/ Safety Studies: The Evaluation of the toxicity and adverse drug reaction of the herbal preparation has been a neglected area, as herbs are considered as natural products and, therefore safe. This lack of information makes it difficult to compare the benefit-risk profile of herbal medicines. Standardization doesn't mean only for the products, but the collection, processing of raw material and the final product should be standardized. Availability of the desired genotype of plant in the required quantity, free from toxic contaminants and with desired therapeutic activity has also very critically considered. This issue gains relevance in the current context were many countries like UK and Canada has been banned the Indian Ayurvedic products, with the allegation that most of these contains metal content, and similar allegation was there regarding some products that they contain steroids. But most of the experts[11] has the opinion that, the problem is actually, created by the simple drugs and compound drugs. Simple drugs the standardization is simple and it can be followed in the modern lines. But in the case of compound drugs it is very difficult to find the therapeutic quality of each and every component. So while in ayurveda when poly herbal product is validated we have a chemical finger printing mechanism for validation up to three ingredients are possible, but difficult. But most of the Ayurvedic medicines, it is very difficult to go for these chemical finger printing. For example the case of *dasamoolarishtam*, one cannot check the quality by taking each and every ingredient of the formulation.

So in the case of standardization, we can follow the efficiency model China has been put forward, through Good Agricultural Practice (at the collection/cultivation level), Good Manufacturing Practice (at the manufacturing level) and Good Clinical Practice (at the trial standardization level). India has already adopted the Good Manufacturing Practice and many firms are following the guide lines set.

Inadequacies with Existing Patent laws and Protection of Ayurvedic knowledge

Inadequacies in the Intellectual Property Regime are of great relevance when the fact of community ownership and secretive nature of Traditional medicine is considered. In addition to this, in the case of traditional medicine, like Ayurveda, how the grass-root innovations, which have high commercial significance, can be protected and equally shared is of major concern. Though we have some successful examples like *Jeevani*[12], at present, the requirements for protection provided under international standards of patent law and most national patent laws are inadequate to protect traditional knowledge and biodiversity. For example, traditional skills in manual and spiritual therapies are different from those in modern practice and there is no record of who was the inventor. Existing conventional patent law can and does protect pharmaceutical products. However, herbal medicines and herbal products are different from chemical drugs. The intellectual property standards established by the Agreement of Trade-Related Aspects of Intellectual Property Rights (TRIPS Agreement) (1994) allows innovation to be protected by the discovery of new chemical components, know-how in producing the product, trademarks and trade secrets. However, for herbal medicines it is difficult to meet all the requirements of patentability due to their intrinsic characteristics.

Firstly, herbal medicines are crude plant materials, such as leaves, flowers, fruits, seeds, stems, wood, bark, roots, rhizomes or other plant parts, which may be entire, fragmented or powdered. As such, it is often not possible to obtain existing patent law protection for nerbal medicines by claiming the discovery of new chemical entities, which are novel, involve an inventive step and are industrially applicable. Secondly, herbal products are powdered herbal materials, or extracts, tinctures and fatty oils of herbal materials prepared by steeping or heating herbal materials in alcoholic beverages and/or honey, or in other materials. The production process is usually simple. There is no know-how or invention in the preparation process that is sophisticated enough to justify protection under existing patent laws. Thirdly, except for pharmaceutical companies and industries, other holders of traditional knowledge, such as research institutes and practitioners, often do not have the financial and human resources that are necessary to obtain protection through trademarks. Fourthly, it is extremely difficult, if not impossible, to keep knowledge a secret, because disclosure of the composition of the product is a prerequisite for registration of herbal medicines before the product can be sold.

The identification of TK/assigning property right to the medicinal knowledge, five major analytical steps have to be considered. (i) subject matter of IPR i.e. information categories that would be called as knowledge in this category, (ii) Identification of beneficiaries, (iii) contribution to biodiversity conservation and appropriate mechanism for the same, (iv) specific attributes of any chosen system of IPR like duration, enforcement mechanism etc and (v) implementation mechanisms.

Regarding these issues major consideration should include, (i) the protective mechanism should take into account the ethic laws of the community, who own the knowledge, (ii) sharing authorities should decide for further proceeding forum depends on the intention of protection, for example, whether we are looking for trade benefits (then WTO), or proceed it as a major health care system and to be incorporated to the 'mainstream' medicine (then WHO), (iii) Immediate need to develop the sharing benefits mechanism of cumulative innovations, which consider all the involved stakeholders. The recent models, like Bhagirathy (2003), are relevant in this concern and (iv) possibilities should be explored not only to develop a *sui generis* system, but inclusion in geographic indication should also be explored.

Easing the Power Relations and Framing an Adequate Export Policy

To an extent, the policy framed by the major export destinations, like USA, UK and other European nations, have the ability to decide the role of Traditional medicine in the world market. Thus the 'selling benefits' from ayurveda largely depend on the destination policies. Many herbal products fall between the far ends of this regulatory range: unlicensed preparations are thought to account for over 80 per cent of herbal sales (De Smet, 1995). European Union legislation requires herbal products to be authorized for marketing if they are industrially produced and if their presentation or their function, or both, bring them inside its definition of a medicinal product. Unfortunately, the drawing of sharp borderline is difficult. Many medicine-like products on the British herbal market remain unregistered for two reasons: acceptable data on efficacy, safety and quality may not be available, and the licensing fee is high (De Smet, 1995). Special licensing procedures for herbal medicines are already in force in Germany, where regulatory evaluations of medicinal herbs have been laid down in more than 300 monographs, and in France more than 200 herbs have been listed as acceptable ingredients of phytomedicines. Australia developed an integral approach to the herbal market that will also cover various non-western herbs. The main registering and regulating body for Western herbal practitioner is the National Institute of Medical Herbalist situated in U.K. Only graduates of approved courses are accepted on to the register, and a strict code of ethics is maintained. The European Herbal Practitioner Association, an umbrella body with about 1000 members, has been set up to encourage greater unity among herbalists. However, it has no formal criteria for screening membership and no published code of ethics yet (Vickers and Zollman, 1999).

What is striking is that WHO has been accepted the Chinese yardstick for standardization of the traditional medicines, which is of a more evidence based and scientific, which compels India to go for the scientific validation of their products. The guidelines set for good practices, in manufacturing, agriculture, validation or clinical trials (GCP< GMP< GAP) are accepted as a common requirement for acceptance. Many countries have been taken very abrasive steps regarding the traditional medicine, might be the pressure from the lobbies of other medicines.[13] From 2000, the EU has drafted a series of directives that seriously restrict the practice of herbal medicine, with the intent of a suitable choice on consumer choice and public safety. A house of lords have been appointed in 1999-00 in Britain to enquire into various science and technology aspects. Since 2000, this British House of Lords and the Government have been working towards a regulatory scheme for Complementary and alternative medicine in Britain, a scheme that will include ayurveda. House of Lords Select Committee on Science and Technology produced six reports, the last of which was entitled 'Complementary and Alternative Medicine[14]' (henceforth the '*Report*'). The report, of which most of the recommendations have been agreed upon by the government have raised a big protests from the CAM practitioners and manufacturers. The report classifies the Traditional medicines into three sections, in which ayurveda has been included in the third category, advocates strong evidence to prove its efficacy (for detailed discussion see Wujastyk, 2004). There are criticisms that this document has prepared without considering the available knowledge about different traditional medical systems, and been not helpful in bringing out more truthful deliberations on the same. It is also regrettable that such a bluntly hegemonic approach to CAM has been the informing principle behind these documents, in stark contrast, for example, to the approaches taken by the WHO (Wujastyk, 2004). So the industry, academia and government have to keep on track of the larger power relations in the world herbal market, because that can be a decisive factor ultimately, though whatever efforts effectively we put up (Banerjee, 2004). US Department of Health and Human Services (DHHS) and the agencies under that, strongly acknowledges the need for scientifically proven CAM practices, to integrate the same to modern medicine and mainly insists on research, outreach and integration. For the effective integration, it has been mentioned as a clause that the published research work will only be considered. So the validation should be in the modern norms.

Since, these kinds of regulations, exist in other countries, the manufacturers are exporting medicines in food supplement and cosmeceuticals category, from which the manufacturers are gaining much. This fetches them additional tax benefits too. Now Ayurvedic medicines are exported to UAE and Malaysia. Singapore and Germany are emerged to be the new destinations and opens new potentials and possibilities.[15]. But the solution will be as we mentioned earlier, proper in house validation and standardization along with our own well-developed modern Ayurvedic pharmacopoeia and bring more transparency in listing the documents and ingredients.

CONCLUSION: LOOKING FOR AN OPTIMAL STRATEGY

This paper mainly focused on the organized sector of ayurveda and its initiatives and prospects for growth in an open economy regime. Here we didn't deal with an equally important sector in size and employment creation in the economy - the unorganized sector of ayurveda, since the paper mainly intends to address the issues face by the organized sector and the information regarding the other is scanty. Most of the issues we have addressed here necessarily call for state's active role, irrespective of its nature, whether standardization of the products, R&D, intellectual property shield for biological diversity etc. Even now the expenditure on Indian systems of Medicine and Homeopathy (ISM&H) is limited to only 2% of the whole health expenditure. This alone shows the increasing disregards to the system. A tangential consideration in the overall development pattern is not sufficient in the case of ayurveda, but need focused strategies to resolve each and every pertinent issue, which hinder the development. Education and the research have been strengthened, with a concerted effort from the private firms than the public and the efforts in the public sector need to get speeded up.

There is a need for vertical integration in the industry and vertical clustering. That may create growth and employment opportunities through linkage effects. To reach a stage where herbal products of assured quality and effectiveness become integrated into mainstream medicinal treatment, several obstacles have to be surmounted. We have pointed out the major issues specifically faced by this industry like standardization, documentation, ideological mismatch and property rights problems, raw material depletion etc. A nodal agency should be formed at state level to carry out the functions and solve these issues. The private initiatives like *CARe Keralam*[16] should be encouraged in this regard. This should be formed at least in the export front as a *single window system*, for standardization and ensure raw materials at the right time etc. This kind of nodal agencies can help not only in solving these specific problems, but to help the medium firms to resolve the problems of economies of scale also. The bigger equipments can be provided by these agencies as a centralized system and can help the medium firms to produce their products without huge fixed costs. This will work as an incentive for those firms, which are not entering into large-scale production, mainly because of high fixed cost and high sunk cost.

Initiatives and incentives for more expenditure in R&D in developing new drugs and extracts other than clinical trials and standardization should be brought in as a new agenda and a national legislation for property rights and grass root innovation should be formed. Other immediate concerns include; (a) Identifying the easily penetratable markets (b) an ideological consensus and (c) strong move in WHO and other international forums for the acceptance etc, again depend mainly on state initiatives. Clearly there is a need to conduct trials which use not just simple, but these complex herbal compounds. The interactions between the constituents in a compound may be crucial to its modus operandi. There is an immediate need for trial promotion in the compound drugs. For these, Chinese Medicine can be a better reference point. There are many internal and external factors, which have a long term impact on the growth of this sector. While aiming at a global market, the major hurdle is found to be the proof of efficacy, and might be because of the same, Traditional Indian Medicine is lagging behind, and not because of its intrinsic inefficiency. The efforts now should be in the direction to understand the world market, standardize the product and toxicity screening as China has succeeded. Possibility of scientific validation, not at the cost of traditional Ayurvedic value, can be pursued with an eye on ruling pharmaceutical power relations.

ENDNOTES

The following major initiatives have been taken by the Central Government for ensuring safety and quality control of ASU (Ayurveda, Siddha and Unani) drugs:

(i) Good Manufacturing Practices (GMP) for ASU drugs were notified on 23rd June, 2000 under Schedule 'T' of the Indian Drugs & Cosmetics Act, 1940 and Rules, 1945 which seeks mandatory compliance from the licensed manufacturers with regard to raw-materials, manufacturing area, manufacturing processes, record keeping, storage of raw-materials and finished products and quality testing. State Governments and all State Licensing Authorities have been advised vide Department of AYUSH order dtd. 13.10.2005 to ensure strict compliance of GMP by ASU drugs manufactures and cancel the license of non-GMP compliant units.

(ii) Provisions relating to proper labelling, packing and conspicuous display of all the ingredients along with the quantities contained in the formulations on the label/container or a leaflet inserted inside the container, have been reiterated for compliance by an order issued by the Department of AYUSH on 10.10.2005 for strict compliance by State Drug Controllers/Licensing Authorities.

(iii) To address domestic as well as international concerns on presence of heavy metals in ASU drugs exporters of purely herbal ASU drugs have been directed to either conspicuously display on the container of purely herbal ASU drugs words "Heavy metals within permissible limits" or furnish the above certificate from an appropriately equipped in-house laboratories or any other approved laboratories along with other consignment papers w.e.f. 1.1.2006. Mandatory testing for heavy metals on purely herbal ASU drugs will also be extended for sale of purely herbal ASU drugs within the country in phases keeping in view the testing infrastructure within the country.

(iv) The issue of safety of herbo-mineral/herbo-metallic Bhasmas/ Compounds is also being addressed by the Central Government. A project has been sanctioned for chemical analysis and safety studies of eight most widely used Rasaushadhis/Bhasmas, namely, Kajjali, Rasmanikya, Nag Bhasma, Rasasindoor, Basantkusumkar Ras, Arogyavardhini Vati, Mahayograj Guggul and Mahalaxmi Vilas Ras by CSIR laboratories under the Golden Triangle Project within a time frame of 18 months.

(v) Use of permissible excipients, preservatives for increasing the shelf-life of ASU drugs has been notified. Draft rules for expiry date of ASU drugs have also been published in November, 2005 and a consultation process is on for finalizing these rules.

(vi) Certain guidelines have also been issued to State Licensing Authorities with a view to curb the mushroom growth of irrational ASU combinations through the patent and proprietary route.

ACKNOWLEDGEMENT

The paper tries to comprehend the problems and prospects of Indian Ayurvedic sector in the free market regime. Ayurvedic sector here, have undergone substantial change in theory and practice either as a survival strategy or as a part of the efforts to create its own space in the global competitive market. But seemingly, this sector is looking for a big leap from marginalization to dominance with the help of innovation, boosted by the modern marketing techniques and diversification of products. Two case studies from Kerala, namely Oushadhi and Pankajakasthuri are evident for this. But to reap the future prospects in the economic front, this industry has to tackle a large number of issues viz. standardization, raw material depletion, intellectual property protection etc. not on priority wise but concurrently, since these all calls for immediate attention. While from a theoretical and ideological ground, this move is very much debatable; from an economic point of view this seems to be inevitable and most importantly state have a comprehensive role in setting the way clear.

NOTES

1. Dabur, Himalaya, Zandu and AVS Kottakkal.
2. EXIM Bank, 2002.
3. In the domestic market 13% is contributed by Homeopathy and in export figure we have included Ayurveda and Unani only. So considering the same share as in the domestic market, we assume Ayurveda constitutes 97% of total exports.
4. Restriction on day to day habits means restriction on food consumption i.e. one cannot intake spicy food, non vegetarian diet needs to be avoided, one cannot consume alcohol etc.
5. *Best rural entrepreneurs award* by National Integration Society of India in 1994-95, *Best herbal medicine award* for Pankajakasthuri granules from the Kerala State Consumer Protection Centre in 1996-97, *best herbal soap in Kerala* in 1997-98 for Kerala Upabhokthru Vedi for Kasthuri herbal soap and *JeevanRaksha Award* in 1997-98 from Human Aids and Cancer Control Society of India.
6. *Harmony* offers readymade Ayurvedic rejuvenation therapies carried out by specially trained masseurs under the supervision of ayurveda physicians. Over a hundred masseurs are currently in the final stages of an intensive 10-month training programme in Thiruvananthapuram. Besides a thorough grounding in various aspects of Ayurvedic massage, the masseurs are also learning yoga, spoken English and other 'soft skills'.
7. *Panacea* is the company's brand of Ayurvedic therapies for various illnesses. For its Panacea brand of Ayurvedic therapies, the company plans to target individuals in the UK, Germany, Italy and West Asia. The launch of the Harmony and Panacea brands is part of an effort to dispel negative impressions about ayurveda and establish a benchmark for the industry. Both brands have been developed based on strict ayurveda treatment protocols.
8. This is an analysis based on the data obtained from the major Ayurvedic manufacturing units of Kerala.
9. This section draws heavily from the ideas of Joy Varghese (discussion with him), Herbal chief of KINFRA.
10. All manufacturers of Traditional Chinese medicine (TCM) were mandated to comply with guide line laid down by the Chinese State Drug Administration (SDA) by 2004 and farms producing raw ingredients must comply with SDA-imposed standards by 2007. As a result 1470 companies have qualified for GMPs. This kind of quality follow up has done even in marketing especially packing and labeling (Patwardhan et al., 2005).
11. They are also of the opinion that, the recent allegations against the Ayurvedic drugs are baseless, because the atmospheric difference in the nations needs different metallic content in food and medicines. For example, in western atmosphere, the metallic content needed is 20 points per million grms, while in India it is almost double. So obviously, in the western norms, the metallic content will be higher.
12. Jeevani is a drug with anti fatigue properties extracted from the lead given by *Kani* Tribe of Kerala about a plant called Trychopus zeylanicus (*arogyapacha* in Malayalam). Tropical Botanical Garden and Research Institute (TBGRI) has successfully presented a model of benefit sharing by sharing the benefits of the commercialization with the Tribe, even acknowledged by UNDP.

13. Efforts of the enquiry committee of British lords to include acupuncture in the highest category of CAM while keeping Chinese Traditional Medicine in the third category, while both need almost same efficacy parameters.
14. See 'General Information about House of Lords' Select Committees' at http://www.parliament.the-stationery-office.co.uk/pa/ld199697/ldselect/ldscgen.htm.
15. Around 6% of the total tourists in Kerala are coming solely for Ayurvedic treatment and this remains to be the second largest reason for tourist visit (TCS, 1999). A case of *Somatheeram* and *Manaltheeram* Ayurvedic Resorts situated at Thiruvananthapuram shows that around half of these tourists belongs to Germany (Harilal, 2004).
16. CARe Keralam is an organization recently formed in Kerala by a number of large Ayurvedic manufacturers to work as a nodal agency for resolving this industry related issues like raw material availability, intellectual property right problems, standardization and marketing problems etc. this is yet to be commissioned.

REFERENCES

Appadurai, A. (1996), 'Commodities and Politics of Value' in Appadurai (ed.) *The Social Life of Things–commodities in Cultural Perspectives*, CUP.

Banerjee, M. (2002), 'Power, Culture and Medicine: Ayurvedic Pharmaceuticals in the Modern Market', *Contributions to Indian Sociology* (n.s) 36, 3.

Banerjee, M. (January 2004), 'Local knowledge for World Market: Globalising Ayurveda' *Economic and Political Weekly.*

Baumol, W.J. (1959), *Economic Dynamics-An Introduction*, The Macmillan Company, New York.

Bhagirathy, Aparna (2003), *Intellectual Property Right for Traditional Knowledge–Economic Analysis of an Incentive System*, SANDCE Project Report.

Bode, M. (2004), *Ayurvedic and Unani Health and Beauty Products: Reworking India's Medical Traditions*, PhD Dissertation, Department of Anthropology, University of Amsterdam.

Chandrakanth, M.G., Suneetha, M.S. (2001), '*Demand and Valuation of Medicinal Plants in the Western Ghats of Kerala–A Resource Economics Study*', Department of Agricultural Economics, University of Agricultural Sciences, Bangalore.

Dadha Mahendra (1992), "IDMA's Memorandum" IDMA Bulletin 23 (5) March.

De Smet PAGM (1995), Should Herbal Medicines-like Product be Licensed as Medicines? *BMJ*, 310, 1023-4.

Devi, Indira, P., Joseph, M.J. (2003), *'Market Economy of Medicinal Plants in Kerala'* at National Seminar on 'Evolving Action Plan to Facilitate the Development and Utilisation of Medicinal Plants', KINFRA.

Gautham Vinayaseel; Raman R.M.V., Kumar, Asish (2002), *Exporting Indian Health care*, EXIM bank, Quest Publications.

Grove, Richard (1998), *'Indigenous knowledge and the Significance of South–West India for Portuguese and Dutch Construction of Tropical nature'*, in Grove, *et.al* edited Nature and the Orient, Oxford University Press.

Harilal, M.S. (2004), *Ayurvedic Manufacturing Industry of Kerala-A Study of its Organised Sector*, Unpublished M.Phil Dissertation, Jawaharlal Nehru University, New Delhi.

Hirschman, A.O. (1958), *The Strategy Ofeconomic Development*, Yale University Press.

Howes, David (ed.) (1996), *Cross Cultural consumption: Global Markets and Local Realities*, Rotledge Publication, New York.

Kumar, A. (1998), *'Medicine and the Raj: British Medical Policy in India, 1835-1911'* Sage Publications, New Delhi, p. 68-73.

Kumar, Anil (2004), 'Research Methodology on Ayurvedic Formulations', Paper Presented in the *Intellectual Conclave on Ayurvedic Research Methodology*, Aluva, Kerala

Langford, J. (2004), *Fluent Bodies: Ayurvedic Remedies for Post Colonial Imbalance*, Oxford University Press.

Leslie (1999), Comments on Alter's Heaps of Health, Current Anthropology, 40 Supplement 61.

Madhav Karki and Radhika Johai (ed.) (2002), *The Role of Medicinal Plants Industry in Fostering Bio Diversity Conservation and Rural Development* MAPPA, IDRC.

Masood E. (February 1997), Medicinal Plants Threatened by over-use, *Nature*, Vol. 385, No. 6617, p. 570.

Panikkar, K.N. (1995), 'Indigenous Medicine and Cultural Hegemony' in *Culture, Ideology and Hegemony-Intellectual and Social Consciousness in Colonial India*, Tulika Publications.

Patwardhan, B., Warude, D., Pushpangadan, P. and Bhatt, N. (2005), *Ayurveda and Traditional Chinese Medicine: A Comparative Overview*, Advance Access Publication, CAM, p. 465-473.

Pushpangadan, P. (2002), 'Future Scope of Herbal Medicine' in *Indian Health Care Tradition: a Contemporary View*, (ed.) Kottakkal Ayurveda Series-53.

Sampath, P.G. (2003), *Defining an IPR on Traditional Medical Knowledge: A Process Oriented Perspective*, Discussion paper INTECH, UN University, Maastricht.

Sanjoy Kumar Pal1, Yogeshwer Shukla (2003), 'Herbal Medicine: Current Status and the Future', *Asian Pacific Journal of Cancer Prevention, Vol 4*.

Sengupta, Nirmal (2003) *Traditional knowledge and Intellectual Property rights*, Paper Presented on IPR at Administrative Staff College, Hyderabad, November 17-18, 2003.

TATA Consultancy Services (1999), *Economic Benefits of Tourism Sector in Kerala*, a Draft Report Prepared for Government of Kerala.

Vargese, J.P. (2005) Report on CARe Keralam, Paper presented in Kerala Study Congress, AKG Centre, Thiruvananthapuram.

Varier, M.R. (2002), *The Rediscovery of Ayurveda-The Story of Kottakkal Arya Vaidya Sala*, Penguin Books.

Varier, N.V.K. (2004) *History of Ayurveda*, Arya Vaidya Sala, Kottakkal Publishing House.

Vickers A. and Zollman C. (1999). ABC of Complementary Medicine: Herbal Medicine. *BMJ*, 319, 1050-3.

WHO *'Strategy for Traditional Medicine 2000-03'*, Geneva, p.vi. (September, 2000).

Wujastyk, D. (2004), 'Policy Formation and Debate Concerning the Government Regulation of Ayurveda in Great Britain in the 21st Century', Available on website.

Chapter - 13

Banking and the Sustainable Development of the Indian Economy: With Special Reference to the Urban Co-operative Banks

S.K. Hegde

SECTION - I

INTRODUCTION

The Indian economy is passing through a crucial phase of economic development with social change in the present context of new economic reforms undertaken in the county. The new strategies of development in India being multidirectional in nature and necessitated a faster growth of primary, secondary and tertiary sectors under public, private and co-operative sectors of the country.

Asection, form the public and private sectors, the co-operative sector is flourishing in the country. The development of co-operative sector gave rise to the growth of co-operative banking which has a distinct role to play in the sustainable development of India.

ROLE OF BANKS IN NATIONAL ECONOMIC DEVELOPMENT

The banks can influence the pace and position of economic growth in well-determined directions in consonance with the national objectives and priorities. Organized banking has always played a very vital role in the economic development of India.

Singh Autar (1977) has rightly pointed out that "the development, welfare and uplifftment of whether it is social, cultural, economic monetary fiscal or political sectors depends on the various financial resources which are available to the country either from within or from outside because finance plays a significant role in the economic development of a country.

Schupeter (1912) the first modern economist, regarded banking system as one of the two key agents (the other being entrepreneurship) in the whole process of development. He described bank credit as the fundamental phenomenon of economic development.

Among various types of banks, the UCBS occupy a significant place in the co-operative movement of the country and constitute and important multi-agency banking system in India. Despite the existence of commercial banks, the UCBs have a distinct status and wider role to play which occupy a strategic position in meeting the requirements of small men in urban and semi-urban regions.

THE PROBLEM

The challenges of changes in the economy and society have great impact on the business operations of UCBs. More than a decade of new economic reforms and the consequent financial and banking sector reforms have paved the way for shift from the closed economy towards a global economy. The banking sector has been the first to be exposed to the market economy due to liberalization, privatization and globalisation. Some of the international prudential norms such as capital adequacy norms, income recognition, asset classification, NPA norms, graduation of banks accounting standards etc have been imposed on UCBs.

Moreover, the life style of urban families is fast changing. Urbnisation and urban development is considered as one of the most complicated changes of the new millennium.

At this crucial juncture, can the UCBs rise up to the occasions, innovate and cope with the emerging trends? Can they discharge their promotional and developemental role properly to meet the millennium development goals? These are the major research questions and the problem areas of research. They have to be carefully studied and solutions are to be found.

REVIEW OF LITERATURE

The survey of existing literature reveals that there are very few studies on the present theme of banking and sustainable development of the Indian economy in the context of new economic reforms. To quote some of them.

Kazim Shamim (1996) has studied the role and problems of UCBs in India in the wake of the recommendations on financial reforms by the Narasimham committee. He has observed that the UCBs occupy a special position in the financial system with their unique structure and character. The author has referred to the new environment created by financial reforms and globalisation and how it has affected the co-operative banking sector.

Warekar (1996) has pleaded for a cautious approach to the privatization of urban banks. He has observed that in the new libaralised environment, every UCB has to decide for itself, once the legal position is clear whether it should be privatized and whether it will be able to serve the members, constituents and the society better.

Joshi (1999) has srudied the impact of banking sector reforms followed by the recommendations of the Narasimham Committee (1991). The author has observed that the introduction of reform process has paved the way for building a strong and efficient banking system'.

Patil (2000) has observed that the fast changing business environment has placed the co-operative banks in a competitive set-up and this has necessitated to achieve efficiency and strategic management.

Dabir Yeshwant (2000) has focused his study on the issue of autonomy and minimizing the role of government. The author has suggested that the UCBs should employ professional experts for managing the affairs of their banks and they have to adopt the latest banking techniques.

Kundan (1999) has observed that financial sector reforms require that the UCBs have to operate on the basis of operational flexibility and functional autonomy with a view to enchancing efficiency, productivity, profitability and sustainability.

Ram Kumar (2003) has studied the causes for the failure of some UCBs in India in recent years in the context of reforming economic scenario. The author has observed that the adverse economic conditions like drought or a general eonomic slow down are responsible for the failure of UCBs.

OBJECTIVES OF THE STUDY

The present study has both general objective and specific objectives:

General Objective

To analyse the role and contributions of UCBs to the sustainable development of the Indian economy

Specific objectives

1. To trace out the progress and performance of UCBs in India.
2. To analyse the impact of urban co-operative bank credit on income and employment generation of the borrowers engaged in different activeties with special reference to the SUCB.

The Specific objectives are linked and integrated to study the general objective

HYPOTHESIS

Based on the review of literature and the objectives of the present study, the following hypothesis is formulated.

1. The intensive urban co-operative bank credit has substantially raised the net income and employment of the borrowers engaged in different activities.

DATA SOURCE AND METHODOLOGY OF THE STUDY

The present study is based on both secondary and primary data. The primary data was collected form the selected 237 borrower respondents by conducting field survey by designing interview schedule to borrower respondents. The before and after approach was used to analyse the impact of urban co-operative bank credit on income and employment generation of the borrowers engaged in different activities.

STATISTICAL TOOLS AND TECHNIQUES USED

In the present analysis, the simple averages, percentages, proportions were widely used. Weighted average was used to remove extremes in values by giving weight age to sample size. Paired 't' test was used for testing the hypothesis.

SAMPLING DESIGN

The present research study is based on a case study and the sample survey method.

The study is undertaken in the North Kanara District of Karnataka state, which is one of the pioneering Districts in the field of co-operation and the co-operative movement is very active here. The Sirsi urban co-operative Bank has been selected purposefully for the present study which is one of the leading UCBs of the District. Three Branches of the Bank have been selected to represent one Branch each form coastal, Malnadu and Plain regions of the District by way of random sapling method. They are Honavar Branch from Coastal region, Sirsi-main Branch from Malnadu region and Mundgod branch from Plain region. Coastal region is more developed, malnadu region is medium developed and the plain region is less developed.

Three sample activities have been selected in order to study the impact of urban co-operative bank credit on income and employment generation by way of purposive sampling method. These are activities for which maximum loans and advances are made by the bank and in which there are highest number of borrowers. They include small-scale industries, retail trade and professional and self-employment.

237 borrower respondents were picked up for interview out of 795 borrowers by way of probability random sampling method. These are the borrowers who borrowed loans in the months of April, May and June 2003 under directed credit programme of the RBI for the priority sector. i.e. 30 per cent of the total borrowers in each of the sample activities from each of the sample branches have been selected for interview.

PERIOD OF THE STUDY

The present research study has been restricted to a period of 8 years starting from 1st July 1997 to 30th June 2005. The period of 8 years covers the 1st generation banking sector reform period from 1997 to 1999 and the second generation banking sector reform period from 1999 to 2005. A comparative analysis could be made between the 1st generation and the 2nd generation reform periods.

REFERENCE PERIODS

In order to collect the primary data two reference periods were taken. One is the period before borrowing and another is the period after borrowing. The year 2002-03 is the period before borrowing and the years 2003-04 and 2004-05 refers to the period after borrowing. The sample borrowers who availed bank loan in the months of April, May and June 2003 were interviewed in the months of April, May and June 2005 respectively. Therefore the interview of borrowers was conducted after two full years from the data of availment of bank loan.

INCOME GENERATION

This is the incremental net income of the borrowers form the load activity during the period after borrowing over the period before borrowing.

EMPLOYMENT GENERATION

This is the increase estimated in gross mandays of work of the borrowers from the loan activity during the period after borrowing over the period before borrowing.

USEFULNESS OF THE STUDY

The present research study would add some new dimensions to the existing literature on the subject of urban co-operation and sustainable development. India being a vast country with different natural, social, cultural temporal and economic characteristics, more and more area specific, local oriented, in-depth and grass root level studies are essential for formulating proper policies, plans and programmes. The study is an attempt in this direction. The study would be useful to the young scientists and the students who have just entered the portals of the significant discipline of the co-operative banking.

SECTION - II

URBAN CO-OPERATIVE BANKING DEVELOPMENT IN INDIA

In non agricultural credit sector of the co-operative movement, the urban co-operative credit in India have come to occupy a significant place not only in the banking sector, but also in the co-operative movement of India.

They have created a niche for themselves in our economy as an instrument of attaining the socio-economic objectives.

One of the most important achievements of UCBs has been the spread of banking knowledge among the unpreviledged classes such as small depositors, small borrowers, women and self-employeds. UCBs are working for national goals and priorities with their unique characteristics.

At present, the UCBs have grown not only in numbers, but also in size and complexity of their operations and are rendering all types of services that are being rendered by commercial banks. A few banks also enjoy the status of scheduled bank and few also deal in foreign exchange. Today, the total business of UCBs is equal to eight per cent of the total business of commercial banks in India. The extablishment of Mahila UCBs and SC/ST UCBs are the bold steps taken in this sector in recent years.

PROGRESS OF UCBS IN INDIA DURING THE STUDY PERIOD

The Progress of UCBs in India during the study period is shown in the table 1. Table 1 reveals that there was a sizeable growth both in numbers of UCBs and their overall performance during the study period from 1997-98 to 2004-2005.

The number of UCBs had grown from 1502 in 1997-98 to 1872 in 2004-05 with 24.63 per cent growth. The amount of owned funds had grown from Rs. 5985 crores in 1997-98 to Rs. 12348 crores in 2003-2004 with 106 per cent growth.

Table 1
Progress of UCBs During the Study Period i.e., from 1997-98 to 2004-05 with some key Financial Indicators

(Amount in Rs. Crores, Ratio in per cent)

Item	*Years as end March*							
	1997-98	*1998-99*	*1999-00*	*2000-01*	*2001-02*	*2002-03*	*2003-04*	*2004-05P*
1. Number	1502	1590	1784	1826	1854	1941	1926	1872
2. Owned funds	5985	7322	9314	10826	13797	9830	12348	NA
3. Deposits	40692	52681	71189	80840	93069	101546	110256	105017
4. Borrowings	886	1041	1475	2069	NA	1590	1484	NA
5. Working capital	'52229	67074	90302	103042	115596	111746	NA	NA
6. Loans outstanding	27807	314214	45995	54389	62060	64880	67930	66905
7. Credit Deposit ratio	68.3	64.9	64.6	67	67	64	62	65.3

P: Provisional NA: Not Available

Source: Report on Trend and Progress of Banking in India, Supplement to RBI Bulletin for the related years.

The deposits of UCBs have increased continuously during this period. It was Rs. 40692 crores in 1997-98 and it has increased to Rs. 105017 crores.in 2004-05 with 158.07 per cent.growth. The borrowings of UCBs during the period had grown slowly. This shows that UCBs in India are not depending too much upon external funds. They are almost self-reliant. The total borrowings of UCBs was Rs. 886 crores in 1997-98 and it was stood at Rs. 1484 crores in 2003-04 with 67 per cent growth.

The working capital of UCBs during the study period has increased considerably. The total working capital was Rs. 52229 crores in 1997-98. It was increased to Rs. 11746 crores in 2002-03 with 114 per cent growth.

Total loans outstanding has also increased from Rs. 27807 crores in 1997-98 to Rs. 66905 crores in 2004-05 with 140.60 per cent growth. The credit-deposit ratio, an important performance indicator was varied from a minimum of 62 per cent in 2003-04 to a maximum of 68.3 per cent in 1997-98 during the study period. The average credit-deposit ratio during the period of 8 years stood at 65 per cent, which is the ideal C-D ratio maintained by the UCBs.

Thus during the study period, the UCBs have shown an impressive progress and performance in India which is a liberalisation era, the 2nd generation banking sector reform period.

CREDIT TO PRIORITY SECTOR AND WEAKER SECTION

Performance of UCBs in the deployment of credit to priority sector is also appreciable. They have crossed the benchmark fixed by the Reserve Bank of India and contributed to economic growth with equity. Their weaker section advance is also above the target fixed by the RBI. The major segments of their lending to priority sector and weaker section includes agriculture and allied activities, cottage and small scale industries, road and water transport operators, private retail trade, retail trade, small business enterprises, professional and self employed, educational loans, housing loans and consumption loans. The table 2 gives details of the priority and weaker section advances by UCBs as on 31-3-2003.

Table 2 reveals that as at end march 2003, UCBs in India had extended Rs. 42633 crores to the priority sector constituting 62.1 per cent of total loans and advances which is above the bench mark fixed by the RBI. Similarly they have extended Rs. 10690 Crores to the weaker section constituting 15.6 per cent of the total loans and advances, which is also above the target prescribed by the RBI.

The segment wise break up shows that the highest percentage of priority sector advances was extended to cottage and small scale industries followed by housing and small business enterprises and the lowest to education purpose. The highest percentage of weaker section advances was extended to housing purposes and the lowest to consumption purposes.

FINANCIAL PERFORMANCE OF UCBS IN INDIA (REGION-WISE)

The region-wise financial performance of UCBs in India as on 31-3-2004 reveals that the UCBs at Mumbai are comparatively performing well. The total share capital, pre reserves, deposits, loans and advances, and investments of UCBs at Mumbai constitutes the highest amount. It is followed by UCBs at Ahmedabad, Bangalore, Nagpur and Chennai. Patna region has recorded a lowest amount in case of all financial indicators. The C.D ratio is the highest in Chennai region (67.7 per cent) and it is the lowest in New Delhi (36.3 per cent). The region-wise financial performance of UCBs in India is shown in the table 3.

Table 2
Priority Sector and Weaker Section Advances by the UCBs: (Segment-wise) as on 31-3-2003 in India

(Amount in Rs. Crores)

Segments	*Priority sector advances*	*Weaker section advances*
1. Agriculture and allied activities	2143 (5)	668 (6.3)
2. Cottage and small scale industries	9252 (21.7)	1373 (12.8)
3. Road and water transport operators	2876 (6.8)	614 (5.7)
4. Private retail trade	3444 (8.1)	866 (8.1)
5. Retail trade	3702 (8.7)	1108 (10.4)
6. Small business enterprises	6043 (14.2)	1441 (13.5)
7. Professional and self employed	5134 (12)	1605 (15)
8. Educational loans	1228 (2.9)	403 (3.8)
9. Housing loans	6835 (16)	2287 (21.4)
10. Consumption loans	1975 (4.6)	326 (3.1)
Total	42633 (100)	10690 (100)
Percentage to total advances	62.1	15.6

Note: Figures in brackets indicates percentages to respective advances.
Source: Report on Trend and Progress of Banking in India (2003-04). Supplement to the RBI Bulletin December 2004. P.103.

Table 3
Financial indicators of UCBs in India: Region-wise as on 31-3-2004

(Amount in Rs. Crore)

Region	*Share Capital*	*Pre Reserves*	*Deposits*	*Advances*	*Investments*	*C.D. Ratio*
Ahmadabad	440	1584	16279	9703	8305	59.6
Bangalore	355	1018	8353	5372	3277	64.3
Bhopal	47	77	1159	613	532	52.9
Bhubaneswar	22	38	606	345	313	56.8
Chandigarh	24	40	568	325	246	57.2
Chennai	146	162	3132	2121	1342	67.7
Guwahati	8	8	276	135	121	48.8
Hyderabad	111	145	2113	1379	924	65.2
Jaipur	59	84	1052	612	442	58.1
Jammu	4	4	184	112	52	60.5
Kolkata	96	107	1750	929	969	53.1
Lucknow	138	262	2310	1442	781	62.4
Mumbai	1468	4957	60725	37424	25842	61.6
Nagpur	239	399	8628	5628	3615	65.2
New Delhi	36	83	850	308	415	36.3
Patna	3	7	30	17	15	56.4
Tiruvananthapuram	71	105	2240	1467	1029	65.5
Total	3267	9082	110256	67930	48220	61.6

Source: Report on Trend and Progress of Banking in India (2003-2004). Supplement to RBI Bulletin December 2004, p. 108.

Table 3 reveals that as on 31-3-2004 the total share capital of UCBs stood at Rs. 3267 crores and the pre reserves at Rs. 9082 crores. The total deposits and advances stood at Rs. 1,10,256 crores and Rs. 67,930 crores respectively. The total investments in government shares and securities stood at Rs. 48,220 crores. The C.D ratio of UCBs at all India level as on 31-3-2004 was 61.6 per cent.

SECTION - III

IMPACT ANALYSIS

In this section and attempt has been made to analyse the impact of urban co-operative bank credit on income and employment generation of the borrowers engaged in different activities with special reference to the SUCB on the basis of the primary data collected from the selected 237 borrower respondents.

DETAILS OF CREDIT BORROWED BY THE BORROWER RESPONDENTS

The borrowers respondents engaged in three different sample activities in the area of operation of the three sample branches of the SUCB have availed bank credit to start or run their activities. Table 4 represents the details of borrowing of the borrower respondents.

Table 4
Branch-wise and Activity-wise Average Amount of Credit Borrowed by the Borrower Respondents

Name of the Bank Branch	*Honavar*		*Sirsi-Main*		*Mundgod*		*Total*	
Details of borrowing name of the activity	*No. of borrower respon-dents*	*Average amount of credit borrowed*	*No. of borrower respon-dents*	*Average amount of credit Borrowed*	*No. of borrower respon-dents*	*Average amount of credit borrowed*	*No. of borrower respon-dents*	*Average amount of credit borrowed*
SSI	8	36750.00	15	33033.33	7	172857.14	30	66649.99
RT	32	30662.50	55	19400.00	60	26528.33	147	24761.00
P&S	19	30657.89	24	25354.17	17	34352.94	60	29583.33
Total	59	31864.44	94	23995.75	84	40305.95	237	31831.22

Source: Primary data based on the field survey.

It can be observed from the table 4 that on an average the amount of credit borrowed by the borrower respondents was Rs. 31831.22. The inter branch comparison shows that the average amount of credit borrowed is the highest in case of Mundgod Branch which stood at Rs. 40305.95 and it is the lowest in case of Sirsi-main Branch which was Rs. 23095.75.

The activity wise borrowing reveals that the borrower respondents engaged in small-scale industries have borrowed the highest amount of bank credit, which was Rs. 66649.99. But the borrower respondents engaged in retail trade have borrowed in the lowest amount of bank credit, which was at Rs. 24761.22.

The amount of credit disbursed in the area of operation of Mundgod Branch is the highest and it is the desirable also from the point of view of regional balance as the Branch lies in the backward region of Uttar Kannada District. It is also quite natural that the amount of credit disbursed by the Branches of the Bank to the industrial sector is comparatively higher than that of the service sector.

INCOME GENERATION

Now let us examine the impact of bank credit on income generation of the borrower respondents i.e. the end use of bank credit. Table 5 presents the Branch-Wise income generation.

Table 5
Branch-wise Income Generation per Borrower per Year
(Amount in Rs.)

Name of the Bank BranchSectioniculars	*Honavar*	*Sirsi-Main*	*Mundgod*	*Total*
Gross income before borrowing	27965.72	22744.68	26369.05	25317.80
Gross income after borrowing	51887.93	39771.28	45113.10	44650.42
Gross Expenditure Before Borrowing	18879.31	16212.77	19047.62	17877.12
Gross Expenditure After Borrowing	33413.79	28545.21	32041.67	30986.23
Net Income Before Borrowing	9086.41	6531.91	7321.43	7440.68
Net Income After Borrowing	18474.14	11226.07	13071.43	13664.19
Incremental Net Income	9398.73	4694.16	5750.00	6223.51
Percentage Increase in Net Income	103.32	71.87	78.54	83.64

Source: Primary data based on the field survey.

It can be observed from the table 5 that on an average the net income of the borrower respondents has increased by 83.64 per cent after borrowing. The pei centage increase in net income in case of Honavar Branch is 103.32 and it is 71.87 per cent and 78.54 per cent in case of Sirsi-Main Branch and Mundgod Branch respectively. The percentage increase in net income of the borrower respondents is the highest in case of Honavar Branch and it is the lowest in case of Sirsi-Main Branch.

The borrower respondents in the area of operation of the Honavar Brach are getting more infrastructure facilities and that is why they have realised more incremental net income after borrowing. Small investment here brings more income as the area of operation of the Honavar Branch is in the more developed region of the Uttar Kannada District.

In case of the area of operation of the Sirsi-Main Branch all the business activities depends upon the prices of Areca nut. Because of the downtrend in the prices of Areca nut, the borrower respondents could not generate much additional income after borrowing. The area of operation of the Sirsi-Main Branch lies in the medium developed region of Uttar Kannada District.

It is interesting to note that even though the area of operation of the Mundgod Branch is in the less developed region of the U.K. District, the borrower respondents were able to generate more income as compared to that of the Sirsi-Main branch and it is desirable also from the point of view of regional balanced development. This is because of the hard efforts made by the respondents in their loan activities. This proves that bank credit would be effective even in less developed or backward regions.

Diagram 1
Branch-wise Incremental Net Income of the Borrowers (in Percentage)

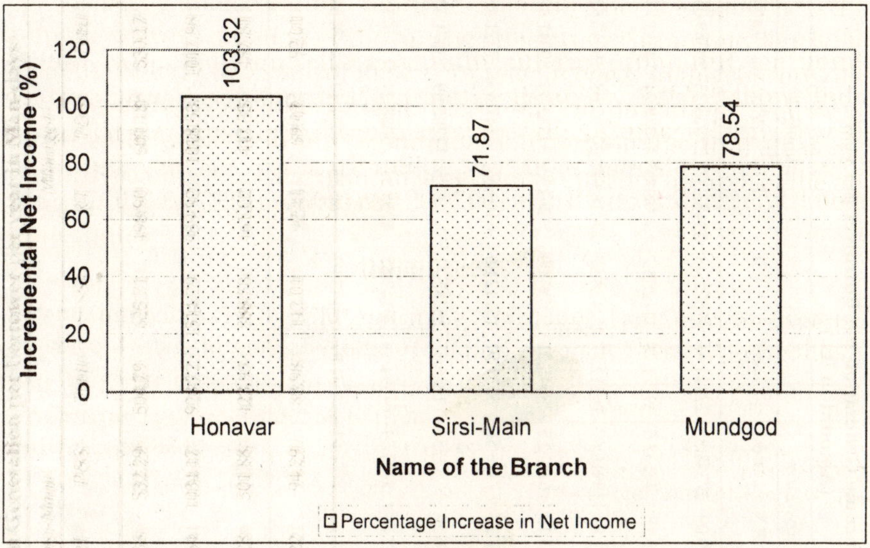

ACTIVITY-WISE INCOME GENERATION

After having discussed the Branch-wise income generation, now let us examine the activity wise income generation of the borrower respondents. The type of activity of the borrowers itself determines the extent of income generation. Table 6 presents the activity wise income generation.

It can be observed from the table 6 that the net income of the borrower respondents engaged in small-scale industries has increased by 92.15 per cent after borrowing. The net income has increased by 72.30 per cent in case of retail trade and by 99.05 per cent in case of professional and self-employment. Therefore, the income generation is the highest in case of professional and self-employment activities and it is the lowest in case of retail trade.

The Branch-wise analysis reveals that in case of Honavar Branch the borrower respondents engaged in professional and self-employment have generated the highest income (144.69 per cent) and it is the lowest in case of small-scale industries (79.39 per cent).

Table 6
Activity-wise Income Generation per Borrower per year
(Amount in Rs.)

Name of the Bank Branch	*Honavar*				*Sirsi-Main*				*Mundgod*				*Total*			*Grand Total*
Activities Sectioniculars	*SSI*	*RT*	*P&S*	*Total*	*SSI*	*RT*	*P&S*	*Total*	*SSI*	*RT*	*P&S*	*Total*	*SSI*	*RT*	*P&S*	
Gross income before borrowing	45625	2445.61	26263.16	27965.52	32400	18109.09	27333.33	22744.68	47571.43	23483.33	27823.33	26369.05	39466.66	21683.34	27133.33	25317.8
Gross incomeafter borrowing	79062.5	43225.81	54578.95	51887.93	57933.33	31418.18	47562.5	39771.28	111285.7	36975	46588.24	45113.1	52683.33	36256.63	49508.33	44650.42
Gross Expenditure Before Borrowing	31375	16903.23	16842.11	18879.31	22866.67	12781.82	19916.67	16212.77	32428.57	17016.67	20705.88	19047.62	27366.66	15407.5	19166.66	17877.12
Gross Expenditure After Borrowing	53500	29387.1	31526.32	33413.79	41533.33	22268.18	64812.5	28545.21	76000	26250	34382.35	32041.67	52766.66	25443.1	33650	30986.23
Net Income Before Borrowing	14250	7548.38	9421.05	9086.21	9533.33	5327.27	7416.66	6531.91	15142.86	6466.66	7117.65	7321.43	12099.99	6275.83	7966.66	7440.68
Net IncomeAfter Borrowing	25562.5	13838.71	23052.63	18474.14	16400	9150	12750	11226.07	35285.71	10725	12205.89	13071.43	23249.99	10813.52	15858.33	13664.19
Incremental Net Income	11312.5	6290.33	13631.58	9387.93	6866.67	3822.73	5333.34	4694.16	20142.85	4258.34	5088.24	5750	11150	4537.69	7891.67	6223.51
Percentage Increasein Net Income	79.39	83.33	144.69	103.32	72.03	71.76	71.91	71.87	133.02	65.85	71.49	78.54	92.15	72.3	99.05	83.64

Source: Primary data based on the field survey.

In case of Sirsi-Main Branch, the SSI have generated the highest income (72.03 per cent) and it is followed by professional and self-employment (71.91 per cent) and retail trade (71.76 per cent).

In case of Mundgod Branch also the SSI have generated the highest income (133.02 per cent) and it is followed by professional and self-employment (71.49 per cent) and retail trade (65.85 per cent).

If all the three Branches and activities are considered together, the percentage increase in net income is the highest in case of professional and self employment in Honavar Branch and it is the lowest in case of retail trade in Mundgod Branch. So, the activity professional and self-employment has proved better to generate income.

Digaram 2
Activity-wise Incremental Net Income of the Borrowers (in Percentage)

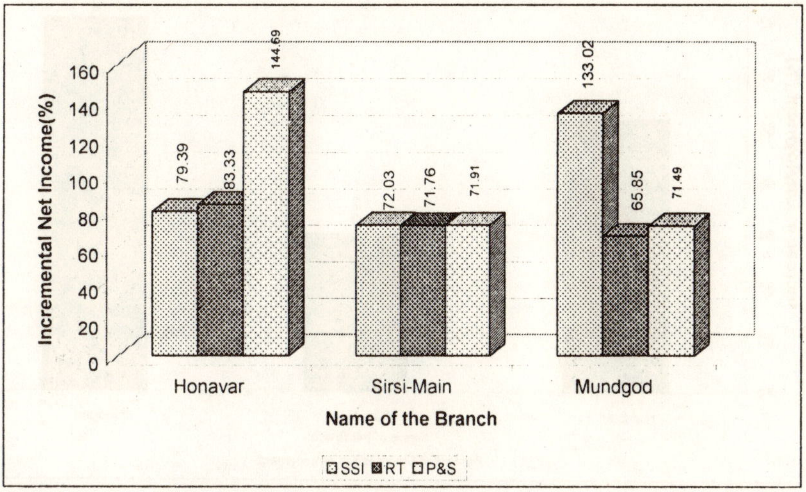

EMPLOYMENT GENERATION

After having discussed the impact of bank credit on income generation, let us examine the impact of bank credit on employment generation of the borrowers engaged in different activities. First let us study the Branch-wise employment generation. Table 7 indicates the Branch-wise employment generation.

It can be observed from the table 7 that on an average the employment of the borrower respondents has increased by 87.99 per cent after borrowing.

The Branch-wise analysis reveals that in case of Honavar Branch the employment has increased by 88.30 per cent. In case of Sirsi-Main Branch the employment has increased by 83.98 per cent and in case of Mundgod Branch, the employment has increased by 92.01 per cent. Therefore, the employment generation is the highest in case of Mundgod Branch and it is the lowest in case of Sirsi-Main Branch.

Table 7
Branch-wise Employment Generation per Borrower per year in Man-days

*Name of the Bank BranchSectionicular*s	*Honavar*	*Sirsi-Main*	*Mundgod*	*Total*
Employment Before Borrowing	564.92	504.79	530.17	528.75
Employment After Borrowing	1063.77	928.72	1017.98	993398
Increase in Employment	498.85	423.93	787.81	465.23
Percentage Increase in Employment	88.3	83.98	92.01	87.99

Source: Primary data based on the field survey.

Diagram 3
Branch-wise Increase in Employment of the Borrowers (in Percentage)

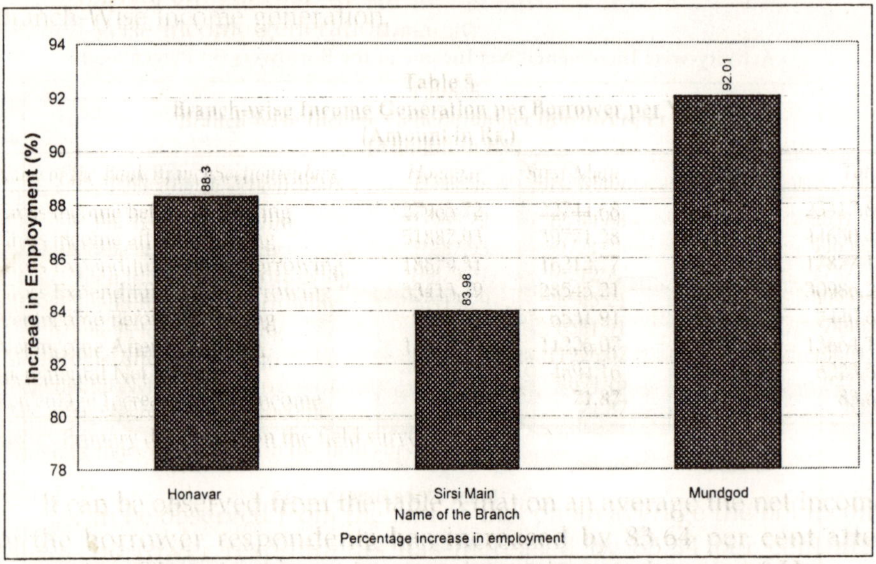

It is interesting to note that even though the area of operation of the Mundgod Branch is in the less developed region of UK District, the borrower respondents could generate sufficient employment out of their loan activities and it is desirable also to restore regional balanced growth. This once again proves that the bank credit is effective even in less developed or backward regions as there is great employment potential.

ACTIVITY-WISE EMPLOYMENT GENERATION

Now let us examine the activity-wise employment generation of the borrower respondents. The type of activity itself can influence the employment generation. Therefore it is interesting to study the employment generation in various economic activities. Table 8 presents the activity-wise employment generation.

It can be observed from Table 8 that in case of small-scale industries, the employment has increased by 91.89 per cent. In case of retail trade,

Table 8

Activity-wise Employment Generation per borrower per year in Man-days

Name of the Bank Branch	Honavar				Sirsi-Main				Mundgod				Total			Grand Total
Activities Sectioniculars	SSI	RT	P&S	Total	SSI	RT	P&S	Total	SSI	RT	P&S	Total	SSI	RT	P&S	
Employment Before Borrowing	775.63	509.38	569.74	564.92	730.00	431.36	532.29	504.79	625.71	498.90	601.18	530.17	717.83	475.91	563.66	528.75
Employment After Borrowing	1493.75	922.34	1120.92	1063.77	1251.67	794.64	1034.17	928.72	1514.29	959.92	1018.53	1017.98	1377.50	889.89	1057.20	993.98
Increase in Employment	718.12	412.96	551.18	498.85	521.67	363.28	501.88	423.93	888.58	461.02	417.35	487.81	659.67	413.98	493.54	465.23
Percentage Increase in Employment	92.59	81.07	96.74	88.30	88.30	84.22	94.29	83.98	142.01	92.41	69.42	92.01	91.89	86.98	87.56	87.89

Source: Primary data based on the field survey.

Diagarm 4
Activity-wise Increase in Employment of the Borrowers (in Percentage)

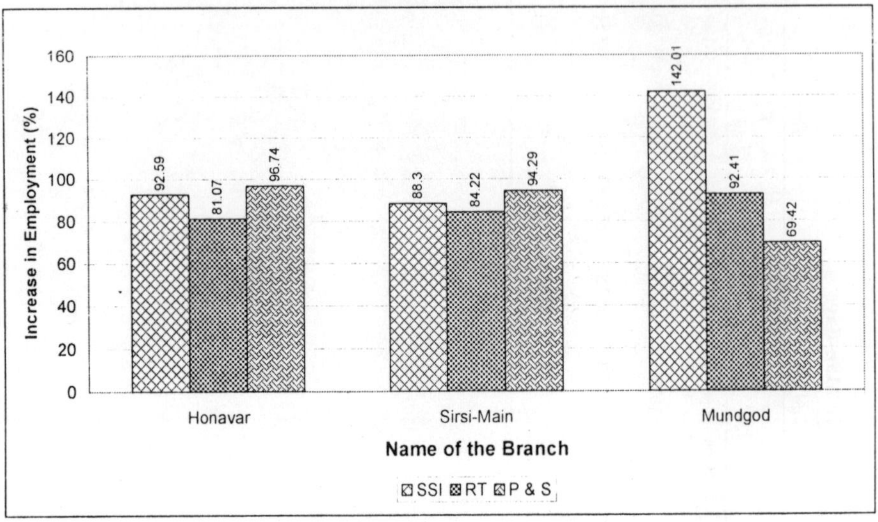

the employment has increased by 86.98 per cent and in case of professional and self-employment, it has increased by 87.56 per cent after borrowing. The employment generation is the highest in case of small-scale industries and it is the lowest in case of retail trade. Small-scale industries are labour intensive and they are employment oriented. So it is quite natural that the employment generation is the highest in case of small-scale industries.

The Branch-wise analysis reveals that in case of Honavar Branch the employment generation is the highest in case of professional and self-employment. (96.74 per cent) and it is the lowest in case of retail trade (81.07 per cent).

In case of Sirsi-Main Branch, the employment generation is the highest in case of professional and self-employment (94.29 per cent) and it is the lowest in case of small-scale industries (71.46 per cent).

In case of Mudgod Branch, the employment is the highest in case of small-scale industries (142.01 per cent) and it is the lowest in case of professional and self-employment (69.42 per cent).

If all the Branches and activities are considered together, the employment generation is the highest in case of small-scale industries in Mundgod Branch and it is the lowest in case of professional and self-employment in Mundgod Branch, itself.

EXPENDITURE ON EDUCATION AND HEALTH BY THE BORROWER RESPONDENTS BEFORE AND AFTER BORROWING

Expenditure on education and health empowers human capital and leads to socio-economic development. According to Panchamukhi PR (1967) the expenditure on health and education either public or private leads to not only the overall development of individuals and their families but also contributes a lot to national economic development. Therefore, an interesting study has been conducted to know the position of expenditure on education and health by the borrower respondents before and after borrowing. A good number of borrowers were able to spend more on education and health care facilities after borrowing. It is because of incremental net income of the borrower respondents from the loan activities. Thus, by generating sufficient income, with the increased expenditure on education and health the Bank has contributed to socio-economic development.

Table 9 presents the details of this

Table 9
Expenditure on Education and Health by the Borrower Respondents Before and After Borrowing (Amount in Rs.)

Sectioniculars	*Average Expenditure on health and education by the borrowers in the Branches of the Bank*			*Total*
	Honavar	*Sirsi-Main*	*Mundgod*	
Expenditure on Education and Health Before Borrowing	6428.84	5375.46	4386.21	5287.07
Expenditure on Education and Health After Borrowing	9746.38	8236.79	7827.63	8467.57
Incremental Expenditure on Education and Health After Borrowing	3317.54	2861.33	3441.42	3180.5
Percentage Increment in the Expenditure on Education and Health	51.6	53.22	78.45	60.15

Source: Primary data based on the field survey.

It can be observed from the table 9 that on an average the expenditure on education and health of the borrower respondents has increased by 60.15 per cent after borrowing.

The Branch-wise analysis reveals that the percentage increment in the expenditure on education and health is the highest in case of Mundgod Branch, which stood at 78.45 per cent because initially the borrower respondents were spending lesser amount on education and health before borrowing.

The percentage increment in the expenditure on education and health is the lowest in case of Honavar Branch, which stood at 51.60 per cent because already they have been spending more on education and health before borrowing.

The percentage increment in the expenditure on education and health of the borrower respondents in case of Sirsi-Main Branch stood at 53.22 per cent after borrowing.

Testing of Hypothesis

For testing of hypothesis, the statistical paired 't' test was used

The Null Hypothesis: The urban co-operative bank credit has not increased the net income and employment of the borrowers engaged in different activities.

The Alternative Hypothesis: The urban co-operative bank credit has substantially increased the net income and employment of the borrowers engaged in different activities.

The paired 't' test values in case of the variables net income and employment in the present study in case of all the activities are greater than the tabulated values. Therofre, the Null Hypothesis has been rejected and the Alternative Hypothesis has been accepted. Therefore the Hypothesis of the present study i.e., *"The urban co-operative bank credit has substantially raised the net income and employment of the borrowers engaged in different activities"* has been proved and accepted.

FINDINGS AND SUGGESTIONS

Findings

1. The contributions of UCBs to the sustainable development is appreciable
2. The number of UCBs had grown from 1502 in 1997-98 to 1926 in 2003-2004 i.,e it had grown by 28 per cent during the study period
3. The priority sector and weaker section advances by the UCBs in India as on 31-3-2003 stood at 62.1 per cent and 15.6 per cent respectively which are above the benchmark fixed by the RBI
4. The average C.D ratio maintained by the UCBs in India during the study period stood at 65 per cent which is considered as the ideal C D Ratio.
5. On an average, the net income of the borrower respondents has increased by 83.64 per cent after borrowing.
6. On an average the employment of the borrower respondents has increased by 87.99 per cent after borrowing.
7. The paired 't' test values in case of the variables net income and employment are greater than the tabulated values in case of all the activities selected for the study. Therefore, the null hypothesis Ho has been rejected and the Alternative hypothesis H_1 has been accepted. So, the hypothesis of the present study i.e., "the urban co-operative bank credit has substantially raised the net income and employment of the borrowers engaged in different activities has been proved and accepted.

Suggestions

The Urban Co-operative banks have occupied a unique place in the co-operative credit structure in India and are expected to assume the leadership in undertaking promotional and developmental programmes for the growth and success of the co-operative movement in urban and semi-urban regions of India.

Urban development is one of the most complicated challenges of the 21st century. The life style of urban people is fast changing. With the growing urbanisation, the consequent problems of urban poor and middle class people engaged in different occupations and their sufferings merit immediate attention and action.

The main objective of UCBs is to provide credit and other facilities to the urban poor and middle class people engaged in small-scale industries, trade and commerce professional and self-employment etc. who have been neglected by the commercial banks and other financial institutions. With their unique characteristics, the UCBs can bridge the gap of commercial banks and they can play a special role in the development of urban and semi-urban regions.

1. Distribution of UCBs: Urban Co-operative banks are unevenly distributed in the country. They are highly concentrated in 5 states of our county viz., Maharashtra, Gujarat, Karnataka, Andhra Pradesh and Tamil Nadu. These 5 states account for 80 per cent of the total urban co-operative banks of the country. So, proper steps are to be taken by the central and states Govt. to increase the number of UCBs in other states of the country so that regional balance in the growth of UCBs could be restored.

2. In the context of liberalisation, privatisation and globalisation framework, sea changes are occurring in the domestic and the world financial markets. International prudential norms have been extended to UCBs also. Therefore, the UCBs should be in a position to provide world class banking services by upgrading and updating their banking technology.

3. UCBs should adopt new techniques of marketing such as identification of customer's need, formulation of marketing policy for the specific area, planning and organising according to policy, advertising and publicity, cost estimation and evaluation etc.

4. Some of the norms of the RBI like, NPAs, capital adequacy, benchmark for priority sector lending and weaker section advances etc. cannot be applied universally to all the UCBs. Every norm should be regional specific and local oriented. It should depend upon the size of population, socio-economic status of the region, size and operation of banks etc.

5. It is the high time that all the UCBs in the country should make a SWOT analysis. UCBs have to strengthen their strengths and weaken their weaknesses. They have to make use of the new avenues and

opportunities properly which are thrown upon them which are very challenging. At the same time they must be cautious about the threats.

6. Social Banking and Development Banking should go hand in hand from the point of view of social justice and economic development.
7. Level playing field should be provided to the UCBs for the development of this sector.

REFERENCES

Dabir Yeshwant V. (2000), "Some Vaxation Issues Concerning urban co-operative Banks, House Magazine the Karnataka State Urban Co-operative Bank's Federation Ltd, Bangalore, Vol. No. XXV-XXVI, Issue No. 4. July-October.

Joshi P.N. (1999), "Banking Sector Reforms" Economic and Political Weekly, Vol. No. 34, Issue No. 14, April 3.

Kazim Shamim (1996), "Challenges of Urban Co-operative Banks in Emerging Financial Environment" House Magazine Karnataka State Urban Co-operative Bank's Federation Ltd. Bangalore, Vol. XIX, Issue No. 2, January.

Kundan H.N. (1999), "Urban Co-operative Banks and Customer Services in New Economic Policy", Maharashtra Co-operatives, January-March.

Panchamukhi, P.R. (1967), "Measurement of the Effects of the Public Expenditures", Ph.D Thesis of University of Bombay.

Patil M.B. (2000), "Urban Co-operative Banks and their Economic Environment", House Magazine, Karnataka state Urban Co-operative Bank's Federation Ltd., Bangalore. Vol. No. XXV-XXVI, Issue No. 4, July-October.

Ram Kumar (2003), "Urban Co-operative Banks", Banking Finance, Vol. No. 16, Issue No. 2, February.

Schumpeter J.A. (1912), 'The Theory of Economic Development'; An Inquiry into Profits, Capital, Credit, Interest and the Business cycle', Translated by Redvers Opie, Harvard University Press, Cambridge (Mass) 1934.

Singh Autar (1977), 'Role of Banks in National Economic Development', The Banker, Vol. No. 24 Issues No. 3, May.

Warekar N.R. (1996), "Privatization of Urban Co-operative Banks" Sahakari Vishwa, Co-operative Week, November.

Chapter - 14

Common Property Resources & Rural Livelihoods: A Study of Selected Villages in Dharwad District

A.R. Kulkarni

INTRODUCTION

Natural resources comprising land, water and forests constitute the basic support system of life on earth. Quite a significant proportion of these resources is used by people in the form of Common Property Resources (CPRs). *In the Indian context CPRs refer to all such resources which are accessible to the whole community and to which no individual has exclusive property rights.* According to NSSO (2000) CPRs include village pastures and grazing grounds, village forests and woodlots, protected and unclassed government forests, waste lands, common threshing grounds, watershed drainage, ponds and tanks, rivers, rivulets, water reservoirs, canals and irrigation channels. Traditionally, CPRs are managed by local communities in a sustainable form through their own indigenous methods based on a variety of cultural, social and religious mechanisms (Noronha, 1997; McKean, 1992; Somanathan, 1991). Ironically, notwithstanding the community interests and environmental concerns of CPRs, they are rapidly being depleted in terms of both area and physical quality (Kadekodi, 2001; Damodaran, 1991; Pasha, 1992; Shiva, 1986; Jodha, 1985; Guha, 1983). The depletion of CPRs has been threatening the sustenance of the rural poor (Chopra & Gulati, 2001; Shiva, 1991; Beck & Ghosh, 2000). Unfortunately, the problems faced by CPRs have not received adequate attention in the past from any section of society and state. In the recent past, sustainability of CPRs has been assigned due importance by the researchers as well as policy makers due to increased awareness about the environment. Against this backdrop, the paper makes an attempt to analyze the overall importance of CPRs to different marginalized groups. To be more specific, the study intends to answer to the following questions: a) how important are CPRs to rural HHs in providing biomass resources (fuelwood, fodder, etc), income and employment opportunities, especially to weaker sections of the society in developed and less-developed villages and 2) does CPR income help to reduce income inequalities created by private property resources (PPRs)? The analysis is purely based on primary data collected from eleven villages of Dharwad district in Karnataka. The paper is organized as follows: Section 1 presents a discussion on the methodology employed in the study. The findings of the study are discussed in section 2. The last section concludes.

METHODOLOGY OF THE STUDY

Karnataka is one of the largest states in the country, occupying an area of 1.91 lakh sq.km. There are three climatic regions in Karnataka: (1) region with arid climate, (2) region with semi arid climate and (3) region with per-humid climate. Most part of the state falls in the arid and semi arid regions. It is found that poverty is more concentrated in arid climatic area and hence the role of CPRs is crucial in sustaining the livelihoods. The districts come under this climatic area are Belgaum, Bellary, Bijapur, Dharwad, Gulbarga and Raichur, which also happen to be the districts of north Karnataka (ACRPU: 1991). Among the districts, Dharwad district is selected for the study due to logistical convenience. Dharwad district is situated in the western part of northern Karnataka. The district comprises of five taluks (i.e. Dharwad, Hubli, Kalaghatagi, Kundagol, and Navalgund) with a total geographical area of 4092 Sq. km. The district has partly *Malnad* and *Dry tract* (*Maidan*), the rest being in the transitional belt. Dharwad is generally considered as Dry district. While the annual rain fall in *Malnad* tract varies between 838 and 939 mm, the transitional belt receives rain fall lesser than 777 mm per annum, the lowest being 612 mm in Navalgund. *Malenadu* is marked by chain of low hills and valleys, comparatively heavy rainfall, paddy crop, forests and streams. The greater part of this region remains sparely populated. The villages of this tract are often of a dispersed pattern. The *Maidan* is marked by extensively cultivated area. Cotton, Jowar, and wheat are the main crops. It supports a good number of populations residing in large and compact villages. Dharwad taluk has both *Malnad* and *Dry tract.* Thus it can become a representative sample of Dharwad district. Therefore, we have selected Dharwad taluk for the study.

In Dharwad taluk there are 108 villages but we have relevant data only for 100 villages. Though there are many development indicators, and our study takes only few because of their non-availability of data for the study period. In order to classify the villages based on level of development, a composite index[1] has been developed using the indicators, female literacy, total literacy, cropping intensity and percentage of main workers to total population. Based on this index, the villages are classified into developed and less developed. Out of 100 villages selected for the study 44 are classified as developed villages and 56 as less developed. 10 per cent of villages are randomly selected from each group for the study. From each selected village, 15 per cent of households are chosen for availing detailed data.

The study is based on both primary and secondary data. The primary data is collected through the household schedule and village schedule. Apart from this, PRA technique has been employed to get in-depth information. Participatory tools such as participatory mapping, focus group discussion, and seasonal diagramming techniques are used. The secondary data, related to land use, cropping pattern, population, etc, are collected from Village Panchayat Office, Taluk Panchayat Office, Tahsildar Office, Land Record Office and Forest Department Office. Table 1 shows characteristics of selected villages.

Chikkamalligawad, Holtikoti, Kogilkere, Murkatti, Haletegur, and Honnapur are in the Malenadu region. These are marked by hills, valleys, forests and streams. Therefore these villages have large extent of CPRs. Village Murkatti is not having forestland in its geographical area but HHs have access to forest of nearby village. HHs in these villages get more number of CPR products. D.M.Narendra, Dandikoppa, Somapur, Heggeri and Singanahalli are the other selected villlages located in the *Bayaluseeme* area. HHs in these villages collect crop residues, which are fallen on the private lands as fuelwood and graze their livestock usually on the roadside. Most of the ponds and wells are depleted and HHs use Hand pumps and public taps for getting water in these villages.

FINDINGS OF THE STUDY

The CPRs commonly found in the selected villages are forest, grazing land, wastelands, ponds, wells and bore wells. Common property resources in land constitute almost 38 per cent of the total geographical area of these villages. Available evidence shows that the area under CPRs in the selected villages has been declined by 5.4 per cent during the period 1990-2000. Figure on the page 6 shows resource map drawn by villagers of Holtikoti. The resource map shows that the forest area has been encroached by the villagers mainly for the purpose of cultivation. Besides, the growth of *Parthenium* in the forest has also caused deprivation of growth of other plants in the forest. To protect forest from animals (pouching) and from farmers (enchroachment), forest department planted eucalyptus trees in the forest area. This has resulted in the decline in the availability of CPR products, such as fruits and nuts.

Table 1
Characteristics of Selected Villages

Name of the Village	Total No of HHs	No. of Selected HHs		Literacy Rate (%)	Cropping Intensity%	Availability of CPRs in the Village			
		Total	SC & ST			Forest	GL	Wells	Ponds
1. Chikamalligawad (LD)	274	41	15	29.9	100.0	134.8	23.5	1	2
2. Holtikoti (LD)	167	26	4	41.1	100.0	2225.8	–	1	1
3. Kogilkere (LD)	197	30	1	35.1	100.0	36.4	–	1	1
4. Murkatti (LD)	142	21	6	30.7	100.0	–	–	–	1
5. Shinganahalli (LD)	381	57	9	15.4	125.4	–	–	1	2
6. Heggeri (LD)	51	8	3	27.3	129.4	–	–	–	–
7. Haletegur (D)	176	26	17	29.2	108.7	4.1	14.6	1	1
8. Honnapur (D)	367	55	12	28.3	100.0	121.4	–	1	1
9. Somapur (D)	188	28	7	50.7	162.0	–	–	4	–
10. Dandikoppa (D)	104	16	3	41.9	191.6	–	–	1	1
11. D.M. Narendra (D)	273	41	6	29.0	172.9	–	–	1	–

Note: LD = Less-Developed, D = Developed.

UTILIZATION OF CPRS

The study shows that households utilized CPRs mainly for collection of fuelwood, fodder, animal grazing, and for collecting water, for household use and for irrigation. Utilisation of these resources for collecting water for household purpose is common in all the selected villages and it is also found that almost all HHs depend on CPRs for this purpose. Table 2 shows that during the year 1999-2000, 68 per cent of the HHs in the study area used CPRs for collection of products, 99 per cent used them for grazing their cattle and 10 per cent for irrigating their private lands.

Table 2
Utilization of CPR in Selected Villages

(% To Total No. of HHs)

Type of Villages	*Landless*	*Marginal*	*Small*	*Medium*	*Large*	*Total*
			Product Collection			
Less-Developed Villages	75	95	86	60	67	78
Developed Villages	61	69	55	39	39	57
Total	69	81	71	52	50	68
			Grazing			
Less-Developed Villages	100	100	100	90	100	98
Developed Villages	100	100	100	94	100	99
Total	100	100	100	92	100	99
			Irrigation			
Less-Developed Villages	0	5	0	7	27	4
Developed Villages	0	18	23	33	30	17
Total	0	12	11	17	29	10

Utilisation of CPRs varied across the villages. households in Chikkamalligawad, Holtikoti, Kogilkere, Murkatti, Haletegur, Honnapur and Murkatti have access to forest and they get more number of CPR products. In D.M.Narendra, Dandikoppa, Somapur, Heggeri and Singanahalli, households get only fuelwood and fodder from the CPRs. In these villages, the private land is being used for collection of CPR products (PPRs as CPRs) like fuelwood (crop residue), and fodder and for public grazing during the post harvest season. This benefits mainly landless, marginal and small cultivator households and is based on cost sharing arrangement of labour. Cotton, Maize, and Jawar are the main crops and after harvesting of these crops stalk of these plants are left in the field. Removing of these stalks require more labours. At the same time, landless, marginal and small cultivator households are in need of this crop residue, which they use as cooking fuel. Therefore, landowners allow these households to collect stalks of these plants. There are no restrictions imposed still now by the owners on collection of these resources.

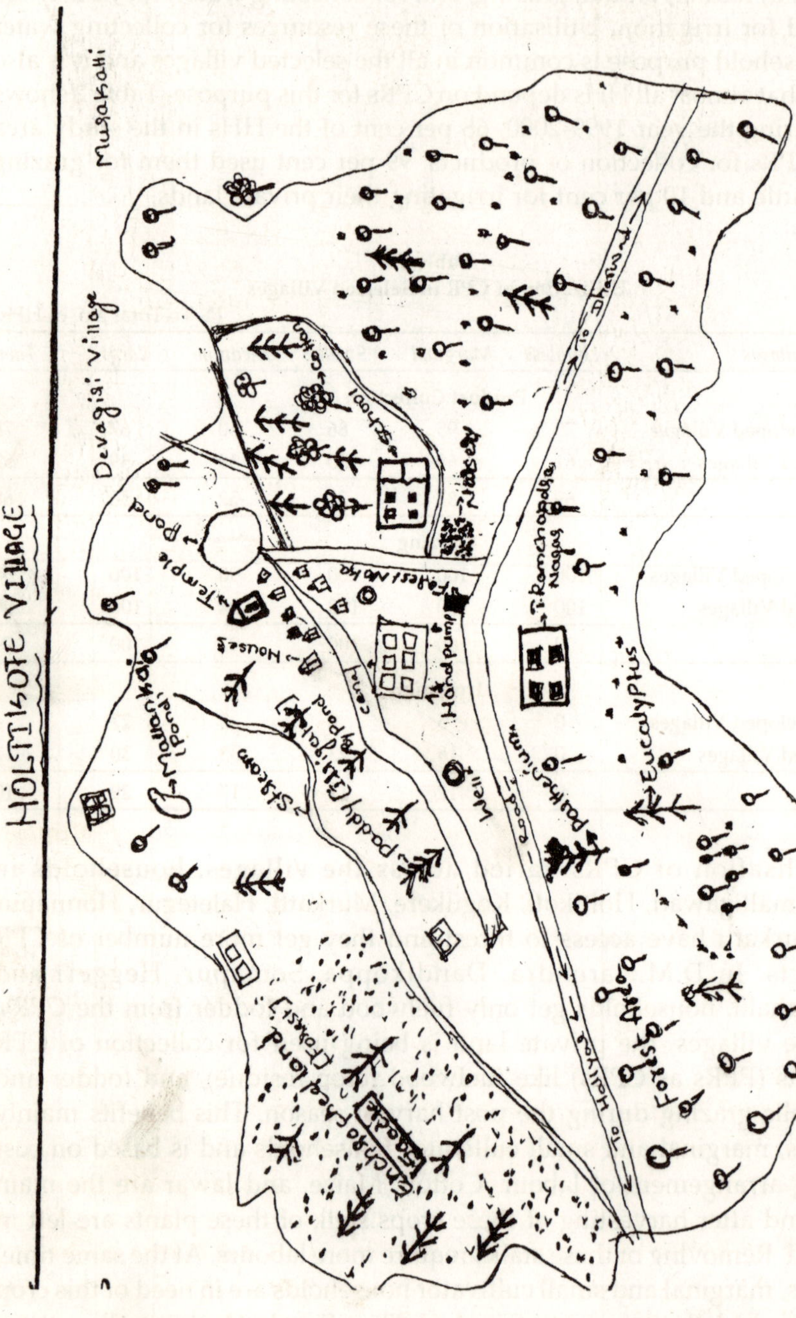
HOLTIKOTE VILLAGE
Musakatti
Devagiri Village
Temple
Pond
Houses
Handpump
Nursery
School
To Dharwad
Eucalyptus
Well
Road
To Haliyal
Forest Area
Stream

SUPPLY OF FUELWOOD

CPRs are the main source of supply of fuelwood to the households in the study area. According to the study, households collected, on an average, 10 quintals of fuelwood having the market value of Rs. 1104 during the period 1999-00. Households in 'less developed' villages collected 12.6 quintals of fuelwood and households in 'developed villages' collected only 7.1 quintals per annum from CPRs.

Table 3
Quantity of Fuelwood Collected From CPRs

Type of Village	*Landless*	*Marginal*	*Small*	*Medium*	*Large*	*Total*
Quantity of Fuelwood Collected (Quintals: Per HH/Annum)						
Less-Developed Villages	11.2	11.8	13.1	14.9	15	12.6
Developed Villages	7.4	7.7	7.3	5.4	6.5	7.1
Total	9.6	9.6	10.4	11.2	9.8	10

The collection of fuelwood has a socio-economic dimension. Women are mainly involved in the collection of fuelwood among households belonging to weaker sections whereas in the other communities men collected fuelwood during the summer season (i.e. after harvesting). The female members belong to weaker sections collect fuelwood everyday (i.e. while returning from the farm work). Even though the family size is more or less the same, the average quantity of fuelwood collection increases with increasing farm size. In 'developed' villages, this trend is reverse i.e. as the farm size increases the quantity of fuelwood-collected decreases. On an average, landless households collected 9 quintals, marginal households 10 quintals, small households 10 quintals, medium households 11 quintals and large households 10 quintals of fuel wood.

The share of CPR fuelwood in total fuelwood consumption can give a better indication about the extent of dependence of households on CPRs.

Table 4
Share of CPR Fuelwood In Total Fuel Wood Use (%)

Type of Village	*Landless*	*Marginal*	*Small*	*Medium*	*Large*	*Total*
Less-Developed Villages	78.2	91.4	77.8	87.1	78.7	82
Developed Villages	63.8	60.7	56.9	32.4	32.9	52.4
Total	73.7	72.9	69.8	63.6	50.3	67.9

Table 4 shows that on an average, households in the selected villages met about 68 per cent of their fuelwood requirement from CPRs. However, the share in the total consumption of fuelwood varies across the villages. It is evident from the table that the share of fuelwood use is significant in developed villages even though its share is less compared to less developed villages. This shows that developed villages also significantly depend on

CPRs for their fuelwood requirements. It is evident from the table that as the farm size of the households increases the share of CPR fuelwood in the total fuelwood consumption decreases. On an average, landless, marginal, small, medium and large cultivator households get 9.5, 9.6, 10.4, 11.2, 9.8 quintals of fuelwood from CPRs and their share in total fuelwood consumption is 72, 74, 69, 65, 52 per cent respectively. This shows that though in absolute terms these households get less, their dependence on CPRs is more compared to other type of households. The study finds a significant supply of fuelwood from CPRs to a large extent, determines the total use of fuel wood. The correlation coefficient between quantity of CPR fuelwood and total fuelwood used is 0.58.

SUPPLY OF FODDER

In the selected villages households depend significantly on CPRs for livestock rearing. In the selected villages CPRs provide very low quantity of fodder. On an average households collected 1.1 quintals of fodder valuing Rs.198 during a year. CPRs also provide space for grazing the cattle. Both medium and large farmers prefer better quality fodder and mostly meet their requirement from PPRs. As medium and large farmers have more cultivable area, they cultivate fodder crops such as jowar, paddy, wheat, groundnut, etc. They use byproduct of these crops as fodder. In spite of this, a significant proportion of livestock depend on CPRs for grazing space. It is observed[2] in the villages that only the cows, buffaloes calves, sheep and goats are allowed to graze in the CPRs (not working bullocks because of less availability of fodder at CPRs). On an average 38 per cent of the animals (in units) depend on CPRs for grazing. This dependency also varies across villages and socio-economic classes. In 'less developed' villages more number of animal units depend on CPRs for grazing compared to 'developed' villages. It is also found that a higher proportion of animals of landless, marginal and small cultivator households depend on these resources.

Table 5
Animals Held on Account of Supply of Free Fodder From CPRs
(Animal Units/100 HHs)

Type of Village	*Landless*	*Marginal*	*Small*	*Medium*	*Large*	*Total*
Less-Developed Villages	41.0	38.7	30.8	17.5	0.0	28.0
Developed Villages	28.4	28.7	49.7	0.0	0.0	25.9
Total	34.4	33.1	39.1	10.5	0.0	26.8

The free supply of fodder helps in keeping extra animals[3]. Table 5 shows that 100 households were able to hold about 27 units of animals on account of free supply of fodder and it was more pronounced among landless, marginal and small cultivators. On an average landless held 34.4

units of animals, while marginal, small and medium cultivator households held 33.1, 39.1, and 10.5, units of animals respectively for 100 households.

EQUITABLE DISTRIBUTION OF ANIMAL HOLDINGS

Free supply of CPR fodder to the poor helps in more equitable distribution of animals among the households despite un-equal distribution of land holdings among different type of households. Table 6 shows that percentage distribution of animal holdings is more than the percentage distribution of land holdings among the landless, marginal and small cultivator households. Table 7 shows that per household animal holdings are more than per household land holdings for landless and marginal farmer households taken together. Thus, it can be concluded safely that free supply of fodder facilitates more equitable distribution of animal holdings than land holdings among these households.

Table 6
Distribution of Cultivable Land and Animal Holdings (%)

Type of Village	*Landless*	*Marginal*	*Small*	*Medium*	*Large*	*Total*
Distribution of Cultivable Land						
Less-Developed Villages	0.0	9.1	18.8	30.5	41.6	100.0
Developed Villages	0.0	9.2	16.7	17.7	56.5	100.0
Total	0.0	9.2	17.7	23.8	49.4	100.0
Distribution of Animal Holdings						
Less-Developed Villages	13.0	18.8	19.7	24.2	24.3	100.0
Developed Villages	8.9	23.6	22.5	13.9	31.2	100.0
Total	11.0	21.1	21.1	19.3	27.6	100.0

Table 7
Per HH Animal Holdings and Land Holdings

Type of Villages	*Landless*	*Marginal*	*Small*	*Medium*	*Large*	*Total*
Animal Holdings (Animal Units)						
Less-Developed Villages	0.9	2.2	2.6	3.7	7.4	2.5
Developed Villages	0.7	2.2	3.0	3.2	5.6	2.5
Total	0.9	2.2	2.8	3.5	6.3	2.5
Land Holdings (Acre)						
Less-Developed Villages	0.0	1.6	3.6	6.9	18.9	3.7
Developed Villages	0.0	1.5	4.0	7.3	18.3	4.5
Total	0.0	1.6	3.8	7.1	18.6	4.1

INCOME FROM CPRs

Income from CPRs is estimated by converting all resources and services provided by them into money terms. The CPR products, namely fuelwood, fodder, leaves, fruits and other items, have been collected largely for domestic consumption. The values of these products have been estimated by imputing the value of physical products collected from CPRs and benefits obtained from the activities based on them. The income from them has been derived by adding up their imputed values. The imputed value of a CPR product has been obtained by multiplying its quantity with local market price quoted by the households. The income from irrigation is calculated by taking into account the additional value of crop production over non-irrigated crops. Thus according to the present exercise, total income from CPRs includes value of CPR products collected and additional value created by irrigation over non-irrigated crops.

Table 8 reports total income derived from CPRs by way of product collection and irrigation. It shows that on an average households in the selected villages earned income of Rs. 1752 per annum. Households in the 'less-developed' villages obtained more income than the households in the 'developed' villages. It is also found that CPR income is positively associated with farm size of households.

Table 8
Income From CPRs: Product Collection and Irrigation

(Rs/HH/Annum)

Type of Village	*Landless*	*Marginal*	*Small*	*Medium*	*Large*	*Total*
Less-Developed Villages	1843	2092	1933	2300	3068	2086
Developed Villages	1473	1288	1336	1359	1470	1383
Total	1689	1661	1648	1937	2101	1752

Though it seems that the CPRs provided less income in absolute terms, in relative terms (share of CPR income in total income of the households) their contribution is significant, which is shown in table 9. The table shows that households earned about 11 per cent of their total income from CPRs. Thus, the share varies across the villages. It is also found that landless, marginal, and small cultivator households get more proportion of income from these resources. This shows that CPR income is more important for the poor household economies.

Table 9
CPR Income As a Percentage of Total Income

Type Of Village	*Landless*	*Marginal*	*Small*	*Medium*	*Large*	*Total*
Less-Developed Villages	15.7	24.5	15.4	13.5	6.7	14.1
Developed Villages	15.8	15.0	7.7	5.2	2.7	7.3
Total	15.8	19.4	11.1	9.4	4.1	10.5

It was expected that CPRs would help in reducing the rural inequalities created by PPRs, however, the study did not support this argument. It is found that the CPR income has not helped to reduce rural inequalities created by PPRs. The calculated value of Gini coefficient also reveals this fact. The Gini coefficient for income from PPR is 0.47 and Gini coefficient for total income (i.e. income from PPRs and income from CPRs) is 0.46.

EMPLOYMENT CREATED BY CPRs

Table 10 shows that CPRs are important source of employment for the rural households in the selected villages. It shows that on an average about '11 percentage of households depended on CPRs for employment. The study also indicates that households in the 'less developed' villages depend more on CPR based employment.

Table 10
Percentage of HHs Who Depend on CPRs For Employment

Type of Village	*Landless*	*Marginal*	*Small*	*Medium*	*Large*	*Total*
Less-Developed Villages	21.9	20.5	20.0	10.0	6.7	18.0
Developed Villages	6.1	2.2	0.0	0.0	0.0	2.4
Total	15.0	10.7	10.6	6.3	2.6	10.6

Table 10 also reveals that landless and marginal and small cultivator households depend more on these resources as a source of employment than medium and large cultivator households.

Table 11 shows days of employment created in income earning activities. On an average male members got 38 days of employment whereas women members got only 32 days of employment. According to study, male members are more interested in income earning activities than product collection for household use.

Table 11
Days of Employment Created in Income Earning Activities
(Days/ Worker)

Type of Village	*M/F*	*Landless*	*Marginal*	*Small*	*Medium*	*Large*	*Total*
Less-Developed	Male	34	58	27	50	2	35
Villages	Female	33	33	20	53	5	30
Developed	Male	39	120	0	0	0	66
Villages	Female	70	0	0	0	0	70
Total	Male	35	70	27	50	2	38
	Female	36	33	20	53	5	32

It is found that landless, marginal and small cultivator households depend on these resources for employment opportunities especially during off-season. They go and collect various CPR products and sell it in the nearby market. Group discussion with villagers of Holtikoti revealed that strong and influential persons only can get employment in government works, (such as road construction, planting trees in forest, etc) whereas any person can get CPR based employment. Thus, CPR based employment opportunities help weaker sections of the society (especially old and women). The CPR generated employment opportunities are higher in village Holtikoti than the employment created by government. In this village, an able bodied person could get 25 to 30 days of employment in government activities whereas a person would get 40 to 45 days of CPR based employment in a year.

Table 12 shows per day income earnings from CPR based activities. It shows that on an average a male member earns Rs.41 and a female member earns Rs.32 per day at the current market prices. It can be seen that in many cases medium and large cultivator members earn more income than landless, marginal and small cultivator household members. The asset holdings (such as carts, tractors, etc) help these households to extract more quantities of CPR products.

Table 12

Income Earnings Of CPR Based Activities (Rs/day)

Type Of Village	*M/F*	*Landless*	*Marginal*	*Small*	*Medium*	*Large*	*Total*
Less-Developed Villages	Male	37	30	58	82	900	48
	Female	35	35	25	28	33	33
Developed Villages	Male	27	0	0	0	0	11
	Female	20	0	0	0	0	20
Total	Male	36	20	58	82	900	41
	Female	33	35	25	28	33	32

Table 13 shows seasonal activities in village Holtikoti. This table is drawn with the help of Participatory Rural Appraisal Technique (PRA) by the villagers (with the help of seasonal calendar). This shows that HHs in the villages can get more employment opportunities with CPRs than government programmes.

Table 13

Seasonal Activities in Village Holtikoti

(Based Upon The Application of PRA Technique)

Sl. No.	*Activities*	*Months (in order)* 1	2	3	4	5	6	7	8	9	10	11	12
1.	Agriculture					x	xx	xx	x	x	xx	xxx	
2.	CPR Based Activities												
	(a) Plantation work in the forest						xx	xx	x	x			
	(b) Leaves collection				x	xx							
	(c) Gum collection	x	xx										
	(d) Fuelwood collection	xx	xx										
	(e) Collection of Hulagal seeds					xx	x						
	(f) Collection of teak seeds				xx	xx							
	(g) Collection of Tendu leaves				xx	xx							
	(h) Nelli collection									x	x		
	(i) Kaulikai collection					xx							
	(j) Fodder collection											xx	x

Note: x shows existence of employment opportunity and more number of x shows higher level of employment opportunity.

CONCLUSION

The study shows that CPRs are of crucial importance to poor people's livelihoods. In the selected villages households utilize CPRs mainly for collection of fuelwood, fodder, leaves, fruits and other products, animal grazing, and water for drinking and for irrigation purposes. The utilization of these resources has a class dimension. More number of landless, marginal and small cultivator HHs collect these resources. Most of these households belong to SC, ST and OBC categories. In the case of irrigation, more number of households belonging to medium and large cultivators utilize CPWRs. Free supply of fodder helps households to hold extra animals and it also helps to distribute animals more equitably among the households despite un-equal distribution of land holdings among different type of HHs. CPRs generated Rs. 1752 per household during the year 1999-00. Though in absolute terms landless, marginal and small HHs get less income than other households, their share in their total income is very high. On an average landless get 15.8 per cent, marginal land holders get 19.4 per cent, and small land holders get 11.1 per cent, medium land holders get 9.4 per cent, and large cultivator households get 4.1 per cent of their income from CPRs. This shows the importance of CPR income to poor households. The study reveals that the CPR income has not helped to reduce rural inequalities created by PPRs. The Gini coefficient for income from PPR is 0.47 and Gini coefficient for total income (i.e. income PPR and income from CPRs) is 0.46. About 2 per cent of the population is depending on CPRs for their direct income earning activities. From such an employment male earned Rs.41 and female Rs. 34 per day. Thus, CPRs are sustaining the rural livelihoods by providing required materials, income and employment opportunities. If these CPRs are developed they can provide higher income and employment opportunities. Presently CPRs are considered only as providing a safety net for those who may not have access to products and services through conventional markets. Positive approach to development requires a focus on providing people the means with which to lead better lives. Therefore CPRs need to be seen not only as a safety net, but also in terms of their contribution to positive opportunities for social and economic development.

ACKNOWLEDGEMENT

This paper is based on the study of common property resources (CPRs) in eleven villages in Dharwad district in Karnataka. The study highlights the importance of CPRs in sustaining livelihoods of rural households (HHs), especially weaker sections of the society. The Participatory Rural Appraisal (PRA) method is adopted to collect information about the use of CPRs apart from collecting information through interview schedule. The study shows that CPRs generated Rs. 1752 per household during the year 1999-00 and it is estimated around 11 percent of total income of HHs. Due to lack of management and hence encroachment, these resources have been depleting very rapidly. The findings of the study show that there are more possibilities of utilizing these resources for employment and income generation, which can lead to sustainable livelihoods of the rural people.

NOTES

1. Taxonomic method has been used; because this method helps to construct such an index, which would be able to rank different villages without assuming any statisticaldistribution (Behara and Mitra, 1996).
2. The working bullocks are not preferred to graze in the CPRs because of their tradition and partly because of degraded condition of CPRs.
3. It is found from the group discussion with villagers and personal observation of the researcher that the open grazing does not provide enough fodder for animals. Therefore, while estimating the contribution we considered only the fodder collected. The extent of contribution would be greater if animal grazing along with the collection of fodder is considered. The number of animals held on account of free supply of fodder is calculated on the basis of proportion of CPR fodder supply to the total HH use. For example, a HH requires fodder based on the number of animals it holds. Taking into account the requirement of each animal in the total and the quantity of fodder obtained from CPR we have tried to link up CPR supported animals in the HH. The total animal units is multiplied by proportion of supply of CPR fodder and is divided by hundred (100) to get animals held on account of free supply of fodder.

REFERENCES

Agro Climatic Regional Planning Unit (1991), "Agro Climatic Regional Planning at State Level" ACRPU, Ahamadabad.

Beck, Tony and Ghosh, Madan G. (2000), "Common Property Resources and the Poor- Findings from West Bengal" *Economic and Political Weekly*, January, 15, pp. 147-153.

Behera, Manaranjan and Mitra, Ajit Kumar (1996), "The Standard of Living in India: An Attempt Towards Inter Regional Study" *Indian Journal of Regional Science*, Vol. 28, No. 2, pp. 1-7.

Chopra, Kanchan and Gulati, S.C. (2001), "Migration, Common Property Resources and Environmental Degradation" Sage publications, New Delhi.

Chopra, Kanchan, et al (1990), "Participatory Development-People and Common Property Resources" Sage Publishers, New Delhi.

Damodaran, A. (1991), "Tragedy of the Commons and Comedy of Common Property Resources" *Economic and Political Weekly*, Vol. 26, No. 38, pp. 2213-2215.

Ghosh, Madan Gopal (1995), "Common Property Resource Use by Poor in West Bengal" Internet.

Iyengar, Sudarshan (1989), "Common Property Land Resources in Gujarat: Some Findings about their Size, Status and Use" *Economic and Political Weekly*, Vol. 24, No. 25, pp. A-67.

Jodha, N.S. (1986), "Common Property Resources and Rural Poor in Dry Regions of India", *Economic and Political Weekly*, Vol. 21, No. 27, pp. 1169-1181.

Jodha, N.S. (1990), "Rural CPRs: Contributes and Crisis "*Economic and Political Weekly*, Vol. 25, No. 26, pp. A-65.

Jodha, N.S. (1985), "Population Growth and the Decline of Common Property Resources in Rajastan, India" *Population and Development Review*, Vol. 11, No. 2, pp. 247-264.

Kadekidi, Gopal (1997), "Regeneration of Degraded and Waste Lands" Institute of Economic Growth, Delhi.

Kadekodi, Gopal (2001), "Common Property Resource Management: Reflections on Theory and Indian Experience" Centre for Multi-Disciplinary Development Research, Dharwad.

Kadekodi, Gopal K. and Gulati S.C. (2000), "Root Causes of Biodiversity Losses in Chilika Lake" Centre for Multi-Disciplinary Development Research, Dharwad, Monograph No. 26.

Karanth, G.K. (1992), "Privatisation of Common Property Resources-Lessons from Rural Karnataka" *Economic and Political Weekly*, Vol. 27, No. 31 and 32, Pp. 1680-1688.

Kumar, Suresh (2000), "Common Property, Community Interests and Environmental Concerns" Manak Publishers, New Delhi.

Pasha, Syed Ajmal (1992), "CPRs and Rural Poor-A Micro Level Analysis" *Economic and Political Weekly*, Vol. 27, No. 46, pp. 2499-2503.

McKean, Margaret A. (1992), "Success on the Commons; A Comparative Examination of Institutions for Common Property Resource Management" *Journal of Theoretical Politics*, Vol. 4, No. 3.

National Sample Survey Organisation (2000), "Sarvekshana" Government of India, Vol. 24, No. 1.

Noronha, Raymond (1997), "Common Property Resource Management in Traditional Societies" in 'The Environment and Emerging Developing Issues, Vol 1, Clarendon Press, Oxford.

Sengupta, Nirmal (1995), "Common Property Institutions and Markets" *Indian Economic Review*, Vol. 30, Issue 2, pp. 187-202.

Shiva, Vandana (1991), "Ecology and Politics of Survival" Sage Publications, New Delhi.

Singh, Karam, Singh, Nirmal and Singh, R.P. (1996), "Utilisation and Development of Common Property Resources–A Field Study in Punjab" *Indian Journal of Agricultural Economics*, Vol. 51, No. 1 and 2, pp. 249-259.

Singleton, Sara and Taylor, Michael (1992), "Common Property, Collective Action and Community" *Journal of Theoretical Politics*, Vol. 4, No. 3.

Somanathan, E. (1991), "Deforestation, Property Rights and Incentives in Central Himalaya" *Economic and Political Weekly*, Vol. 26, No. 3, pp. PE-37-45.

Swanson, Timothy M., Ed (1996), "The Economics of Environmental Degradation-Tragedy for the Commons?" UNEP, Edward Elgar Publishing Company, Cheltenham, UK. Brookfield, US.

United Nations (1996), "Rural Poverty Alleviation and Sustainable Development in Asia and the Pacific" United Nations, Economic and Social Commission for Asia and the Pacific, pp. 11-12 and 54-66.

Chapter - 15

Empowerment of Women: Some Conceptual and Measurement Issues

Sanjeev D. Kenchaigol

INTRODUCTION

Advocacy on women's development is not a new phenomenon. From the celebrated classic book of Mary Wollstonecraft[1] to Ester Boserup[2], the writings on gender have laid much emphasis on women's contributions for economic development. Women's movements, that began to generate constant debates and critics on women's well-being and agency around the world, introduced whole new concepts and paradigms in the gender literature, of which the concept of empowerment is fundamental. (Stein 1997, Batliwala 1994). Unfortunately the term 'empowerment', now, has become more a 'buzzword' (Bose 2000) only because it has been driven by different contexts rather than by any known theory (Beteille 1999). The contexts differ due to historical, social, political, economic, cultural and geographic factors the region and accordingly the concept of empowerment is being shaped in India and elsewhere.

In the development process, women's empowerment strategy has its own role in achieving enhanced concentration on women's wellbeing which could transform their status from being mere passive recipients of benefits to active agents of change, which in turn can alter the lives of both women and men (Sen 2001, Mahmud 2003). It is in this context, empowerment is taken as a development strategy, which in turn eliminates or reduces gender inequalities and female deprivation. Since the applicability of the empowerment process still is in it's infancy, one can debate on alternative methodologies to measure the well-being including the methods of UNDP-HDR, 1995.

To begin with, at the micro-level, gender sensitive indicators of well-being based on Amartya Sen's *'functionings and capabilities'* approach[3] give a space to develop a framework and the measurement of well-being outcomes of empowerment (Saith et al 1999).

Poverty has many bearings with its implications on female disadvantages. During the 1990s there were many attempts to interlink both the gendered poverty and empowerment mainly because the latter loaded with powers could successfully be used to eliminate the persistent gender inequalities. This, however, is reflected in various development approaches of international agencies such as the World Bank and the UNDP. Such means of *power*, which are discussed in various writings of Amartya Sen, are nothing but the human capabilities and functionings- or in brief, reflect on what people can actually *do* and *be* (Dreze and Sen 1989: 42).

The capabilities approach can also be contrasted with that of basic-needs and physical quality of life approaches advocated by M D. Morris. He assessed and integrating three indicators-*infant mortality, life expectancy at age one,* and *basic literacy*-into the composite Physical quality of Life Index (PQLI), whereas the concept of human development advocated by United Nations Development Programme (UNDP 1990) focuses on the three distinct aspects of life namely, health, per capita income, and literacy/ education. UNDP HDR 1995, for the first time, uses the gender sensitive indicators for measuring the state of women's empowerment (UNDP HDR 1995).

To take forward the discussion, the paper is organised into four different sections. In the second section, the meaning and conceptual issues of empowerment are looked into. A broad literature review explores the meaning and conceptual issues of empowerment with a special focus on ways and means of measuring empowerment. It also considers the identification of various gender sensitive indicators, particularly focusing on the important components of empowerment viz., *resources, women's agency,* and *achievements* or *well-being outcomes.* The third section goes on describing the understanding of the *functionings* approach, which uses three broad indicators: *being healthy, being nourished* and *being educated.* It further focuses briefly on the composite assessment of well-being proposed in the UNDP methods of Gender development Index (GDI) and Gender Empowerment Measure (GEM). The fourth section ends up with the concluding remarks on the importance and usefulness of micro level indicators of well-being.

CONCEPT OF EMPOWERMENT

In varying contexts of socio-economic, political and cultural diversities, how to introduce a meaningful concept of empowerment? One can make a good beginning if we understand the nature and usage of the term 'power'. The emergence of empowerment as a drive emerged all over the world, partly due to women's movements. The different schools of thought (Townsend *et al* 1999)[4] on empowerment emerged initially out of experiences of working with women's groups in America and Europe and in South Asian countries.

During the 1970s, the writings of Paulo Freire, on the *Concientisation* approach, advocating the liberation of poor through raising awareness (Karlekar 2004) influenced the two original schools of thought. The first school namely American *Community Psychologists (hereafter CP for short),* mainly consists of the authors such as M.A. Zimmerman, Paulo Freire, Julian Rappaport among others, whereas the second school includes the feminist thinkers such as Batliwala (1994), Kabeer (1999), among others. The CP school authors see empowerment process as humanising the society by increasing inclusion and equality. Both the schools display a sharp technical difference between their approaches. For instance, if the American Psychologists propose for the psychological empowerment of individual at the organisation and community level, the writers at Tapalehui advocate the personal empowerment at the familial and collective levels. (Townsend et al 1999).

The historical emergence of empowerment concept goes back to the thoughts of Paulo Freire's theory of *Concientisation,* which were also widely adopted by the proponents of feminist "popular education" in Latin America. The defined goals of the latter, as Srilatha Batliwala puts it were:

> *...To unambiguously take the standpoint of women; (and) ...demonstrate to women and men how gender is constructed socially, ...and ...can be changed...[to show] through the lived experience of the participants, how women and men are gendered through class, race, religion, culture etc;*
>
> *...To build collective and alternative visions for gender relations...and deepen collective analysis of the context and the position of the women ... locally, nationally, regionally and globally...To develop analytical tools ...to evaluate the effects of certain development strategies for the promotion of women's strategic interests...To help women to develop the skills to assert themselves... and to challenge oppressive behavior... which can pressurize for change (Batliwala 1994: 128).*

By 1980, according to the feminist critics, Freire's strategies completely failed to make expected changes to the lives of poor women. Another important approach is the writings of Molyneux, which shed some thoughts on women's "practical" and "strategic" interests. Here the practical needs according to the author are: food, health, water, fuel, childcare, education, improved technology and so forth. To fulfill these needs, he gave some suggestions...

> *... Analysis of women's subordination and to bring some alternative, more satisfactory set of arrangements to those exist... such as the abolition of sexual*

> *division of labor, to alleviate the burden of domestic labor and child care... freedom of choice over child bearing ... and male violence and control over women.*

It is from these ideas the notion of empowerment emerged and was more clearly articulated in 1984 by DAWN (1994: 129) activists from Bangalore, in south India.

> *To put it more broadly in the words of Jane Stein, a CP school thinker, "...the roots of empowerment lie in the multifaceted efforts of many of those who experienced the domination to achieve self determination and free themselves from external control... Gandhi's Satyagraha movement in India, ... Mao Tse-tung, uniting China...Black Africans' struggle for freedom from the British, the Spanish, the Germans, the French, the Portuguese and the Afrikaners...these strategies – non-violence, the use of group -process to increase political consciousness and ethnic or racial pride directly affected the civil rights movements in the USA and can be seen as precursors of the women's empowerment movement" (Stein 1997: 54).*

The roots of emergence of empowerment as a development strategy (movement) to affect changes were influenced by the powerful thoughts and ideas of several leaders of the world, which incidentally also influenced by the civil rights movements in the USA and the latter is the main precursor for the empowerment movements.

MEANING OF EMPOWERMENT

As an NGO activist Srilatha Batliwala puts it: 'I like the term empowerment because no one has defined it clearly yet; so it gives a breathing space to work it out in action terms before we have to pin ourselves down to what it means'. (Cited in Kabeer 1999: 436). Sociologist Andre Beteille says, "The idea of empowerment may be invoked in virtually any context: in speaking about human rights, about basic needs, about economic security, about capacity building, about skill formation or about the conditions of dignified social existence (Beteille 1999: 590). The process of empowerment, as we discussed earlier ought to address the "conditions" of the women in the society, in which they live, which could affect their own "position". In the context of increasing intra-household gender inequalities, and female deprivation at all strata of life, we will attempt to explore a more suitable, (workable) meaning and definition of the term empowerment.

The most indispensable component of empowerment is the term *power.* Power has widely been defined as one's capacity to influence or control others (Singh Roy 1995). According to Srilatha Batliwala power is defined as control over material, intellectual resources, and ideology. The material assets over which control can be exercised may be physical, human, or financial, such as land, water, forests, people's bodies and labor, money, and access to money. Intellectual resources include Knowledge, information and ideas. Control over ideology signifies the ability to generate, propagate, sustain and institutionalize specific sets of beliefs, values, attitudes, and behavior - virtually determining how people perceive and function within given socio-economic and political environments (Batliwala 1994).

In developing countries, women are living in conditions of acute poverty; increased male dominance; lack of knowledge, basic education, healthcare, vulnerability; lack of control over financial or other forms of resources such as a piece of land (Agarwal 1994), skilled labour etc; lack of control over their own body and sexuality; and their silent suffering against the patriarchal system of living. Many of these are-not in their control; hence the decisions taken by others would greatly affect their lives every day. In this respect, Srilatha Batliwala puts as 'the process of challenging existing power relations, and gaining control over the resources of power', may be termed as '*empowerment*'. Whereas Naila Kabeer says 'my understanding of the notion of empowerment is that it is inescapably bound up with the condition of disempowerment and refers to the process by which those who have been denied the ability to make choices acquire such an ability. In other words, empowerment entails a *process of change*. People who exercise a great deal of choice in their lives may be very powerful, but they are not *empowered* in the sense in which I am using the word, because they were never disempowered in the first place' (Kabeer 1999:436-437). By this, what Kabeer is likely to mean is that it is the marginalised poor, and disadvantaged sections of the society, in general, and women in particular, who are already in the state of vulnerability and destitution. By *disempowerment,* we mean lack of abilities to make *choices.* When the powerless are given such powers by a strategic process, it can be termed as empowerment.

Bina Agarwal (1994) who advocates women's rights to land assets and property (as resources) for the achievement of gender equality and empowerment, defines empowerment in the context of women's "position" relative to men and particularly with women's ability to challenge male oppression within home and in the society, as *a process that enhances the ability of disadvantaged ('powerless') individuals or groups to challenge and change (in their favour) existing power relationships that place them in subordinate economic, social and political positions.* Here, Agarwal argues that land rights would enhance women's 'freedom to achieve' or (capability to function) in non-economic spheres as well.

Empowerment is a process that challenges the existing power relations. As Sharma (cited in Batliwala, 1994) writes, the term empowerment refers to a range of activities from individual self-assertion to collective resistance, protest and mobilisation that challenge basic power relations. For individuals and groups where class, caste, ethnicity and gender determine their access to resources and power, their empowerment begins when they not only recognise the systematic forces that oppress them, but act to change existing power relationships. Empowerment, therefore, is a process aimed at changing the nature and direction of systematic forces, which marginalise women and other disadvantaged sections in a given context.

In the present context, where women's status is worsening, where millions of women are missing from our population (Dreze and Sen 1995), where intra-household gender inequalities (Sen 2001) in food distribution and intake persist, control over resources is lacking (Agarwal 1994), male dominance in decision making in the families and in the society prevails, lack of control over their sexuality and mobility and their reproductive rights including having their own say on how many children to bear (Batliwala 1994) are dominant; the conditions of acute poverty and destitution (Das Gupta 1995), where over burden of unpaid domestic work is still prevailing, and the contexts, where, women's positions as second class citizens and their roles as housewives (Boserup Ester 1971) are still dominant, we have a complex case of disempowerment. In such contexts, women's *empowerment* may be defined as:

> *Women's empowerment is a process that gives the power to the powerless (disadvantaged and marginalized) women (individuals or groups) by which they can gain the abilities to exercise choices or to control resources, which could help them to challenge and change (in their favour) existing power relationships that would place them under subordination, which, in turn could enhance their capability to function and hence, to achieve their own well-being and well being of their family and groups.*

CONCEPTUALISING EMPOWERMENT

Until now, we have discussed the meaning of women's empowerment with reference to prevailing discourses in the development literature. Naila Kabeer (1999) puts it as "a wide gap that separates the processual understanding of empowerment from the more instrumentalist forms of advocacy which have required the measurement and quantification of empowerment".

Naila Kabeer who comes from Bangladesh, with a wider experience of working with the NGOs, discusses the valuable insights with regard to the conceptual and measurement issues of empowerment (Kabeer, 1999). It would be useful to reproduce her expression of empowerment, which reads as 'notion of empowerment is about change, it refers to the expansion in people's ability to make strategic life choices in a context where this ability was previously denied to them'. But she identifies three important prerequisites of the ability to exercise the choice as:

1. Resources *(Preconditions)*
2. Agency *(Process)*
3. Achievements *(Outcomes)*

Chart 1
Empowerment Process

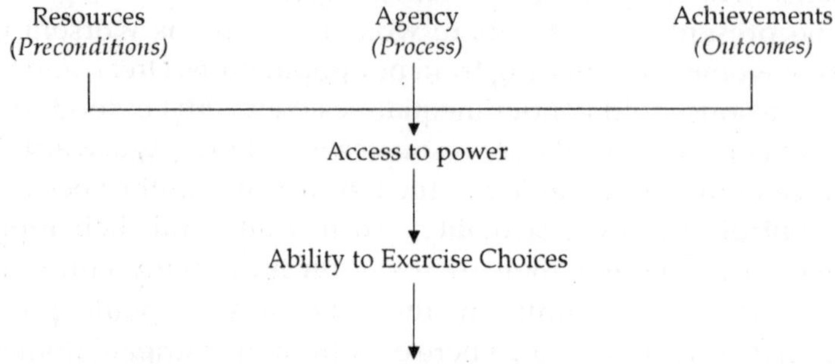

Resources: not only material resources but also the various resources, which serve to enhance the ability to exercise choice.

Agency: The ability to define one's goals and act upon them. Agency or ' power from within', is operationalised as 'decision-making' process in any given context.

The author tries to link up the 'ability to make choice' with that of Amartya Sen's "functionings and Capabilities" approach. She writes "Resources and agency together constitute what Sen (cited in Kabeer, 1999) refers to as capabilities: the potential that people have for living the lives they want, of achieving valued ways of 'being and doing".

Nature of the Choice: Since the ability to exercise choice is the ultimate manifestation of empowerment, we are more concerned with the prevailing inequalities and opportunities in making choices by people rather than in the *differences* in the choices they make. For the measurement purposes, we have to focus on certain universally valued basic functionings of women's survival strategies and well being. For instance, proper nourishment, good health and shelter are treated as very basic needs. This is the strategy suggested by Sen (2000). There may be some shortcomings confronted with inequalities in exercising choices. The methods of measuring such gender inequalities adopted in UNDP's human development Index (HDI) and Gender empowerment Measure (GEM) are more relevant to the present context. Another important but critical character of choice is that women's acceptance of being subordinated to their husbands and in-laws, which can have adverse implications on their well being and well being of other female family members. (Kabeer 1999).

Achievements: Seen in terms of human well-being with the selected indicators.

MEASURMENT OF WOMEN'S EMPOWERMENT

The understanding of empowerment on three important dimensions of power or ability to make choices, such as resources, agency and achievements is basic to any analytical method on measurement.

Measurement of Resources

The dimension of resources and their power sharing often dictates the status of women. Many studies (Boserup 1971, Agarwal 1994, and Panda and Agarwal 2005) have showed that the entitlements on resources to women will enhance their ability to make choices. Entitlement enables access. Such 'access' to resources, for instance, land inheritance, as a resource of power can help women to exercise greater degree of autonomy, where they enjoy some rights over land (Agarwal 1994) However, there are some doubts while dealing with the resources that are entitled to women. How resources can be defined so that it could spell out the potential for human agency? How to define 'access', 'control' and 'decision making'?

UNDP methodology to assess Human Development Index (HDI) has come up with three broad indicators such as life expectancy to measure longevity, Educational attainment to represent Knowledge; and an appropriately adjusted real GDP per capita to serve as a surrogate for command over *resources* (Shiva Kumar 1996, Seeta Prabhu et al 1996). Many authors used several other non-conventional indicators to assess human well being (see Rustagi 2000, 2004: 293; see also Indira Hirway et al 1996; Sonpar and Kapur 2001, Vishwanathan 2001 among others). For operational reasons, we may treat 'resources' as 'human, material and intangible sources of power (Kabeer 1999) that can determine the ability to exercise human choices'. This notion is reflected in the definitions of 'power' aired by several authors (see Batliwala 1994, Batliwala et al 1998 and Kabeer 1999).

When it comes to gender equality and role in decision-making, both 'access' and 'control' are important. To define access, Batliwala et al (1998) opined that in the context of material, human and intangible resources, the term 'access' refers to the opportunity available to use the resource'. Control over certain resources can act as a bargaining power to determine the use of that resource. 'Control' means, they observe, 'an acknowledged and socially sanctioned equal share in decision making, in both the private and public spheres' (Batliwala et al 1998: 18).

Measurement of "Agency"

In the literature of empowerment, 'agency' is often attached to the decision making process in both the private and public arenas. Women's agency plays very vital role in enhancing capabilities to affect their living. Sen has profound observations here. He writes...

> *...Focusing on women's agency may be precisely the role that such an agency can play in removing the inequalities that depress the well being of women. Empirical work in recent years has brought out very clearly how the relative respect and regard for women's well being is strongly influenced by such variables as women's ability to earn an independent income, to find employment outside*

the home, to have ownership rights and to have literacy and be educated participants in decisions within and outside the family. ...These different aspects may at first sight appear to be rather diverse and disparate. But what they all have in common is their positive contribution in adding force to women's voice and agency–through independence and empowerment (Sen, 2000: 191).

As an agent of social change women's well being is closely connected to capabilities, which could influence the well being of the family members, particularly of children and also of the elderly and adult members (Mahmud 2003). As the development discourses have emerged with the goals of women's well being, (on par with men) their agency has been given greater prominence with the notions of well-being.

MEASUREMENT OF ACHIEVEMENTS: FUNCTIONINGS APPROACH

Pure income related approaches to the measurement of poverty led to think on other alternative approaches of measures. In this respect, the alternative approaches developed either by Morris (Morris, 1979, cited in Razavi, 1999, Batliwala, 1994, and Saith et al, 1999), or by Sen (Sen, 1985a) can be viewed as the first set of alternative responses to income based measurements of well-being. For the purposes of gender inequalities, the same can be made more specific. (Razavi 1999). A number of efforts have been made by feminist thinkers to explore persisting gender inequalities and female disadvantages including that on 'missing females' (Mari Bhat 2002) and 'missing girls' (Premi 2001). Amartya Sen's notion of 'functionings and achievements' (see Saith et al 1999, Mahmud 2003, and Razavi 1999) could prove to be better approaches to assess the achievements or the well being of the women.

Assessment of well-being

An important reason behind adopting the framework of Sen's pioneering contribution of 'functionings' is directly based on the relationship between the basic 'functionings' and the respective achievements. It has to be distinguished from the commodities, which are used to achieve those functionings (Sen 1985a: 7). The framework examines three basic functionings namely: being healthy, being nourished and being educated.

Being Healthy

The notion of health ranges from good health to morbidity to acute ill health. (Saith et al 1999) have worked on the Sen's basic functionings indices: being healthy, being nourished and being educated and their contextual relevance to the developing countries. What the authors' findings say is that apart from these basic functioning indicators, indices such as anthropometric measures are potentially useful and makes much more demands on micro level research. Under different categories of basic functionings, the authors have recommended several social indicators to assess the achievements of respective functioning. For instance, other sub indicators that are shown through the chart 2 explain the functioning of 'being healthy'.

Chart 2
Indicators of 'being healthy'

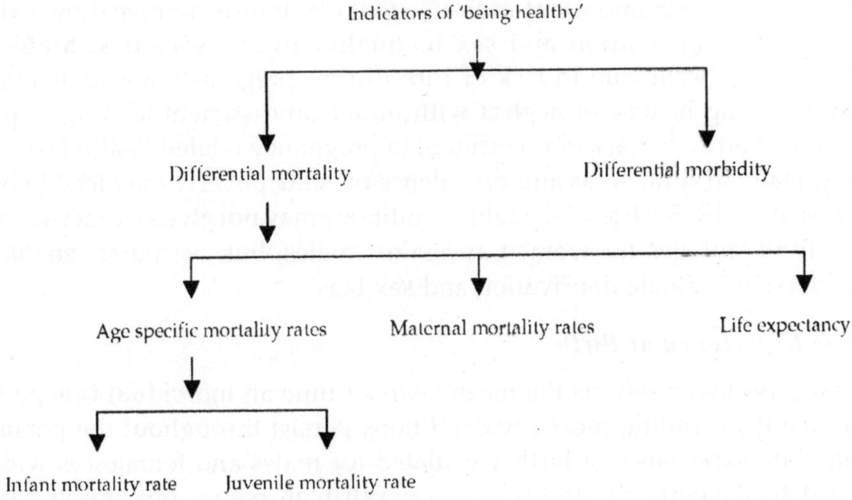

Mortality Indicators

Differential Mortality Rates

These gender sensitive indicators of health reveal different aspects of demographic situations of people in which they are living. The sex differential in mortality rates itself is a direct evidence of female disadvantages in terms of gender treatments, health care facilities and neglect of girl child. Decline in sex ratio, i.e., the ratio of female to male population (henceforth, FMR for short) is another good indicator of health, as a direct evidence of this fact. There is also much evidence in India that the phenomenon of declining sex ratios are due to the relative neglect of health and well-being of women (particularly young girls including female infants), leading to survival disadvantages of women vis-à-vis men over long periods (Dreze and Sen 1995: 141). The concept of 'missing women' (even also 'missing girls') conveys that due to conditions of women's adversity in mortality and due to female disadvantages in well-being compared to males, significant differential mortality rates are observable. In the context of intra household comparison, the FMR could be used for all such micro level researches to explain the persisting gender inequalities.

The age specific death rates are another set of health related indicators, which are calculated for groups of five years; especially the groups of 0-4, and 5-9 have greater impact on overall FMR. These indicators could prove reliable, since they depict a picture of poorer antenatal care, unsatisfactory health delivery system (Agnihotri 1997 cited by Saith et al 1999) and increased availability and use of gender determination of foetuses (Sen 2001).

Maternal Mortality Rate (MMR)

MMR is another important indicator that can indirectly reveal the extent of female deprivation and sex inequality in our societies. Maternal mortalities occur due to lack of care during pregnancy and delivery as well as long history of neglect with under nourishment leading to poor physical growth. Lack of investment in pregnancy related health facilities, especially in rural areas and prevalence of acute poverty may lead to high rates of MMR. Such sex inequality conditions may not give an exact account of disadvantages for women as against males, but, of course, enable to understand female deprivation and sex bias.

Life Expectancy at Birth

Life expectancy reflects the mean years of time an individual is expected to live if prevailing mortality conditions persist throughout the person's life. Life expectancy at birth, calculated for males and females, is widely used to measure differentials in overall well-being. But this index is criticised as the higher female mortality in India up to the age of 35 is disguised by the estimated female life expectancy at birth (Chatterjee 1990, cited by Saith et al 1999). Therefore, overall female life expectancy is the best indicator of development, and also useful in it's usage to capture gender differences in well-being and hides age specific differentials in mortality.

Morbidity Indicators

Morbidity indicators may be grouped into two categories. First, comprising the conditions that are sex specific such as reproductive disorders. But it suffers from the same constraints as the MMR. The second group contains the conditions that are applicable to both the sexes. Often the conditions may be more specific to either sex. For instance, (a) some physical disorders of working women in factories, (b) gendered environments, as for example, in rural Karnataka, where the males work in the open air while females work around the 'dark, smoke filled kitchen' this makes the exposer to infection gender specific (Caldwell and Caldwell 1987, cited by Saith et al 1999), or (c) differentials in medical care and nutrition.

Being Nourished

Indicators under this heading are categorised under two headings: Indicators of intake and indicators of outcome.

Indicators of Intake

Consumption of the sources of macro-nutrients (Carbohydrates, proteins and fats) and micro nutritients (vitamins and minerals) can be considered as an intake indicator. Since the quantity of food consumed is measurable directly this reflects a commodity-based approach. Yet, in this approach, there are many limitations associated with it such as:

- Collecting data on estimated food intake is biased and time consuming,

Estimation of workload of women (while assessing gender differentials in nutrition) could result in an underestimation of any existing female disadvantage. (Saith et al 1999).

Indicators of Outcome

Here, apart from other methods, the anthropometric measurements are more popular.

The anthropometric approach rests on the presumption that people's appearance reflects their nutrition (and health) status, e.g. if their body intake and expenditure balance at too low a level, this will show in their body constitution. Instead of energy intake nor the expenditure, the body structure and constitution would suffice. The anthropometric approach is therefore more direct and simple and less reliant on data collection than the dietary approach (Svedberge 1991, cited in Saith et al 1999). On the other hand, Anuradha Khati Rajivan (1996) observes that 'measures based on anthropometric data should ideally serve as indicators of the physical condition of individuals–male and female–and allow us to draw inferences about inequalities in their functioning capabilities'.

The indicators of anthropometric approach however, suffer from certain drawbacks. Many studies show the provenance excessive female mortality, but not reflected in anthropometric indicators (Saith et al 1999).

Being Educated

A vast literature from micro level research is available on the essence of formal education for the day-to-day living of people, next, on the causes of low overall literacy and prevailing gender inequalities in this functioning. But these micro-level studies often do not investigate the issues of gender sensitivity of differential indicators of education (Saith et al 1999). Following a study by of Saith et al 1999, we present these indicators of education.

Indicators of education are broadly divided into two groups, indicators of access or indicators of participation and indicators of content and purposes. This can be seen through the flow chart below.

Chart 3
Indicators of 'Being Educated'

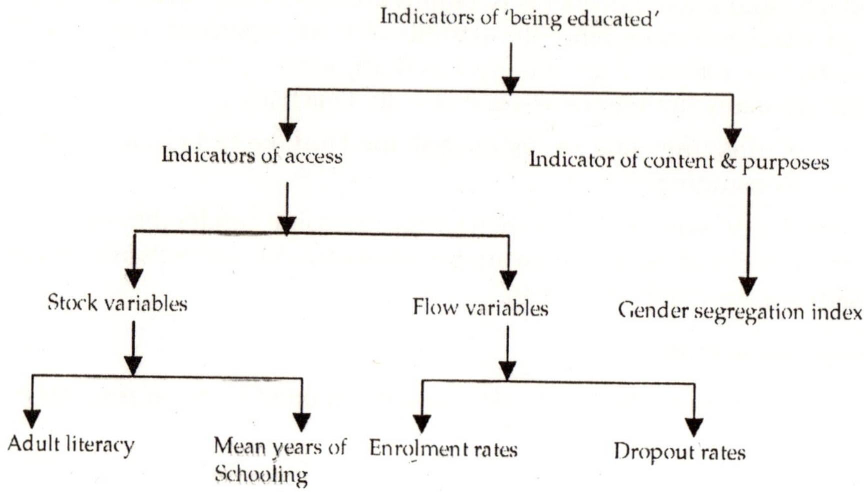

Indicators of Access

These indicators represent the accessibility of education from basic literacy up to tertiary education and they can display the inequalities in terms of access. Indicators of access are subdivided into stock and flow variables.

Stock Variables: These give information about the older population. 'Adult literacy' refers to persons (15 years and above) who can understand read and write. Literacy rates have been criticised on several grounds, particularly on the definition they bear. The 'mean years of schooling (average number of years of schooling received per person aged twenty-five and over) overcomes this problem. These two variables reflect past investments and accessibility to education.

Flow Variables: These include gross enrolment, net enrolment and dropout ratios at the primary, secondary and tertiary levels. The gross enrolment ratio (GER) is the total enrolment in any level of education (regardless of age), divided by the population of the age group. The net enrolment ratio refers to enrolment with respect to the official age group for that level.

Indicators of Content and Purposes: In most of the South Asia and sub-Saharan African countries, gender differentials in primary and secondary levels are in favour of males and widen at tertiary level. Such gender differences have been studied in both the poor and rich countries subjected to quantification by UNESCO, which has developed the Gender Segregation Index. These indices are based on macro level studies.

CONCLUDING REMARKS

An attempt is made here to discuss the term 'empowerment'; it's conceptualisation and the measurement issues particularly proposing Amartya Sen's 'functionings and capabilities ' approach to measure basics of well-being functionings. The literature shows that the emancipation and victimization of women with respect to their labour and status within the house and in the society have led to the emergence of women's movements for recognizing their status, dignity and quality of life. Thus emerged the concept of empowerment. The kind of empowerment we discussed here is aimed at the process of social change, which gives power to the powerless, particularly poor women. In the measurement of well-being, three basic functionings viz; being healthy', 'being nourished' and 'being educated' are used to develop with respect to certain composite indices. We also discussed the relevance of UNDP composite indices of GDI and GEM as the valid measures of well-being.

The main purpose of 'functionings' approach is its validity and reflectivity in the measurement of human well being as we have seen in the UNDP methodologies. There is however, a criticism that indicators of single functioning as with each of the indicators may give false impression of equality in one, while there is inequality in other functionings. In such situations, efforts to develop alternative methods of assessing quality of life as per the demands of different contexts could prove most useful in poor countries. This holds true more so in case of micro level researches, with composite indices the qualitative assessment of persisting gender inequalities and deprivation could help us to understand the different dimensions of well-being. The non-conventional indicators for GDI and GEM are the most well come tools to assess female disadvantages relative to that of men. Since the UNDP indices do not capture the *micro-level* realities of gender deprivations, the former efforts hold true in different contexts of diverse societies and cultures. Efforts on the qualitative explorations at the micro level researches could be of more relevance to assess the well-being in more meaningful ways. Despite all these constraints, the composite indices of UNDP may still prove the first cut of tools, measuring human functionings and capabilities provide other estimates of gender well being, inequalities and deprivations are also developed to capture the micro-level realities.

ENDNOTES

This paper is part of my on going PhD research work on *empowerment of women in Karnataka* under the supervision of Prof Gopal K Kadekodi, Director, Institute for Social and Economic Change (ISEC), Bangalore and I am very grateful to Prof Kadekodi for his valuable comments and suggestions to improve the earlier version of this paper. My sincere thanks are also due Prof Padmini Swaminathan for her valuable comments on the paper during the 5th Development Convention of Southern ICSSR Institutions organized at CMDR, Dharwad, 27-28 April 2006. The researcher is only responsible for any errors remaining in the paper.

NOTES

1. See Sen, (2000:189). Reprinted in 2001.
2. For the first time, this pioneering work brought the critical picture of women's engagement both in the (rural and urban) agrarian and industrial sector and their contribution for the economic development in different parts of the world. The author condemned the tendency of planners to see women as secondary earners and to concentrate on their roles as housewives. See for e, g; Boserup (1971) and for some remarks on women's social independence, see J.S. Mill (1848). In his *Principles of Political Economy,* Mill speaks about the social independence of women for the welfare of laboring classes. See Mill, '*Principles of political Economy*' first published in 1848 and reprinted in 1985 by Penguin Classics, London.
3. The concept is heavily drawn on the writings of Amartya Sen on human capabilities and functionings. For detailed discussion and rich references cited there, see Sen, 1995, 1999, and 2001 among other contributions. See also Sudhir Anand 1994, Saith *et al* 1999, and Razavi 1999.
4. Janet Townsend brings about the two important schools of thought on 'empowerment' writings. One is the Community Psychologists (PC) School from United States, which includes the authors such as Zimmerman MA, Paulo Freire, Julian Rappaport and Jane Stein among others. The second school is based on the writings of Srilatha Batliwala, Naila Kabeer and others (or Tapaļehui). One sharp difference between these two groups lies in the recommended levels of analysis. If the CP school strongly believes in psychological empowerment of individual at the levels of the organisation and the community, the latter advocates the personal empowerment at the familial and collective levels. For a clearer but a brief observation see the appendix by Janet Townsend and for the detailed look-see chapters two and eight in Townsend *et al* (1999).

REFERENCES

Agarwal, Bina (1994), *A field of One's Own: Gender and Land Rights in South Asia,* Cambridge University Press, Cambridge, New York.

Batliwala, Srilatha (1994), 'The Meaning of Women's Empowerment: New Concepts from Action', in Gita Sen, Adrienne Germain, Lincoln Chen (Eds), *Populations Policies Reconsidered: Health, Empowerment and Rights,* Harvard Center for Population and Development Studies', Cambridge, pp. 128-138.

Batliwala, Srilatha, B.K. Anitha, A. Gurumurthy and C.S. Wali (1998), *Status of Rural Women in Karnataka,* National Institute of Advanced Studies, Bangalore.

Beteille, Andre (1999), 'Empowerment', *Economic and Political Weekly,* March 6-13, pp. 589-597.

Bose, Ashish (2000), 'Empowerment of Women: How and When?' *Economic and Political Weekly,* August 19, pp. 3005-3007.

Boserup, Ester (1971), *Women's Role in Economic Development*, George Allen and Unwin, London.

Das Gupta Partha (1995), *An Inquiry into Well-Being and Destitution*, Oxford India Paperbacks, New Delhi.

Dreze, Jeane and Amartya Sen (1989), *Hunger and Public Action*, (fourth reprint 1999) Oxford India Paperbacks, New Delhi.

Dreze, Jeane and Amartya Sen (1995), *India Economic Development and Social Opportunity*, Oxford India Paperbacks, New Delhi.

Hirway, Indira and Darshan Mahadevia (1996), 'Critique of Gender Development Index: Towards an Alternative', *Economic and Political Weekly*, October 26, pp. WS 87-96.

Kabeer, Naila (1999), 'Resources, Agencies, Achievements: Reflections on the Measurement of Women's Empowerment' *Development and Change*, Vol. 30, pp. 435-464.

Karlekar, Malavika (2004), 'A Note on the Empowerment of Women', *Indian Journal of Gender Studies*, 11:2, pp. 145-155.

Khati Rajivan Anuradha (1996), 'Measurement of Gender Differences Using Anthropometry', *Economic and Political Weekly*, October 26, pp. WS 58-62.

Mahmud, Simeen (2003), 'Actually how empowering is Micro Credit?' *Development and Change*, Vol. 34 (4), pp. 577-605.

Mari Bhat P.N. (2002), 'On the Trail of 'Missing' Indian Females I: Search for Clues', *Economic and Political Weekly*, December 21, 2002, pp 5105-5118.

Mill, J.S. (1848), *Principles of Political Economy* Reprinted in 1985, by Penguin Classics, London.

Panda Pradeep and Bina Agarwal (2005), *'Marital Violence, Human Development and Women's Property Status in India'*, Working Paper Series No. E/256/2005, Institute of Economic Growth (IEG), New Delhi.

Prabhu, K. Seeta, P.C. Sarkar and A. Radha (1996), 'Gender-Related Development Index for Indian States: Methodological Issues', *Economic and Political Weekly*, October 26, pp. WS 72-79.

Premi Mahendra K. (2001), 'The Missing Girl child', *Economic and Political Weekly*, May 26, 2001, pp 1875-1880.

Razavi, Shahra (1999), 'Gendered Poverty and Well-being: Introduction', *Development and Change*, Vol. 30, 465 - 497.

Rustagi, Preet (2004), 'Significance of Gender Related Development Indicators: An Analysis of Indian States', Indian Journal Of Gender Studies, 11:3, pp. 291-343.

Rustagi, Preet (2000), 'Identifying Gender Backward Districts Using Selected Indicators', *Economic and Political Weekly*, November 25, pp. 4276-4286.

Saith, Ruhi and Barbara Harriss-White (1999), 'The Gender Sensitivity of Well-being Indicators', *Development and Change*, Vol. 30, 465-497.

Sen, Amartya Kumar (1985a), *Commodities and Capabilities*, Oxford India Paperbacks, New Delhi.

Sen, Amartya Kumar (2000), *Development as Freedom*, Oxford India Paperbacks, New Delhi.

Sen, Amartya Kumar (2001), 'Many faces of Gender Inequality', *Frontline*, November 9, 2001, pp 4-14.

Shiva Kumar, A.K. (1996), 'UNDP's Gender-Related Development Index: A Computation for Indian States', *Economic and Political Weekly*, April 6, pp. 887-895.

Singh Roy, Debal K. (1995), 'Peasant Movements and Empowerment of Rural Women', *Economic and Political Weekly*, September 16, pp. 2306-2307.

Sonpar, Shobna and Ravi Kapur (2001), 'Non-Conventional Indicators: Gender Disparities under Structural Reforms', *Economic and Political Weekly*, January 6, pp. 66-77.

Stein, Jane (1997), *Empowerment and Women's Health: Theory, Methods and Practice*, Zed Books Ltd., London.

Townsend Janet, Emma Zapata, Jo Rowlands, Pilar Alberti and Marta Mercado (1999), *Fighting Patriarchies and Poverty: Women and Power*, Zed Books Ltd., London.

United Nations Development Programme (1995), *Human Development Report, 1995*, Oxford University Press, New Delhi, for UNDP.

Vishwanathan, Renuka (2001), 'Development, Empowerment and Domestic Violence: Karnataka Experience', *Economic and Political Weekly*, June 16, pp. 2173-2177.

Chapter - 16

National Rural Employment Guarantee Act: A Panacea to End Poverty in India

Himanshu Sekhar Rout

I

INTRODUCTION

In September 2000 the largest ever gathering of heads of state ushered in the new millennium by adopting the UN Millennium Declaration (United Nations, 2000) is know as the Millennium Development Goals (MDGs). The Goal 1 (eradication of poverty and hunger) of the MDGs states that halve, between 1990 and 2015, the proportion of people whose income is less than one dollar a day[1] (Target 1) and halve, between 1990 and 2015, the proportion of people who suffer from hunger (Target 2). But the goal is unlikely to be achieved, as two UN reports–one by the Food and Agricultural Organization (FAO), noting that the number of hungry people is rising, and another by International Labour Organization. For the first time since independence, the last decade witnessed a decline in per capita output in agriculture. The per capita net availability of pulses declined to less than half of what it was in the 1950s (Shah, 2004). According to FAO, over 225 million Indians remain chronically undernourished. The National Nutrition Monitoring Bureau has estimated that in 2000-2001 about half of the rural children below five years of age suffer from malnutrition and forty per cent of adults from chronic energy deficiency (Radhakrishna, 2005). India has the highest percentage of anaemic pregnant women in the world. Reports of starvation deaths suicides by farmers abound in the media. In this connection the National Rural Employment Guarantee Act (hereafter the Act) is a panacea for it. Another argument in favour of the implementation of the act is that there will be a significant number of poor who will not be absorbed in the mainstream economy even at the end of Tenth Plan (and also in the Eleventh Plan) (Hirway, 2004). There is an urgent need to support these people to enable them to come out of poverty.

The paper has seven sections. Section II states the concept and design of the act briefly. Section III analyses the financial implications and suggests some of the methods to finance the act. Section IV explains the benefits of the National Rural Employment Guarantee Scheme. The act will be a panacea for poverty eradication, if it will create awareness among the rural poor, stated in section V. Some critical questions pertaining to the act are discussed in Section VI. Section VII presents the concluding remarks.

II

THE ACT

The policy agenda outlined in the National Common Minimum Programme (NCMP) of the United Progressive Alliance (UPA) government begins with the following pledge:

> *"The UPA government will immediately enact a National Employment Guarantee Act. This will provide a legal guarantee for at least 100 days of employment to begin with on asset-creating public works programmes every year at minimum wages for at least one able-bodied person in every rural, urban poor and lower middle-class household" (NCMP, 2004).*

The amended National Rural Employment Guarantee Bill, introduced in Lok Sabha in 2004 by the government, was moved by Rural Development Minister Raghuvansh Prasad Singh amid the thumping of desk (The Hindu, 2005) on 18th August 2005. Describing it as a "historic bill", the Prime Minister Dr. Manmohan Singh said it aimed at banishing poverty through assured employment.

According to the act, every household in the rural areas[2] of India[3] shall have a right to at least hundred days of guarantee employment every year for at least one adult member (eighteen years and above) for doing casual labour, at sixty rupees per day as minimum wage and receive it there of within seven days of the week during which work has been done. In case of any delay in the payment of wages, labourers shall be entitled to the payment of compensation as per the payment of wage act. It shall be the responsibility of the state government to provide employment in accordance with the provision of the programme to every such person within fifteen days of receipt of an application. If the applicant is not provided with employment within fifteen days of receipt of an application, he or she shall be entitled to a daily unemployment allowances at such rate as may be fixed by the state government from time to time with the approval of the state council[4], but not less than one third of the prevailing statutory minimum wage of agricultural labourers in the state.

The entitlements of labourers employed under the programme are, firstly, labourers on public works under the will be entitled for medical treatment and hospitalization costs in case of injury at work, along with a daily allowance of not less than half of the statutory minimum wage rates. In case of death or disability of a worker, an exgratia payment shall be made to these legal heirs in the manner laid down in the Workmen Compensation Act. Secondly, facilities to be available at work sites will be (1) safe drinking water, (2) shades for small children and workers for rest, (3) first aid box with adequate material for emergency treatment for minor injuries, strokes, body ache and other health hazards, and (4) crèche for babies. Thirdly, in case of any delay of payment of wages, (payment latter than seven days), labourers will be entitled to the payment of compensation as per the Payment of Wages Act. Fourthly, a proportion of wages, not exceeding five per cent, may be deducted as a contribution to welfare schemes like health insurance, accident insurance, survivor benefits, maternity benefits and social security schemes.

III

FINANCIAL IMPLICATIONS

In the "Baseline Scenario[5]", presented in the preliminary estimates of the financial implications of the act proposed by the National Advisory Council (NAC), whereby a nation-wide Rural Employment Guarantee Programme is gradually introduced over a period of four years, the total cost of the programme rises from 0.5 per cent of the Gross Domestic Product (GDP) in 2005-2006 to one per cent of GDP in 2008-2009. The cost can brought down, if needed, by raising the labour-material ratio, stretching the inception phase beyond four years, or taking measures to reduce the "Participation Ratio[6]". However, these cost-reducing measures are best avoided. One per cent of Country's GDP is not a high price to pay to protect the bulk of rural population from hunger, insecurity and extreme poverty - once and for all (Dreze, 2004).

Dreze (2004) assumes that each person-day of employment generated costs one hundred at 2004-05 prices. This would roughly consist of Rupees sixty for wages and Rupees forty for the non-labour component including administrative costs. The National Rural Employment Guarantee Scheme (NREGS), and these costs, are modeled on a similar scheme, which has been implemented successfully for twenty years in Maharastra. But the preceding calculations assume a labour material ratio of 60:40. The corresponding ratio is much lower in Maharastra, and unit cost could come down with more labour intensity. The material costs including administrative cost could be managed with twenty to twenty five, as experienced in Maharastra, and reduced the total cost of the NREGS by Rs. 6,000 to Rs. 8,000 crore.

The figure of Rupees sixty for the wage component is quite close to the population-weighted average of state specific statutory minimum wages for agricultural labourers in different states (See Table 1).

Table 1
Statutory Minimum Wages in Different States (in Rupees)

States	*Minimum Wages*	*States*	*Minimum Wages*
Andhra Pradesh	80	Madhya Pradesh	53
Assam	46	Maharastra	45
Bihar	59	Orissa	50
Chhatisgarh	53	Punjab	82
Gujarat	60	Rajastan	60
Haryana	80	Tamil Nadu	54
Himachal Pradesh	60	Uttar Pradesh	58
Jharkhand	63	Uttaranchal	58
Karnatak	46	West Bengal	62
Keral	91	All States (Population weighted average)	59

Source: Dreze (2004).

Table 2
Cost of A National Rural Employment Guarantee Act: Baseline Estimate

Total Rural Population, 2001 (in Crores)	74.2
Proportion of rural population below the poverty line[a] (in percentage)	26.8
Estimated Rural Population below the poverty line[b], 2001 (in Crores)	20.0
Total number of rural households below the poverty line[c] (in Crores)	04.0
Total person-days to be generated assuming "100 days per poor household on average"[d] (in Crores)	400
Cost per day at 2004-05 prices (in Rupees)	100
Total cost of the Employment Guarantee Programme (in Crores)	40, 000
Total costs as a percentage of India's GDP in 2004-05[e]	01.3

(a) Official estimates (Planning Commission) for 1999-2000.
(b) 26.8 per cent of 74.2 crores.
(c) Assuming an average household size of five.
(d) See the above paragraph for further discussion of this benchmark.
(e) GDP = Rs.3, 104,857 Crores (Budget Estimate, reported in Government India, 2004, p. 33)

Note: These calculations assume that there has been no decline (more precisely, no change) in the *absolute number* of poor households since 2001. This is likely to introduce a small upward bias in the cost estimates, since the trend decline in poverty, according to official estimates, implies a *decline* in the number of poor households over time.

Source: Dreze, 2004.

If "hundred days per household on average" is the useful benchmark for the initial goal of an Employment Guarantee Programme, which is not an ambitious goal, but it could have a major impact on rural poverty. Combining the benchmark of "hundred days per household on average" with the assumed unit cost of Rupees hundred per day, it is easy to estimate the cost of the full-fledged Employment Guarantee Programme. This simply involves multiplying the number of households below the poverty line by Rs. 10,000. The relevant calculation is given in Table 2. The estimated cost is Rs. 40,000 crores per year at 2004-05 prices or 1.3 per cent of GDP.

An alternative set of calculations by Abhijit Sen starts by looking into the source of demand for employment. There would be demand for employment from two categories of labourers: those who are unemployed at present and those who would unemployed due to wage rate being higher than prevailing marketing wage. Given that about two-thirds of casual labourers received less than Rs. 40 a day in 1999-2000 (as per NSSO 55th round Data), Sen estimates that about twelve per cent of rural adults (three crore) would demand employment in the programme at a wage rate of Rs.60 per day. Assuming the wage component to be sixty per cent of the cost and guarantee of hundred days of work the total cost of the programme would be Rs. 30,000 crore (Ganesh-Kumar et el, 2004).

Given the current level of India's GDP' all the above alternative estimates of the financial cost of the programme range between 0.5 to one per cent of current GDP or three to six per cent of central government's total expenditure. In this juncture, the question arises "is it possible for India to spare one per cent of its GDP for an Employment Guarantee Programme, four years from now"?

As discussed in a number of Expert Committee Reports in recent years there are vast possibilities for increasing the tax-GDP ratio in the near future, arising inter alia from (a) the introduction of VAT, (b) the extension of indirect taxation to services (which account for more than fifty per cent of GDP and are virtually untaxed to day), (c) the rapid trend growth of income tax revenue (both individual and corporate), (d) the extensive of information technology to broaden the tax net and improve compliance, and (e) ample opportunities to crack down on tax evasion, arbitrary exemption and other forms of erosion of the tax base. If these possibilities are well used, plan expenditure could be raised much more than one per cent of GDP during the next four years[7] (Dreze, 2004). Finance Minister P. Chidambaram said the government would meet the requirement for NREGS by "normal increase" in budgetary support, savings from present employment schemes and additional allocation in gross budgetary support to states (The New Indian Express, 2005). Besides the measures suggested by the Finance Minister, an "Employment Guarantee Tax" (Direct Tax) could be designed to impose on the high-income group, say those who have income equal to or more than Rs. 4,00,000. Many economists are also optimistic that it is not difficult to manage one per cent of the country's GDP for NREGS.

IV

THE BENEFITS

The benefits of the NREGS depend on the awareness and the precautionary measure discussed in the next section. Firstly, the world as a whole is on track to achieve the first goal of MDG–reducing by half the proportion of people living on less than one Dollar a day–thanks mainly to rapid economic growth in India and China, where many of the world's poor live[8] (World Bank, 2003). The NREGS, definitely, accelerates the process of achieving the above said goal. Secondly, this programme will provide at least two square meals to the persons who were deprived of it. Thirdly, it will produce productive assets for the society such as road, ponds, plantation et cetera. Fourthly, the labour intensity can be high in such works as watershed development, land regeneration, and prevention of soil erosion. This would not only protect environment, it would enhance land productivity and promote rural employment in the future. Fifthly, such plans would have positive second round effects on household incomes, by raising agricultural wages and investment in human capital. Sixthly, by increase in income, people can improve their health standard, which has multiple effects. Seventhly, one of the major reasons that the children of poor parents drop out of school is because the parents can not afford the direct and indirect costs of education, raising family income would reduce school drop outs.

V

CREATION OF AWARENESS

Generally, the rural poor in India are illiterate, ignorant, involved in the local nasty politics and biased by the local immature politicians. Therefore, they should be properly *trained* and *aware* about the following sections and sub-sections of the act for the proper implementation of the scheme.

1. The eligible beneficiaries under the scheme shall apply for employment in the prescribed application form supplied by and submitted to the Grama Panchayata and the Programme Officer. They are bound to accept valid applications and *issue a dated receipt* to the applicant.
2. It is the responsibility of the State government to provide employment in accordance with the provision of the programme to every such person *within fifteen days of receipt of application.*
3. Employment shall be provided within a radius of *five kilometers* of the village where the applicant resides at the time of applying. In case where employment is provided outside such radius, it must be provided *within the Block and transport allowances and daily living allowances* shall be paid in accordance with the programme rules.
4. If the applicant is not provided with employment within fifteen days of receipt of an application, he or she shall be entitled to a *daily unemployment allowances* at such rate as may be fixed by the state government from time to time with the approval of the state council, but *not less than one third of the prevailing statutory minimum wage* of agricultural labourers in the state.

5. If the Grama Panchayata is satisfied, after due verification, that a person has registered by making *false declarations* of name, age or residence, it may recommend this person's name to the Programme Officer and the Programme Officer, after giving reasonable opportunity to the person concerned of being heard, *delete his/her name* from the register.
6. The *four entitlements* of labourers discussed in section II.
7. Any applicant who is provided with employment and *does not report for work* within fifteen days of being notified or who is *absent from work* for more than one week *without a valid application* for exemption, shall stand *debarred* from applying for work or receiving unemployment allowances for a period of fifteen days.
8. The details of each project, including a summary of expenditure and labour employed, shall be prominently displayed on a board close to the site after completion of the work. Similar information shall be painted on the walls of the Gram Panchayata Office. Public can get the copies of all accounts and records relating to the programme on demand at cost price.

VI

CRITICAL EVALUATION

The NREGS, if properly implemented, may give *temporary* relief to the rural poor. But, freedom from illness and freedom from illiteracy are two of the most important ways poor people can escape from poverty (World bank, 2003), *permanently,* and contribute significantly to the economic growth. Government should concentrate more on the development of health and education sector.

The main objective of the act is to guarantee at least hundred days of employment every year for at least one adult member (eighteen years and above) for doing casual labour, at sixty rupees per day as minimum wage to reduce poverty. This is a narrow aspect of the act, having short-term focus and temporary relief from the problem of unemployment and poverty. The objectives could be three fold-*poverty reduction, construction of productive assets and promoting mainstream employment subsequently* (Hirway, 2004). The act needs to include this long-term focus for sustainable development of the country.

There is tremendous variation in the statutory minimum wage rates across states[9]. The statutory minimum wage rate fixed for the act is Rupees sixty. Many states with a larger number of rural poor-such as Jharkhand, Chhattishgarh and Bihar - have a minimum wage that is less than Rupees sixty. Others such as Rajasthan have a rate that is a little higher (Varadarajan, 2005). In a state, where the statutory minimum wage rate is less than Rupees sixty, it is fine, and labourers will be happy to work under the act. But, employing a labourer, under the act, in a state where the minimum wage is more than Rupees sixty would constitute forced labour and violation of Article 23 of Indian Constitution. In this case, state may be allowed to provide a higher wage rate if they could supplement the additional funding from their own source.

According to the act, every household in the rural areas of India shall have a right to at least hundred days of guarantee employment every year for at least one adult member (eighteen years and above) for doing casual labour. In India, most of the poor are working poor. Providing employment to them for hundred days in a year at Rupees sixty comes Rupees six thousand per year and monthly Rupees five hundred only, which could potentially raise two-thirds of Indian's population of poor above the poverty line (Mehrotra, 2004). It is not desirable and has no logic to provide guarantee only for hundred days, as there is no need to put any ceiling to alleviate poverty. It is not also easy to implement the ceiling of hundred days, which will add to the burden, and costs of administration.

Urban poor are excluded from the employment guarantee programme. One can argue that resource commitment for the programme, that is politically feasible, is limited and consequently, the need to focus on the poor and vulnerable sections of population would make rural poor as the obvious choice. (Kundu and Sarangi, 2005). But starting from the Finance Minister to economists all are argued financing the programme is not a constraint (see Section III), then why should it not extend to urban poor also.

State government has crucial role in the implementation of the Act. Concurrence of the state governments and their willingness to abide by the operational implications of the act are essential. The role of state in the act is not clear. The act has nothing to say about the criteria for determining the funds to be allotted to districts, and their constituent Panchayats, and for ensuring that funds are transferred to them. Nor does it say whether these matters are subject to national guidelines or left to the discretion of states (Vaidyanathan, 2005).

According to the act, the Panchayata should be made responsible for registration of applicants for work and all projects should be decided, implemented and monitored by Panchayati Raj Institutions (PRIs) or through PRIs. But, the current position is that mandated elections are not held regularly, elected Panchayatas are superseded at the whim of state governments, and there is concerted and intense opposition from politicians holding or aspiring for positions at state and central levels in transferring authority, resources and responsibility for local level development projects to Panchayatas.

The rural poor will get guarantee employment in different "Productive works[10]", as decided by the Gram Panchayata and the Gram Sabha, and produce public as well as private productive assets, (of course, private works should be undertaken after the completion of public works) for the future income generation. In creation of private assets, first preference should be given to the asset less small and marginal farmers. There should be adequate and proper institutional framework to maintain the public assets, which is not discussed in the act.

"The tragedy of the current Employment Guarantee Bill, 2004 is that it is a deliberate bureaucratic dodge which is almost bound to discredit itself" (Bhaduri, 2005). In India, this statement is not correct. According to Mahatma Gandhi "Politics encircles us today like the coil of a snake from which one cannot get out, no matter how much one tries". In implementation of the act, the Chief Executive Officer (CEO) or District Collector (DC) shall be accountable to the Zilla Parisad and the Programme Officer (PO) shall be answerable to the Panchayata Samiti. In a recent survey, it is found that seventy per cent of the Chairmen of the Zilla Parisad are not able to read and write. They are puppets in the hand of seasoned politicians. In such a situation, how shall a CEO/DC be accountable to the Zila Parisad. But in the developed countries, it is wise, where people are very conscious and educated, the bureaucrats could be accountable to people's representatives.

VII

CONCLUSION

The Goal 1 (eradication of poverty and hunger) of the Millennium Development Goals (MDGs), the decline in per capita output in Indian agriculture in the last decade, the failure of the series of wage employment programmes in India since 1960s are the general, and the policy agenda outlined in the National Common Minimum Programme (NCMP) of the United Progressive Alliance (UPA) government is the immediate cause of the emergence of the National Rural Employment guarantee Act, 2004, the "Historic Bill" on employment, introduced in Lok Sabha last year by the government, and was moved by Rural Development Minister Raghuvansh Prasad Singh amid the thumping of desk on the 18th August 2005, which guarantees every household in the rural areas of India shall have a right to at least hundred days of employment every year for at least one adult member (eighteen years and above) for doing casual labour, at sixty rupees per day as minimum wage. There is consensus that finance for the programme is not a problem for government of India. One per cent of Country's GDP (the cost of the programme as calculated by Dreze) is not a high price to pay to protect the bulk of rural population from hunger, insecurity and extreme poverty-once and for all. The paper states that if it will create awareness among the rural poor, and take care of the controversies of objectives (poverty reduction, construction of productive assets and promoting mainstream employment subsequently); minimum wage rates; ceiling of hundred days of employment; exclusion of urban poor; role of states; role of Panchayatas; and political pressure, the act will be a panacea for the malady of unemployment in India.

NOTES

1. Whose income is less than one dollar a day is called below poverty line.
2. Rural areas include 'B' and 'C' class municipalities.
3. Except the state of Jammu and Kashmir
4. For the purpose of regular monitoring and review of implementation of the act at the state level, each state government shall constitute a state council to be called the State Employment Guarantee Council.
5. See Table 2
6. Participation Ration is defined as the number of persons employed on an average day as a proportion of the total population below the poverty line.
7. The tax revenue projection presented in Government India (2004), based on wide ranging tax reforms aimed at rising the tax-GDP ratio, make room for an increase of Rs. 1,10,000 crore in plan expenditure between 2004-05 and 2008-09 (this is in nominal terms, equivalent to roughly Rs. 90,000 crore at today's prices.
8. Taking the world as a whole hides the fact that Sub-Saharan Africa is off track in reaching the income poverty goal.
9. There is controversy regarding the statutory minimum wage rates across states. Dreze (2004) calculated the population weighted average wage rate for the act at Rs. 59 by taking the statutory minimum wage rates of major nineteen states where Keral has the highest statutory minimum wage rate at Rs. 91 and Maharastra has the lowest at Rs. 45 (See Table 1). In the Editorial (2005) states that the statutory minimum wage rates vary between Rs. 25 in Nagaland and Rs.134 in Keral whereas Varadaranjan (2005) states Keral heading the list at Rs.126 and Meghalaya at the bottom with Rs. 26.
10. Productive work means any work, which, in the opinion of State Council, will directly or indirectly contribute to the increase in production, creation of durable assets, the preservation of environment, or improvement in the quality of life.

REFERENCES

Bhaduri, Amit (2005), Guarantee Employment and the Right to Information, *Economic and Political Weekly*, January 22, pp. 269.

Dreze, Jean (2004), Financial Implications of an Employment Guarantee Act: Preliminary Estimates, *Mimeo*, National Advisory Council, New Delhi.

Editorial (2005), Employment Guarantee: Setting Legislation Right, *Economic and Political Weekly*, Vol. XL, No. 32, pp. 3556.

Ganesh-Kumar, A., Srijit Mishra and Manoj Panda (2004), Employment Guarantee for Rural India, *Economic and Political Weekly*, Vol. XXXIX, No. 51, December 18, pp. 5360.

Hirway, Indira (2004), Providing Employment Guarantee in India: Some Critical Issues, *Economic and Political Weekly*, Vol. XXXIX, No.48, November 27, pp. 5117.

Kundu, Amitabh, and Niranjan Sarangi (2005), Issues of Urban Exclusion, *Economic and Political Weekly*, August 13, pp. 3642.

Mehrotra, Santosh (2004), Job Law can Sharply Cut Poverty this Decade, *Economic and Political Weekly*, Vol. XXXIX, No. 51, December 18, pp. 5357.

National Common Minimum Programme (NCMP) (2004): *http://nac.nic.in/ncmp.htm*, Accessed on August 18, 2005.

Radhakrishna, R. (2005), Food and Nutrition Security of the Poor: Emerging Perspectives and Policy Issues, *Economic and Political Weekly*, Vol. XL, No. 18, pp.1817.

Shah, Mihir (2004), National Rural Employment Guarantee Act: A Historic Opportunity, *Economic and Political Weekly*, Vol. XXXIX, No. 50, December 11, Pp.5287.

The Hindu (2005), *'Historic' Bill on Jobs in Lok Sabha*, August 18, pp. 1.

The New Indian Express (2005), *Government will Fund Rural Job Scheme: Chidambaram*, August 18.

United Nations (2000), United Nations Millennium Declaration, United Nations General Assembly Resolution 55/2. *www.un.org/milleennium/declaration/ares552e.pdf*, Accessed on December 1, 2004.

Vaidyanathan, A. (2005), Need for Involvement of States, *Economic and Political Weekly*, August 13, pp. 3648.

Varadarajan, Siddharth (2005), Minimum Wage Must be Treated as Sacrosanct, *The Hindu*, August 23.

World Bank (2003), Making Services Work for Poor, *World Development Report 2004*, Washington D.C.

Index